Tom Pickering.
4/1/88.

WORD
Perfect

WORD
Perfect

A dictionary
of current
English usage

John O. E. Clark

HARRAP'S *REFERENCE*

First published in Great Britain 1987
by Harrap Ltd
19–23 Ludgate Hill, London EC4M 7PD

ISBN 0 245–54562–X (cased edition)
ISBN 0 245–54601–4 (plastic edition)

To Gill: for the title and the patience

*Printed in Great Britain
at the Bath Press, Avon*

Preface

This book has evolved gradually from notes and observations made during nearly thirty years working as an editor and writer for various British and American publishers. Many of the "style sheets" encountered over those years have been silent sources of inspiration, and I remain indebted to them and their creators. The result is a guide to current English usage, arranged alphabetically to make it easy to look things up. It is intended to be of help to learners of English, to writers and to editors. But any editor who attempts to prepare such a guide is soon made embarrassingly aware of the adage that warns anybody living in a glass house of the danger of throwing stones. Nevertheless a senior editor can – and sometimes should – be uncompromisingly prescriptive; a publisher's house style should not be intended to address itself to the rights and wrongs of stylistic decisions so much as to establish editorial consistency.

Although *Word Perfect* can therefore be regarded as primarily an editorial guide to English writing style, I have also tried to make it something more. I believe that for general purposes – that is, where visible authorship is not desirable – a good writing style is characterized by ease of access (what some people call readability). This is, in effect, the absence rather than presence of any noticeable style. In preparing material for this book I have tried to offer advice that encourages a writing or editing style that is unobtrusive yet acceptable to most readers of modern English. A basic assumption is that the chief object of the written or printed word is to communicate; anything that detracts from this purpose is consequently criticised or even deplored.

Despite this aim, sometimes the demands of the pedant or purist, on the one hand, and the vagaries of fashion, on the other, compete for precedence. Often the difficulty can be avoided or a fair judgement made by acknowledging the overriding importance of usage – that ill-defined influence which breathes life into the language and ensures that it continues to evolve as a dynamic, vital thing.

With regard to one decision, however, I have remained fairly firmly traditional: this is with regard to the gradual Americanization of English. During my working experience I have probably produced as many books in American English as in the European kind, and have frequently translated from one to the other. With less awareness of the differences I might have been more inclined to advocate an amalgam. As it is, I believe that such an attempt produces more problems than solutions, and – more seriously and dangerously – makes students and practitioners of the language uncertain and confused. In terms of spelling and punctuation there is, certainly, a "mid-Atlantic" style that causes least offence to either side. But the important point is that it is a compromise, and nobody should believe that by making it all the problems have been solved.

For practising editors, this book also includes definitions and explanations of technical terms common in publishing, printing and papermaking. Within Europe there is a continuing move towards standardization, but again many of these standards have yet to find favour in North America. Nevertheless, the Americanization of the English language is undeniably proceeding apace. The dominant medium of mass communication is television, and in this medium American usage prevails. Apart from newspapers and magazines, most print either comes from or must also be sold in North America, and the commercial logic for a common style is inescapable. But until that common standard is clearly established, I contend that it is more valuable – because it is less confusing and therefore more practical – to have a "home base" to relate to. This is one thing I have tried to provide.
J.O.E.C., London 1987

A

A (indefinite article) *See* **a or an**.

Å is the abbreviation of angstrom (a unit of length equal to one hundred millionth of a centimetre, used to measure interatomic distances and wavelengths of light).

a/an can be used to mean **per**, and is less formal. E.g.:
three times *per* week   three times *a* month
80 kilometres *per* hour   30 miles *an* hour
With imprecise numbers, *a* is preferred (e.g. "several times a year").
For *a/an* as indefinite articles, *see* **a or an**.

a-/an- *See* **negative prefixes**.

abacus (pl. abacuses).

abate, abatable, abatement, abater.

abattoir (= slaughter-house, which is preferred to the French euphemism).

abbreviate, abbreviator.

abbreviations As a general rule, abbreviations should be avoided in narrative text. Despite the list of exceptions described later, the most important fact to note is the formal difference between an abbreviation and a contraction (*see* **contractions**). A contraction ends with the final letter of the word when it is spelled in full; an abbreviation does not, and thus requires a full point. E.g.:

a.m.	*d.* (died)	Ho.	Q.C.
b. (born)	e.g.	*ibid.*	R.I.P.
c. (circa)	etc.	i.e.	Sq.
Co.	fig.	p.m.	u.c.
c.v.	*fl.* (flourished)	Prof.	Ven.

Unfortunately, there are very many exceptions.

abbreviations

1. Names, titles, honours and acronyms for organizations; the preferred modern style is without full points:

AA	FOC	MA	SOGAT
BA	FRCO	MBE	UNESCO
BBC	GLC	MP	UNICEF
BSc	GPO	NATO	UNICEF
CH	HMS	OBE	UK
DD	HMSO	OM	USA
DDT	ILEA	RAC	USSR
EFTA	ITV	RAF	VC
EEC	KLM	QE2	WRAC
			YMCA

(Some publishers prefer to retain full points in B.A., B.Sc., M.A., etc.).

2. Measurements and units:

bhp	gm	lb (pound)	mm
cc	km	m (metre)	mph
cm	kg	mg	oz
ft	l (litre)	min	sec

(Note that the abbreviations of these measurements are both singular and plural; *see also* **units**).

3. Miscellaneous:

AD BC (set in small capitals)

N S E W NNE SSW (*see also* **compass directions**)

MS PS

CAT-scan L-dopa Rh+

General notes:

The abbreviations e.g. and i.e. should be avoided in running narrative text (but are usually allowable in parentheses, tables, and so on).

Use uranium-235, carbon-14, etc. for first mention but U-235, C-14 thereafter (do not use an initial capital letter for spelled out names of chemical elements).

In astronomical works, Messier numbers (M) are set with no space before the catalogue number (e.g. M32, M109).

New General Catalogue numbers (NGC), however, do have a space (e.g. NGC 54, NGC 7332).

Note mph (miles per hour) but km/h (kilometres per hour).
S. Giorgio (S. = San) but Sta Maria (Sta = Santa) and Ste Juliette (Ste = Sainte) for names of Italian, Spanish, Portuguese or French saints. The abbreviation S for the English word Saint has the plural SS (= Saints).

Abbreviations of British county names should be avoided and used only as a last resort when pressed for space in captions (*see* **counties**). Similar advice applies to the names of American (USA) states (*see* **US states**). Similarly, avoid using abbreviations of American states. Avoid abbreviations of months and days of the week but, if necessary (e.g. in tabular matter), use:

Jan Feb March Apr May June July Aug Sept Oct Nov Dec
Sun Mon Tues Wed Thurs Fri Sat (all without full points).

Do not use ' and " as abbreviations of foot (feet) and inch(es), although these symbols are correct for minutes and seconds of arc.

Plurals of abbreviations:

BAs MAs MPs O-Levels (not BA's etc.)
p. (page) pp. (pages)
f. (folio or following page) ff. (folios etc.)
v. (verse) vv. (verses)
w. (word) ww. (words)
MS. (manuscript) MSS (manuscripts)
sp. (singular species) spp. (plural species)

This Dictionary includes abbreviations of common weights and measures, and other abbreviations commonly encountered in publishing. *See also* **contractions**.

abet, abetting, abettor.

abide is archaic when it is used to mean *wait for*, and is colloquial for *live, remain, stay, endure* or *tolerate*, any of which is preferred.
   Abide by (= adhere to, conform) is acceptable usage; e.g. "A good sportsman abides by the rules of the game". The past tense and participle of the former is *abode*, of the latter is *abided by*.

ability = power to do or skill in doing something;

capability = **capacity** (non-technical) = capability or the inborn power of a person to learn something, or of a thing to do something. E.g.:

"He has outstanding ability as an editor, but his capacity for biology is negligible."

-ability and -ibility are the endings of nouns formed from adjectives ending in *-able* or *-ible*. The usual spelling difficulty is *a* or *i*? For a list, *see* **-able and -ible**.

ab initio (italics) = from the beginning; this Latin form should be avoided.

abjure = to renounce an oath, repudiate, recant; **adjure** = to charge on oath, appeal in a solemn way. E.g.:

"He must abjure Roman Catholicism before joining the sect."
"I adjured him to think twice before joining the sect."

able, like **competent,** takes an infinitive (e.g. "She was able to go", "He was competent to do it"); **capable** takes *of* and a gerund (e.g. "It was capable of moving quickly").

-able and -ible One of the most vexatious problems in English spelling occurs when verbs (and some nouns) are converted into adjectives by adding the suffix *-able* or *-ible*. There are some general rules, but unfortunately there are also many exceptions (for this reason, many such adjectives are included in this Dictionary).

1. Words ending in a *y* preceded by a vowel retain the *y*; e.g. *buyable, deployable, layable, payable.*

2. Words ending in a *y* preceded by a consonant have an *i* for the *y*; e.g. *deniable, dutiable, justifiable, variable* (exception *flyable*).

3. Words ending in a silent *e* usually drop the *e*; e.g. *solvable, usable.*

4. Words ending in an *e* retain the *e* if it is necessary as an aid to pronunciation; e.g. *blameable, chargeable, gaugeable, likeable, noticeable, pronounceable, rateable, replaceable, tuneable.*

5. Words ending in *-ee* usually retain both *es*; e.g. *agreeable.*

6. *-ible* is the suffix on certain words of Latin origin, and these have to be learned. Examples include:

accessible	destructible	indelible	reprehensible
adducible	digestible	intelligible	repressible
admissible	dirigible	irascible	reproducible
audible	discernible	legible	resistible
avertible	dismissible	miscible	responsible
collapsible	divisible	negligible	reversible
combustible	edible	ostensible	revertible
compatible	eligible	perceptible	risible
comprehensible	exhaustible	perfectible	seducible
contemptible	expressible	permissible	sensible
contractible	extensible	persuasible	susceptible
controvertible	fallible	plausible	tangible
convertible	feasible	possible	transmissible
corrigible	fencible	prehensible	vendible
corruptible	flexible	producible	vincible
credible	forcible	reducible	visible
deducible	fusible	reflectible	
deductible	gullible	remissible	
defensible	includible	rendible	

and their opposites (*inaccessible*, *inadmissible*, and so on).

ablution(s) = the act of washing onself; it should be reserved for religious contexts and not used as a pompous way of describing a simple routine act.

abnormal = any difference from normal; **subnormal** = below normal; **supranormal** = above the normal.

abode is precious for **house** or **home**, either of which is preferred.

abolish, abolishable, abolishment, abolition, abolitionist. *Abolishment* and *abolition* (preferred) both = doing away with or ending something, usually of official or legal status. An *abolitionist* was someone who believed in the abolition of slavery.

aboriginal (adj. and noun, sing.; pl. aborigines) = an original inhabitant of a country; but Australian Aborigines (initial capital letters).

Aboriginal words *See* **Australia and New Zealand**.

about, applied to dates, can be represented by *c.* (the abbreviation of *circa*). *See also* **around**.

above/below Do not write "...as described above (or below)"; write instead "...as described earlier (or later) in this article." But *above/below* is correct in captions. *Above* or *below* should not be used to mean *more than* or *less than* when referring to specific quantities (e.g. write "more than 20km" or "less than 3cm"); but "above/below zero, boiling point, etc." is correct. **Above** = *at/on a higher level* can be synonymous with *over* (e.g. "above the window", "over the window"), just as **below** (= *at/on a lower level*) can mean *under*.

abridge, abridgement (preferred to abridgment).

abscess

absence = state of being not present, not existing, missing;
    lack = shortage, deficiency, insufficiency. E.g.:

"We could not continue because of the absence of materials."
"We could not finish because of lack of time."

absent, absentee, absence.

absinthe is the liqueur flavoured with the wormwood plant **absinth**.

absolutely = unconditionally, separately; it should not be used as an intensifier. E.g.:

in "The text is absolutely perfect" delete *absolutely*;
in "She was absolutely overcome" substitute *completely* for *absolutely*.
"His co-operation is guarantee absolutely" is correct usage.

absorption = the taking up of one substance within the structure of another (like water into a sponge); **adsorption** = the taking up of a gas or vapour on the surface of a solid (as gases into charcoal). The corresponding verbs are *absorb* and *adsorb*, with *absorbent* and *adsorbent* as adjectives and nouns (not absorbant).

abstain = to go/do without, to refrain from doing something; **abstinent** describes someone who abstains (i.e. has none); **abstemious** describes someone who eats or drinks sparingly, who is not overindulgent (i.e. has some, but not too much). Thus *abstention* is having none, whereas *abstemiousness* (or in its strict meaning *temperance*) is having some but in moderation.

abstemious *See* **abstain**.

abstinent *See* **abstain**.

abuse (verb) = use wrongly (usually something that is abstract); **misuse** = use incorrectly (usually something that is visible or tangible). E.g.:

"He abused his authority by using his official car to go shopping".
"He so misused his car that it soon needed a new clutch."

abut, abutment, abutting, abuttal.

abyss = deep trench or cavity, deep ocean; **abyssal** = relating to the ocean depths; **abysmal** = relating to an abyss, bottomless, extremely low in merit/quality/interest.

AC is the abbreviation of alternating current.

acanthus (pl. acanthuses).

accelerate, accelerator.

accents and diacritical marks All accents and diacritical marks should be unambiguously marked in the text, by hand if they cannot be typed. Common accents include acute (*é*), cedilla (*ç*), circumflex (*ê*), grave (*è*), tilde (*ñ*) and umlaut (*ü*). In certain languages there are means of avoiding accents. In French only, capital letters do not (have to) have accents. In German only, vowels with an umlaut (¨) can be spelled as vowel + *e*; e.g. *über* = *ueber*, *schön* = *schoen*. In Danish and Norwegian only, *å* can be spelled *aa*; e.g. Århus = Aarhus. These rules should not be transferred to other languages. *See also* **foreign words and phrases**.

accentuate = make prominent, throw into relief, draw attention to; it does not mean *worsen* or *increase*. E.g.:

"The continuing bad weather accentuated the sale of umbrellas" is incorrect.

accept, acceptable, accepter (but acceptor in law/chemistry/ electronics), acceptance. **Accept** = to receive or take; **except** (verb) = to exclude.

access, accessory, accessary, accessible, accession.
Access = means of entry, act of approach; *accession* = attaining office, power or status, an increase, an addition. E.g.:

"A gap in the hedge provided access to the next field."
"The holiday was to celebrate the anniversary of the king's accession."
Both *accessary* and *accessory* can be noun or adjective. The former is an accomplice or helper; the latter is usually an additional (but non-essential) feature. E.g.:

"He was charged with being an accessary to murder."
"She ordered a radio as an accessory for her new car."

accident, accidental, accidentally (not accidently). **Accident** = an unforeseen (usually unfortunate) event; it should not be used to describe the outcome. E.g.:

"She could not draw because of an accident to her hand" should be "... because of an injury to her hand" or "... because she had an accident involving her hand."

acclimatize, acclimatization.

accommodate, accommodation.

accompany *by* another person or people; **accompany** *with* another thing or things. The noun (in music) is **accompanist**.

accomplish *See* **attain**.

account, accountable, accountant. When *accountable* is used to mean *responsible*, it should be applied only to a person or persons (e.g. "The officer is accountable for his actions"; the actions are not accountable). *See also* **responsible**.

accredit *See* **credit**.

accrue = accumulate gradually, increase piece by piece, happen to one's advantage; the word should not be used of any, particularly sudden, increase. The corresponding noun is *accrual*.

accumulate, accumulator, accumulation.

acknowledge, acknowledgeable, acknowledgement (preferred to acknowledgment).

acme = peak (of perfection); **acne** = pimply disorder of the face.

acoustics, the science, is singular (e.g. "Acoustics is the science of sound"); when used to describe the sound properties of, say, a concert hall, it is plural (e.g. "The acoustics of the Festival Hall are excellent").

acquaint with seldom means more than **tell** or **inform**.

acquiesce(nce) *in* (not acquiesce(nce) *to*).

acquit, acquittance (let off a debt), acquittal (found not guilty).

acre, acreage.

acronym = pronounceable word from the initials or opening letters of a name or phrase – not merely any set of (unpronounceable) initials, which constitute an abbreviation. Acronyms consisting of capital letters should be printed without full points and typeset close up. Particularly in computer technology, phrases are sometimes selected so that they make memorable acronyms (such as ERNIE = *E*lectronic *R*andom *N*umber *I*ndicating *E*quipment). E.g.:

AIDS	(*a*uto*i*mmune *d*eficiency *s*yndrome)
EFTA	(*E*uropean *F*ree *T*rade *A*ssociation)
EOKA	(*E*thnikē *O*rganōsīs *K*yprīon *A*gōniston)
FORTRAN	(*for*mula *tran*slation)
NASA	(*N*ational *A*eronautical and *S*pace *A*dministration)
SALT	(*S*trategic *A*rms *L*imitation *T*reaty)

Acronyms that have passed wholly into the language are treated as ordinary words (usually without an initial capital letter). E.g.:

bren (gun)	(*Br*no and *En*field armouries)
laser	(*l*ight *a*mplification by *s*timulated *e*mission of *r*adiation)
qwerty	(standard keyboard, named after the first six letters on it)
radar	(*ra*dio *d*irection-finding *a*nd *r*anging)
sonar	(*so*und *n*avigation *a*nd *r*anging)

See also **abbreviations**.

acrophobia = neurotic fear of heights; **agoraphobia** = neurotic fear of open spaces. These are terms in psychology relating to specific mental disorders, and should not be used of mere dislike of heights/open spaces.

act (noun) = law as passed (enacted) by Parliament; **bill** = proposed law submitted to Parliament for debate/approval.

action-packed

activate = bring about, cause to act, inspire; **actuate** = start or use a mechanism (i.e. cause to act), motivate. E.g.:

"He actuated the series of switches that activated the rocket's firing sequence."

active, activate, activation, activeness (to be avoided), activity (preferred).

actual, actually. These overworked and often superfluous words should be avoided. *See also* **really**.

acute = an accent, as in *café*. See **accents and diacritical marks**.

AD (the abbreviation of *anno Domini*) is usually typeset in small capital letters, indicated <u>AD</u>, before the relevant date.

adapt, adapter (general), adaptor (gadget), adaptation; *adaption* does not exist. **Adapt** = make suitable; **adept** = skilled, expert; **adopt** = take as one's own.

add, addable, additive.

addendum (pl. addenda).

adduce, adducible.

add up to usually = **mean** or **come to**, which are preferred. E.g.:

"It all adds up to a disaster" is better put as
"It means a disaster."

adequate = sufficient in quantity, enough (which is preferred);
adequate *to* = sufficient in quality, suitable. E.g.:

"The quantity of material was adequate for the task"
"The quality of the workmanship was barely adequate to the task."

adequate enough is a tautology (omit either word).

adhere, adhesion, adhesive, adhesiveness, adherence (which takes *to* not *of*), adherent [noun, preferred to adherer] (which takes *of* not *to*), adherent [adj.] (which takes *to* not *of*). E.g. (correct use):

"He proclaimed his adherence to the faith."
"He was an adherent of the faith."
"The tar was adherent to his shoes."

adhesive binding *See* **perfect binding**.

ad hoc (italics) = for a special purpose, improvised.

ad infinitum (italics) = to infinity; the Latin form should be avoided.

adit = tunnel or sloping shaft at the entrance to a mine. The word is found mainly in crossword puzzles; mining engineers prefer the term *entrance* or *entrance shaft*.

adj. is the abbreviation of adjective. In this Dictionary, *adjective* or *adjectival* is used of any describing word. Thus in the expressions "small blue car", "in the pouring rain", "pour on melted butter" and "systems analyst", *small* and *blue* are adjectives whereas *pouring* and *melted* are verbs and *systems* is a noun, all three being used adjectivally.

adjacent = near, neighbouring; **contiguous** = bordering, touching.

adjective order It is unusual to find four or more adjectives before a noun, but when adjectives do accumulate there is a conventional order. Of the two phrases
    1. the old green Chinese jade perfume bottle
and 2. the green perfume jade Chinese old bottle,
(1) makes sense whereas (2) does not. The usual order is (using the same example):

the	**old**	**green**	**Chinese**	**jade**	**perfume**	**bottle**
article	(e)	(d)	(c)	(b)	(a)	noun
	age	colour	origin	material	purpose	
	shape	texture	ownership	composition	function	
	size					
	hot/cold					

adjectives *See* **-able and -ible; comparitives and superlatives; -wards**.

adjure *See* **abjure**.

ad lib (= *ad libitum*) should be avoided for *extemporize*.

administrate, administrator (but administratrix, fem. legal), administrative, administration, administrable (not administratable).

admit, admissible, admission, admittance. *Admit to* should be reserved for meaning "allow physical entry" (e.g. "She admitted him to her room"); in the meaning "confess" (e.g. "She admitted to letting him in"), *to* is redundant and should be omitted.

admonish, admonition (preferred to admonishment).

ad nauseam (italics) = to a sickening extent; the Latin form should be avoided.

adolescent *See* **baby.**

adopt, adopter, adoption, adoptive (describing the parents of an adopted child), adoptee (describing the adopted child). *See also* **adapt.**

adrenalin (preferred to *adrenaline* in ordinary writing; the usual North American term for the hormone is *epinephrine*).

adulate, adulator.

adulterate = spoil by adding a foreign or poisonous element; **adulteration** = act of adulterating; **adultery** = extra-marital sexual relations; **adulterer** = someone who commits adultery (for **adulteress,** *see* **gender**).

adv. is the abbreviation of adverb. Most adverbs are formed by adding -*ly* to an adjective (e.g. quickly, slowly, happily, tearfully). A few retain the spelling of the adjective in one sense. E.g.:

"a *hard* apple" (adjective);
"she worked *hard*" (adverb);
"she *hardly* worked" (different adverb).

advance (noun) = forward movement, progress, loan (in anticipation of income); **advancement** = promotion, furthering (of a cause).

advent should be reserved for a coming that is of great importance or significance, and not used merely as a grand alternative to the neutral **arrival.** E.g.:

"A profusion of flowers heralded the advent of spring."

"A whistle announced the arrival of the train."
When it describes the coming or second coming of Christ, *Advent* has an initial capital letter.

adventitious = happening by chance or accident; **adventurous** = involving adventure.

adventure = exciting experience, remarkable occurrence; **venture** (noun) = (speculative) business undertaking.

adverse = unfavourable; **averse** = unwilling, opposed to, against. Both words take *to* in adjectival constructions. E.g.:

"Slippery fallen leaves on the road contributed to the adverse driving conditions."
"She was averse to driving a car on the slippery road."

advert (noun) is colloquial for advertisement, and should be avoided; **ad** with the same meaning is even less acceptable. **Advert** (verb) = refer to.

advise (verb), advisable, adviser, advisory, advice (noun).

-ae- This vowel sound, in words from Greek or Latin, should be written (and printed) as separate letters, not as the ligature *æ* (e.g. Aesop, Caesarian, formulae, haemoglobin), although *æ* is retained in Old English. In a few modern words, the vowel has been reduced to a single *e* (e.g. ether, medieval, hyena). *See also* **-oe-**.

aeon is the preferred spelling, not **eon**.

aerial *See* **antenna**.

aerie The preferred spelling is **eyrie** (= an eagle's nest).

aerobic = capable of life only in an oxygen-containing environment; **aerobics** = type of physical exercise.

aeroplane is generally being replaced by **aircraft**. An *aeroplane* is a fixed-wing aircraft, whereas the term *aircraft* can include rotating-wing machines (such as a helicopter). *Plane* (not 'plane) is now an accepted short form; *airplane* is an Americanism, to be avoided.

aerosol

aetiology (not etiology). *See also* **-ae-**.

affect = to have an effect on; **effect** (verb) = to bring about, produce, accomplish; **effect** (noun) = the result of an action, impression produced. E.g.:

"Moisture affects the conductivity of carbon."
"Moisture effects a colour change in cobalt salts."
"The effect of moisture is to alter the colour."

affectation = pretence, adoption of an unreal or unnatural appearance; **affection** = love, attachment. E.g.:

"His cultured accent was an affectation to disguise his humble background."
"His affection for language is reflected in his precise enunciation of English."

affinity *with* or *between* people or things, not affinity *for* or *to*. *Affinity for* is correct in scientific usage.

affirm = to state or declare that something is true; **confirm** = to ratify or corroborate an existing statement (already taken to be true).

afflict = to distress, cause to suffer, torment; **inflict** = to impose suffering or punishment; **inflect** = to turn off course, to bend in, to modulate (the voice). The corresponding nouns are *affliction, infliction* and *inflexion*. *See also* **-ection**.

affluent = abundant, well provided; it should be avoided as a synonym for the simpler *rich* or *wealthy*.

affranchise, affranchisement.

Afghanistan The derived adjective and noun is *Afghan* (not Afghani).

aficionado (italics) = enthusiast; the Spanish form should be avoided.

aforementioned is archaic for (as) **mentioned before**; it is retained in legal contexts but should be avoided in ordinary writing.

aforesaid is archaic (and legal) for **previously mentioned**, which should be used.

Afro-English etc. (with a hyphen).

after, afterbirth, after-care, afterlife, afternoon, after-thought.

aftermath, originally meaning a second crop of grass or an unpleasant consequence, is now used of any result or after-effect.

afterwards is preferred to **afterward**.

agate = obsolete name for $5\frac{1}{2}$-point type. For others, *see* **type sizes**.

age, aging.

agenda is singular (even though it is the Latin plural of *agendum*); its plural is *agendas*.

aggravate = to worsen, increase (an evil). The sense to *tease* or *irritate* is colloquial. The verb should not be used to mean *spoil*, *upset* or *endanger*. E.g.:

"Hot water merely aggravates the condition" is correct;
"He turned up the volume to aggravate his neighbour" is colloquial;
"His attitude aggravated their friendship" is incorrect.

aggression (= an opening act of hostility), aggressive (= initiating hostility, attacking), aggressiveness (= displaying aggression). The key ideas of aggression are displaying hostility and acting first. Thus such expressions as "continuing aggression" and "an aggressive response to their attack" are strictly incorrect.

agitate, agitator, agitation.

agnostic = someone who believes that the existence of God cannot be proved; **atheist** = someone who denies the existence of God.

agony, agonize.

agree, agreeable, agreement.
Agree is traditionally an intransitive verb taking the preposition *with*, *on* or *to*, although the word can be used transitively. E.g.:

"I agree with your comments on the text" (intransitive),
"We must agree on an agenda" (intransitive);
"I agree to your commenting on the text" (intransitive),
"I agree your figures" (transitive);
the last form should be used sparingly.

agriculture, agriculturist (not agriculturalist).

AH is the abbreviation of *anno Hegirae* (the year of Hegira, the flight of Mohammed in AD 622). It is typeset in small capitals, indicated AH in copy.

aid = to help, assist; **aide** = an assistant.

aide-mémoire (italics) = reminder; the French form should be avoided.

aim *at* a target; **aim** *to* achieve something. E.g.:

"The wicketkeeper aimed the ball at the stumps."
"The charity aims to provide food for starving children."

ain't should not be used for **am not** in formal writing. *See* **non-standard English.**

air, airborne, air-conditioning, aircraft, airfield, airflow, airgun, airman, airless, airlift, airline, airliner, airport, air-pump, air raid, airship, airtight, air-to-air (missile), airworthy, airworthiness.

aircraft names should be typeset in roman face with an initial capital letter; e.g. Concorde, Boeing 747, Hurricane, Messerschmitt, Vulcan. Names given to individual aircraft should be italicized; e.g. *Spirit of St Louis*; *Lucky Lady*. *See also* **aeroplane.**

air-knife coating = papermaking term for a method of applying a thick coating to paper using a stream of high-pressure air, which levels the coating and blows away any surplus. It reduces the need for subsequent polishing of the paper surface by supercalendering. *See also* **paper.**

airmail = thin paper (of weight less than 40 gsm), often coloured blue, used for lightweight stationery.

airplane is an Americanism for **aeroplane**; *aircraft* is the preferred current term.

akin *to* (not akin *with*).

à la (italics) = in the manner/style of (e.g. *à la* Strauss); the French term (an abbreviation of *à la mode de*) should be avoided.

a large extent seldom means more than **much** or **most**, which are preferred. **To a large extent** usually means merely **mostly.**

albedo (pl. albedos).

albeit *See* **howbeit.**

albino (pl. albinos), albinism.

ale = drink made by fermenting a watery mash of malt (germinated barley), with the yeast on top; **beer** = drink made by a similar process to that used for ale but with added hops (for flavour) and the yeast at the bottom of the brew; **bitter** = light non-sweet beer; **lager** = extra-light beer, traditionally kept for six months before use; **mild** = dark beer, sweeter than bitter and with no hops; **pilsner** (sometimes abbreviated to **pils**) = lager-type beer, originally from Pilsen in Czechoslovakia; **porter** = dark beer made using roasted malt; **stout** = extra-strong porter. *Porter* is archaic, as (according to the *OED*) is *ale* although the word has long been preserved in the terms *light* or *pale ale* and *brown ale* (usually bottled versions of bitter or mild with added gas) and in the draught bitters proprietarily called *India(n) Pale Ale* (IPA). The revived interest in "real" ales has also revived *ale* from its archaic status. The American term **malt liquor** is usually applied to a strong, gassy light beer sold in cans; bottled strong, dark beer is called **barley wine** in Britain.

alexia = loss of the power to read; **dyslexia** = inability to learn to read (properly).

alfalfa is an alternative (and American) name for the fodder crop **lucerne**, which is preferred.

alfresco (one word preferred) = in the open air; the Italian expression should be avoided.

alga (pl. algae).

alias (pl. aliases).

alibi (pl. alibis) is a defence based on the plea that the accused was elsewhere at the time of the alleged offence; it should not be used to mean merely *excuse*.

alien, alienate, alienable (not alienatable), alienator, alienation.

alive = living; **live** (adj.) = energized (e.g. a live electricity cable, live ammunition), not recorded (e.g. a live performance), living (e.g. a live specimen).

alkali (pl. alkalis), alkaline.

all- Most compound adjectives with the prefix *all-* are hyphenated; e.g. all-American boy, all-day event, walk on all-fours, all-in wrestling, all-night garage, all-out effort, all-over roof, all-powerful ruler, all-risks policy, all-round sportsman (an all-rounder), all-time low.

all alone, like **all by her/him/itself,** is usually a tautology (omit *all*).

allay = to relieve or calm; **alleviate** = to mitigate, give temporary relief. The former is usually permanent, the latter is always temporary. E.g.:

"Appointment to the permanent staff allayed his fears of redundancy"
"The soothing lotion alleviated the itching of the rash."

allegiance = loyalty to a person; **alliance** = pact or treaty between nations.

allergic should be reserved for reference to a true (medical) allergy, and not misused to express dislike or antipathy.

alleviate, alleviator.

alliance *See* **allegiance**.

all in = exhausted; **all-in** = inclusive, taken as a whole. E.g.:

"By the time we had climbed the hill we were all in."
"I bought the day's travel and meals for an all-in price of £17."

all in all (e.g. "All in all it is a good result") is, like **by and large,** a cliché to avoid.

allot, allotted, allottable, allotment.

all over Consider the following sentences:
"He tipped his cup and spilled tea on the chair."
"He knocked over a bottle and spilled milk over the floor."
"He tripped over a bucket and spilled water all over the floor."
"The song became popular all over the world."
The first three, using *on, over* and *all over*, correctly convey the idea of an increase in volume spilled with increasingly serious consequences. In the fourth sentence, *all over* means *throughout*, a use to be avoided in formal writing.

allow *See* **permit**.

all ready *See* **already**.

all right is the preferred form of **alright**.

All Saints' Day, All Souls' Day (but All Souls College, Oxford).

all together *See* **altogether**.

allude, allusion *See* **illude**.

allure = to entice, attract as by a lure (noun); **lure** (verb) = to attract someone or something to his/its disadvantage, to entrap.

alluvium (pl. alluvia).

almanac (not almanack).

almost is an adverb and should not be used to qualify a thing, for which use **virtual** (or *near*). E.g.:

"The virtual (or near) certainty that . . ."
Avoid **almost never** (use *hardly ever* or *very seldom*). *See also* **already**.

alms (= charity) is a singular word. The related adjective (meaning charitable, or to do with alms) is the unlikely word *eleemosynary*.

aloes (= a bitter drug), although a plural form, is regarded as singular (e.g. "Aloes is used on the fingers to discourage nail-biting").

alone = unaccompanied, single, on one's own; **lone** = solitary, isolated. The meanings overlap, although the former tends to be used of people and the latter of things (and is usually preceded by *a*). E.g.:

"She preferred to eat alone, not with the crowd";
"All he contributed to the discussion was a lone idea about schedules."

A person who prefers to be alone is a *loner*. Alone can also mean *only*, as in "She alone knew he was lying." *See also* **lonely**.

alongst is archaic for **along**, which should be used.

a lot of *See* **lots of**.

alpha, alpha-numeric (characters on computer displays), alpha particle (= a helium nucleus), alpha rays (streams of alpha particles).

alphabetization Words in a list or index should be alphabetized by considering each word letter by letter to the first comma (or other punctuation mark), ignoring spaces, apostrophes, accents, diacritical marks and hyphens.

Names that include *de, van, von* and the like, should be listed under the most commonly used form of the name. Thus the German statesman Otto von Bismarck should appear as *Bismarck, Otto von*, whereas the Dutch painter Vincent van Gogh should be under *Van Gogh, Vincent*, preferable with a cross-reference from *Gogh, Vincent van*.

M', Mc and *Mac* are listed as if they were spelled *Mac*. Thus the political scientist *McBain, Howard Lee* precedes the Scottish king *Macbeth*, who precedes the American senator *McCarthy, Joseph* (in each instance the letters after the *Mc* or *Mac* determine the alphabetical order). Exceptions to this rule are African names beginning with *M'*; they are listed in strict alphabetical order: *M'Ba, Mbandaka, M'bour, Mdina*, and so on.

Abbreviations are alphabetized as if they were spelled out (e.g. *S*. is alphabetized as San, and *St* is alphabetized as Saint). Therefore, the heading *St Clair, Arthur* is listed before *Saint Clair, Lake*, which precedes *St Denis, Ruth* and the Dutch island *Saint Eustatius*. Again, in each instance the first letters of the word after Saint determine the alphabetical order.

If the same spelling occurs two or more times, alphabetize the words by category in the order persons, places and things. Thus, in a series headed Washington, the person *Washington, George*, precedes the place *Washington*, state, and the latter precedes *Washington, Treaty of* (thing).

The order of listing for persons of the same name is determined by rank: saints, popes, emperors, kings, followed by titled nobility, such as crown prince, duke or count, baron, baronet, and so forth. Monarchs of the same name are listed numerically and alphabetically by country: *Charles X*, King of France (and all the other French Charleses) appears before *Charles III*, King of Naples, who in turn precedes *Charles III* of Spain. In family articles, alphabetize people with identical names chronologically (by birth date).

Identical place-names are alphabetized in order of population.

alphanumeric characters = computer term for letters and numbers, which may be displayed on a screen (VDU) or provided as *hard copy* by a printer (*see* **printer**).

already is an adverb; **all ready** is adjectival. E.g.:

"They are all ready there" (i.e. all of those people are ready);
"They are already there" (i.e. even by this time they are there).
Almost and *all most* are analogous. Compare
"It is all most useful" and "It is almost useful".

alright should be avoided; use **all right**.

altar = table for offerings in a church or temple; **alter** = to change.

altercation = a (verbal) quarrel, not a (physical) fight.

alternate(ly) = by turns; **alternative(ly)** = in a way that offers a choice. E.g.:

"The lights flashed alternately red and green."
"Show a red light, or alternatively show a green one."
As a verb, **alternate** = to take it in turns. *See also* **alternative**.

alternative involves the use of *or* or *and*; **choice** involves the use of *between* or *of*. E.g.:

"The alternative is to walk or to run."
"The alternatives are to walk and to run."
"The alternatives are walking and running."
But note "The choice is between walking and running."

and "He had the choice of walking or running."

The word *alternative* should, strictly, be used to describe one of two possibilities; e.g. "You can choose between the two alternatives, tea and coffee" (not "tea or coffee"). Increasingly usage permits more than two possibilities; e.g. "The vending machine offered six alternatives, from which I chose coffee." In this example, you would strictly choose *among* the six (or make a choice *from among* the six), not *between* them.

although It does no harm if, with a few exceptions, **although** is used consistently instead of **though**, and many publishers' style sheets insist on this. Exceptions include the combinations **as though** (often better put as *as if*), **even though**, and inverted constructions such as "Harmless though it seems, . . .". Phrasing such as "Do not change it, though" (= "But do not change it") is clumsy and should be avoided.

alto (pl. altos).

altogether = entirely, wholly; **all together** = together in time, place or thought, as one body. E.g.:

"The team's performance deteriorated altogether" (completely); "The team lost heart all together" (each member at the same time).

AM is the abbreviation of amplitude modulation (in radio).

a.m. is the abbreviation of *ante meridiem* (before noon).

amateur = non-professional, not done/performed for payment; **amateurish** = inept, to a poor standard.

amazing = causing amazement (i.e. great surprise and wonder); in its overworked guise this word seldom means more than **surprising**. E.g. in "She ate an amazing amount – two portions!", mere *surprising* would probably be emphatic enough. *See also* **surprise**.

ambidextrous (preferred to ambidexterous).

ambiguity = statement capable of more than one interpretation. Ambiguities should be avoided at all costs. More than 200 years ago, a commentator said "... where different, or perhaps contrary meanings are signified by the same word, how easy is it for a mind, prone to error, to take the wrong one?" Eric Partridge quoted this and expressed a similar thought: "... and whenever two or more meanings are confused, we inevitably render hazardous the way of communication." Both writers were, I think, citing an important application of Murphy's law:

"If a word or sentence is capable of two interpretations, the reader will choose the wrong one."

So writers and editors should make sure that all text permits only one interpretation. There is a difference, however, between ambiguity and **vagueness** in writing (although the two terms are sometimes confused). In vague writing the (intended) meaning is unclear because of imprecision and woolliness, not – as in ambiguity – because there are two possible meanings.

ambivalent = having in mind simultaneously two irreconcilable desires. It should be kept as a psychoanalytical term, and not used as a pretentious synonym of *with mixed feelings*.

amenable *to* requires a noun; it should not be followed by a verb. E.g.:

"She is amenable to persuasion" is correct; "He was amenable to listen" is incorrect.

amend = to improve something (that is imperfect); **emend** = to remove errors from a passage of text or a numerical calculation. E.g.:

"He amended the design to make the photograph more prominent";
"She emended the text before it was typeset."

America, strictly, = North America and South America (also called The Americas). The people who live there are Americans. North America = Canada and the United States, although it is sometimes taken to include also Central America (Mexico *et al.*). In English text, *American* usually describes anything pertaining to the United States (as opposed to, say, Canadian), and may be abbreviated to US in tables, etc.

Americanisms English – that is, British English – contains various words from the Americas. These include some derived from Carib, Inuit (Eskimo), North American Indian and South American Indian languages. E.g.:

avocado	hickory	pecan	tamarack
barbecue	hurricane	pemmican	tanager
cannibal	igloo	petunia	tapioca
canoe	jaguar	peyote	tapir
cashew	kayak	piranha	terrapin
caucus	llama	poncho	tobacco
chilli	maize	potato	toboggan
cocoa	moccasin	puma	tomahawk
chipmunk	moose	quetzal	tomato
chocolate	musquash	quinine	totem
coyote	pampas	raccoon	toucan
coypu	papaya	rumba	wampum
curare	papoose	sequoia	wapiti
hammock	parka	skunk	wigwam

Others were taken or modified from the languages of voluntary or involuntary immigrants (for instance, from Africa), sometimes via Portuguese or Spanish. E.g.:

banana	cola	okra	tote
banjo	hamburger	prairie	voodoo
bongo	hokum	pretzel	zombie
boss	hoodlum	rodeo	
caribou	jazz	sleigh	
chaps	limbo	tango	

Modern America has also supplied some words of its own. E.g.:

blurb	gimmick	lynch	teenager
bobcat	hobo	motel	tuxedo
bunkum	jive	maverick	
commuter	know-how	stetson	
gerrymander	lifestyle	stunt	

or influenced English spelling (such as the terms *analog*, *disk* and *program* as used in computer technology). Words in all but the last group are standard English. Words in this last group, the use of totally American expressions (such as "candy store" for "sweet shop", "presently" for "at present" and "truck" for "lorry") and even words that have fallen into disuse in English but are still current in North America (such as "closet" for "cupboard", "gotten" for "got" and "raise" for "rise" in pay) are examples of Americanisms, which should be avoided in normal English writing.

When the Americans and British have different words for the same thing, ignorance of each other's terms generally leads merely to an absence of understanding. Thus what is in the United States termed a *beltway* is called a *ring road* in Britain, *janitor* (USA) is *caretaker* (UK), and *straw boss* (USA) is *assistant foreman* (UK); an Englishman who does not know what a straw boss is will be at a loss if he comes across the term. But when the same spelling means different things in the two countries, misunderstanding can be total (because a person in each country thinks that he *does* know what the other intends). Thus an American in Britain who ordered chips would be surprised to receive French fries, just as a Briton in the United States who asked for a cot for the baby would wonder why he was given a camp bed. Here are some more examples that have taken on a different meaning on each side of the Atlantic Ocean.

word	meaning in the USA (expressed in British terms)	meaning in the UK
bathe	take a bath	take a swim
bill	banknote	account, invoice
blank	form (paper)	gap
bureau	chest of drawers	small fold-down desk
casket	coffin	lidded box
clippings	newspaper cuttings	hedge/hair trimmings
closet	cupboard	private room
cord	electric flex	strong string
cracker	biscuit (usually sweet)	dry biscuit
crib	cot	notes (memory aid)
drawers	underpants	part of furniture, knickers
dry goods	drapery	non-liquid groceries
electric fire	blaze caused by electrical fault	electric room heater
fender	mudguard/car wing	fireplace surround
first floor	ground floor	first floor

Americanisms

formula	baby's feed	mathematical or chemical symbols
garters	man's sock supporters	woman's elastic stocking-supporters
gas fire	blazing petrol	room heater fuelled by gas
grip	holdall	firm hand-hold
help	servant	aid
hood	car bonnet	head covering
jelly	jam	fruit-flavoured gelatine
knickers	boy's breeches	girl's/woman's underwear
loafer	slip-on shoe	idler
lot	plot of land	item at auction
momentarily	in a moment, soon	for a moment
motor	aircraft/car engine	electric motor
notions	fancy goods	ideas
pants	trousers	underpants
paraffin	paraffin wax	paraffin oil, kerosene
pavement	road	footpath alongside road
pit	fruit stone	hole in the ground
porch	veranda	entrance shelter
presently	at the present time, now	in a short time, soon
private school	public school	non-State school
public school	council school	private school
purse	handbag	money holder
raise	a rise	to lift
rubbers	overshoes	erasers
shorts	underpants	short trousers
squash	vegetable marrow	fruit drink
subway	underground railway	underground walkway
suspenders	braces	stocking supporters
switch	railway points	electric switch
trailer	caravan	towed goods carrier
trunk	car boot	large piece of luggage
vest	waistcoat	undershirt

veteran	ex-serviceman (any age)	old soldier
wash up	wash oneself	wash the dishes
5/6/87	6 May 1987	5 June 1987

Words from column one used with the meanings of column two, and words spelled in the American way (e.g. tranquilizer, woolen), are Americanisms.

American spellings Use American words, phrases and spellings only in editions intended for sale in the United States. Retain American spellings when quoting an American source (*see also* **Americanisms**; **quotations**). *See* **units** for American units and measurements.

American states *See* **US states**.

amiable = agreeable or good-natured (of a person); **amicable** = friendly (of relationships or arrangements). E.g.:

"Amiable people generally have amicable relationships."

amid *See* **mid**.

amoeba has the preferred plural **amoebas** (not *amoebae*).

amok is the preferred spelling (not **amuck**).

among should be used consistently instead of **amongst**. *See also* **between**.

among other reasons/things should be avoided; the usual meaning is "along with other ...", "apart from other ...", "besides" or, most often, "in addition to other ..."

amoral = non-moral, lacking in morals; **immoral** = wicked, corrupt. E.g.:

"Someone of amoral upbringing may develop immoral tendencies."

amortize(= spread initial cost over many repayments).

amount applies to mass or bulk (or money), not to number. E.g.:

"A large amount of timber" but "A large number of tables."

amp. is the abbreviation of ampere.

ampersand (&) should be avoided in ordinary text unless it is part of a direct quotation (e.g. "The company of Jones & Co."). Do not use *&c.* for *etc.*

amuck *See* **amok**.

an *See* **a or an**.

anaesthesia, anaesthetic, anaesthetize.

analogous = having analogy, resembling in certain circumstances or effects, parallel; **similar** = having a resemblance or likeness, of like kind. Both words are used with *to*. E.g.:

"The action of the elbow joint is analogous to that of a hinge."
"The bones of the fingers are similar to those of the toes."

analogue = something of like appearance or function;
analogy = point of correspondence between things that are otherwise different. E.g.:

"The elbow and a hinge are analogues, because they allow movement in only one plane."
"The past participle of *strive* is *striven*, by analogy with *drive* and *driven*."
Increasingly in computer technology, *analog* is being spelled in the American way. *See also* **data**; **disk**.

analogy = figure of speech that compares two things or makes them equivalent. It is a useful device for giving explanations (of the unfamiliar in terms of the familiar) without having to resort to formal definitions. E.g.:

"In many of their chemical reactions, rubidium and caesium behave much like sodium and potassium."

(Thus readers who know all about sodium and potassium now know something about rubidium and caesium). *See also* **simile**.

analysis (pl. analyses), analyse, analyst, analytic(al).

anatomical/biological/medical terms are set in lower case unless they include a proper noun or adjective; e.g. Adam's apple, Fallopian tube, Golgi apparatus, Huntington's chorea, islets of Langerhans.

ancient refers to the remote past – it is the opposite of modern; **antiquated** refers to something that is no longer used or is no longer in style/fashion; **archaic** refers to things that were used in the past and are used now only in historical reconstruction; **obsolete** refers to things that are no longer used because they have been superseded (supposedly by something better); **obsolescent** refers to things that are becoming obsolete.

Ancient Egyptians/Greeks etc. need an initial capital letter on *Ancient*.

ancillary (not ancilliary).

and Avoid beginning a sentence with *and*, although it is not forbidden; never begin a paragraph with *and*. Do not use a comma before *and* at the end of a list (unless the last-but-one item on the list comprises two things linked by *and*). See **punctuation** (comma).

and/or should be avoided in ordinary writing; e.g. "He will give it to his brother and/or sister" is better put as "...to his brother or sister, or to both of them."

and which, if used, should be preceded by another *which* clause; e.g. "The dog, which had bitten him and which continued to bare its teeth, stood its ground." Usually the second *which* in such constructions can be omitted.

anecdote = short account (about an event or person); **antidote** = medicine to counteract/treat poisoning.

anemone

anent is archaic for **about** or **concerning**, either of which should be used.

aneurysm is the preferred spelling (not **aneurism**).

angry *at* things or events; **angry** *with* people. E.g.:

"She was angry at the damage, and with the driver for having caused it."

angst is a term in psychology and psychiatry; it is better left there and not used as a synonym for ordinary anxiousness or anxiety.

annex (verb) = to take over, add on; **annexe** (noun) = an addition (usually to a building).

annoyed *at* a thing or occurrence; **annoyed** *with* a person. E.g.:

"I was annoyed at the error and with myself for making it."

annul, annulled, annulling, but annulment.

annunciation = proclamation, announcement; **enunciation** = method of or distinctness in pronunciation.

anon is archaic for **soon**, which should be used.

another should not be used for plain **other**; e.g. "some way or another" is incorrect. Neither misuse **another** for **one other**; e.g. "There is only another page to go" is also incorrect. **Another** should not be used for a second number unless it is identical to the first one. E.g.:

"Nearly 3,000 people attended the meeting and another 3,000 waited outside" is correct;
"About 10,000 people died of starvation and another 30,000 are suffering from malnutrition" is incorrect
(say ". . . an additional 30,000 are" or ". . . 30,000 others are").

ante- = before (in place or time); **anti-** = against (opposed to). E.g.:

antechamber, antedate, antenatal (= prenatal), ante-room;
and anti-aircraft, antibiotic, anticline, anticlockwise, antidote,
antifreeze, anti-hero, antimatter, antiparticiple, anti-Semitic, anti-
Semitism, antitoxin.

The spelling of anticipate (which *see*) appears illogical.

antedate *See* **predate**.

antenna, = a radio or radar aerial, has the plural *antennas*; **antenna,**
 = a "feeler" of an insect or other animal, has the plural *antennae*.

anthology = book containing a collection of items (particularly poems
or songs), usually selected by one person; **atlas** = collection of maps
in book form; **compendium** (pl. compendiums, not compendia) =
book containing a collection of abstracts from a single larger source
or from various sources; **dictionary** = a book listing words and
their meanings, or their equivalents in another language, sometimes
with pronunciations and definitions and almost invariably arranged
in alphabetical order; **encyclopaedia** = a book that provides
information about all branches of knowledge, as a series of articles
arranged alphabetically or thematically; **gazetteer** = alphabetical
list of place-names, usually with their locations and a brief
description or acting as an index to an atlas etc.; **glossary** =
collection of definitions of specialist terms usually as an alphabetic
list in a book; **index** = alphabetical list, usually at the end of a book,
of topics and the page numbers on which they can be found;
lexicon = dictionary; **omnibus** = book containing a collection of
previously published items, usually by one author and often sold at
a lower price than the total cost of the individual publications. The
terms *compendium, lexicon* and *omnibus* are now seldom used. But in
their search for new titles for reference books, publishers have
extended the meaning of some of the other terms. For instance an
atlas may be a book with only some maps or even none at all, a
dictionary may be any book in which the collection of items is listed
alphabetically, and an *encyclopaedia* may be devoted to the various
aspects of a single subject; a *compendium* is more often a collection
of games or puzzles. *See also* **encyclopaedia**.

anti- *See* **ante-**.

anticipate = to act before someone else, notice a need and act in advance. It should not be used to mean merely **expect**; e.g. "I anticipate that the article will be finished by Friday" is incorrect.

anticlimax = figure of speech that employs a sudden drop in importance or emphasis following a gradual rise. E.g.:

"Thin clouds thickened and gathered, became increasingly heavy and dark, and then dissolved away."
See also **climax**.

antipathy = strong dislike bordering on hatred; **antithesis** (pl. antitheses) = opposite of. E.g.:

"I have an antipathy to firearms"
"The demonstration was the antithesis of non-violence".

antiquated *See* **ancient**.

antithesis = figure of speech that contrasts opposite terms or statements, usually to emphasize a point. E.g.:

"Rush the planning and you slow the production."

antonomasia Figure of speech in which a term (epithet) stands for a person (e.g. "Virgin Queen" for Elizabeth I, "Iron Duke" for the Duke of Wellington, "Iron Lady" for Margaret Thatcher).

antonyms = words of opposite meaning (e.g. *hot* and *cold*); **synonyms** = words of the same meaning (e.g. *gorse* and *furze*). *See* **homonym**; **synonym**.

anxious = worried, feeling or displaying anxiety; the word should not be used to mean merely expectant or eager, particularly if it is pleasurable expectation. E.g.:

"The convicted man was anxious to hear the sentence of the court" (correct);
"She was anxious to receive the prize" (incorrect).

anyone = anybody (which is preferred) should be distinguished from **any one**, as in "The poison can kill anyone (anybody)" and "The poison could kill any one of us." *Anyone, anybody, no one, nobody,*

some one and *somebody* are all singular and conventionally
represented by a masculine pronoun, unless specifically female.
Some publishers, however, insist on the "he or she" formula. *See*
gender.

anything/something can be replaced by **any thing/some thing**
when contrasted with any person or the pronouns in the preceding
entry; e.g. "He will buy anything" and "He will not paint people or
animals but he will paint any thing you ask him to" (better as
". . . anything else . . ." "or. . . any object . . .").

anyway = in any case, and is often a non-essential part of a sentence;
any way = in any manner, by any method. E.g.:

"I did not use the illustration – it was poorly drawn anyway."
"She can do the illustration any way we like."

a or an (indefinite article)

1. Before all normal vowels (and dipthongs), use *an*:

an animal	an aim	an authority
an easel	an 8-year-old	an entertainer
an illness	an opening	an unusual

2. Before a silent *h*, use *an*:

an heiress	an honorary	an hour

(which are pronounced as if spelled "airess", "onorary", "our").

3. Before an aspirated *h*, use *a*:

a habitual	a heraldic	a heroic
a historical	a hotel	a hypothesis

which, in older usage, would have taken *an* (because the first
syllable of each is unaccented; old usage would have been "an
history" and "an historical").

4. Before a syllable beginning with a vowel but with the sound of
w- or *y*-, use *a*:

a eucalpytus	a ewe	a once-only
a one-off	a unity	a useful

5. Before all normal consonants, use *a*.

6. With letters or groups of letters, be guided by pronunciation:

a BBC broadcast	a D-shaped part	an FA Cup Winner
a KLM flight	a NATO conference	an OPEC country
an RAC rating	an S-bend	a U-turn

ape, aped, aping, apish.

apex (pl. apexes).

aphis (pl. aphides, although *aphis* is increasingly being used also as the plural form).

apiary = place for keeping bees; **aviary** = place for keeping birds.

apostrophe = punctuation mark or figure of speech. The punctuation mark indicates the omission of letters or possession (genitive case); e.g. "can't" (omission), "John's book" (possession). *See also* **ellipsis**; **punctuation** (apostrophe). As a figure of speech, apostrophe is usually employed only in conversation, in which an inanimate object is addressed as if it were a person (or an absent person is addressed as if he or she were present); e.g. "This typewriter is always making mistakes – 'Why do you do it to me?'" *See also* **personification**.

Apothecaries' weights and measures *See* **units**.

apparatus (pl. apparatuses).

appease, appeasement.

appendix, meaning an addition to a book, has the plural *appendixes*; as a term in medicine, it has the plural *appendices*.

appetite, appetize, appetizer, appetizing.

appliqué, appliquéed, appliquéing.

apposite = appropriate, apt, suited to its purpose; **opposite** = opposed, directly contrary, face to face.

appraise = to evaluate; **apprise** = to inform, make award; **apprize** (archaic) = to (estimate the) value (of).

apprehensive = dreading something that is to come; **timid** = lacking self-confidence; **timorous** = timid but shrinking (habitually) because of lack of courage.

appropriate, as an adjective, is overused. Take the appropriate action and try *right, suitable, fitting* or *proper*, for a change.

approve = confirm, think well of, ratify (noun *approval*); **endorse** = to note on a document or to assign (in writing), give one's name to, sanction (noun *endorsement*).

approx. is the abbreviation of approximate(ly).

approximate(ly) = very close(ly). It should not be used when *about* or *roughly* will do; nor should it be applied to figures that are not approximate (but exact). The absurd expression *very approximate* should be avoided; it means, if anything, *not* very approximate.

apt *See* **liable**.

aquarium (pl. aquariums).

Arabia The preferred adjective and noun for the people is *Arab* (not *Arabic*, which should be reserved for the language, or *Arabian*, except in names such as Arabian desert). *See also* **Arabic words**.

Arabic numerals are the "ordinary" numbers 1, 2, 3, 4, 5, 6, 7, 8, 9 and 0. *See also* **numbers and counting; roman numerals**.

Arabic words that have contributed to the English vocabulary include several that incorporate the definite article *al-* (admira*l*, *al*chemy, *al*cohol, *al*cove, *al*embic, *al*gebra, *al*kali). Many other words can be traced to Arabic origins – possibly by way of India, Persia or Turkey or even via French or Spanish. Sometimes they present spelling difficulties, so here, for interest and as a spelling check, is a list of examples:

arsenal	fez	marabou	sequin
burnous	gala	mattress	sheikh
cadi	gazelle	minaret	sherbet
caftan	giraffe	mocha	sirocco
camphor	ghoul	monsoon	soda
candy	harem	mosque	sofa
caracal	henna	muezzin	sugar
carafe	hookah	mufti	sumac
carat	howdah	mullah	tabby
caraway	jar	mummy	tamarind
carob	jasmine	nadir	tarboosh
caviare	jerboa	orange	tare
cipher	jumper	popinjay	tariff
coffee	kebab	quintal	turban
dhow	kismet	racket	vizier
divan	lemon	realgar	wadi
djellaba	lilac	saffron	yashmak
douane	loofah	saker	zenith
elixir	lute	saluki	zero
fakir	magazine	sash	

arbitrate, arbitrator (= someone who impartially and with given authority resolves a dispute), arbiter (= someone who comments on matters of taste or gives an expert opinion in a dispute), arbitrary, arbitration. *See also* **mediate**.

arbor = spindle for holding a rotating tool or workpiece; **arbour** = bower of trees, tree-shaded area.

arc (noun) = part of a circle, spark between two electrodes; **ark** = (wooden) chest, Noah's vessel.

archaeology is the preferred spelling (not **archeology**).

archaic *See* **ancient**.

archaisms are old-fashioned words that should by now have passed on, but are sometimes preserved as a single use in a cliché or used in "precious" writing. Several common examples, such as *betwixt,* *nigh* and *wont,* are included in this Dictionary, usually with the advice to avoid them. *See also* **non-standard English**.

archipelago (pl. archipelagos).

Arctic has an initial capital letter when it is used for the region round the North Pole (which also has initial capital letters); e.g. "the weak Arctic sunshine", "the cold Arctic seas". **Arctic Circle** also has initial capital letters.

aren't should not be used for **are not** in formal writing.

Argentina The derived adjective and noun is *Argentine* (not Argentinian).

argot, often regarded as the same as **cant,** is a type of slang restricted to a particular group of people, such as criminals. *See* **non-standard English; slang**.

argue, arguing, arguable, argument.

arise has the past tense **arose** and past participle **arisen**. *See also* **raise**.

armadillo (pl. armadillos).

aroma is usually precious for **smell** or **odour,** either of which is preferred.

around should be avoided as a substitute for **about** (e.g. "It was built around the 1800s" is better put as "... about the 1800s") and not used for **round** (e.g. "He passed the salt around the table" should be "... round the table"). In general, *around* should refer to something moving or placed in an extensive area (e.g. "The horses galloped around the moors") whereas *round* should indicate motion in a circular path (e.g. "The horses galloped round the final bend").

arouse = engender, give rise to, stimulate, wake from sleep; **rouse** = stir from dormancy or inaction. E.g.:

"The national music aroused feelings of patriotism."
"The sudden threat roused him into action."

arpeggio (pl. arpeggios).

arrange, arrangeable, arrangement.

arras = hanging tapestry screen; **arris** = horizontal, triangular rail of a fence, sharp-edged stone; **arête** = sharp rocky ridge (on a mountain).

arrest, arrestable, arrestment (rare).

art, artistic, arty-crafty (= pretentiously artistic), artful (= deceitful, cunning), artless (= innocent, naive). *See also* **inartistic**.

artboard = papermaking term for a gloss-coated (polished) board, similar to art paper but weighing more than 220 gsm, used for high-quality printing. *See also* **paper**.

art deco/art nouveau (no initial capital letters).

artefact is the preferred spelling (not **artifact**).

article *See* **a or an**.

artificial satellites Italicize their names and use Arabic numerals; e.g. *Early Bird, Comsat, Telstar, Skylab 1*.

artist = someone who draws, paints sculpts, etc.; **artiste** = a professional entertainer.

artless = innocent, ingenuous, naive, "uncrafty"; **ignorant** = lacking in knowledge (often used pejoratively).

art paper = type of paper with a heavy china clay coating and polished (gloss-coated) by supercalendering to a highly smooth finish; used for high-quality printing. *Imitation art* is a paper with a similar finish achieved by incorporating a heavy loading of china clay in the pulp before the paper is made. *See also* **paper**.

artwork *See* **A/W**.

as should not be misused for **because**, a use that often leads to
ambiguity. E.g. "He could not read as he was lying in bed" is
capable of two interpretations (or four with the additional
ambiguity of *lying*). *See also* **than**.

ascend, ascender, ascendant, ascendance, ascendancy, ascension.

ascender (typography) *See* **x-height**.

ascent = a going up; **assent** = agreement, consent.

ASCII (usually pronounced "*as-key*") = acronym for *A*merican
*S*tandard *C*ode for *I*nformation *I*nterchange, an advanced
computer language used by most modern computerized typesetting
systems.

ascribe = to assign, reckon; **attribute** (verb) = to impute, consider as
belonging. The meanings overlap and the words are near
synonyms.

ascus (pl. asci).

A series = range of ISO (formerly DIN) international paper sizes.
See **paper sizes**.

as far as ... is/are concerned should be avoided as an alternative to
a simpler preposition such as **for**; e.g. "There are some attractive
clothes as far as the younger age groups are concerned" is better
put as "... clothes for younger people."

as follows is the correct form of introducing one or several listed
items. E.g.:

"The most popular choice is as follows: English."
"The most popular choices were as follows: English, Biology and
History" (not "as follow:").

Asia The derived adjective and noun is *Asian* (not Asiatic).

aside from should be avoided in the sense *except* or *apart from.*

asinine

asperate *See* **aspire.**

asphalt (not ashphalt, asphalte).

asphyxia, asphyxiate, asphyxiation.

aspire, aspirant (who aspires), aspirate (=breathe, pronounce the letter *h*), aspirator (=apparatus for producing a flow of gas), aspiration (=hope, breathing, pronouncing an *h*, or action of an aspirator); **asperate** (=roughen), asperity (=roughness, extreme coldness).

assassin, assassinate, assassination.

assay (verb), an archaic word for **try,** now means testing metals/ores; **assay** (noun)=a (scientific) test; **essay** (verb)=to attempt, to try; **essay** (noun)=an attempt (archaic), a prose composition.

assess, assessable, assessor.

asset = valuable possession, advantage; **assets** = property.

assign, assignee (preferred to assignor), assignment, assignation. An *assignment* is an alloted task; and *assignation* is an arranged meeting (often furtive, sometimes amorous).

assimilate *See* **simulate.**

assist, assistant (preferred to assister; assistor, legal). Assist someone *in* doing something, not assist someone *to do* something.

assume = to adopt, (take for granted); **presume** = to take as true without definite proof, (take upon onself, take for granted). These verbs are often interchangeable, especially in their secondary meanings. E.g.:

"He assumed the role of dictator."

"He saw your car outside and so presumed you were there."
"He saw your car outside and so assumed you were there."
Assumption and **presumption** are also similar in some of their meanings.

assure, assurable, assurer (who gives assurance), assuror (an insurance underwriter). *See also* **insure**.

asterisk (*) *See* **footnotes**.

asthma, asthmatic.

as though *See* **although**.

astonish *See* **surprise**.

astound *See* **surprise**.

astronomical terms Constellations, planets, stars and other named celestial bodies have an initial capital letter(s); e.g. Great Bear (= Ursa Major), Venus, Earth, Sun, Moon, Dog Star, Orion Nebula, Milky Way (*see also* **Earth**; **Moon**).
Messier numbers are typeset with no space before the catalogue number (e.g. M42); New General Catalogue numbers do have a space (e.g. NGC 332).

asymmetry, asymmetric(al). **Asymmetry** = lack of symmetry; **dissymmetry** = asymmetry, or the symmetry of right and left hand, of an object and its mirror image.

at should not be used for *in* in the construction "She was born in England/London/Kensington/Cromwell Road." Note also "He went to university *in* London", "He studied *at* Queen Mary College" and "He graduated *from* the University of London."

atheist *See* **agnostic**.

atlas *See* **anthology**.

atm. is the abbreviation of atmosphere (unit of pressure).

at. no. is the abbreviation of atomic number.

atom bomb is the preferred form (editorially speaking) of **atomic bomb**.

atomic *See* **nuclear**.

atomize, atomization.

atrium (pl. atria).

atrocious should be reserved to describe an *atrocity* (= a brutal, barbaric or extremely wicked act), and not used to mean merely poor quality or bad (as in "The player made an atrocious mistake").

attaché

attain = to reach, gain, achieve; **accomplish** = to perform (a task), succeed in (an undertaking). E.g.:

"To attain the target amount you must accomplish something every day."

attend, attendant, attendance.

attended *by* another person; **attended** *with* another thing or things.

at the end of the day is a modern cliché (equivalent to the older ones "when all is said and done" and "when it comes down to it") meaning, if anything, *finally* or *ultimately*. They should all be avoided. *See also* **basically**.

at the present time, like **at this moment in time,** = now (or today), which should be used.

attire, like **garb,** is precious for **clothes** or **dress,** either of which is preferred.

attribute (verb). *See* **ascribe**.

attune = make to correspond, arrange in a suitable way; **tune** = put in tune or (figuratively) put in accord with, adjust something to a required form or state. Thus the usual meaning of the former overlaps with the figurative meaning of the latter. E.g.:

"He found it difficult to attune his views to hers";
"She decided to tune her attitudes to those of the rest of the group."

at. wt. is the abbreviation of atomic weight, which may more accurately be presented as atomic mass (at. mass) or atomic mass number (at. mass no.).

AU is the abbreviation of astronomical unit.

audible, audio.

auditorium (pl. auditoriums).

au fait (italics) = acquainted, instructed; the French term should be avoided.

auger = tool for boring; **augur** = Roman fortune-teller.

aught = anything, in any way (archaic); **ought** = should. E.g.:

"I doubt that it will come to aught."
"Ought it to come to anything?" (= "Should it come...")

aunt = sister of one's parent and, by extension, wife of one's uncle. *See also* **family relationships** (diagram).

aural = pertaining to the ear or hearing; **oral** = pertaining to the mouth, the voice or speaking. *See also* **oral**.

auspicious = with good omens for success, favourable, of good auspices; the word should not be used as a synonym of memorable (as in the cliché "auspicious occasion").

Australia and New Zealand have English as their official language. Early British settlers in these countries adopted some words from the local people (particularly names of indigenous animals), and these are now part of English. For example, Australian Aborigines donated boomerang, budgerigar, dingo, kangaroo, koala, kookaburra, wallaby, wallaroo and woomera, whereas kauri, kiwi, mana, moa and tuna (eel) are Maori words, and lei, taboo, tattoo and ukulele are from various Pacific island languages.

autarchy = despotism, absolute sovereignty; **autarky** = national (economic) independence; **autocracy** = government by a single absolute ruler.

authoress Most female authors prefer to be called *authors*, although *lady author* (like *lady doctor*) is accepted by some. *See also* **gender**.

authority, authorize, authorization, authoritative (not authoritive), authoritarian. An expert is an authority *on* something; someone in power has authority *over* someone else – he or she has authority *to* do something or *for* doing something. E.g.:

"He is an authority on silver snuffboxes."
"She has authority over the other workers."
"She has authority to organize their work."
"She has the authority for checking their work."

autobahn (pl. autobahns, not autobahnen). *See also* **motorway**.

autocracy = absolute rule or government (by an individual); **autonomy** = self-rule or self-government.

automaton (pl. automatons, preferred to automata).

automobile is no longer the usual American word for car (for which the usual word now is *car*). It is retained in such expressions as automobile industry which, in both Britain and the United States, is being replaced by automotive industry (although this is a wider term, including lorries (ever more commonly being called *trucks* in English) and sometimes agricultural and earth-moving vehicles).

auxiliary (not auxillary).

avant-garde

avenge another person (take vengeance on behalf of someone else);
  revenge oneself upon (take revenge on).

average (= arithmetic *mean*) of a set of *n* numbers is their sum
  divided by *n*. The **mode** is the number that appears most
  frequently in the set. The **median** is the number that has exactly
  the same number of values larger than it than there are values
  smaller than it. Average should apply to a quantity, not to a person
  (e.g. "The English drink an average of 50 gallons of tea per person
  every year", not "The average Englishman drinks 50 gallons of tea
  each year.").

averse *See* **adverse**.

avert, avertible, aversion.

avocation = ancillary occupation, side-line; **vocation** = main
  occupation, calling.

Avoirdupois weights *See* **units**.

A/W (or a/w) = abbreviation of artwork, the publishing term for any
  non-photographic, non-typeset illustration – line or tone, black-
  and-white or colour. The term is sometimes extended to
  mechanicals and other pasted-up material prepared for reproduction
  and plate-making. *See* **CRC**; **mechanical**.

awake, awaken, wake, waken These four verbs should be inflected
  as follows:

awake	awoke	awaked (not awoke or awoken)
awaken	awakened	awakened (not awoken)
wake	woke	woken
waken	wakened	wakened

Simplification can be achieved by using only two verbs: *wake* and
wake up, which inflect the same way.

award = something given as a result of a judgement or arbitration,
  possibly after a trial or competition (e.g. a football referee can
  award a free kick, an Ombudsman can award compensation);

reward = something given in recognition (e.g. an insurance company may offer a reward for the recovery of stolen property).

awe, awesome, awful, awe-inspiring. *Awful/awfully* have been so grossly overworked as pejorative terms that *awe-inspiring* now has to be used of things that inspire awe. As the Fowlers said; "*Awfully nice* is an expression than which few could be sillier."

axel = jump in ice-skating; **axil** = angle between a leaf-stalk and its stem; **axle** = spindle holding a wheel or wheels.

axis (pl. axes).

ay = yes; **aye** = always (both archaic). *Ayes* is the plural of *ay* ("The ayes have it").

aye-aye (Madagascan lemur).

B

b. (italics) is the abbreviation of born.

baby is usually used for a child up to the age of about 2 years; *newborn* may be used for a baby in the first few months of life. From the age of 2 to about 4 or 5 the term *infant* (or, increasingly, *pre-school child*) is generally employed. Pre-pubescent children aged 5 to about 11 (corresponding to those in infant, junior and primary schools in Britain) are best described as *schoolchildren*. For children after puberty (those in the secondary school), the term *adolescent* or *teenager* can be used, possibly becoming *young man* or *young woman* at the upper end of the teenage scale. *Young person* or *young people* are also acceptable terms, although *a youth* should be avoided unless the reference is specifically to a boy. The expression *little child* should be avoided (use *young child*). The conventional singular pronoun when referring to a baby or infant is *he* (and is preferred to *it*). If this is objected to for sexist reasons, use *he or she* or one of the other devices described under *he*. *See also* **gender**; **pupil**.

baccy = tobacco (slang); **bakkie** = pick-up truck (in South Africa).

bacillus (pl. bacilli) (= rod-shaped **bacterium**; which *see*).

backache, backbender, backbite, back-boiler, backbone, backbreaking, backchat, back-cloth, backcross, back door (noun), back-door (adj.), back-draught, backdrop, back-end, backfire, back-formation, back garden, background, backhand, back-handed, back-hander, backlash, back-list, backlog, back-number, back-pedal, backrest, back room, back-scratcher, back seat, backside, backslide, backstage, backstitch, backstroke, backtrack, backwash, backwoods(man), back yard.

back-list = book publisher's term for previously published titles, kept in stock (and reprinted if necessary) because they have a continuing sale (*see also* **edition**); **back-number** = magazine or newspaper publisher's and retailer's term for unsold copies of a previous issue, usually made available to purchasers on request.

back matter *See* **prelims**.

back-slang = form of slang in which words are pronounced backwards or given their totally opposite meaning (e.g. *cool* = look, *yob* = boy; *bad* or *wicked* = good). *See also* **slang**.

backward can be an adjective (e.g. "a backward child") or an adverb (e.g. "move backward"), although **backwards** is the preferred form of the adverb. *See also* **-wards**.

bacterium (pl. bacteria).

baggage is a singular word, meaning suitcases and so on taken by passengers travelling by air or sea; **luggage** is also singular, used by travellers by land (car, coach or train). *Baggage* used to mean *luggage* is an Americanism. A plural can be achieved by the construction "items of luggage/baggage".

bail (noun) = money or other security lodged with a court to secure the temporary release of a prisoner before trial, or one of the crosspieces on cricket stumps; **bail** (verb) = to provide or release on bail, to remove water from a boat; **bale** (noun) = a large bundle; **bale** (verb) = to make bales, or (with *out*) to parachute from an aircraft. A person who bails water is a *bailer*; a person or a machine that makes bales is a *baler*. These are the preferred forms, although *bale* is an alternative spelling of the verb *bail* (but not vice versa). *Bale* is also an archaic word for *evil* (*see* **baleful**).

bailey = part of a castle; **bailie** (or baillie) = Scottish magistrate.

Bahamas The derived adjective and noun is *Bahamian*.

Bahrain The derived adjective and noun is *Bahraini*.

balance, balanceable. Balance should not be used to mean *remainder* or *rest*; e.g. "I shall make the first three articles; you must make the balance" is incorrect. **Balance** (verb) = to put in equilibrium, to

apportion equally; **balance** (noun) = equilibrium, scales for
weighing; **unbalance** (verb) = to put out of equilibrium;
imbalance (noun) = lack of equilibrium. *Unbalance* should be
avoided as a noun, and *imbalance* should be avoided as a verb.
Unbalanced often means mentally unstable. *Inbalance* should never
be used – particularly because it could be confused with *in balance*.

balcony = railed off and elevated platform projecting from the
outside wall of a building, reached by a window or French window;
gallery = railed off and elevated platform projecting from the
inside wall of a building, a long narrow room. The "layers" of seats
in a theatre are called *stalls* (ground floor), *dress circle*, *balcony* and
gallery (uppermost level).

bale *See* **bail**.

baleful = evil, hurtful, malignant; **baneful** = poisonous, harmful,
destructive. Both words now have an old-fashioned ring to them.

balk (noun and verb) is the preferred spelling of **baulk** (except in
billiards and snooker).

ballot, balloted, balloting.

bamboo (pl. bamboos).

Bangladesh The derived adjective is *Bangladeshi*; the people (as a
nation) are *Bangalees*; many of them (as an ethnic group) are
Bengalis.

banister = a (usually wooden) upright that supports the handrail of a
(usually indoor) staircase; **banisters** = the whole rail and its
(wooden) supports; **baluster** = a (usually stone) upright that
supports a (usually outdoor) coping or rail; **balustrade** = the whole
rail and its (stone) supports.

banjo (pl. banjos).

bank, in papermaking, = a type of flimsy thin paper, used
principally for making carbon copies (although less frequently used

since the introduction of photocopiers). It gets its name from its resemblance to paper for banknotes (in transparency, but not in strength); bank paper usually has a weight of less than 60 gsm (*see* **gsm**).

banzai = Japanese battle-cry; **bonsai** = technique/art of growing miniaturised trees in containers.

baptize, baptism, Baptist, baptistry (not baptistery).

bar, used to mean *but* or *except*, is at best a colloquialism and should be avoided. E.g.: in "They all came bar the twins", *bar* should be *except*.

Barbados The derived adjective and noun is *Barbadian*.

barbecue (not any of the many variants).

bar code = pattern of thick and thin lines on a document, package or book cover which can be "read" by an optical character reader (OCR) and translated into electronic signals for processing by a computer. It is an increasingly common method of computerizing stock control and may be an obligatory part of a book jacket or cover. *See also* **OCR**.

bare (verb) = to uncover, expose (e.g. 'He bared his chest''); **bare** (adj.) = uncovered, naked (e.g. "He displayed his bare chest"); **bear** (verb) = suffer, endure, carry or give birth to (e.g. "She bears pain in silence"; "He bears arms for the queen"; "Most mammals bear their young in spring"); **bear** (noun) = large furry mammal (e.g. "Bears are reputed to like honey"). For past tenses and participles, *see* **bear**.

bar mitzvah

baron holds a **barony**; **baronet** holds a **baronetcy**.

barque is the preferred spelling of **bark** (a sailing vessel).

barrel, barrelled, barelling, barrelage.

bases is the plural of both *base* and *basis*.

basically is often included in a sentence for no purpose (e.g. in "Basically, there are three options . . ." or "There are basically three options . . .", delete *basically*).

basinet = light metal helmet; **bassinet** = (old-fashioned) pram or cradle.

basis (pl. bases).

bath (verb) = wash in a bath; **bathe** = moisten with liquid, wash a wound, swim (in the sea). E.g.:

"Please bath the dog."
"Please bathe the dog's injured paw."
The past tenses are spelled the same (e.g. "I bathed the dog"; "I bathed the dog's paw"), but pronounced differently.

bathos = figure of speech involving a sudden transition from the sublime to the ridiculous; it should be used only for humorous effect. E.g.:

"The archbishop looked magnificent in his mitre, golden robes and blue woollen socks showing over his shoes."

baton = a stick, staff, truncheon; **batten** = a strip of (sawn) timber.

battle-axe, battle-cry, battledress, battlefield, battleground, battleship.

baud = unit of speed in data transmission (equivalent to one "piece" per second); **bawd** = brothel-keeper or prostitute.

baulk *See* **balk**.

bayonet, bayoneted, bayoneting.

bay window sticks out from a wall; **bow window** is a curved bay window.

bazaar = (Eastern) market; **bizarre** = strange, odd, extravagant.

BC (abbreviation of before Christ) is usually typeset in small capital letters without full points, indicated <u>BC</u>, after the relevant date.

bear (verb, meaning "give birth to") has the past tense **bore** and past participle **born**. When **bear** = to carry, the past tense is still **bore** but the past participle is **borne**.

beat (verb) has the past tense **beat** and preferred past participle **beaten** (not *beat*).

beau (pl. beaux).

beauty, beautiful, beauteous (avoid), beautify.

because should not be misused for **that** e.g. "The importance of science is because it broadens the mind" should be "The importance . . . is that it broadens the mind." Avoid beginning a sentence with *because*. *See also* **as; for**.

become has the past tense **became** and past participle **become**.

bedbug, bedclothes, bedcover, bedfellow, bed-jacket, bedpan, bedpost, bedridden, bedrock, bedroom, bedside, bed-sitter (-sitting-room), bedsore, bedspread, bedstead, bedtime.

bedouin (= desert-dwelling Arab) does not need an initial capital letter – neither does *bushman* (Australian) nor *nomad*, although *Bushman* (of a particular South African group) does.

beef has the plural **beefs** when it means kinds of beef, cuts of meat; it has the plural **beeves** when it means cattle or oxen.

beer *See* **ale**.

beforehand (one word).

befriend = act as a comforter to; it does not mean "to make friends with", for which use *make friends with*.

begin has the past tense **began** and the past participle **begun**. *See also* **commence; start.**

beg the question *See* **question.**

behest is archaic for **command, request** (as in the cliché "at his behest"); either of the modern alternatives should be used.

behindhand, = in arrears (with), can usually be replaced by the simpler **behind** (as in "I am behindhand with my work").

behove is archaic for *to be fit or proper for* (used impersonally with *it*: e.g. "It behoves me to pass judgement in this matter"); the alternative spelling **behoove** is now an Americanism; **behoof** is archaic for *behalf* or *benefit*. All three words should be avoided.

Belgium The derived adjective and noun is *Belgian*.

belief *in* something, not belief *of*.

believe, believable. *See also* **make-believe.**

bell code = coded command, on the keyboard of a typesetting computer, which allows a larger number of different signals than would otherwise be available.

bellicose = warlike, liable to wage war; **belligerent** = waging war. E.g.:

"The new republic was worried by its neighbour's bellicose attitude."
"The neighbouring country continued its belligerent action with daily air raids on the capital."

bellows (noun) is a plural word; "a pair of bellows" achieves a singular construction.

below *See* **above; beneath.**

bend (verb) inflects *bend – bent – bent.*

beneath = lower than; it should not be misused for **under** (as in "Miners work beneath the ground", which is incorrect).

benefactor

benefit, benefited, benefiting.

benzene = liquid hydrocarbon (a single substance, which is the basis of aromatic organic chemistry); **benzine** = mixture of petroleum hydrocarbons (used as a general solvent), and containing no benzene, **benzoin** – natural hard resin from various south-east Asian trees.

bequeathe, bequeather (= testator), bequest.

bereave is a little-used verb meaning to deprive, cause to be orphaned or widowed; its preferred past tense and participle is **bereaved**, although *bereft* is retained as an adjective (as in the cliché "bereft of beauty"). It should be remembered, however, that someone can become bereft only of something he or she once possessed; the woman of the cliché is bereft of beauty only if she was once beautiful (if she was never beautiful she is merely *plain* or perhaps even *ugly*).

beseech is archaic for **entreat** (which also now sounds old-fashioned) and precious for **ask**; the simple **beg** usually serves instead. If *beseech* must be used, the old past tense and participle *besought* is probably more in keeping than the more modern form *beseeched*.

beside = at the side of; **besides** = as well, in addition to (but not *other than*). Both words are used incorrectly in these examples:
"There were two girls beside the twenty men there" (in which *besides* = *in addition to* is intended);
"The reaction must have been caused by something besides an acid" (in which *other than* is intended). *See also* **by**.

best known etc. is hyphenated when it precedes a noun (e.g. "best-known designer", "best-loved hymn") but unhyphenated when following a verb (e.g. "design for which she is best known").

bête noire (italics) = pet aversion, bugbear; either of the English
forms is preferred to the French expression.

bethink (past tense and participle **bethought**) is archaic for to reflect
or remind (oneself), and should be avoided.

better is the comparative of **good** (of which the superlative is **best**)
and so requires *than* and both the things/persons being compared;
e.g. "Evergreen trees provide better protection" – better than
what? Note also **better** = person who bets (not *bettor*), often called
a *punter*.

between applies strictly to only two persons or things, and they
should be linked by *and*. E.g.:

"Between 20 and 30 people came" is correct;
"Between 20 to 30 people came" is incorrect;
"The guests included between 20–30 men" is incorrect.
For more than two alternatives, **among** is preferred. E.g.:

"He shared the wine among all the guests, but divided the cheese
between only two of them."
According to some authorities, *between* can be used to express the
relation of one thing to many surrounding ones individually; *among*
expresses a relationship to them collectively and vaguely. E.g.:

"The area between the three trees."
"A giant among men."
See also **among**; **in between**.

betwixt is archaic for **between**, which should be used. The
tautologous **betwixt and between** should not be used.

bevel, bevelled, bevelling.

beverage can nearly always be replaced by **drink**, which is
preferred.

bhp is the abbreviation of brake horsepower.

Bhutan The derived adjective and noun is *Bhutanese*.

bi-, as a prefix, takes a hyphen only as an aid to reading and pronunciation (*bi-iliac* is the usually quoted example). Before a vowel, it may become *bin-* (e.g. binaural, binocular). For *bi-* or *di-* as prefixes meaning *two, see* **numerical prefixes**.

biannual = half-yearly; **biennial** = two-yearly; *Half-yearly* and *two-yearly* should be used to prevent possible confusion.

bias, biased, biasing.

Bible (capitalized) when referring to the Old Testament or New Testament, but **biblical** (uncapitalized).

bible paper = extremely thin paper, strong yet opaque, used for printing small-format dictionaries, bibles, and so on, for which low bulk and weight are required.

biblical citations should take the form of book, chapter and verses (inclusive); e.g. "Genesis 3:4–8" (Book of Genesis, Chapter 3, verses 4 to 8 inclusive). The preferred style for numbered books is I Kings, II Kings.

biceps is a singular word; both the Latin plural *bicipites* and the "English" *bicepses* would confound many readers – perhaps "two (or several) biceps muscles" achieves a more acceptable plural construction. The same comment can be made about **triceps**.

bid (verb) has the past tense and participle **bid** (not *bad, bade* or *bidden*).

bight = wide bay, bend in a rope; **bite** (noun) = wound made by teeth, a piece bitten off.

bigot, bigoted.

bijou (pl. bijoux) = a trinket, "toy"; the French term should be avoided.

bike is slang (or at least colloquial) for **bicycle,** and should be avoided.

bill *See* **act**.

billet, billeted, billeting.

billiards is a singular word; "games of billiards" achieves a plural construction.

billion = 1,000 million in the United States (a number formerly known as a *milliard* in Britain); originally a billion = 1 million million in Britain, but is increasingly being used in the American sense. Therefore, to prevent possible ambiguity, use "thousand million" or "million million". Scientific texts may use 10^9 and 10^{12}.

bin- *See* **bi-**

bind has the past tense and participle **bound** (not *binded*); *bounden* is retained as an archaic adjective (as in the cliché "bounden duty").

binoculars (noun), like *spectacles*, is a singular word. *Binocular* is the adjective (= two-eyed), as in 'binocular vision."

biological nomenclature *See* **Latin classification**.

birdbath, birdcage, bird-lime, birdseed, bird's-eye view, bird's-foot (trefoil), bird-song, bird-table.

Biro (= ball pen) is a trade name and should have an initial capital letter; note *ball pen* (which avoids the trade name) is preferred to *ball-point pen*. See also **trade names**.

birth control, birth date, birthday, birthmark, birthplace, birth rate.

birth date = date on which somebody was born (date of birth); **birthday** = anniversary of somebody's birth.

bison (pl. bison) = species of European or North American ox (the European animal is also called **wisent**); **buffalo** (pl. buffaloes) = species of ox found in southern Africa (= Cape buffalo) or Asia (= water buffalo). The use of *buffalo* for the North American bison is an Americanism, and should be avoided except in historical contexts (e.g. "An American buffalo hunter").

bit = abbreviation of binary digit, one of the two characters (0 or 1) in the binary notation used by digital computers. A group (of usually eight) bits is a **byte** (which *see*).

bite (verb) has the past tense **bit** and preferred past participle **bitten** (not *bit*) – except in the cliché "the biter bit". *See also* **bight**.

bivouac, bivouacked, bivouacking, bivouacker.

bizarre *See* **bazaar**.

black (no capital letter) is the preferred term for dark-skinned people from, or originally from, Africa, the United States or the West Indies. The term Coloured (with a capital letter) should be reserved for South African people of mixed ancestry. The word Negro and its derivatives should be avoided. *See also* **native**.

black-and-blue, black-and-tan (and Black-and-Tan(s)), black-and-white, black art, blackball, black belt, blackberry, blackbird, blackboard, black box, blackcap (bird), black cap (judge's headgear), black-coated, black comedy, Black Country, blackcurrant, Black Death (plague), black eye, Blackfoot, blackguard, black-hearted, black humour, blackjack, blacklead, blackleg, blacklist (verb), blackmail(er), Black Maria, black market(eer), black mass, blackout (noun), black powder, black pudding, Black Rod, black sheep, Blackshirt, blacksmith, black spot, blackthorn, black velvet, Black Watch, blackwater fever, black widow.

blade coating = papermaking term for a speedy method of applying a coating to paper using a thin steel blade to produce an even surface, which may be left matt or smoothed further by calendering (polishing with smooth rollers) or supercalendering (two-stage polishing). *See also* **paper**.

blame, blameable. Blame someone *for* something, not blame something *on* someone.

blanch = to make or become white; **blench** = to shrink from, flinch. The words are only coincidentally interchangeable (e.g. when given a fright, someone might blanch *or* blench – or both). A valid alternative to *blanch* is *bleach*, although this word should be used only of objects, not people; the usual gardening and culinary term is *blanch*.

blancmange

blanket, blanketed, blanketing.

blasé

blatant = falsely noisy or showy, obviously contrived (for effect); **flagrant** = outrageous, shockingly objectionable. The words are close in meaning. E.g.:

"I saw him in the restaurant yet he said he stayed at home all day because he was ill; he told me a blatant lie."
"She deliberately lit a cigarette although she knew that smoking is forbidden in the works kitchen; it was a flagrant breach of regulations."

bleach *See* **blanch**.

bleed inflects *bleed – bled – bled*.

bleed = printer's term for an illustration that runs off the edge of a page. Such images are made larger (by about 3mm or $\frac{1}{8}$ inch) than the trimmed page size to ensure a clean cut-off in manufacture.

blench *See* **blanch**.

blend with (not blend *into*).

blessed is the preferred past tense and participle of the verb *bless* (not **blest**).

blind blocking (printing) *See* **blocking**.

blitz (noun and verb) is now accepted English (German *Blitzkrieg* = lightning war).

bloc = a group of people or nations; **block** = a (usually cuboidal) piece of solid material, etc.

blocking = bookbinder's term for type matter or a design that is stamped into the binding of a book, often using metal foil to give a gold or silver finish. In *blind blocking* no foil is used, thus leaving merely the impression of the design. The die that stamps the blocking is known as a **brass**.

blond (masc.) and **blonde** (fem.) retain their genders in English.

blood bank, blood-bath, blood-brother, blood cell, blood count, blood-curdling, blood donor, blood feud, blood group, bloodhound, blood-letting, blood-lust, blood orange, blood-poisoning, blood pressure, bloodshed, bloodshot, blood sports, bloodstain, bloodstock, bloodstream, bloodsucker, blood supply, blood test, bloodthirsty, blood transfusion, blood vessel.

bloom = an individual flower, especially on a plant grown for its flowers; **blossom** = a collection of flowers, especially ones that will lead to fruit (roses are blooms, apple trees bear blossom).

blow (verb) has the past tense **blew** and past participle **blown**.

blue, blueing, bluish, blueprint.

blues = American term for an Ozalid proof (*see* **Ozalid**).

blurb = publisher's and advertiser's term for a short description of a book, usually on its jacket (originally American slang, but not now condemned by the *OED*).

bn is an abbreviation of billion (which *see*).

bodge *See* **botch**.

bogey = designated number of golf strokes for a hole or course;

bogie = wheeled undercarriages; **bogy** = goblin; **bougie** = candle, surgical instrument.

bold face (type) *See* **weight**.

bole = tree trunk; **bowl** = basin, deep dish or wooden ball.

bona fide(s) = in good faith, genuine(ness); the Latin term should be avoided.

bond, in papermaking, = a type of strong white paper, so-called because it was once used for printing bonds. It usually has a weight of more than 60 gsm (*see* **gsm**).

bonhomie (italics) = pleasant (good) nature; the French term should be avoided.

bon mot(s) (italics) = "clever" saying, witticism; the French term should be avoided.

bonnet, bonneted, bonneting.

bonus (pl. bonuses).

book-binder, bookcase, book club, book-end, bookie, bookkeeper, booklet, booklouse (-lice), bookmaker, bookmark, bookseller, bookshelf, bookshop, bookstall, book-token, bookworm.

book block = printer's and publisher's term for a partly made book before the *case* (covers) is added; the printed sections of the book have been folded, *gathered* (collated), *sewn* or otherwise bound together and *trimmed* (cut to size on three sides). It is then ready for *casing-in* (having the case and binding added). *See also* **books**.

booklet = small book with the pages fixed in the binding (often saddle-stitched, with wire staples like a slim magazine, rather than sewn); **leaflet** = a single (unstitched) leaf or page of printed matter, possibly folded; **pamphlet** = small book with the pages stitched but not bound (i.e. with no separate cover); **brochure** = slightly "posh" name for a pamphlet or leaflet (usually advertising/promoting a product or service).

books Technical terms for various parts of a book are explained in the diagrams on the opposite page.

born = brought into life; **borne** = carried (past tense and participle of *to bear*).

born *in* is preferred to **born** *at* (in biographical text).

borrow = have temporary use of an object or money (the object is *borrowed* or *on loan*, the money is a *loan*); **lend** = to make an object or money temporarily available to someone else (the object/money is *lent*). If A borrows from B, B lends to A. *Borrow* and *lend* are verbs; *loan* is a noun.

Börse = West German Stock Exchange.

bortsch is the preferred spelling of **borsch** (Russian beetroot soup).

bosom is an archaic euphemism for **breast**, which is preferred.

botch (= make or repair badly) is preferred to **bodge**.

both should not be misused for **each**; e.g. "There is a large building on both sides of the street" is incorrect for "... on each side of the street"(unless it is a building with a street through the middle of it).

bouillon *See* **bullion**.

bounce, bouncy, bounceable.

bourgeois, bourgeoisie. **Bourgeois** is also an obsolete name for 9-point type. For others, *see* **type sizes**.

bourrée

Bourse = French Stock Exchange.

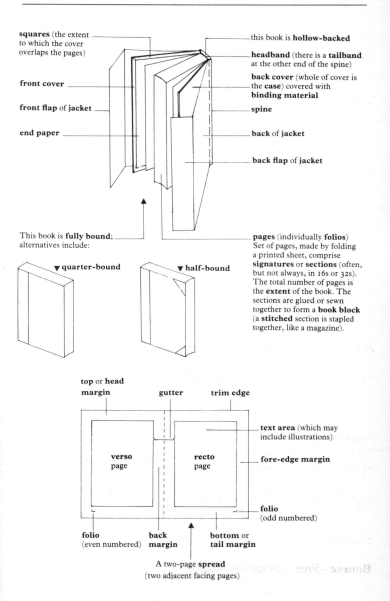

squares (the extent to which the cover overlaps the pages)

this book is **hollow-backed**

headband (there is a **tailband** at the other end of the spine)

front cover

back cover (whole of cover is the **case**) covered with **binding material**

front flap of jacket

spine

end paper

back of jacket

back flap of jacket

This book is **fully bound**; alternatives include:

▼ **quarter-bound**

▼ **half-bound**

pages (individually **folios**) Set of pages, made by folding a printed sheet, comprise **signatures** or **sections** (often, but not always, in 16s or 32s). The total number of pages is the **extent** of the book. The sections are glued or sewn together to form a **book block** (a **stitched** section is stapled together, like a magazine).

top or **head** margin

gutter

trim edge

text area (which may include illustrations)

verso page

recto page

fore-edge margin

folio (odd numbered)

folio (even numbered)

back margin

bottom or **tail margin**

A two-page **spread** (two adjacent facing pages)

boutique (not italics).

bowdlerism *See* **non-standard English**.

bowl *See* **bole**.

bow window *See* **bay window**.

boxed head *See* **subheadings**.

b.p. is the abbreviation of boiling point.

bra is now an accepted short form of **brassière**.

bracket = structure for supporting or holding (up); **brackets** = square brackets []; round brackets () are properly called **parentheses**; **braces** are {}. For use of parentheses, *see* **punctuation** (parentheses).

brain-child, brain drain, brainpower, brainstorm(ing), brain-teaser, brains trust, brain-wash(ing), brainwave.

braise = to cook (using steam, in a closed pan); **braze** = to join metal using heat and a high-melting solder; **brazier** = someone who brazes, a worker in brass, a container for hot coals.

brand names *See* **capitalization**; **trade names**.

brass (printing) *See* **blocking**.

brasserie (not italics).

bravado = behaviour that is boastful, ostentatiously bold or seemingly courageous; **bravery** = genuine courage (in adversity), heroism; **bravura** = brilliant but showy performance. E.g.:

"His offer to climb the tall tree was an act of bravado he soon regretted."
"She was awarded a medal for her bravery in rescuing a drowning child."

"The juggler ended his act with a bravura sequence using flaming torches."

bravo The *OED* prefers **bravoes** as the plural in the rare use of the word to mean "hired ruffian, desperado" but **bravos** when it is a cry of approval. It is simpler, and no less correct, to use **bravos** for both (incidentally, the plural of *desperado* is *desperados*).

breach = breaking of a rule etc., a split, a gap in fortifications; **breech** = rear end of a gun barrel, buttocks (as in breech-birth); **breeches** = knee-length trousers.

breadth = width; **broad** = wide, coarse or dialectal (e.g. a broad river or a broad accent); **broadness** = coarseness (not *breadth*).

break (verb) has the past tense **broke** and past participle **broken**.

breakword = editor's jargon for a word broken (hyphenated) between the end of one column or page and the top of the next, usually to be avoided in quality publishing.

breath is the noun; **breathe** is the verb.

breathalyse, breathalyser (with an *s*).

breech/breeches *See* **breach**.

breed (verb) inflects *breed – bred – bred*.

brethren is archaic for **brothers**, except in certain religious contexts, and should be avoided.

brevier = obsolete name for 8-point type. For others, *see* **type sizes**.

briar The preferred spelling is **brier**.

bribe, bribable, bribery.

bric-à-brac

brief = lasting a short time, concise (of a speech etc.); **short** = of little duration (= brief), but also = of little length (opposite of long); e.g. "a brief interlude", "a short article" and "a short stick".

brier is the preferred spelling of **briar**.

brilliant = obsolete name for 4-point type. For others, *see* **type sizes**.

bring inflects *bring – brought – brought*. *See also* **fetch**.

bring to a conclusion = **conclude**, which should be used.

brioche = small round cake; *broche* = piece of meat; **brochette** = small piece of meat or the skewer it is cooked on. Only the second term retains enough Frenchness to still require italicization.

Britannia, Britannica (not Britania, Britanica).

British = to do with Britain, i.e. Great Britain, i.e. The United Kingdom of Great Britain and Northern Ireland (as opposed to French, American, Irish, etc.); or = to do with the British Isles (the United Kingdom and the Republic of Ireland). *British* should not be used when English (or Welsh or Scottish) is more accurate or intended. A derived noun is **Briticism** (or Britishism), the name given in North America to imported English words (the converse of an *Americanism*).

broach (verb) = to pierce, break into, introduce; **broach** (noun) = a tapering tool; **brooch** = ornamental pin (originally for fastening clothes).

broadcast (verb) has the past tense and participle **broadcast** (not *broadcasted*).

broad etc. The adjectives broad, deep, high, long and wide form the nouns *breadth, depth, height, length* and *width*; only *height* does not have the *-th* ending.

broccoli

brochure *See* **booklet**.

bronchus (pl. bronchi).

bronco (pl. broncos).

Bronze Age (initial capital letters).

brooch *See* **broach**.

brother-in-law *See* **in-laws**.

browse = to read desultorily, to feed on leafy vegetation. *See also* **peruse; scan**.

brunch *See* **lunch**.

B series = range of ISO (formerly DIN) international paper sizes. *See* **paper sizes**.

budget, budgeted, budgeting.

buffalo (pl. buffaloes). *See also* **bison**.

buffet (verb) buffeted, buffeting.

bug = mistake or malfunction in a computer program. The removal of such errors is termed debugging. *See also* **insect**.

build inflects *build – built – built*.

bulk refers to volume or mass; it should not be misused for **most**.

bulk, in papermaking, = a term that refers to the thickness of a given type of paper. Formerly it was arrived at by measuring the total thickness of a designated number of sheets of a given *substance*. Thus a bulk of "29/32 for 320 pages s/o 30 × 40 60lb/512" corresponds to a thickness of 29/32 of an inch for 320 pages (= 160 sheets) of paper substance of (s/o) 60lb per 512 sheets measuring 30 by 40 inches. This example is known as a *29 basis* paper. Not surprisingly, this rather cumbersome way of expressing paper thickness has been largely superseded by *calliper* = the average thickness of a single sheet, usually now expressed in microns or millimetres (formerly in thousandths of an inch). *Bulk* and *bulk basis* are still used in the United States, often expressed as ppi (pages per inch). *Volume number* = thickness in millimetres of 100 sheets of 100 gsm paper. *See also* **gsm**; **paper sizes**; **substance**.

bullet = typographic term for a large dot, asterisk or similar device used for ornament on a printed page, often before headings or items in a list.

bullion = bulk precious metal (gold, silver), often cast in the form of ingots; **bouillon** = meat broth, soup.

bull's eye = printers jargon for a type of hickey, an imperfection on a printed sheet (*see* **hickey**).

bumptious

buoy, buoyage, buoyant, buoyancy.

bur = prickly seed-head that sticks to fur or clothing; **burr** = rough edge left on metal after cutting, a dental drill; **burin** = engravers tool.

bureau (pl. bureaux), bureaucracy, bureaucrat(ic).

bureaucratic English, or officialese, = convoluted, verbose and often unhelpful language used by some civil servants and other bureaucrats; it is one of the worst kinds of **jargon** (which *see*).

burger = abbreviation of hamburger; **burgher** = foreign townsman. *Burger* is given by the *OED* as colloquial and of mainly American usage; it is currently fully entrenched in English and looks as if it is here to stay – but so have many other now defunct words.

burgh is the usual Scottish term for **borough**.

Burma The derived adjective and noun is *Burmese*.

burn Preferred past tense and participle is **burned** (not burnt), although *burnt* is retained as an adjective (e.g. "burnt offering").

burst *See* **bust**.

bus (pl. buses), bused, busing. *Bussed, bussing* = kissed, kissing (archaic) in English; in North America *bussing* describes the compulsory transport of black and white children to give a better racial balance in schools.

bushman *See* **bedouin**.

business = commercial or industrial undertaking, trade or profession; **busyness** = state of being busy (a spelling introduced to distinguish between the two words).

bust used as a verb (with the past tense and participle *bust* or *busted*) is an Americanism, retained in British English only in such expressions as *bust-up*. The correct English verb is burst, which inflects *burst – burst – burst*.

butte (two *t*s, despite the pronunciation which rhymes with *flute*).

buy inflects *buy – bought – bought*.

buzz-word *See* **vogue words**.

by *See* **x** (multiplication sign); **with and by**.

by and large *See* **all in all**.

bye (noun) = secondary issue, extra (e.g. at cricket). The preferred form of the phrase meaning "in passing" is *bye the bye* (not by the by), although the apparent anomaly can be avoided by using *by the way*.

by-election (preferred to bye-election), bygone(s), by-lane, by-law (preferred to bye-law), byline, byname, bypass, by-play, by-product, by-road, bystander, byway, byword.

byte (in computers) = eight bits (a *bit* is one binary digit).

C

c. (italic) is the abbreviation of *circa* (= about), and is preferred to *ca.*

°C = degrees Celsius (formerly centigrade). *See* **Celsius**.

cabriole = curved ("Queen Anne") furniture leg; **cabriolet** = carriage or motor car with a folding hood.

cacao = tropical American seed-bearing tree; **cocoa** = extract from seeds of cacao tree used to make the drink cocoa and to make chocolate; **coca** = South American shrub whose leaves contain a stimulant; **coco** = palm tree that bears coconuts.

cache is now used to mean any hiding place, not merely an underground one (for provisions).

cachet = distinguishing mark; **cachou** = scented sweet (to perfume the breath).

cactus (pl. cacti).

caddie = someone who carries someone else's golf clubs; **caddy** = container for tea.

café

cage, caged, caging, cagey, cagily, cageyness (preferred to caginess).

calculate, calculator, calculable (and incalculable, not -atable).

calculus = a "stone" in the body (pl. calculi) such as a kidney stone, or a system of mathematics (pl. calculuses).

calendar = chart or book of dates; **calender** = to make smooth. A machine that calenders is also a **calender**; a person who calenders is a **calenderer**. (A *calender* is also a Persian or Turkish dervish.)

calf (pl. calves).

calibre = diameter of a bullet or shell, internal diameter of a tube (such as a gun barrel), status or importance (of a person). *See also* **calliper**.

calico

calligraphy is pretentious for **handwriting** (and incorrect unless the writing is artistically beautiful).

calliper (preferred to caliper) = a metal leg splint which enables a disabled person to walk, or a technical term in papermaking for the thickness of paper or board (plural callipers), usually expressed in microns or millimetres. *See also* **bulk**. **Callipers**, = compasses for measuring internal or external dimensions, is a plural word; "a pair of callipers" achieves a singular construction.

callus (pl. calluses) = patch of hard skin, corn; **callous** is the corresponding adjective, with the additional figurative meaning of unfeeling, unsympathetic, hard (in attitude), cruel.

calorie (with a lower case *c*) is a unit of heat in physics (equals originally the amount of heat required to raise the temperature of one gram of water through one degree centigrade, but now redefined in terms of joules); **Calorie** (with an initial capital letter) = 1 kilocalorie (= 1,000 calories). In dietetics, the energy unit of foods is the Calorie, although its initial letter is often not capitalized.

calyx (pl. calyces) is the preferred spelling (not **calix**).

camel There are two kinds: the one-humped *Arabian* camel (from northern Africa) and the two-humped *Bactrian* camel (from central Asia). A **dromedary** is a kind of Arabian camel, originally bred for racing and riding.

camellia (although pronounced to rhyme with *steelier*).

cameo (pl. cameos) = precious stone or shell carved in relief; **intaglio**

(pl. intaglios) = design carved in relief in any material (and a method of printing, *see* **printing processes**).

camera ready copy *See* **CRC**.

can implies an ability to do something; **may** implies permission to do something or reflects doubt (= **might**). E.g.:

"The boy can ride a bicycle" (has the ability to).
"May the boy ride his bicycle to school?" (has he permission to?).
"They may get to school early" (there is a possibility that).

canal, canalize, canalization.

canapé = toast or pastry case with a savoury filling; **canopy** = "roof" projecting, supported or suspended over a throne etc., or an aircraft cockpit cover.

cancel, cancelled, canceller, cancelling, cancellation. **Cancel** = printer's term for the correction of a serious error by removing a leaf or leaves from a printed book (or book block) and replacing them with a reprinted version (usually by pasting in).

candelabra, although originally a plural word, has the plural candelabras.

cannibal, cannibalize, cannibalization.

canoe, canoeing, canoeist.

canon = churchman; **cañon** = ravine; **cannon** = gun, shot at billiards; **canyon** = ravine (preferred to cañon). **Canon** is also a name for 48-point type. For others, *see* **type sizes**.

cant = jargon, often applied to that spoken by criminals. *See* **jargon; non-standard English**.

can't should not be used for cannot in formal writing.

canto (pl. cantos).

canvas = strong, coarse cloth; **canvass** = to solicit support (for).

capable *See* **able**.

capacity *See* **ability**.

capers, like *chives*, was originally a singular word (e.g. "Chives is a plant of the onion family"), although some dictionaries now list *caper* and *chive* as singulars. **Pease** (pl. peason) was once similar and gave rise to *pea* as another singular form, which has to be given the plural *peas*; the old singular survives in various compounds, such as pease-blossom and pease-pudding. *See also* **lens**.

Capitalization Unnecessary capitalization should be avoided, and if in doubt do not capitalize.

1. The state, government, politics:
The rules are best illustrated by examples: the state, state control; Parliament; the Government (a specific one, but no capital when used adjectivally; e.g. government control); the House of Commons; the Labour Party; the Conservative Party (etc.); Prime Minister or President when followed by the name of the office holder – prime minister, president when referring to the office or constitution; Communist Party (but communism).

2. Gods, religions:
Again, examples:
God, but he, his, him of God or Jesus ("pagan gods"); (The) Bible, but biblical; hell; Devil of The Bible; Roman Catholic (but catholic taste); Buddhism; Christianity; Protestant(ism); Puritan (but puritan morals); the established Church (but "an old stone church").

3. Titles and ranks:
Capitalize titles and ranks when followed by a proper name; e.g. Field Marshal Lord Alexander, Pope John, President Carter, Prince Charles, Queen Victoria. Also capitalize titles when they stand for the office holder's name; e.g. the Pope, the President, the King of France (but kings and queens in the general sense, the king, several American presidents, Roman Catholic popes), Professor of Chemistry, the Minister of Health. Spell out all ranks

the first time they are used. Thereafter continue to use them in full, except for those with an abbreviation here:

Navy: Able Seaman (AB), Petty Officer (PO), Chief Petty Officer (CPO), Sub-Lieutenant, Lieutenant-Commander, Commander, Captain.

Army: Private, Lance-Corporal (L/Cpl), Corporal, Sergeant, Warrant-Officer (WOI and WOII; note that CSM and RSM are appointments, not ranks), Second-Lieutenant, Lieutenant, Captain, Major, Lieutenant-Colonel, Colonel, Brigadier, Major-General (pl. Majors-General), Lieutenant-General, General, Field Marshal.

Air Force: Aircraftman (note, no "s"), (AC2, AC1, LAC, SAC), Corporal, Sergeant, Flight Sergeant, Warrant-Officer (WO), Pilot Officer, Flying Officer, Flight Lieutenant, Squadron Leader, Wing Commander, Group Captain, Air Commodore, Air Vice-Marshal, Air Marshal.

4. Proper names:

William Shakespeare, the Bard of Avon; the Mother of Parliaments; Father, Mother, etc. when used in speech as a form of address. The particles de, de la, du, des, van, von, etc. are generally lower case except at the beginning of a sentence. There are, however, some exceptions; e.g. Charles de Gaulle but De Gaulle, Thomas De Quincey and De Quincey.

"Dutch" names, where appropriate, appear as Van unless preceded by a Christian first name or initial; e.g. Vincent van Gogh but Van Gogh. Some North Americans with Van use a capital "V".

5. Geographical areas:

Do not capitalize points of the compass except as an abbreviation; the north of England, south-eastern England (not southeastern or southeast), in a north-westerly direction (not northwesterly), in the east of the county (but Western civilization, the wisdom of the East). *See* **compass directions**. Note also the following examples:

the Continent	South-East Asia (political)
the Lake District	South India
the Netherlands (not Holland)	the Soviet Union (not Russia)
North America	the United States (not America)
Northern Ireland	the West Country
North India	Western Australia
the Orient; the Occident	West Germany
South America	the West Indies

Western, Eastern, Central or Northern Europe when discussed as a political/social/cultural entity – but uncapitalized when used as an ordinary adjective.

6. Trade names:

Trade names should always be capitalized; although some have become generic terms and may, with care, be used uncapitalized (e.g. nylon, polythene). *See* **trade names**. *See also* **aircraft names; car names; locomotive and train names; ships' names, space rockets and missiles.**

7. Adjectives and nouns derived from proper names:

Capitals should be used for adjectives derived from proper names; e.g. Victorian, French, Junoesque. But where the connection has become remote, use lower case:

alpine	roman (type)
chelsea bun	venetian blind
china clay	victoria (a carriage)
french window	wellington boots

In adjectives with prefixes, the prefix is generally uncapitalized; e.g. anti-Hitlerian, pre-Columbian (but note Pre-Raphaelite Brotherhood), trans-Atlantic, mid-Atlantic (but the American Mid-West). *See also* **named effects and laws.**

8. Eras in history and historical events:
Note the following examples:

the Boston Tea Party	the Ottoman Empire
the British Empire	the Renaissance
Byzantine	the Roman Empire
Carboniferous	the Seven Years War
Classical	the South Sea Bubble
the Dark Ages	the Wars of the Roses
the Middle Ages	World War I (not First World War)
early Minoan	World War II

9. Other points of capitalization:
Few major periodicals have the definite article as part of their titles, except *The Times, The Economist, The Bookseller, The Listener*. Planets, stars, constellations and so on are capitalized (**see astronomical terms**). In named effects and laws, capitalized the

person but not the law; e.g. Newton's law, Pascal's principle
(*see* **named effects and laws**).
Taxonomic groupings except species, race and variety are
capitalized (*see* **Latin classification**).
Names of chemical elements are uncapitalized; e.g. arsenic, zinc.

capo (pl. capos).

carafe

carat = measure of purity of gold (24-carat is pure gold, 9-carat is
therefore $\frac{9}{24}$ gold and $\frac{15}{24}$ another metal, such as copper) or weight of
gemstones (1 carat = 0.2 grams); **caret** = editor's and proofreader's
mark that indicates the position of an omission in text (the mark $\wedge$
or $\hat{\ }$); **carrot** = a vegetable.

carburettor

carcase is the preferred spelling (not **carcass**).

cardboard = type of board made from mechanical pulp.
See **mechanical pulp**; **paper**.

card punch = machine that makes holes in punched cards at the
input or output terminal of a computer. A **tape punch** does the
same for paper tape.

card reader = computer terminal device for inputting data on
punched cards, or for converting data on punched cards so that it
can be read by a human being (e.g. by displaying it on a VDU
screen or by producing *hard copy* on a printer). A **tape reader**
does the same for perforated paper tape.

care about = be concerned or worried about; **care for** = look after,
take care of, like; **care to** = want to, like to. E.g.:

"She cares about the quality of her work."
"She cares for her invalid mother at home."
"She seldom cares to go out in the evening."

carefree = without a care, unworried; **careless** = without taking care, unheeding, sloppy. E.g.:

"Her work was good, despite her carefree attitude to it."
"Her work was poor because of her careless approach to it."

caretaker = someone who looks after (empty) premises such as a school or offices; **care-taker** = anyone who looks after and raises a child (originally a sociological term). The hyphen is necessary in the latter (new) word to distinguish of from the former. Such a care-taker may be a parent, guardian, permanent child-minder, and so on.

cargo (pl. cargoes).

caribou (pl. caribous) = North American name for the reindeer (*Rangifer tarandus*).

Carib words that have become part of English are included in the examples under **Americanisms**.

caries, the medical term for *decay*, is a singular word (e.g. "Dental caries is the most common disorder in the Western world"); "cases of caries" achieves a plural construction (e.g. "Cases of caries are increasingly common in children under five"), although "Caries is increasingly common..." would serve as well). The adjective is **carious** (not **carous**).

car names should be given initial capital letters (and typeset in roman face); e.g. a Ford Escort, Volkswagen Golf. Names of individual cars should be italicized; e.g. *Bluebird*.

carpal = to do with the wrist; **carpel** = leafy part of a flower.

carte blanche (italics) = a free hand, full discretion; the French term should be avoided.

carton = (thin) cardboard box; **cartoon** = drawing (usually humorous).

cartridge = type of strong paper of high opacity used for printing high-quality publications and, in its thicker forms, as drawing paper. It is so called because it was first used for making paper cartridges (for muzzle-loading rifles).

casino (pl. casinos).

cassock = long garment worn by clergy or choristers; **hassock** = small stool or cushion for kneeling on in church.

cast-coating = papermaking term for a method of drying a coating on paper by squeezing it against a hot polished roller. It produces a smooth glossy finish with excellent ink-holding properties without the need for supercalendering. *See also* **paper**.

caster = someone who casts, a casting machine; **castor** = oil-bearing plant, small wheel, beaver, sugar sprinkler (although fine sugar is usually known as *caster* sugar).

casual = informal, off-hand; **causal** = that causes, being the cause.

catabolism is the preferred spelling (not **katabolism**).

cataclasm = violent break, disruption; **cataclysm** = deluge, violent upheaval.

catalysis, catalyse, catalyst.

catastrophe = disaster of great magnitude; it should not be used of events that are merely *serious* or *severe*.

catch (verb) inflects *catch – caught – caught*.

Catholic should not be used when **Roman Catholic** is intended, particularly at the first mention; catholic (with no initial capital letter) = wide-ranging, universal (e.g. "a person with catholic tastes in music").

cat-o'-nine-tails

catsup The preferred spelling is **ketchup**.

cattle is plural (e.g. "The cattle are lowing"); "a herd of cattle" achieves a singular construction.

cause = the (non-human) factor responsible for an event or outcome; **reason** = (human) justification of an action or belief, a distinction that is not always preserved. E.g.:

"Heavy rain was the cause of the landslide."
"Her wish to see her mother was the reason she went."

cauterize, cautery (an instrument or chemical that cauterizes), cauterization.

cavil, cavilled, cavilling, caviller.

cayman (pl. caymans).

cc is the abbreviaton of cubic centimetre, which for ordinary liquids is equivalent to a millilitre (ml).

-ce and -cy are noun endings which generally are not interchangeable. E.g.:

agent	agency	diligent	diligence
avoid	avoidance	ignorant	ignorance
belligerent	belligerence	intelligent	intelligence
clement	clemency	latent	latency
decent	decency	magnificent	magnificence
different	difference	vacant	vacancy

For a few words, both the -ce and -cy forms exist and have the same meaning:

consist	consistence, consistency
inconsistent	inconsistence, inconsistency
irrelevant	irrelevance, irrelevancy
resilient	resilience, resiliency
valent	valence, valency

For yet others, the two forms have different meanings:

depend	dependence (= be dependent on in general)

	dependency (= a country that is dependent on another)
emerge	emergence (= a coming out)
	emergency (= unexpected happening)
excellent	excellence (= state of being excellent)
	excellency (= diplomatic title)

cede, ceder (who cedes); the tree is a **cedar**.

-cede is the usual verb ending (e.g. concede, recede) except in *exceed*, *proceed* and *succeed*.

cedilla = an accent which, in French, softens the sound of *c* before the vowels *a, o* and *u*, as in *garçon*. In Turkish, it converts a sibilant *s* to the sound *sh*, as in *Gelişm*.

celebrate, celebrator, celebrant (who celebrates, say, mass), celebrity (who is celebrated).

celibate = unmarried (usually applied to men); **chaste** = abstaining from sexual intercourse, although not necessarily virgin (usually applied to women).

cello (pl. cellos), cellist.

Celsius temperatures (abbreviation °C) should now generally be used in "scientific" texts, rather than centigrade temperatures (which are numerically identical). For conversion of Celsius to Fahrenheit and vice versa, *see* **units**.

Celtic words have contributed to the English language, mainly by way of Gaelic, Irish, Scottish and Welsh – in addition to a huge influence and borrowings from French (*see* **French words**). The following examples form an interesting list:

banshee (female fairy)	Irish *bean sīdhe*
bard (poet)	Gaelic *bàrd*
bog (marsh)	Gaelic *bogach*
brogue (shoe)	Gaelic *brōg*
cairn (pile of stones)	Gaelic *càrn*

ceilidh (folksong/dance meeting)	Gaelic
colleen (girl)	Irish *cailín*
coracle (boat)	Gaelic *curach*
corgi (dog)	Welsh *cor ci*
corrie (hollow)	Gaelic *coire*
cromlech (stone circle)	Welsh *crom llech*
dolmen (tomb)	Cornish *tolmēn*
drumlin (long mound)	Gaelic *druim*
flummery (trifle(s))	Welsh *llymru*
galore (abundance)	Irish *go léor*
glen (valley)	Gaelic *gleann*
leprechaun (little imp)	Irish *luchorpán*
loch (lake)	Gaelic *loch* (Irish *lough*)
menhir (standing stone)	Breton *men hir*
pikelet (cake)	Welsh *bara pyglyd*
plaid (cloth)	Gaelic *plaide*
poteen (illicit whiskey)	Irish *poitín*
shamrock (plant)	Irish *seamróg*
shillelagh (club)	Irish (place-name)
slob (stupid person)	Irish *slab*
slogan (catch word)	Gaelic *sluagh gairm*
Tory (now Conservative)	Irish *tóraighe*
trousers (garment)	Gaelic *triubhas*
whiskey (drink)	Gaelic *uisge beatha*

cement = binding agent consisting of an anhydrous powder that sets solid after the incorporation of water (and by extension any adhesive); **concrete** = rock-like solid made from a mixture of sand, gravel (aggregate) and cement; **mortar** = substance used to bind together bricks or masonry, made from sand and cement (or, formerly, sand and lime). *Cement* is not a synonym of *concrete* or *mortar*.

censer = incense vessel; **censor** = official who can suppress part (or whole) of a letter, film, play, book, etc.; **censure** = to condemn, blame.

centi- is the metric prefix for a hundredth ($\times 10^{-2}$), as in *centimetre* (*see* **units**).

centigrade *See* **Celsius**.

central, centralize, centralization.

central processor (computers) *See* **CP**.

centre of a circle; **middle** of a line. Middle is less precise and can apply to time; e.g. "middle of the field" is vaguer than "centre of the field", "middle of the week" cannot be changed to "centre of the season". Avoid **centre round**; use **centre on** (or **centre in** for exactness or precision). Other forms are **centred** and **centring**, but note **centering** for an arch.

ceramics (= the making of pottery etc.) is singular; **ceramics** (= pots etc.) is plural.

cereal = a grain crop (barley, millet, oats, rice, rye, wheat etc.); **serial** = story or radio/television drama that appears as regular separate episodes. *See also* **grain**.

ceremonial (adj.) describes a ceremony or other formal occasion; **ceremonious** describes a person or people when they behave as they might at a ceremony (even if this is inappropriate). E.g.:

"The Queen's coronation was a colourful ceremonial occasion."
"He donned his robes of office and made a ceremonious entrance."

certainty = the state of being certain or having conviction; **certitude** = the state of having conviction – i.e. the former can mean the latter, but the latter shares only one meaning with the former. E.g.:

"It was a certainty that the tidal wave would engulf the ships in the harbour."
"Despite the mood of the meeting, he expressed his views with certitude."

cervix (pl. cervixes, not cervices) has the adjective *cervical*. It can

cession = handing over (to another); **session** = period of time, meeting.

apply to the neck (e.g. cervical ribs, cervical vertebrae) or to the neck of the womb (e.g. cervical cancer).

cf. is the abbreviation of *confer* (compare).

Chad The derived adjective and noun is *Chadean.*

chafe, chafing (= wearing by friction); **chaff**, chaffing (= bantering).

chairperson *See* **gender**.

chambré (italics) = at room temperature.

chamois has the same form in the singular and plural. When applied to a type of soft leather, the word can also be spelled **shammy** (in accord with its pronunciation in this meaning).

champagne = the sparkling wine; **champaign** = a plane, flat open ground.

chance *See* **possibility**.

change, changeable, changeling.

channel, channelled, channelling.

character, characteristic, characterize.

chassis has the plural **chassis** (only the pronunciation changes).

chaste *See* **celibate**.

château (pl. châteaux).

chauvinism *See* **gender**.

cheap is an adjective meaning *inexpensive*; **cheaply** is an adverb meaning *inexpensively*. E.g.:

"She bought a cheap pair of shoes."

"She has new shoes, which she bought cheaply."
On the cheap is slang, and should be avoided.

check-in, check-list, check-out, check-up (all nouns); but check in, check out, check up as verbs.

chemical pulp = cellulose fibres for papermaking broken down from the raw material (such as various kinds of wood, grass or leaves) by a chemical process, rather than by grinding. *See also* **mechanical pulp; paper**.

chequer, chequered, chequering (= patterned with squares). Avoid using *checkered* etc. (although *checker* is correct meaning someone who checks goods and so on).

cherub (pl. cherubs, preferred to cherubim).

chickenpox (one word).

chicory (*Cichorium intybus*) has long, smooth pale yellow leaves and a slightly bitter taste; its roots are roasted as a coffee additive/substitute. **Endive** (*Cichorium endivia*) has curly or wavy leaves. Both are used in salads (and, in this context, have their meanings reversed in the United States).

chide, an archaism for *scold*, has the preferred past tense and participle **chided** (not the original *chid* and *chidden*).

chilblain

child *See* **baby**.

childbirth, childhood, childlike, child-minder, child-proof.

childish = puerile, not suitable/becoming for an adult; **childlike** = having the innocence/candour/good qualities of a child.

chilli (pepper) has the plural **chillies**.

Chinese words that have found a permanent place in English include:

cheongsam	ketchup	pekinese	tea
chop suey	kowtow	sampan	typhoon
chow mein	kung fu	silk	wok
cumquat	lychee	soya	yin
kaolin	mandarin	tai chi	yang

chipboard = papermaking term for grey board made from recycled waste paper. It may be *lined* to give it a white finish on one side of the sheet, suitable for printing. *See also* **paper**.

chirrup, chirruped, chirruping.

chisel, chiselled, chiselling.

chives *See* **capers**.

chivvy is the preferred spelling (not **chivy** or **chevy**).

choice *See* **alternative**; **option**.

choir, chorister. *See also* **quire**.

choose, choosy. **Choose** has the past tense **chose** and past participle **chosen**.

chord = harmonious set of notes, line joining points on a curve; **cord** = strong string (and spinal cord, umbilical cord, vocal cords).

chordate = any member of the group (phylum) of animals that includes vertebrates; **cordate** = heart-shaped; **cordite** = propellent explosive made mainly from gun-cotton ("nitrocellulose").

chorus, chorused, choral (to do with a chorus or choir), chorale (a piece of music), chorister.

chou (pl. choux) = cabbage, decorative "rose" made of ribbon; **choux** = light, rich pastry.

Christian name can be an objectionable term to a non-Christian person and is best avoided. Of the alternatives, *first name* is preferred to *forename* or *given name*, except in official documents or for peoples who traditionally state their family name or surname first.

chronic = long-term, long-standing; **acute** = of sudden onset, short-term.

cicero = unit of type measurement used mainly in Continental Europe. In this system, 1 cicero = 4.511mm (approximating to an "English" pica = 4.21mm). *See also* **didot; pica; point**.

cine- is preferred to **kine-** as a prefix (e.g. cinematograph).

cipher (= zero, monogram) is the preferred spelling of **cypher**.

circumcise, circumcision.

circumflex = an accent, as in *fête*.

cirrhosis

cist = prehistoric burial chamber; **cyst** = lump, growth or sac.

cite = refer to, quote; **site** = place, position.

civil, civilize, civilizable, civilization.

clack = sharp sound (like two pieces of flat wood struck together); **claque** = hired applauders. *See also* **click**.

claim to be requires an object to refer to the claimant; it does not mean to **assert**. E.g.:

"She claims to be happy" (correct, the happiness is possibly hers); "They claim to be rich" (correct, the richness is possibly theirs); "You claimed the work to be late" (incorrect, *late* refers to *work*, not *you*, and the sentence should be rephrased as "You asserted that the work was late").

clamour, clamorous.

clang, clanger, clangour, clangorous.

clay, clayey.

cleanliness = the routine or habit of keeping something clean; **cleanness** = the state of being clean. E.g.:

"The maintenance of strict cleanliness reduces the risk of contamination."
"After the contamination, the cleanness of the apparatus was in question."

cleave There are two different verbs of opposite meaning with this spelling. One = to divide, split, hack apart; the other = to stick (to), unite. The first has the past tense **clove** and past participle **cloven,** although *cleft* is also retained as an adjective (e.g. "a cleft stick"). The second verb has the past tense and participle **cleaved.**

clench *See* **clinch.**

clever = ingenious, adroit, quick-witted; it should strictly not be used to mean knowledgeable, well educated, well informed (as in "He must be a clever man to know Latin grammar").

cliché = a stereotyped expression, a well-worn and thus overexposed idea. Clichés should be avoided like the plague, if you see what I mean. Often they are refuges of **archaisms** (which *see*). The adjective is *clichéd. See also* **inseparable pairs; metaphor.**

click = a short, sharp sound; **clique** = exclusive group of people. *See also* **clack.**

client = someone who commissions a lawyer, estate agent or somesuch – i.e. purchases a professional service (although a doctor has *patients*); **customer** = someone who purchases goods or a tradesman's services; thus a consultant has clients, a plumber and a grocer have customers. A group of customers may properly, if a little affectedly, be referred to as **clientele.**

climatic = to do with climate; **climactic** = to do with a climax;
  climacteric = to do with a critical period (usually the menopause).

clime is archaic for climate (as in the cliché "sunnier climes");
  climate should be used.

climax = figure of speech that involves a series (of terms or
  statements) of gradually increasing importance or emphasis. E.g.:

  "She asked, begged, cajoled and finally compelled him to accept her
  point of view."
  See also **anticlimax**.

clinch = to embrace, to settle (a deal); **clench** = to close tightly (teeth
  or fist), to secure a nail or rivet.

cling inflects *cling – clung – clung*.

close *See* **shut**.

cloth (noun = textile material, fabric) has the plural *cloths* (e.g.
  "cloths for wiping the top of the table"); **clothe** (verb) = to dress,
  cover (with fabric) (e.g. "clothed in silk"); **clothes** (plural
  noun) = garments (e.g. "he wore his best clothes"). The verb
  clothe has the preferred past tense and participle **clothed**,
  although *clad* is retained in certain technical terms (e.g. "tile-clad
  elevation").

cloth-centred paper = strong paper consisting of three layers, with
  linen sandwiched between two sheets of paper, used for maps and
  so on which have to be refolded many times; **cloth-lined
  paper** = two-layer paper consisting of a sheet backed with linen or
  muslin – not as strong as cloth-centred paper but used for similar
  purposes.

club, clubbable.

club line = editor's jargon for the first line of a paragraph that falls as
  the last line of a column or page, usually avoided in quality
  publications.

cm is the abbreviation of centimetre.

Co. is the abbreviation of County and Company, for which it should be used only if the abbreviated form is the company's style. The same rule applied to "& Co.".

coal-dust, coal-face, coalfield, coalfish, coal gas, coalman, coal-mine, coal tar.

coarse (adj.) = rough, base, unrefined; **course** (noun) = track or ground to be covered (e.g. racecourse, golf course, course of action), series of lessons/lectures (e.g. A-level course), dishes (e.g. a meal of three courses), doses of medicine (e.g. a course of antibiotics), a row of laid bricks or dressed stones (e.g. damp course).

coastal = to do with the coast (e.g. "coastal defences" against the action of tides); **costal** = to do with the ribs (e.g. "costal muscles" used in breathing).

coaxial, coeducation(al), coefficient, coequal, coeval, coexist(ence), coextensive, coheir(ess), cotangent. Most other words with the prefix *co-* have a hyphen.

coccus (pl. cocci); its compounds have similar plurals.

coccyx (pl. coccyxes).

cockatoo (pl. cockatoos).

codex (pl. codices).

codicil *See* **corollary**.

coelom (pl. coelomata). Note also coelacanth, coelenterate.

coequal should be avoided in favour of plain equal.

coeval (not coaeval).

coffee-table book = usually large-format, lavish illustrated book with many four-colour illustrations, once regarded as more for ostentatious display (on the coffee table) than for serious reading.

cogitate is an affected synonym for **ponder** and an inaccurate one for **think**.

cohere, coherent, cohesion (= sticking together), coherence (= consistency, logical connection).

coiffure (italics) = hair-style or the more familiar hair-do; the French term should be avoided.

coign *See* **quoin**.

coir *See* **quire**.

colic, colicky.

collaborate = work (willingly) with someone else for a common purpose; it is pejorative, with implications of treason, if the collaboration is with an enemy. **Corroborate** = (provide evidence to) confirm someone else's claim/statement. *See also* **collusion**.

collapse, collapsible.

colleague = someone who works with a professional person, such as a doctor, solicitor, teacher, and so on. Strictly it should not be used for someone who works with a tradesman or manual worker (who is termed a fellow-worker or workmate). *See also* **client**; **skilful**.

collect, collector, collectable. **Collect** = gather, bring together; it should not be misused for **fetch** (which *see*).

collective words often pose problems about number – are they singular or plural? Group collectives, such as *audience, class, committee, company, congregation, corporation, council, crew, department, family, firm, gate* (at a sporting event), *government, majority, minority, personnel, population, staff, team*, and so on may be regarded as singular or plural, depending on context. Singular is better when referring to the collection as a whole (e.g. "The department was held to be responsible"); plural is better when the emphasis is on the individual members (e.g. "The council were given front-row seats"). But once the choice has been made, it should remain consistent throughout the text. The use of a pronoun to refer to such a collective may force the verb into singular or plural. E.g.:

"The family was unable to agree about its holiday."
"The family were told to take off their coats."
(One cannot say "The family was told to take off its coat.")

Words for groups of similar things, people or animals, such as *flock* (of birds), *heap* (of things), *herd* (of animals), *horde* (of people), *pack* (of dogs/wolves), *pile* (of sand, stones etc.), *shoal* (of fish), and so on, are singular. E.g.:

"The herd of antelopes has begun to migrate."
"A flock of gulls is flying overhead."

Some animal collections in this category are specific; many sound precious or affected and are best avoided by using a neutral term such as *group* or a more general one such as *flock, herd* or *shoal*. E.g.:

bevy of quails
brood of chickens
cete of badgers
charm of finches or goldfish
clamour of rooks
colony of ants, gulls, etc.
covey of grouse or partridges
drove of oxen
exultation of larks
flight of doves, swallows etc.
gaggle of geese (on the ground or in water)
hive of bees
host of sparrows
kindle of kittens
leap of leopards

litter of cubs or puppies
mob of kangaroos
murmuration of starlings
muster of peafowl
nest of mice or rabbits
plump of waterfowl
pod of seals or whales
pride of lions
rookery of rooks or seals
school of porpoises or whales
siedge of herons
skein of geese (in flight)
skulk of foxes
swarm of bees or flies
troop of kangaroos or monkeys
unkindness of ravens

So-called distributive collective words (such as *folk*, *people*) and generalizing collectives (usually occupations such as *the clergy, the police*) are regarded as plural. E.g.:

"The people are upset."
"The police have taken action."

Nouns of "mass" or class collectives (uncountable nouns for groups of different things that together form a category) are singular – indeed they have no plural. Examples include *baggage, clothing, crockery, cutlery, furniture, garbage, glassware, hardware, ironmongery, kitchenware, luggage, machinery, software* (computers), *stationery*. E.g.:

"All baggage is weighed."
"No cutlery has been washed."
"Much stationery was missing."

Expressions such as "items of clothing" and "pieces of furniture" achieve a plural construction, if needed.

collision occurs when a moving object hits a stationary one;
  collusion occurs when two or more people conspire to deceive or defraud (straightforward open co-operation is *collaboration*). E.g.:

"My car was dented in a collision with a tree."
"The witnesses' accounts were identical down to the last detail, suggesting collusion between them."

colloquialism = non-formal English, usually reserved for speech and to be avoided in formal writing. *See also* **non-standard English; slang.**

collotype = old printing process that used sheets of gelatin or gelatin-coated printing plates. The gelatin was made light-sensitive, a photographic image (line or tone) transferred to it, and prints made by lithography. It allows only a relatively few copies (short run) but, because there is no half-tone screen involved, can produce continuous-tone prints.

collusion = (secret) agreement in order to deceive; it should not be used as a synonym for co-operation, which may be open and praiseworthy. *See also* **collaborate; collision.**

colon *See* **punctuation**.

colony, colonial, colonize, colonization. **Colony/colonials** should not be applied to former British overseas territories or their citizens (*colonial* is pejorative). Some nations are properly called *Dominions*, many are republics and *Commonwealth* countries. Hong Kong (until 1996) has the official status of a Crown Colony.

colophon = publisher's symbol, usually printed on book jackets, spines and title pages. A letter symbol is also known as a **logo** (short for *logogram* or *logo type*).

coloration (and discoloration); other words (except decolorize) derived from *colour* keep *-ou-*.

colour bar = printing term for a row of colours and tones along the edge of a four-colour proof or printed sheet (outside the image area), on which ink densities can be measured.

comatose = affected with coma, unconscious; **comose** = hairy, tufted, resembling the head of a comet.

combat = a fight between enemies; a **contest** or **competition** may be between neutrals or friends (at worst they are rivals). Other forms are combated, combating, combative.

combust, combustible, combustion. *See also* **inflammable**.

come has the past tense **came** and past participle **come**.

comic describes someone or something that is deliberately funny; **comical** describes someone or something that is unintentionally funny or amusing. E.g.:

"He wrote a comic sketch for the student review."
"Her make-up ran in the rain, giving her face a comical expression."

coming and going = printer's jargon for a method of printing in which the imposition scheme produces two copies (e.g. of a book) from one set of printing plates. *See also* **imposition**; **printing processes**.

comma *See* **punctuation**.

commando (pl. commandos).

comme il faut (italics) = as it should be, proper; the French expression should be avoided.

commence should be reserved for the beginning of a formal ceremony or procedure; otherwise **begin** or **start** should be used. *See also* **start**.

commentate, commentator.

commercialese = pejorative term for the jargon of business and commerce, particularly in letter-writing, with its abbreviations such as *inst., prox.* and *ult.* and use of expressions such as *in respect of, per, re,* and so on. It is universally and soundly condemned by advocates of good style in writing. *See also* **jargon**.

commit, committed, committing, committee, commission (= act of committing, authority to commit), commitment (= obligation, order for sending to prison), commital (= pledge, order for sending to trial).

common *See* **mutual**.

commoner is the noun; **more common** should be used as the comparative of **common**. *See also* **comparative and superlative**.

common names (of plants and animals) *See* **Latin classification**.

common sense is the noun form, **common-sense** is the adjective; *commonsense* should be avoided.

communiqué

Comoros The derived adjective and noun is *Comorian*.

comp = printer's and typesetter's jargon for a **compositor** who originally composed (assembled) individual pieces of type ready for printing. Since the advent of typesetting machines and then photocomposition machines, a compositor (or *typesetter*) works at a keyboard resembling that of a typewriter, and with the introduction of computers into the technology is more likely today to be called a *keyboard operator*.

comparative and superlative forms of short (monosyllabic and disyllabic) adjectives are usually formed by adding -er and -est (or -r and -st if the adjective ends in *e*):

small, smaller, smallest
large, larger, largest.

Adjectives ending in a consonant usually have a double consonant in the comparative and superlative:

big, bigger, biggest
hot, hotter, hottest.

Adjectives ending in a *y* change the *y* to an *i*:

funny, funnier, funniest
happy, happier, happiest.

Most polysyllabic adjectives have *more* and *most* to form the comparative and superlative:

beautiful, more beautiful, most beautiful
uncooperative, more uncooperative, most uncooperative.

Irregular comparatives and superlatives have to be learned. Common examples include:

bad, worse, worst
good, better, best
little, less, least
old, elder, eldest (although older, oldest also exist).

compare *to* (= to liken something to something else) has a different meaning from **compare** *with* (= to point to resemblances and differences between two things); **contrast** = to note only differences. E.g.:

"I could compare his handwriting to an infant's scribbles."
"Compare the galley proof with the typescript."
"Contrast the attitudes of the English and the Americans".
Other forms are comparable, comparative, comparison.

compass directions The basic terms north, south, east and west
(without capital letters, abbreviated to N, S, E, W, without full
points) give rise to northern, northerly and northward(s) (*see*
-wards), and similar forms for the other directions. Compounds
have hyphens: E.g.:

"in north-eastern China" (not north-east)
"a south-westerly direction" (not south-west).

Note compounds such as a "north-facing window" (preferred to
northerly-facing or northward(s)-facing).
Exceptions are established national or political units, which are
usually also distinguished by capitalization. E.g.:

South Africa (the nation), but southern Africa (the southern part of
the continent in general);
South-East Asia (politically), but south-eastern Asia (generally).

Note that a *southerly* wind blows a sailing vessel on a *northerly*
course (to the north).

compatible

compendium *See* **anthology**.

compère (with accent). The term *commère* for a woman compère
should be avoided.

competent *See* **able**.

competition *See* **combat**.

complacent = self-satisfied; **complaisant** = obliging.

complete and utter is a tautology and should be avoided. E.g. in
"He made a complete and utter fool of himself", delete *complete* or
utter (and the *and*).

complex (adj.) = made up of many parts, intricate; it is often used as a synonym for **complicated**, which can have the additional meaning *confused* (e.g. "a complex problem with a complicated solution"). **Complex** (noun) = group of psychological symptoms, a group of buildings (e.g. "sports complex").

complexion is one of the few words that should be spelled *-exion* (not *-ection*).

compliment = flattering comment; **complement** = that which fills or completes, an integral part or portion. *See also* **supplement**.

compose, composer (of music), compositor (of type), composition (= the result of composing either music or type), composure (= calmness of temperament).

compositor *See* **comp**.

compound words Most compound words are formed from adjective-noun combinations (e.g. blackboard, hardcore) or noun-noun combinations (e.g. cupboard, schoolboy). But, to quote G. H. Vallins, "when two nouns really coalesce to become one (armchair, bookcase), when they are linked by a hyphen (plate-rack, pen-holder), and when they remain separate are questions that in the present state of usage are past the wit of man to answer." Here are some general rules:
Hyphens should be used as little as possible, and then only when needed to avoid confusion in sound or comprehension. E.g.:

re-cover and recover
re-creation and recreation
re-count and recount
re-form and reform
re-enter and co-operate (to prevent the same two vowels occurring together).

Use hyphens for compound adjectives, the parts of which, if not separated, could lead to miscomprehension. E.g.:

hot-metal typesetting
fried-fish shop

good-sized house
red-hot poker
poverty-stricken town
red-brown dust.

A hyphen is not needed for an adverb-adjective combination when the meaning is clear: E.g.:

a richly endowed church
the rumour was ill founded
a beautifully phrased sentence
a fully grown bear (but full-grown bear preferred)
a swiftly flowing stream.

A hyphen is often needed for a verb-adverb combination used as a noun. E.g.:

make-up   mark-up   paste-up   take-off
but note: breakdown, getaway, handout, layout.

A hyphen is needed for numbers and fractions when they are spelled out. E.g.:

twenty-eight   fifty-four   one-and-a-half
two-thirds   fifteen-sixteenths   two-and-a-half.

A hyphen is needed to avoid repetition in such expressions as:

single- or double-jointed
a two-, three- or four-colour process
forward- and rear-facing windows.

A hyphen is usually desirable in compounds of which the first element ends with a vowel and the second element begins with a vowel (e.g. aero-elastic, sea-urchin), or in which the first element ends with the same consonant as that beginning the second element (e.g. part-time). Exceptions include words used so commonly that the hyphen can be omitted (e.g. coeducation, earring, radioactive). Many unhyphenated two-word compound nouns take hyphens when they are used attributively. E.g.:

boiling-point measurement
engine-room officer
freezing-point determination
melting-point temperature

nickel-silver alloy
right-angle(d) triangle
test-tube baby.

Note: In text for typesetting where an obligatory hyphen happens to come at the end of a line, mark it " = " to distinguish it from a non-obligatory hyphen of a word break. E.g.:

"... and they co =
operated in marking up the copy."

See also **well-**; **word breaks**.

comprehend, comprehensible (= understandable), comprehensive (= wide-ranging, complete).

comprise = consist of, contain, include, be composed of; e.g. "The staff comprises nine people". *Comprise* should not be used to mean to form or to make up; e.g. "Nine people comprises the staff" is incorrect. *See also* **consist of**.

compromise

compulsion = irresistible urge or action (adj. *compulsive*);
impulse = spontaneous (but resistible) thought or action (adj. *impulsive*).

compute is now acceptable for what a *computer* does; it should not be used as a synonym for **calculate** or **estimate**, particularly if performed by a human being. Similarly **computation** should be avoided when **calculation** is intended. The verb for to convert (a system) to computer use/control is **computerize**.

computer terms The introduction of computers to aid or control typesetting, reproduction and printing processes has increasingly made some computer terms part of the jargon of publishing. Terms commonly used in this context have separate entries in this Dictionary.

concave = domed in, like the inside of a spoon; **convex** = domed out, like the outside of a spoon. The corresponding nouns are *concavity* and *convexity*.

concensus The correct spelling is **consensus** (derived from consent, not census).

concerned *in* or *with* = having to do with; **concerned** *for* or *about* = worried. E.g.:

"He was not concerned in the crime."
"Arithmetic is concerned with numbers."
"The pupils were concerned for the teacher after her accident."
"He was concerned about the consequences of his actions."

concertina, concertinaed, concertinaing.

concerto (pl. concertos, not concerti).

conch (a shell), (pl. conchs).

conclave = private or secret assembly; **enclave** = area of land surrounded by foreign territory.

concreter = someone who concretes, part of a sugar refinery.

concur *with* someone *in* something; e.g. "He concurs with me in praising your work." Other forms are concurred, concurring, concurrent, concurrence.

condensed face, or condensed type, = typeface in which the characters are narrower than in the normal parent face. Formerly made as separate founts, condensed faces can now be generated (to any required percentage of condensation) by phototypesetting machines. *See also* **expanded face; weight.**

condominium = joint sovereignty. The word is being imported (from the United States) as a name for a jointly owned and occupied building, usually split into flats (apartments).

conducive *to* (not conducive *of*).

conduct, conductor (all uses).

confer, conferred, conferring, conferrable; but conferment, conference.

confetti is singular (despite being the Italian plural of *confetto*).

confidant (fem. confidante) = someone to whom one entrusts a confidence (secret); **confident** = exhibiting or feeling confidence (assurance). Both words derive from **confide** (which *see*), but reflect two meanings of *confidence*.

confide *in someone* (= confess); **confide** something *to* someone (= entrust).

confirm *See* **affirm**.

conga (pl. congas) = a dance; **conger** = an eel.

congenial = of the same taste, sympathetic, kindred; **congenital** = present at birth; **genial** = affable, cheering, kindly; **genital** = pertaining to generation or reproduction, of the genitals.

Congo The derived adjective and noun is *Congolese*.

conjure, conjuror (preferred to conjurer for the performer).

connect, connection (not -exion). *See also* **-ection**.

connive, connivance.

connoisseur.

conquer, conqueror.

conscience takes only an apostrophe (not *'s*) to form the possessive (e.g. "for conscience' sake").

conscious is better put as **aware** (of) in such constructions as "He became conscious that it was raining."

consensus is the correct spelling (not **concensus**).

consequent takes the preposition *on* (e.g. "He was charged with the crime consequent on his confession"). The phrase has a stilted ring to it, and the simpler "...*as a result of* his confession" or "...*after* he confessed" is preferred. *See also* **following** (which should be avoided as an alternative to *consequent on*).

conserve, conservation, conservationist (not conservationalist), conservatory.

consider (= regard as) does not need an additional "as" or "to be". E.g.:

"I consider style important" is sufficient and correct (not "consider as important" or "consider to be important").

considerable should be avoided when being used to mean *great* or *large* (e.g. "a considerable number of people"), thus reserving it to mean "worthy of consideration".

consistent = compatible, fixed, uniform – hence **consistently** = uniformly, without exception; **persistent** = on-going, enduring, continuous – hence **persistently** = continuously, without interruption.

consist of = to be made up of; **constitute** = to make up; e.g. "A whole consists of the parts; the parts constitute the whole." **consist in** = have its essence in; e.g. "The popularity of the book consists in its humour."

consommé

constrain = to compel someone (to do something); **restrain** = to hold back someone (or oneself). E.g.:

"She constrained him to go to the meeting."
"She restrained him from interrupting the meeting."

constructional = pertaining to construction; **constructive** = helpful (opposite of *destructive*). E.g.:

"The building collapsed because of a constructional fault."

"The building inspector made constructive suggestions about how to maintain the schedule."

consume = to use up (= destroy), not merely to **use**. **Consume** (applied to human beings) is, like **partake of**, precious for **eat** or **drink**, which are preferred.

contact (verb) = to touch, bring into contact; some people do not approve of its use to mean *communicate* (as in "He contacted me last week"), although it is an almost exact synonym for the idiomatic *get in touch with*.

contagion/contagious *See* **infection/infectious**.

contemplate, contemplative (not contemplatative).

contemporary (not contempory).

contemptible = worthy of derision, despicable; **contemptuous** = scornful, haughty. E.g.:

"His efforts at building a wall were contemptible."
"When asked about the quality of the work, the builder gave a contemptuous reply."

content (noun) refers to the type of material in a container; **contents** refers to all of it. E.g.:

"It was a large basket and the major content was fruit."
"The basket held fruit and the entire contents were rotten."

contest *See* **combat**.

contiguous *See* **adjacent**.

continual = always going on, although not necessarily without interruption; **continuous** = non-stop, unbroken in time or sequence. E.g.:

"The monsoon season brings continual rain."
"The mechanism provided for a continuous movement from floor to ceiling."

continuation = a "going-on", resumption, that which continues; **continuity** = the state of being continuous, unbroken, uninterrupted. E.g.:

"They agreed to meet again tomorrow for a continuation of their discussion."
"They agreed to talk all night to preserve the continuity of their discussion."

continuo (pl. continuos, not to be confused with *continuous*).

contra (= against) forms compounds without a hyphen except in the medical terms contra-indication and contra-suggestible.

contractions end with the final letter of the word when it is spelled in full, and so do not need a full point. E.g.:

Ave	Bt or Bart	Ct	cwt	Dr	Fr
ft	hr	Ltd	Mlle	Mme	Mr

St (street and Saint; plural SS for Saints) yd

The usual style for dates is not 1st, 2nd etc. but 1 January 1986. Verbal contractions (e.g. *can't* for *cannot*, *shan't* for *shall not*) should be avoided in formal writing. *See also* **abbreviations** (particularly under measurements and units); **units**.

contralto (pl. contraltos, not contralti).

contrast *See* **compare.**

contretemps is a singular word meaning **mishap** (usually involving embarrassment); it does not mean *argument* (as in "We had a contretemps about who should pay the bill"). The French term should be avoided.

contribute, contributor.

control, controlled, controller, controlling, controllable.

controvertible

convenience takes only an apostrophe (not *'s*) to form the possessive (e.g. "for convenience' sake").

converse, conversation, conversationalist. **Converse** is precious for **talk,** which is preferred. *See also* **inverse**.

conversion factors *See* **units**.

convert, converter, convertible, conversion.

convey, conveyer (who conveys), conveyor (which conveys).

convince = make someone believe something, give them conviction; **persuade** = make someone do something, using persuasion. E.g.:

"He could convince me that black was white."
"He could persuade me to do anything he wanted."
The derived adjectives are *convincing* and *persuasive*.

cony is the preferred spelling (not **coney**), except in Coney Island.

co-operate, co-operation, co-operative (with hyphens); but note non-co-operation (two hyphens) and uncooperative (no hyphen).

co-ordinate, co-ordination (with hyphens); but note uncoordinated (no hyphen).

copier paper = dust-free paper for use in photocopying machines.

copyright (noun) = the legal right to publish or reproduce a work (text, drama, music, film or television); **copyright** (verb) has the past tense and participle **copyrighted**; **copywrite** = to write copy (text), particularly for advertising or the press. *See also* **plagiarism**.

core = central part; **corps** = group of (uniformed) people; **corpse** = dead body. **Corps** has the same form in both singular and plural.

co-respondent = the person named in a divorce action as the alleged adulterer's extramarital partner; **correspondent** = a person who writes a letter or newspaper report.

corgi (pl. corgis).

corn is an American term for **maize**, and a common term elsewhere for any cereal crop. **Corn on the cob** is a seed-head of maize, also known as **sweet corn**. *See also* **grain**.

cornflour/cornflower *See* **grain**.

corollary = conclusion drawn from something already proved, a natural consequence; **rider** = amendment or supplement to a proposition or document; **codicil** = rider to a will.

corpulent is a euphemism for fat, as are *adipose, portly, rotund, stout* and *well-built* (of which the last seems to be the least offensive to fat people). *Well-covered* is colloquial for *fat*; *well-endowed* is colloquial for *buxom*. **Obese** is the medical term for *overweight*, often used in everyday language to mean very fat, grossly overweight.

corpus (pl. corpora).

corps *See* **core**.

corrasion = term in geology that describes local land erosion; **corrosion** = gradually eating or wearing away (as of a metal by acid or rust).

correct, correction, corrector (who corrects), corrective (which corrects), correctness, correctitude (archaic for correctness of manner/conduct).

corrections On a typescript, any corrections should preferably be made in the body of the text, in the space above the word or line being amended, and not in the margins with carats as with proof-reading marks (this is one reason why copy should be typed with double-line spacing, to allow room for corrections). Any typesetting instructions should be put in the margin and ringed round (this is why typescripts should have generous margins).
On printers' proofs, use standard proof-reading marks (*see* **proof-**

reading). All corrections should be marked clearly in ink or ball pen, in the margins. In the usual conventions, printer's errors are marked in red; author's and publisher's emendations should be in blue or any other colour other than the one the printer's reader (if any) has used. This can be important for calculating correction charges. Lengthy additions and instructions are best typed on a separate sheet and attached to the proof; the additions should be labelled and their exact positions clearly indicated in the text.

correspond, when making comparisons, takes *to*; when it means to write, it takes *with*. E.g.:

"An annual bonus of £5,200 corresponds to £100 a week."
"My daughter corresponds with a boy in Germany."

corrigenda (sing. corrigendum) = list of corrections in a book. Strictly they should consist of last-minute changes by the author to statements in the text as originally written and printed. *See also* **errata**.

corrigible

corrupt, corruptible, corrupter, corruption.

cortège

cortex (pl. cortices).

cosset, cosseted, cosseting.

cosy (not cozy).

cotter = retaining pin; **cottar** = villein.

couch = long upholstered seat (originally with a half-back and an arm at one end), as used by doctors and so on; **divan** = long seat with no back or ends, now used mainly of a bed (with no headboard); **settee** = long upholstered seat with a back and ends (arms); **sofa** = settee (but with an old-fashioned ring to it).

counsel (verb), counselling, counsellor (adviser), but councillor on a council.

counter (= opposite, duplicate) generally forms compounds without a hyphen except in counter-attack, -attraction, -claim, -clockwise, -espionage, -intelligence, -offensive, -productive, -revolution, -tenor; note also Counter-Reformation.

counties of England, Wales and Northern Ireland, and districts of Scotland, were established with their present names and boundaries in 1974. They should be spelled in full in ordinary text, although some of the longer names can be abbreviated in tables etc. The correct titles are as follows:

ENGLAND
Avon
Bedfordshire (Beds)
Berkshire (Berks)
Buckinghamshire (Bucks)
Cambridgeshire (Cambs)
Cheshire
Cleveland
Cornwall
Cumbria
Derbyshire (Derbs)
Devon
Dorset
Durham
Essex
Gloucestershire (Glos)
Hampshire (Hants)
Hereford and Worcestershire (H & W)
Hertfordshire (Herts)
Humberside
Isle of Wight (IOW)
Kent
Lancashire (Lancs)
Leicestershire (Leics)

Lincolnshire (Lincs)
Manchester, Greater
Merseyside
Norfolk
Northamptonshire (Northants)
Nottinghamshire (Notts)
Oxfordshire (Oxon)
Shropshire (Salop)
Somerset
Staffordshire (Staffs)
Suffolk
Surrey
East Sussex
West Sussex
Tyne and Wear (T & W)
Warwickshire (Warks)
West Midlands
Wiltshire (Wilts)
North Yorkshire (North Yorks)
South Yorkshire (South Yorks)
West Yorkshire (West Yorks)
Channel Islands (CI)
Isle of Man (IOM)

WALES

Clwyd	Mid Glamorgan
Dyfed	South Glamorgan
Gwent	West Glamorgan
Gwynedd	Powys

NORTHERN IRELAND (for which the abbreviation
Co. = County is permissible)

Antrim	Fermanagh
Armagh	Londonderry
Down	Tyrone

SCOTLAND

Borders	Lothian
Central	Orkney
Dumfries and Galloway	Shetland
Fife	Strathclyde
Grampian	Tayside
Highland	Western Isles

counting *See* **numbers**.

countless should not be used to describe something that can (or could) be counted; often *many* is all that is intended.

country names, adjectives from Adjectives derived from country names are commonly formed by adding *-n* or *-ian* to the name of the country (e.g. an Angolan, Jordanian). Often the same word serves as a noun for the name of the people (e.g. Angolan, Angolans; a Jordanian, Jordanians). There are many exceptions (e.g. Dutch, French, Swedish/Swede), and many of the less familiar ones are included in this Dictionary.

coup = sudden successful move, take-over of the government; **coupe** = shallow bowl; **coupé** = two-seater closed (hard-topped) car; **coupee** = salute to a dancing partner.

coup de grâce (italics) = finishing stroke; ***coup de main*** (italics) = sudden successful attack; ***coup d'état*** (italics) = violent (subversive) take-over of government; the French terms should be avoided, but *see* **coup** (non-italics).

course *See* **coarse**.

courtesy = polite behaviour, act of respect; **curtsy** = act of obeisance, usually by a standing woman bending her knees.

cousin = child of an uncle (parent's brother) or aunt (parent's sister), also called *first-cousin*; **second-cousin** = child of parent's first-cousin; **first-cousin once removed** = child of first-cousin; **first-cousin twice removed** = grandchild of a first-cousin. In each case, the term is defined from the standpoint of the person using the expression. *See also* **family relationships**.

covert (noun) = bushes etc. that provide shelter for birds such as partridges and pheasants; **covey** = group of birds such as partridges.

cowrie is the preferred spelling (not **cowry**). *See also* **karri**.

CP or **CPU** is an abbreviation of central processor or central processing unit, the "heart" of a computer in which data can be processed. In word processors and typesetting computers, the storage capacity of the CPU determines the amount of text that can be worked on at one time. This capacity, often in the form of a random access memory (RAM), is usually designated in terms of kilobytes (K). Thus a 128K RAM in the CPU of a personal computer or word processor has a capacity of 128,000 bytes (equivalent to approximately 18,000 to 20,000 ordinary text words). *See also* **RAM**.

CPI = abbreviation of characters per inch, an average for a given typeface and type size used to estimate the number of characters in a printed line of a particular length; **CPP** = abbreviation of characters per pica, used in a similar way to CPI (*see* **pica**).

crackpot *See* **mad**.

crape *See* **crêpe**.

crave is too strong a word to serve as a synonym for **ask** or **beg**; a **craving** is an irresistible desire, not merely a *liking* for something.

craven = cowardly, lacking courage; **graven** = engraved, carved.

CRC = abbreviation of camera ready copy – that is, an accurate paste-up of reproduction quality type matter and possible (line) illustrations ready for conversion to film and plate-making for printing.

crèche

credence = belief or trust; **credibility** = quality of being believable; **credulity** = quality of being ready to believe anything.

credible = believable; **creditable** = praiseworthy, to someone's credit; **credulous** = gullible; **credit-worthy** = of sufficient financial status or reputation to be given credit.

credit, creditor, creditted, credit card. **Credit** (verb) = to believe, trust, lend on trust or for a fee; **accredit** = to accept or prove to be true, vouch for, provide with credentials.

credo (pl. credos).

creep inflects *creep – crept – crept.*

crematorium (pl. crematoria).

crêpe (as in crêpe paper, crêpe Suzette), although **crape** is preferred for the fabric.

crescendo (pl. crescendos).

crevice = any cleft, rift or small fissure, a split; **crevasse** = a deep, often wide fissure in a glacier.

cringe, cringeing.

crisis (pl. crises).

criss-cross

criterion (pl. criteria).

critic, criticism, critique, criticize. A **critic** = someone who produces a **criticism** or **critique** (i.e. a knowledgeable review of the quality/merit of a work), often also termed a *review* or *survey*. Because the verb **criticize** is now more often used to mean *find fault* (rather than *give a balanced judgement*), the words *critic* and *criticism* have also attracted negative connotations.

crochet (needlework), crocheted (pronounced *"kro-shayed"*), crocheting.

crocus (pl. crocuses, not croci). *See also* **gladiolus**; **narcissus**.

croissant (not italics).

crosier is the preferred spelling of **crozier**.

cross-head *See* **subheadings**.

cross-references to other headwords or articles in alphabetically arranged matter such as a dictionary, encyclopaedia, glossary or index should be distinguishable typographically. A common style is to set *see* or *see also* in italics and the title referred to in small capitals or bold face; e.g. *see* CAPITALIZATION, or *see also* **capitalization**. *See* should be used to direct the reader directly to the location of the information being sought. E.g.:

> **trade names** *See* **capitalization**.

See also should be employed to direct the reader to additional or ancillary information. E.g.:

> **trade names** should be spelled with an initial capital letter. *See also* **capitalization**.

The abbreviation *cf* (*confer*) means "compare (with)" and should, strictly, direct the reader to contrasting information and be distinguished from *see* or *see also* as previously defined, although it is nearer the latter than the former.

croûton

crow (verb) has the preferred past tense and participle **crowed** (not *crew*).

crown, in printing, is a size of paper (named after the design of its original watermark). *See* **paper sizes**.

crucial = decisive, testing, critical (from *crux* = turning point); it should not be used to mean merely **important**.

crucify, crucifix, crucifixion.

crumpet = round cake made from dough containing yeast, baked (on a baking sheet) on one side only and with holes in the top; **drop scone** = small thick pancake, containing baking powder and turned during baking so that it is cooked on both sides; **muffin** = round doughy cake cooked on both sides; **pancake** = very thin, large "cake" made with eggs and flour (batter) and fried on both sides; **pikelet** = crumpet; **scone** = small cake made from an unsweetened mixture containing flour or oatmeal and baking powder, usually baked in an oven; **Scotch pancake** = drop scone; **teacake** = round flat bun made from a sweetened mixture containing yeast, often with added fruit (currants or sultanas). Crumpets, muffins and teacakes are usually toasted before being eaten; pancakes may be served with either sweet or savoury dishes.

crutch = a prop or support (as used by the lame); **crotch** = the fork of the body.

crux (pl. cruxes).

crystal, crystallize, crystallization.

C series = range of ISO (formerly DIN) international sizes of envelopes and folders. *See* **paper sizes**.

-ction *See* **-ection**.

cubical = shaped like a cube; **cubicle** = small room or cupboard.

cudgel, cudgelled, cudgelling.

cue, cueing. **Cue** = a hint, stick for striking a ball at billiards, pool or snooker; **queue** = a line of people waiting, pigtail.

cul-de-sac (pl. cul-de-sacs, not culs-de-sac).

cuneiform

cupful (pl. cupfuls).

curb This spelling should be used for the verb, **kerb** for the noun (kerbstone).

cure, curing, curable.

curio (pl. curios).

currant = a small fruit; **current** = a flow of air, electricity or water. *Current* is also an adjective meaning contemporary, up-to-date.

currency *See* **money.**

curriculum (pl. curricula).

curse = to wish someone evil; **swear** = to take or utter an oath, to use swearwords. E.g.:

"May you rot in hell" is cursing someone;
"God damn it!" is swearing.
Contempt of God or Jesus is also termed *blasphemy.*

cursive (in printing) = typeface with joined-up characters that imitate handwriting, also called a script face.

curtsy *See* **courtesy.**

cuscus = millet grain, Indian grass fibre; **cus-cus** = Malaysian marsupial; **couscous** = North African dish of steamed wheat flour and meat.

Customary Units (USA) *See* **units.**

customer *See* **client**.

cut-back binding *See* **perfect binding**.

cut line = printer's jargon for a line appearing on plate-making film or a proof resulting from the reproduction of (shadows from) the edge of a piece of paper pasted down on camera-ready copy (*see* **CRC**); **strip line** = similar flaw resulting from sticking down (assembling) pieces of film before plate-making. The two terms are often interchanged.

cut-off (adj. and noun), meaning the point at which something ceases to apply or happen, is a vogue term (e.g. "We cannot spend any more time on the task – we have reached the cut-off point"). *See* **vogue words**.

c.v. is the abbreviation of *curriculum vitae*.

cwt is the abbreviation of hundredweight(s).

cyclopaedia *See* **encyclopaedia**.

cypher The preferred spelling is **cipher**.

Cyprus The derived adjective and noun is *Cypriot*.

cyst *See* **cist**.

czar The preferred spelling is **tsar**.

Czechoslovakia The derived adjective and noun is *Czechoslovak* (not Czechoslovakian); the words *Czech* and *Slovak* should be reserved for the two major languages.

D

d. (italic) is the abbreviation of died.

dado (pl. dados).

dagger (†) *See* **footnotes**.

dago (pl. dagos), but avoid.

dahlia (plant named after Anders Dahl).

daily = of or on each day; **diurnal** = opposite of nocturnal, occupying one whole day (e.g. "a planet's diurnal rotation").

daisy-wheel printer *See* **printer**.

damage (noun) occurs to a thing; **injury** occurs to a person.

dandy roll = wire mesh cylinder on a papermaking machine which gives a texture to one surface of the paper. It can impress a *watermark* or create a *laid* finish (with parallel watermark lines). *See also* **paper**.

dare has the preferred past tense and participle **dared** (not *durst*).

dare say should be spelled as two words (i.e. not *daresay*).

dash *See* **punctuation**.

data can be singular in computer technology (*see* **plurals**).

database = information stored in a computer memory in such a way that individual items can be replaced, up-dated or withdrawn without affecting the rest of the content. It is the basis of computerized information retrieval, and the ideal of many reference book publishers.

date, datable.

dates *See* **time**.

datum (pl. data, which *see*).

day-bed, day-book, day-boy, day-break, day-dream, day-girl, daylight, day-long, day-school, daytime.

DC is the abbreviation of direct current.

de, as part of a French proper name, usually has no initial capital letter (except at the beginning of a sentence); e.g. Charles de Gaulle. In many other languages it is capitalized; e.g. Cecil B. De Mille. Follow the style of the name's owner, if this is known.

deacon, deaconess, deaconship, diaconate.

deadly = (capable of) causing death; deathly = resembling death. E.g.:

"The berries contain a deadly poison."
"Eating the berries gave her a deathly pallor."

dead reckoning, originally a nautical term, means a method of reasoning based on estimation/calculation rather than on (precise) measurement/observation. Its result can be (and often is) imprecise – it is not "dead on".

deaf-and-dumb (adj.) describes a **deaf-mute** (noun), someone lacking the senses of hearing and speech.

deal inflects *deal – dealt – dealt*. When it has a preposition, write deal *in* goods or, commodities, but deal *with* people, a topic.

death-bed, death-blow, death-cap, death duties, death's door, death's-head, death-rate, death-trap, death-watch, death wish.

debacle (no accents).

debar = to prohibit, prevent; **disbar** = to expel from the (legal) bar.

debate, debatable.

debauch = to corrupt, lead astray; **debouch** = issue forth (especially from a confined space into a larger one).

debit, debited.

debris (no accent).

debt, debtor.

debug *See* **bug**.

debut, debutant(e).

deca- is the metric prefix for ten times (× 10), as in *decametre*. *See* **units.**

deceive, deception, deceptive, deceit, deceitful. **Deceitful** = intended to deceive; **deceptive** = which deceives (perhaps unintentionally). E.g.:

"The child was reprimanded for her deceitful behaviour in blaming her sister."
"The deceptive coloration of the insect made it almost invisible against the mottled background."

decent = proper, seemly, modest; **descent** = going down, ancestry; **dissent** = disagree(ment).

deci- is the metric prefix for a tenth (× 10^{-1}), as in *decilitre*. *See* **units.**

decided (adj.) = definite, clear, without question; **decisive** = positive, showing a clear decision. E.g.:

"The designer's drawing skills gave her a decided advantage."
"The editor took decisive action and rejected the manuscript."

decidedly = without doubt, definitely; **decisively** = without hesitation, conclusively. E.g.:

"It is decidedly colder on the northern face of the mountain."
"He grabbed his coat and decisively strode out into the snow."

decimal, decimalize, decimalization. For decimal point, *see* **fractions**.

decimate = to destroy one in ten (i.e., 90 per cent survive); strictly, it does not mean to wipe out entirely, maul or cut up. The noun is **decimator**.

decline, declinable, declension (of nouns), declination (of stars).

decolorize, decolorization.

décor

decorate, decorator, decorative.

decorous = seemly, with decorum; **decorative** = providing decoration; **decorated** = having decoration.

decry = state one's strong disapproval of something, disparage; **descry** = catch sight of something (from a distance), catch on.

deduce = infer, draw a (logical) conclusion; **deduct** = take away, subtract. The verbs are not confused as often as the adjectives **deducible** (= may be inferred) and **deductible** (= may be taken away). And to add to the confusion, the two verbs share the same noun: **deduction**. E.g.:

"From the size of the paw prints and their spacing, the zoologist was able to deduce that they were made by a leopard."
"The identity of the animal was deducible from its paw prints."
"I persuaded the salesman to deduct his commission and so lower the price."
"The commission was deductible from the price."
Both the zoologist and the salesman made deductions.

deep-rooted, deep-seated.

deface, defaceable.

defecate, defecation (but faecal, faeces).

defect, defective, defector.

defective = imperfect (in quality); **deficient** = insufficient (in quantity).

defend, defender, defendant, defence, defensible (= that may be defended; defendable in law), defensive (= intended to defend).

defer, deferred, deferring, deferrable, deferrer, but deference, deferment, deferential.

define, definable.

definite = certain, precise; **definitive** = final, beyond change or criticism. E.g.:

"Her book expresses her definite views on singing."
"Her book has become the definitive work on singing."

definitely *See* **really**.

deflect, deflection (not deflexion).

degrade, degradable, degradation.

de-ice (remove ice), de-iced, de-icing.

déjà vu (italics, two accents).

de La, as part of a French proper name, usually has a capital letter only on *La* (except at the beginning of a sentence, when the *De* also has a capital); e.g. Jean de La Fontaine. Other languages vary; e.g. Walter de la Mare, Lord De La Warr. Follow the style of the name's owner.

delay *See* **dilate**.

delicatessen

delimit = to impose a limit (not to remove one).

delineate, delineable (not delineatable), delineation.

deliver, deliverer, deliverance (from evil), delivery (of coal).

delusion = a (lasting) belief that the false is true; **illusion** = a false conception of an idea or circumstance, deceptive appearance (illusions are believable, delusions are believed). *See also* **illude**.

delve is archaic for **dig**, which is preferred.

demarcation is the preferred spelling (not **demarkation**).

demean = to lower in dignity/reputation, to humble oneself, to conduct oneself; **demeanour** = bearing (towards others); **demesne** = a landed estate.

demi- Little-used prefix meaning *half* (as in demigod, demisemiquaver); more common are *hemi-* and *semi-* (*see* **numerical prefixes**).

demise = death (which is preferred); it should not be used to mean merely *decline* (as in "A gradual increase in vandalism has accompanied the general demise of discipline in the schools").

demobilize, demobilization.

demon, demonic (not demoniacal).

demonstrate, demonstrable (not demonstratable), demonstrator, demonstration.

demount = remove something from its mounting (such as a photographic transparency); **dismount** = unmount, get off a horse (or other animal). Then the transparency is *demounted*; the person on foot is *unmounted*.

demur, demurred, demurring, demurral, demurrage. **Demur** *at* or *to* = hesitate (because of uncertainty), object to; **demure** = sober, modest, grave (noun demureness). E.g.:

"She demurred at the invitation to go to the party."
"She wore a demure, high-necked dress to the party."

demy, in printing, = a size of paper. *See* **paper sizes.**

denarius (pl. denarii); Latin origin of the abbreviation **d** for the (now defunct) British penny.

denationalize, denationalization.

denizen is old-fashioned, and informal, for **inhabitant** (as in the cliché "denizens of the deep"); *inhabitant* is preferred.

dénouement

deny, deniable, denier, denial. **Deny** = to assert the falsity of a statement; **refute** = to prove the falsity of an accusation or theory.

deodorize, deodorizer.

département (of France).

depend, dependable, dependence, dependant (one who depends on another for support), dependent (conditional on, contingent). *Depend* linked to a condition requires the preposition *on* (preferred) or *upon* (e.g. "It depends whether we have enough time" is incorrect); when *depend* = *hang down* the preposition is *from.*

depict, depicter, depiction.

deplete = to empty, exhaust, use almost entirely; **reduce** = to make less.

deplore people's attitudes or actions, but not the people themselves.

depolarize

deposit, depositor (who deposits), depository (to whom a deposit is made, or in which a deposit is made), deposition (= the act of depositing or the act of deposing).

depot (no accents).

deprecate = to plead earnestly against; **depreciate** = to belittle, fall in value (opposite of *appreciate*).

depress, depressant, depressible.

depute, deputy, deputize.

derange, derangement, derangeable.

deride, derider, derision, derisible (= laughable), derisory (= scoffing, deserving derision, ridiculously small), derisive (= expressing derision).

de rigueur (italics) = required by custom or etiquette; the French term should be avoided.

descend, descendant (who or which is descended from), descendent (which descends or is descending), descender, descendible.

descender (typography) *See* **x-height**.

descent *See* **decent**.

desert = arid region; **deserts** = something deserved; **dessert** = pudding. All three words are singular; the first and third add an *s* for the plural, the second has the same spelling for the singular and the plural.

desertification, a comparatively new word meaning the formation of desert (through ecological mismanagement), is preferred to **desertization**.

desiccate, desiccation (not dessicate, dessication).

desire, desirable (= worthy of desire, wanted), desirous (of)(= full of desire (for)).

desman (pl. desmans).

desolate = barren, forlorn, uninhabited; **dissolute** = immoral, loose.

despatch The preferred spelling is **dispatch**.

desperado (pl. desperados).

desperate (not desparate) = feeling beyond hope, in despair, fraught with danger; **disparate** = different in character or quality. E.g.:

"They had not eaten for four days and were desperate for food."
"The twins looked almost identical but held disparate views about the way they should dress."

despise, despicable (not despisable).

despite is preferred to **in spite of**.

despite the fact that = **although**, which should be used.

despoil = to plunder (it does not mean to spoil).

destroy, destroyer, destruction, destructible.

detect, detector, detection, detective, detectable.

detent = mechanical catch; **détente** = improvement in formerly strained diplomatic relations.

deter, deterred, deterring, deterrent, determent.

detour (no accent).

detract (from) = take away (from); **distract** (from) = divert attention (from). E.g.:

"Misspellings detracted from the quality of the article".

"Misspellings distracted the reader from the point being made".

de trop (italics) = unwanted or superfluous, either of which is preferred.

develop, developed, developing, developer, development, developable.

developing countries This term is preferred to *undeveloped* or *underdeveloped countries*.

deviate, deviation, deviant (preferred to deviator).

Devil (capital letter if synonymous with Satan), devilish, devilment, devilry.

devil (verb), devilled, devilling.

devise (verb), deviser (who devises), devisor (who bequeaths), devisee (who receives a bequest); **device** is the noun. *See also* **divide**.

devitalize

dextrous (= nimble-fingered) is the preferred spelling of **dexterous**.

diagnose, diagnosis (pl. diagnoses). **Diagnosis** is the identification of a fault or disorder (from its symptoms or from test results); **prognosis** is the prediction of the course of a disorder and its probable outcome (from experience of similar conditions).

diagram, diagrammed, diagrammatic, diagrammatize.

dial, dialled, dialling, dialler.

dialect = (usually regional) variety of a language, often with some words unique to its vocabulary; **dialectal** = to do with dialect; **dialectic(s)** = branch of logic concerned with methods of reasoning; **dialectical** = to do with dialectics. *See also* **non-standard English**.

dialogue (= conversation between two people) is a vogue word and should be avoided in figurative use (*see* **vogue words**).

dialysis (pl. dialyses), dialyse, dialyser.

diamanté

diamond = obsolete name for $4\frac{1}{2}$-point type. For others, *see* **type sizes**.

diarrhoea (other *-rrhoea* words are analogous).

Diaspora (= the dispersion of Jews outside Palestine or Israel) should not be capitalized in its modern (vogue) use to mean any or all people at large.

diatribe = invective, vicious criticism; the word should not be used for merely any verbose statement.

dice (noun) is now the accepted form of both the singular and the plural; the use of *die* as a singular of *dice* is archaic (except in such expressions as "straight as a die"). The adjective is *dicey*.

dichotomy = separation into opposite/contrasting categories; it should not be used to mean merely **ambivalence** or **dilemma** (which *see*).

dictionary *See* **anthology**.

dictum (pl. dicta).

didot = unit of type measurement used mainly in Continental Europe. In this system, 1 point = 0.376mm (1 "English" point = 0.351mm). *See also* **cicero**; **pica**; **point**.

die *of* is preferred to **die** *from* (e.g. "They died of the plague").

dietitian is the preferred spelling of **dietician**.

differ, meaning *to be different*, requires the preposition *from*; when it is used to mean *disagree*, it can take *from* or *with*. E.g.:

"The possession of retractable claws is the main way in which cats differ from dogs"
"I often differ with my children".
Do not use *differ to. See also* **diverge**.

different *from* is increasingly becoming preferred usage to **different** *to*; do not use *different than*.

diffraction = splitting of light into (coloured) bands by passing a beam close to an edge or through a narrow slit (verb *diffract*); **dispersion** = splitting of light into spectral colours by passing a beam through a prism or grating (verb *disperse*); **refraction** = bending of light rays (possibly with the formation of colours) by passing them from one transparent medium to another (verb *refract*). Even physicists sometimes confuse these terms (which can also be applied to other forms of radiation and to sound).

dig inflects *dig – dug* (preferred to digged) – *dug. See also* **delve**.

digest, digester, digestible, digestion.

digit, digitize, digitization, digital.

digraph *See* **ligature**.

dike The preferred spelling is **dyke**.

dilate, dilatable, dilation (but dilatation in medicine), dilator (not dilatator); all derive from *dilate* = to make/become wider. The words dilatory, dilatorily and dilatoriness derive from *delay* = put off (in time).

dilemma involves a choice between two equally undesirable alternatives. The word should not be used to describe merely any difficult choice or problem.

diminish = to lessen; **minimize** = to make as little as possible.

DIN = Deutsche Industrie Norme, the standards institute of West Germany. It gave rise to the standard DIN paper sizes A series, B series, and so on (now renamed ISO = International Standards Organization). *See* **paper sizes**.

dinghy = small (rowing or sailing) boat; **dingy** = gloomy, grimy.

dingo (pl. dingoes).

dinner = main meal of the day, formally eaten in the evening (although to many people *dinner* is a mid-day meal; a smaller evening meal is called *supper*). A person who eats dinner in a restaurant is a *diner*. *See also* **lunch**.

diphtheria

diphthong *See* **ligature**.

diplomat = someone who represents a government or state; **diplomate** = someone who has been granted a diploma.

direct (adj.) = straight, straightforward. The logical related adverb is **directly,** but this means *immediately* and so *direct* has to do duty also as the adverb meaning *straight*. E.g.:

"She made a direct approach to the problem" (adjective);
"He felt unwell and went directly to bed" (adverb);
"They flew direct to Frankfurt, with no break at Paris" (adverb).

directions *See* **compass directions**.

dirigible = steerable; as a noun it is applied to early airships.

dis- *See* **negative prefixes**.

disadvantaged is sociologist's jargon; like **underprivileged**, it seldom means more than *poor* (e.g. "the disadvantaged sector of society" = "poor people").

disagree *See* **differ**.

disarmed = having had arms (weapons) taken away; **unarmed** = not bearing arms; **disarming** = charming, winsome.

disarrange, disarrangement.

disassemble = to take to pieces, to strip (down a machine); **dissemble** = to disguise, to hide one's feelings.

disassociate The preferred spelling is **dissociate**.

disaster, disastrous.

disbar *See* **debar**.

disbelief = state of not believing; **disbelieve** = to refuse to accept as truth; **disbeliever** = someone who rejects belief in something (having given it due consideration); **unbeliever** = someone who does not believe, often merely through disinterest.

disburse, disbursement.

disc is the preferred spelling of **disk** (although both are correct English); American spelling favours *disk* as, increasingly, do computer engineers (who call a small disk a *diskette*).

discern, discernible.

disclose = to declare, reveal; **expose** = to unmask, put in jeopardy.

discoloration (but discolour, discoloured).

discomfit = to thwart, disconcert, defeat in battle; **discomfort** = to disturb, upset; **discomfiture** = a defeat.

discover = to come across or find (out) something that already exists; **invent** = to make something new, to originate (something that did not previously exist); e.g. "Scheele discovered chlorine" but "Nobel invented dynamite".

discreet = prudent, circumspect, using care with (personal) information (its opposite is **indiscreet**); **discrete** = separate, individual, distinct (its opposite is **indiscrete** = continuous, homogenous). E.g.:

"The manager is a discreet father-figure to his staff."
"A sugar lump is composed of small discrete crystals."

discretionary hyphen, in text prepared or keyed for computer typesetting, is a hyphen for a word break that the machine includes only if necessary to achieve a particular line ending (e.g. to make the correct measure in justified setting). If the hyphen is not needed, the machine omits it. An *obligatory hyphen* is always included. *See also* **hyphen**; **word breaks**.

discriminating = discerning, selective in an experienced way; **discriminatory** = unfair, biased. E.g.:

"She is usually discriminating in her choice of clothes."
"He was often discriminatory in preferring to employ men rather than women."

discus = disc-shaped object thrown by an athlete; **discuss** = to debate, examine in detail.

disfranchise is the preferred form of **disenfranchise**.

dishevel, dishevelled.

disinterested = impartial; **uninterested** = not interested.

disk *See* **disc**.

dislodge, dislodgement.

dismiss, dismissible.

disorganize, disorganization.

dispassionate = calm, without passion; **impassioned** = showing passion, highly enthusiastic; **impassive** = unemotional, apathetic. E.g.:

"Throughout the trial he put his client's case in a dispassionate way."
"At the end of the trial counsel made an impassioned plea for clemency."
"Throughout the trial the defendant maintained an impassive expression."

dispatch is the preferred spelling of **despatch** (noun and verb).

dispense, dispenser, dispensable, dispensary, dispensation.

dispersal = the act of dispersing, distributing, spreading out; **dispersion** = the result of dispersing, distributing, spreading out. *See also* **diffraction**.

dispose = arrange in a particular way, adjust – its noun is *disposition*; **dispose of** = give/throw away – its noun is *disposal*.

disremember should be avoided as a synonym of *forget*; **misremember** = to remember incorrectly.

disrepair = state of needing repair/mending; **misrepair** = to repair incorrectly/badly.

disruption *See* **eruption**.

diss = printer's jargon for **distribute**, meaning to disassemble type (after printing) and return individual characters to their type cases.

dissect, dissection (but bisect, bisection).

dissemble *See* **disassemble.**

dissent *See* **decent.**

dissociate is the preferred form of **disassociate** in ordinary text, and the only form in chemistry.

dissolute *See* **desolate**.

dissolve, dissolvable (which is preferred to *dissoluble*, but equivalent to *soluble* in this sense).

dissymmetry *See also* **asymmetry**.

distaste, distastable, distasteful.

distend, distension (not distention).

distil, distilled, distilling, distillation, distillery.

distinct = separate, individual, unique; **distinctive** = characteristic, distinguishing; **distinguished** = eminent, famous (person). E.g.:

"She assumed a distinct air of indifference."
"I noticed the distinctive smell of petrol."
"The chairman greeted our distinguished visitor."

distract has the past tense and participle **distracted**, although **distraught** is retained as an adjective. *See also distrait*.

distrait (italics) = absentminded; **distraught** = agitated (in mind). The former should be avoided.

distribute, distributer (who distributes), but distributor (in a car).

disused = no longer used (although formerly used); **unused** = not been used (yet), or unaccustomed; **misused** = used incorrectly; **ill-used** = used badly, ill-treated.

ditto Do not use the symbol " or the abbreviation *do*, even in tabular matter.

diurnal *See* **daily**.

divan *See* **couch**.

diverge = to move apart; **divergent** = getting farther apart. These two words do not mean the same as *differ* and *different*. E.g.:

"The editor and designer held divergent views" is incorrect if their views were different.

divide, divisible (preferred to dividable), division, divider (who or which divides, generally), divisor (maths). *See also* **devise.**

djellaba is the preferred spelling (not djellabah, jellaba).

do (verb) has the past tense **did** and past participle **done. Do** (noun) has the plural do's (as in do's and don'ts).

do should not be used as an abbreviation of ditto.

docket, docketed, docketing.

doctor = someone qualified to practise medicine (and, with an initial capital letter, is a form of address for anyone with a doctorate such as a DD or PhD). In Britain, a doctor whose practice is available to the general public is called a *family doctor* or *general practitioner.* In a hospital, a *physician* treats systemic disorders, a *surgeon* performs operations; either may be a *consultant* (to whom patients are usually referred by the family doctor) and/or *specialist* (who concentrates on a particular group of disorders). A *dental surgeon* is usually referred to as a *dentist.* By convention, doctors are addressed as *Doctor*, dentists and consultants as *Mister.*

doctor, as a verb, has to work extremely hard. It can mean treat medically ("I doctored myself"), castrate ("I had my dog doctored"), patch up ("I doctored the crack in the window"), interfere with ("I doctored his drink"), or falsify ("I doctored the accounts"). Most uses are colloquial and should be avoided in formal writing.

doctrine = principle or belief; **dogma** = doctrine laid down with authority; **doctrinaire** = theoretical, carried to a logical but unworkable extreme; **dogmatic** = asserting positively, overbearing.

dodo (pl. dodos).

dog biscuit, dog-cart, dog-collar, dog-days, dog-eared, dogfight, dogfish, doghouse, dog-Latin, dogleg, dog-rose, dogsbody, dog star, dog's-tooth (plant, ornament), dog-tooth (canine tooth), dog-watch, dogwood.

doggie = a (little) dog; **doggy** = to do with a dog or dogs.

dogma (pl. dogmas).

dolman (pl. dolmans) = robe or mantle, type of sleeve; **dolmen** (pl. dolmens) = prehistoric stone slab or tomb.

dolour, dolorous.

domestic = pertaining to the home; **domesticated** = modified to be home-loving; e.g. a dog is a domestic animal, a tame water buffalo is a domesticated animal.

dominating = masterful; **domineering** = bullying; **predominant** = outstanding, principal; **dominant** = prevailing, outstanding, opposite of recessive. The correct form is dominated *by*, not dominated *with*.

dominoes (the game), although strictly plural, is usually treated as a singular form (e.g. "Dominoes is a game for two or four players"). When referring to the playing-pieces, the word is an ordinary plural (e.g. "Most modern dominoes are made of plastic").

don't should not be used for **do not** in formal writing. As a noun, it has the plural **don'ts** (as in *do's and don'ts*).

dope, doper, dopy.

dose, dosage, dosimeter.

dote, dotage.

dot-matrix printer *See* **printer**.

double = two times as many, twice as much; **duple** = twofold, double; **duplex** = duple. The words have the same meanings, although *duple* and *duplex* are now seldom seen or heard. **Treble** and **triple**, however, are both alive and often interchangeable; a subtle difference can be ascribed by making *treble* = three times as many (as in the treble on a dart-board) and *triple* = consisting of three parts (as in triple time in music). *Triplex* is now rare, except as a trade name for a type of safety glass. A set of three is a **triplet** (or are *triplets*), but **doublet** usually refers only to an old type of waistcoat or to two words of common origin but different spelling (such as guardian and warden). An ordinary set of two objects is usually known as a **pair** or **brace**.

double entendre (italics) = double meaning (often indecent); the pseudo-French form should be avoided.

doubt, used in a positive statement, requires *whether* or *if*; in a negative statement, it takes *that* or *but that*. E.g.:

"I doubt whether she will finish on time"
"I have no doubt that she will finish on time".

douse (with) = pour water over, extinguish; **dowse** (for) = to search for water (by divining).

dovecot is the preferred spelling (not **dovecote**), and reflects the correct pronunciation.

dowel, dowelled, dowelling.

downbeat, downcast, down-draught, downfall, down-hearted, downhill, down-market, downpour, downright, downstairs, downstream, down time, down town, downtrodden, downward(s), downwind.

down-market is salesman's jargon, usually for goods of low price and/or inferior quality; it should be avoided in formal writing. The opposite is **up-market**.

draft = plan, preliminary sketch, group of men (drawn from others); **draught** = a pull, something drawn (pulled), current of air, depth of a ship's keel. A **draughtsman**, however, draws lines, not pulls things; a **drayman** carries things in a truck or cart, originally pulled by *draught* horses.

dragée

dragoman (pl. dragomans).

drama, dramatize, dramatization.

drastic = severe, strongly-acting, vigorous (e.g. "drastic measures"); the word should not be used to mean merely *large* (as in "a drastic waste of paper").

draw (verb) has the past tense **drew** and past participle **drawn**.

drawers, an old-fashioned term for knickers, is a plural word; "a pair of drawers" achieves a singular construction.

dreadful should be reserved for things or circumstances that invoke dread (= great fear), and not used of something that is merely *unpleasant* or *disagreeable* (as in "she looked dreadful in her new dress").

dream (verb) The preferred past tense and participle is **dreamed** (not *dreamt*).

dress The names of types and parts of garments seem to have attracted into the language more foreign words and personal or place-names than any other group of things. Here, for curiosity value and as a reminder of any capitalization and preferred spellings, is a list of such terms and their origins:

aba (robe)	Arabic
anorak (jacket)	Eskimo
Balaclava (hat)	Balaklava (Crimea)
belcher (neckerchief)	Jim Belcher, boxer
beret (hat)	French
billycock (hat)	William Coke
biretta (priest's hat)	Italian
bloomers (loose trousers, knickers)	Amelia Bloomer

blouson (jacket)	French
bolero (jacket)	Spanish
bowler (hat)	Maker's name
blucher (shoe)	General Blücher
brassière (breast support)	French
Burbery (raincoat)	Maker's name
burka (robe)	Arabic
burnous (hooded cloak)	Arabic
caftan (robe)	Turkish
cagoule (jacket)	French
calash (hooped hood)	French
camisole (vest)	French
cardigan (jacket)	Lord Cardigan
Capris (shorts)	Capri (Italy)
cashmere (shawl)	Kashmir (India)
chaparajos (= chaps)	Mexican
cheongsam (dress)	Chinese
chesterfield (overcoat)	Lord Chesterfield
chopin (clog)	Spanish
cloche (hat)	French
culottes (shorts)	French
cummerbund (waist-sash)	Persian via Hindi
denims	de Nîmes (France)
derby (US bowler hat)	Lord Derby
dhoti (loin-cloth)	Hindi
dirndl (dress)	German
djellaba (robe)	Arabic
Dolly Varden (hat)	Dickens's character
dolman (sleeve, robe)	Turkish
duffel (coat)	Duffel (Belgium)
dungarees (breeches)	Hindi
epaulet (shoulder ornament)	French
Eton collar, jacket, suit	Eton College
fedora (hat)	*Fédora* (a French play)
fez (hat)	Fez (Morocco)
fichu (cape)	French
garibaldi (blouse)	Giuseppe Garibaldi
glengarry (hat)	Glengarry (Scotland)
havelock (neck-cover)	General Henry Havelock
Homburg (hat)	Homburg (Germany)

ihram (pilgrim's robe)	Arabic
Inverness (cloaked overcoat)	Inverness (Scotland)
jeans	Genoa (Italy)
jodhpurs (riding breeches)	Jodhpur (India)
kaffiyah (head-shawl)	Arabic
kente (robe)	Ghanaian
kepi (hat)	French
khaddar (robe)	Hindi
kimono (robe)	Japanese
leotard (one-piece costume)	Jules Léotard, French acrobat
mackintosh (raincoat)	Charles Macintosh
Mae West (inflatable life-jacket)	Mae West, Hollywood actress
mandarin (coat, collar)	Chinese official
manta (cloak)	Spanish
manteau (gown)	French
mantilla (veil)	Spanish
moccasin (slipper)	American Indian
mufti (civilian garb)	Arabic
Norfolk jacket	Norfolk (county)
obi (sash)	Japanese
Oxford (baggy trousers, shoe)	Oxford (city)
panama (hat)	Panama (country)
parka (jacket)	Eskimo
peplum (overskirt)	Greek (*peplos*) via Latin
petersham (overcoat)	Lord Petersham
poncho (cloak)	Spanish American
putee (bandages gaiter)	Hindi
raglan (coat, sleeve)	Baron Fitzroy Raglan
sari (robe)	Hindi
sarong (robe)	Malay
serape (cloak)	Mexican
shako (hat)	Hungarian
sombrero (hat)	Spanish
spencer (jacket, vest)	Earl Spencer
Stetson (hat)	Maker's name
surtout (coat)	French
taj (cap)	Arabic
tallith (prayer shawl)	Hebrew
tam o-shanter (= tam) (hat)	Burns' character

tarboosh (hat)	Arabic
topi (hat)	Hindi
toque (hat)	French
trilby (hat)	*Trilby* (Du Maurier's novel)
tutu (ballet skirt)	French
vandyke collar	Anthony Van Dyke
wellingtons (boots)	Duke of Wellington
Windsor (-knot, tie)	Windsor (Berkshire)

drink (verb) has the past tense **drank** and the past participle **drunk**.

drive (verb) has the past tense **drove** and the past participle **driven**.

drivel, driveller, drivelled, drivelling.

dromedary *See* **camel**.

drop cap = abbreviation of dropped capital, a typesetter's term for a capital letter at the beginning of a line which is larger than, and extends below, the letters on the rest of the line.

drug names Generic names (approved names) should normally be used, not trade names or proprietary names (e.g. write diazepam, not Valium; soluble aspirin, not Disprin). If trade names must be used, they should have an initial capital letter (*see* **trade names**).

dry, drier, driest (adjectives), drily, dryish. **Drier** is the preferred spelling of the noun (not **dryer**).

duel, dueller, duellist, duelling.

due to, like **owing to,** are adjectival and strictly should not be used as prepositions equivalent to *because of* or *on account of*. E.g.:

"I was late due to a delay on the railway" is better put as "I was late because of a delay on the railway."

dummy = printer's and bookbinder's term for a sample of a book made from blank (unprinted) paper.

duotone = printer's term for a two-colour image made from a single-colour (black-and-white) original using a pair of halftones of different screen angles.

dupe *See* **original**.

during the period from = **from**, which should be used.

Dutch words assimilated into English seldom cause difficulty, because most are well established and familiar. So, more for interest than instruction, here is a list of words – many to do with the sea and ships – that began life in the Netherlands:

boor	easel	sketch	tarpon
brandy	foist	skipper	trigger
caboose	gin	sledge	waffle
cruise	kit	sloop	wagon
deck	landscape	splice	yacht
decoy	loiter	splinter	
dock	maelstrom	split	
drill	marlin	spool	

Other Dutch words, such as *boss* and *sleigh*, probably arrived in Britain via North America; still others travelled from South Africa by way of the Afrikaans language, such as:

aardvark	boomslang	rand	trek
apartheid	commandeer	spoor	veld
boer	klipspringer	springbok	wildebeest

duty, dutiable.

dwarf (pl. dwarfs).

dwell is archaic for to **live** (somewhere), which should be used, although the noun **dwelling** serves as a blanket term for any home or living-place.

dyad, or double, = a pair of words that are almost always found together. *See* **inseparable pairs**.

dye, dyed, dyeing (cloth).

dyke is the preferred spelling of **dike**.

dynamo (pl. dynamos).

dys- *See* **negative prefixes**.

dysentery

dysfunction is medical; **malfunction** is general.

dyslexia *See* **alexia**.

E

E 13 B = type fount whose characters can be "read" by magnetic character recognition machines (MICR), as commonly used on cheques. *See also* **MICR**.

each and **every** are singular words; e.g. "The team made errors and each member is to blame for the defeat; every member later admitted his responsibility." A preference for plural verbs and pronouns can be expressed by substituting *all* (or *both*) for *each* (or *every*): "The team made errors and all the members are to blame for the defeat; all subsequently admitted their responsibility." *See also* **both; either**.

each other applies to two persons or things; **one another** applies to three or more; e.g. "The two boys argued and then hit each other; all four parents arrived and shouted at one another." The possessive forms are **each other's** and **one another's**.

earache, ear-drum, ear-like, earmark, earphone(s), ear-piece, earplug, earring.

Earth, the planet, should be spelled with an initial capital letter (*see* **astronomical terms**).

earthly = to do with the planet Earth; **earthy** = to do with the soil; **earthen** is an archaic form of *earthy*, retained in such expressions as "an earthen floor" and in the compound word *earthenware*.

earthnut = pignut (plant of the carrot family); **groundnut** = peanut (plant of the pea family).

Earth satellites *See* **artificial satellites**.

east, eastern, etc. *See* **compass directions**.

Eastern Hemisphere (spelled with initial capital letters).

easy-going

eat has the past tense **ate** (not *eat*) and past participle **eaten**.

eatable *See* **edible**.

echo (pl. echoes), echoing, echoer, echo-location, echo-sounder, echo-sounding.

éclair

éclat = brilliant success, showy fame; the French term should be avoided.

eclectic = freely chosen from available sources, non-exclusive; it does not mean specially selected to include only the best.

economic = pertaining to (the) economy; **economical** = pertaining to economics; neither word should be used to mean **inexpensive** or **cheap**.

economy, economize.

ecstasy, ecstatic.

-ection is the preferred spelling to **-exion** in such words as confection, connection, deflection, reflection (thus avoiding such combinations as "deflexion of a section" and "in connexion with the election"). Words that should be spelled *-exion* include complexion, genuflexion and inflexion. Note also crucifixion, fluxion. *See also* **reflect** (and *reflexive*).

Ecuador The derived adjective and noun is *Ecuadorean*.

eczema

-ed *See* **suffixes**.

edema The preferred spelling is **oedema**.

edge, edging, edgy.

edible = can be eaten without harm, fit to eat; **eatable** = presented in a way that tempts one to eat. The opposites are *inedible* and *uneatable*.

edifice rarely means more than simply **large building**, which is preferred.

edition etc. **First edition** = first printing of a book; **impression** = a reprint with no change, the first of which is the *second impression* (often now called a *reprint*), and so on. An amended or corrected version is the **second edition** of the book, subsequent impressions of which are numbered again from one (*second edition, first impression* and so on).

educate, educator, educatory, educatable, educative, education, educational, educationist (not educationalist).

educe, educible.

e'er is a (poetic) abbreviation of **ever**, and should be avoided; **ere** is archaic for **before**, and should also be avoided.

effect, effecter (who effects), effector (which effects). *See also* **affect**.

effeminate is properly applied to a man who is womanish, unmanly; it is not a synonym of **feminine** (*see* **female**). The corresponding term, applied to woman, is *mannish*.

effete = worn out, exhausted; it does not mean *effeminate* or *sophisticated*, and is probably best avoided.

efficient = achieved without waste, capable; **proficient** = executed to an accepted (defined) standard; e.g. "His writing was extremely small, making efficient use of the paper, but it revealed that he was not proficient in the use of English". **Efficiency** and **proficiency** are sometimes similarly confused. *Efficient* has also been confused with **effective** (= producing the desired/required effect) and **effectual** (= able to produce an effect) and even **efficacious**

(= producing the required (medical) result, with implied rapidity); e.g. "The machine ceased to be efficient so the mechanic poured on some oil which, although effective in reducing friction, was not effectual in reducing fuel consumption; when swallowed by the mechanic, the same oil was efficacious in relieving his constipation."

e.g. is the abbreviation of *exempli gratia* (for example). It should not be confused with **i.e.** (= *id est*, that is).

egoism = theory that self-interest is (or should be) the basis of morality – an adherent is an *egoist*; **egotism** = overuse of the pronoun *I*, talking about oneself too much – someone who does so is an *egotist*.

-ei- The child's rule of thumb is: "I before E except after C". It is not an inflexible rule; all the following words have *-ei-* not after C in their spelling:

being	feign	meiosis	seizure
blueing	feint	neigh	shoeing
caffeine	foreign	neighbour	singeing
casein	forfeit	neighbouring	skein
canoeing,	freight	neither	sleigh
canoeist	heifer	non-pareil	sleight
codeine	heigh-ho	obeisance	surfeit
counterfeit	height	plebeian	swingeing
cuneiform	heinous	protein	their
deign	heir, heiress	reign	tyreing
dyeing	hoeing	reindeer	veil
eider	inveigh	Seidlitz	vein
eidograph	inveigle	(powder)	weigh, weight
eight, eighty	kaleidoscope	seige	weir
etc.	leisure	seigneur	weird
either	madeira	seize	

The following words *do* have *i* before *e*, even after *c*, and therefore also break the rule:

ancient	omniscience, omniscient
coefficient	prescient
conscience	proficient, proficiency

deficient
efficient, efficiency
glacier
inefficient, inefficiency

science
species
stupefacient
sufficient, sufficiency

Eire, like Southern Ireland, should not be used for the Republic of Ireland or, simply, Ireland. **Northern Ireland** is the correct term for the Irish part of the United Kingdom (formally the United Kingdom of Great Britain and Northern Ireland), for which the term **Ulster** should not be used. *See also* **counties.**

either applies to one of two (persons or things) and is singular; e.g. "There are two applicants: either (of them) is suitable." If the choice is not between two but among three or more, use *any* or *any one* (two words); e.g. "Five teams competed: any (one of them) could have won."
Do not misuse *either* for **each**; e.g. "There are houses on either side of the street" is incorrect; say "... on each side of the street" or "on both sides of the street". (But "There are no houses on either side of the street" is correct and slightly better than "There are houses on neither side of the street", which is an example of a sentence that is an unfulfilled promise.) *See also* **alternative.**

eject, ejector.

eke (out) = to make something last by adding to it (not to make it last by "stretching" or husbanding it, without supplement).

élan (italics) = dash, impetuousness; the French form should be avoided.

elapse = to pass, expire; **lapse** (verb) = to err, fail, fall (temporarily) into disuse (e.g. time may elapse, a person's manners may lapse).

elect, elector (fem. electress), election.

electrolysis, electrolyte, electrolyse, electrolytic.

elegy = poem, funeral song; **eulogy** = lavish written or spoken praise. The corresponding verbs are elegize, eulogize.

element, elemental = pertaining to the elements (either the chemical ones or the classical earth, air, fire and water), elementary (= basic, primary).

elephant, in printing, = size of paper (named after the design of its original watermark). *See* **paper sizes**.

elevator, in English, should be reserved for a machine for lifting goods (e.g. freight elevator, grain elevator); a machine for people is a **lift** (= *elevator* in American).

elf (pl. elves).

elicit = to draw out, evoke; **illicit** = unlawful, improper.

eligible = meeting the requirements for appointment/election/ selection; **legible** = clear, easily read; **illegible** = written or printed so badly as to be incapable of being read (*see* **unreadable**).

eliminate = to remove something from something; **isolate** = to separate something from among other things; **exclude** = to ignore/shut out completely.

elision = omission of a sound, usually a vowel, in pronouncing a word or words; the missing component is indicated by an apostrophe (e.g. can't, didn't, he'll, I'm, Len's arrived, won't). Elided words should be avoided in formal writing. *See also* **ellipsis**.

élite, élitist.

elk = large deer of northern Europe and Asia (*Alces alces*), the North American race of which is called a *moose*. Americans use the term *elk* for a different animal, the wapiti or North American elk (*Cervas canadensis*). *See also* **caribou**.

ellipsis (pl. ellipses) Omissions in a quotation, list or mathematical series are indicated by three full points, preserving any adjacent punctuation. E.g.:

"On the first day of Christmas . . . a partridge in a pear-tree."

January, February, . . ., November, December.

$x_1, x_2, x_3, \ldots, x_n$

See also **elision**.

El Salvador The derived adjective and noun is *Salvadoran*.

else when paired with a pronoun such as *anybody* (anyone), *everybody* (everyone), *nobody* (no one), *somebody* (someone) or *who* forms the genitive (possessive) **else's** (e.g. "anybody else's book", "who else's book is torn?").

elucidate, elucidator.

elude *See* **illude**.

elusive = difficult to understand/capture; **illusive** = not as valuable/real as it seems. *See also* **delusion**.

em = printer's measure equivalent to the width of a lower case letter m in the given typeface. A 12-point em = 1 pica (*see* **point**); an em dash is a long dash.

embalm, embalming, embalment, embalmer.

embargo (pl. embargoes).

embarrass, embarrassment.

embed, embedded, embedding.

embezzle, embezzlement.

embrocation = healing lotion, liniment; **imbrication** = set of overlapping shapes (like tiles on a roof or scales on a fish).

embryo (pl. embryos).

emend *See* **amend**.

emerald = obsolete name for 14-point type. For others, *see* **type sizes**.

emerge, emergent, emergence (= act of emerging), emergency (= happening that emerges unexpectedly).

emigrant and **immigrant** The correct use of these words depends on where you are standing. If you are in Britain, an incoming Nigerian is an immigrant and an outgoing Englishman, who intends to settle in Nigeria, is an emigrant. To a Nigerian in Nigeria, the appellations would be reversed. Both people are **migrants** (as are animals that move long distances, whether they be coming or going). The corresponding verbs are **emigrate, immigrate** and **migrate**.

émigré

eminent *See* **immanent**.

emollient = something that softens the skin, a lotion; **emolument** = pay for holding an office, salary.

emotion gives rise to the adjectives *emotional* and *emotive*. The former is used to mean displaying emotion, the latter to mean stimulating emotion. E.g.:

"Her sensitive singing produced an emotional response in those who heard it."
"The crowd stirred to the emotive sound of military music."

empannel, empannelled, empannelling.

emphasis (pl. emphases), emphasize.

emporium (pl. emporia).

empty = containing or carrying nothing; **vacant** = unoccupied, expressionless; e.g. "An empty cupboard in a vacant flat."

emulate = to try to equal or better (not merely to **imitate**). E.g.:

"He emulated his boss and assembled two machines in an hour."
"He imitated his boss and was dismissed for insubordination."

en = printer's measure equal to half an em (*see* **em**; **point**); an en dash
is longer than a hyphen but shorter than an em dash.

enable = to make able; it does not mean to make possible. E.g.:

"The completion of the work on time enabled us to keep to the
schedule" is correct;
"...enabled the schedule to be kept" is incorrect.

enamel, enamelled, enamelling, enamaller.

en bloc (italics) = wholesale, as a unit; the French form should be
avoided.

enclave *See* **conclave**.

enclose/enclosure are preferred to **inclose/inclosure**.

encrust, incrustation.

encyclopaedia, encyclopaedic. The (American) spelling *encyclopedia*
is gaining ground among British publishers (although probably
more with an eye to the North American market than a desire for
simplification). The old term **cyclopaedia** (= a short or shortened
encyclopaedia) has largely fallen into disuse. *See also* **anthology**.

endive *See* **chicory**.

end matter *See* **prelims**.

endocrine etc. is preferred to **endochrine** etc.

endorse, endorsable, endorsement (**endorse** is preferred to
indorse). *See also* **approve**.

endpapers = strong (sometimes coloured or printed) paper pasted
inside the front and back covers of a book to secure the book-block

into the case; **self-ends** or **own-ends** = use of first and last pages of a book-block to form the endpapers.

endure, endurable.

energy, energetic, energize.

enervate = to sap the strength or energy of, to devitalize; it does not mean to put nerve into, invigorate.

enforce, enforceable.

enfranchise

English = obsolete name for 14-point type. For others, *see* **type sizes**.

engrain, ingrained.

enigma (pl. enigmas).

enliven is preferred to **liven up**.

en masse (italics) = all together, in (as) a body; the French form should be avoided.

en- or in- The *en-* form is preferred to *in-* as the prefix of *enclose, encrust* and *endorse*; the words *ensure* and *insure* coexist with different meanings (*see* **insure**); the *in-* form is preferred for *inquire*.

enormity = serious crime, great wickedness. The word should not be used to mean hugeness, large size; e.g. "The enormity of the supertanker..." is incorrect.

enough *See* **adequate**.

enquire The preferred spelling is **inquire** (and **inquiry** is preferred to **enquiry**).

enrol, enrolled, enroller, enrolling, but enrolment.

en route (italics) = on the way; the French form should be avoided.

ensue, ensuing.

en suite (italics) = in a set, forming a unit (with); the French form, beloved of estate agents, should be avoided in formal writing.

ensure *See* **insure.**

entente (italics) = understanding or agreement between nations.

enterprise

enthral, enthralled, enthralling, enthraller, but enthralment.

enthuse should be avoided as a verb meaning **show enthusiasm** (for).

entitle(d), = name(d), is preferred to **title(d).**

entomology = the study of insects; **etymology** = the study of words.

entrance (noun) = the act of going in; **entry** = the result of going in; both = the way in. E.g. "He made an entrance to gain entry".

entrap, entrapped, entrapping, but entrapment.

entrecôte

entrée

entrepôt

enumerable = countable; **innumerable** = uncountable, and should not be used instead of **many** of things that can (or could) be counted.

enunciate, enunciator, enunciation. *See also* **annunciation**.

envelop is the verb; **envelope** is the noun.

enviable = (capable of) arousing envy; **envious** = showing/feeling envy. E.g.:

"She had an enviable reputation for speed and accuracy."
"He was envious of her ability to work quickly and accurately."

environs is a plural word; it has no singular.

envisage = to imagine/visualize something planned but not created, to view. The word should not be used as a grandiose way of saying to *think, describe, estimate*, and so on. Examples of misuses include: "I envisage that the article will occupy two pages" (use *estimate/ expect*);
"The article envisaged two applications of..." (use *described*);
"He envisaged that train fares might rise" (use *thought/predicted*).

eon The preferred spelling is **aeon**.

epaulet (not epaulette).

épée

ephemera is singular (pl. ephemeras).

epitomy, epitomize.

eponym = someone who gives his name to a place or institution, now applied to any word formed from a person's name; e.g. *boycott* (Charles Boycott), *guillotine* (Dr. J. Guillotin), *lynch* (Capt. W. Lynch), *maverick* (S. A. Maverick), *shrapnel* (General H. Shrapnel), *zeppelin* (Count von Zeppelin). For two lists containing eponyms, *see* **dress**; **personal names**.

equable = even, regular, unflappable; **equatable** = can be equated, regarded as equal; **equitable** = just, fair (note the spelling of *equitable*, which derives from *equity*).

equal, equalled, equalling, equalize, equalization, equaliser. **Equal** takes *to*, not *as* or *with*. *See also* **coequal**.

equally does not need *as* before the word it qualifies; e.g. in "His version was equally as good", delete *as*.

equator (no initial capital letter when it refers to 0 latitude).

equinox (pl. equinoxes).

equip, equipped, equipping, equipment, equipage (archaic).

equitable *See* **equable**.

equivocate, equivocator.

-er *See* **comparative and superlative; -or; suffixes**.

eradicate = to root out (and thus destroy); **irradicate** (rare) = to root, fix firmly; **irradiate** = to expose to radiation/such as light or X-rays.

erase, erasion, erasure (preferred). **Erase** = rub out, scrape away; **raze** = destroy completely, level with the ground, sweep away.

ere is archaic (and poetic) for **before**, which should be used. *See also* **e'er**.

erect, erecter (who erects), but erector muscle.

errata (sing. erratum) = list of corrections in a book. Strictly they should consist of typesetting errors in the printed book which the author failed to correct on proof. *See also* **corrigenda**.

erstwhile is archaic for **former**, which should be used.

eruption = a breaking out (like a pimple or volcano); **irruption** = a breaking in (as of the sea through a broken sea wall); **interruption** = something that breaks (in) between;

intervention = coming between two people or parties;
disruption = a shattering, interruption.

escalate, used to mean *increase* or *intensify* (e.g. "His remarks
escalated their differences"), is a vogue word and should be avoided
(as should *escalation*). *See* **vogue words**.

Eskimo (pl. Eskimos, not Eskimoes, Esquimaux). North Americans
and linguists prefer the term Inuit.

esoteric = intelligible only to the initiated, secret; **exoteric** =
intelligible to the uninitiated, commonplace.

especially *See* **specially**.

esprit de corps (italics) = loyalty to a group (of which one is a
member), high morale, pride/faith in a cause. There seems to be no
English term for this "typically English characteristic";
nevertheless, the French term should be avoided.

essay *See* **assay**.

-est *See* **comparative and superlative**; **suffixes**.

estimatable = can be estimated; **estimable** = worthy of esteem;
inestimable = too large to be estimatable. E.g.:

"There is insufficient information to make the cost estimatable."
"His estimable contribution enhanced the quality of the work."
"We could not thank her enough for her inestimable contribution
to the work."

estimate (noun) = knowledgeable guess (of cost, worth, quantity
required, etc.), or the figure arrived at; **estimation** = the act of
making an estimate, judgement of worth. Both are made by an
estimator. E.g.:

"I can make an estimate of the time the task will take."
"In my estimation the task will take three weeks."

Possible confusion can be avoided by using the verb to estimate. E.g.:

"I cannot estimate how long the task will take."
"I estimate that the task will take three weeks."

et al., the abbreviation of *et alia*, *et allii*, etc. (meaning "and other persons"), should be avoided in narrative text. *See also* **et cetera**.

etc. is the abbreviation of *et cetera* (which *see*).

et cetera is nearly always used as its abbreviation etc. This term should be avoided in formal text – use a phrase such as "and so on" instead. If etc. must be used, remember that it means "and other similar things" and therefore should not, strictly, be appended to an incomplete list of people (*see* **et al.**), animals or plants. Also good style requires a comma before *etc*. E.g.:

"There were various makes of cars: Fords, Fiats, Bentleys, and many others" is correct;
"There were many makes – Fords, Fiats, Bentleys, and so on" is also correct;
"There were many cars: Fords, Fiats, Bentleys, etc." is acceptable but should be avoided;
"There were several of the senior managers: Jones, Smith, Brown, Green, etc." is strictly incorrect.

eternal *See* **temporal**.

etiology The preferred spelling is **aetiology**.

étude (italics) = study; the French form should be reserved for use as a musical term.

étui (= a needle-case, which is preferred).

etymology *See* **entomology**

eulogy, eulogize. *See also* **elegy**.

euphemism *See* **non-standard English**.

evade, evadable (= can be evaded), evasion (= act of evading, hedging), evasive (= difficult to pin down), evasiveness (= quality of being evasive).

even should be placed next to the word it qualifies; misplaced it can lead to ambiguities similar to those created by a misplaced **only** (which *see*). Consider how the position of *even* affects the meaning when it is inserted into the sentence "Children are writing books":

"Even children are writing books"	(let alone adults);
"Children are even writing books"	(let alone reading them);
"Children are writing even books"	(let alone essays).

even though *See* **although**.

even working *See* **working**.

ever, intensifying a noun or pronoun, does not take a hyphen (e.g. "Best ever result", "Largest ever found", "Was the poorest ever", "Who ever told you?", "What ever happened?"). If **ever** is used to generalize a pronoun, it joins it to form one word (e.g. "Come whenever you like", "Whatever interests you", "It is wrong, whoever told you", "It will take time, however you do it").

every is singular (e.g. "Every draughtsman has his own drawing-board"). *See also* **each**. **Everybody, everyone, everything** are similarly also singular (e.g. "Everybody is welcome to his share"). **Everyday** (one word) is an adjective (e.g. "A delay in getting through is an everyday occurrence"); in other contexts, **every day** (two words) should be used (e.g. "Delays occur every day").

evince = to show or prove something (using argument or evidence), and should not be used merely as a synonym for **show**; **evoke** = to summon, call forth.

evocative = reviving memories, stimulating emotions; **provocative** = stimulating interest, causing annoyance/anger (usually with mischievous intent). E.g.:

"The evocative smell of wood smoke reminded her of home."
"He responded angrily to the provocative remark about his ability."

evolve, evolvable, evolution.

ex- (prefix) The preferred term is **former** (which *see*).

exacerbate = make worse; **exasperate** = annoy to distraction. E.g.:

"The herbal remedy only exacerbated his illness."
"She was exasperated by his childish behaviour."

exalt, exalter. **Exalt** = elevate in rank or status, fill with pride; **exult** = rejoice.

excavate, excavator.

except is archaic when used for **unless**; e.g. in "He will not go except I go with him", *unless* should be used. *See also* **bar**.

exceptionable = to which exception may be taken, open to objection. **exceptional** = which is an exception (hence *unexceptionable* = unobjectionable; *unexceptional* = not worthy of special note).

excessive = in excess; **excessively** = in an excessive manner, immoderately; **exceedingly** = greatly, very much, extremely.

exchange, exchangeable.

excise, excisable.

excite, excitement (= state of being excited emotionally), excitation (= act of exciting, usually in science), excitable, exciter (= who or which excites, but excitor nerve).

exclamation mark (!) should be avoided in formal writing except in direct quotation (e.g. *Hello, Dolly!*, Westward Ho!).

exclude *See* **eliminate**.

excuse, excusable.

execute, executer (who executes something), executioner (who executes somebody), executor (who executes a will; fem. executrix).

exemplary = serving as a model to be imitated (e.g. "His exemplary behaviour became a standard for the others"); **excellent** = having/showing excellence, of best quality. The former word should not be used for the latter.

exempt (adj.) = not liable; **immune** = not liable to infection/danger; **excused** = free from blame/guilt/responsibility.

exercise = make use repeatedly of one's muscles, improve through practice, enforce a right; **exorcise** = drive out an evil influence (by invoking a deity).

exert, exertion.

ex gratia (italics) = **as an act of grace**, i.e. without prejudice (as in "an *ex gratia* payment"); the Latin term should be avoided.

exhausting = causing exhaustion; **exhaustive** = full, complete, thorough; **exhaustible** = can be exhausted. E.g.:

"Finding the goats involved an exhausting climb."
"Finding the goats involved an exhaustive search."
"Petroleum is an exhaustible resource."

exhibit, exhibitor, exhibition.

exigent = urgent, pressing, rigorous; **exiguous** = small, scanty.

-exion *See* **-ection**.

exist, existent, existence, but extant.

exit, exited (exit = he/she goes out; exeunt = they go out).

exorcize, exorcism.

expand, expansive, expansible (not expandable).

expanded face, or expanded type = typeface in which the characters are wider than in the normal parent face. Formerly made as separate founts, expanded faces can now be generated (to any required percentage of expansion) by phototypesetting machines. *See also* **condensed face**; **weight**.

expect, expector, expectable, expectant, expectancy, expectation. *See also* **anticipate**.

expectorate is a euphemism for **spit**, which today rarely gives offence as a word.

expel, expelled, expelling, expellent.

experiment, experimenter.

expertise

expiate, expiatable.

expire, expiration (of breath), expiry (of life or a fixed term).

explicit = stated directly (not merely implied), fully expressed; **implicit** = implied (although not stated), entirely/unquestioningly relying on.

explosion = a bursting outwards, often used to describe the bang made by a chemical explosion (verb *explode*); **implosion** = a bursting inwards (verb *implode*).

export (verb) = to send out (goods to another country); **import** (verb) = to bring in (goods from abroad); the goods are **exports** or **imports**; **import** (noun) = the meaning of an action or statement (e.g. "Her remarks had a greater import than I first thought").

exposé

express, expresser, expressible, expression.

expropriate = to dispossess (take away someone's property); **misappropriate** = to take (dishonestly) for oneself, to put to wrong/illegal use.

extant = still existing, surviving (*see also* **exist**).

extempore (usual adv.), extempory (usual adj.), extemporize, extemporization.

extend, extender, extensible (preferred to extendible), extension, extensor muscle. **Extended** = stretched, made larger (e.g. "an extended tour"); **extensive** = wide-ranging, comprehensive (e.g. "an extensive search").

extent = publisher's and printer's term for the number of pages in a book.

exterminate = destroy completely, and should therefore apply to the whole of a group, not merely part of it (e.g. "The insecticide exterminated most of the dog's fleas" is incorrect).

extol, extolled.

extort, extortion, extortioner.

extract, extractor, extractable, extraction.

extreme(s), extremely. The latter is a useful alternative to the overworked intensifier *very*.

exult *See* **exalt**.

eyeball, eyebath, eye-bolt, eyebrow, eyeful, eyeglass, eyelash, eyeless, eyelid, eye-opener, eyepiece, eyesight, eyesore, eye-strain, eye-tooth, eyewash, eye-witness. Note also eyed, eyeing.

eyrie (= an eagle's nest) is the preferred spelling (not **aerie**).

F

-f For plurals of words ending in *f*, *see* **plurals**.

°F = degrees Fahrenheit. *See* **Fahrenheit**.

fable = fictitious story (sometimes of known authorship), often with animals as characters and generally with a moral; **legend** = traditional story with an assumed historical basis, usually involving "real" people (even though possibly fictitious); **myth** = traditional story, usually involving supernatural "people" (gods) or creatures (mythical beasts) and their influences on mortals; **saga** = usually heroic adventure story, often from Iceland or Ireland, originating in medieval times. The derived adjectives from the first three are *fabulous, legendary* and *mythical* which, like the nouns, should be used with care in their figurative senses; fabulous should not be used to mean *excellent* (as in "The rock group gave a fabulous performance"). **Legend** is also a printer's term for an annotation, label or caption.

façade

facet, faceted, faceting.

facia = dashboard of a car, shopkeeper's nameboard; **fascia** = board beneath roof-eaves.

facility = ease, amenity; **faculty** = knack, ability, university department. E.g.:

"He has a facility for drawing" implies he has a pencil; "He has a faculty for drawing" means he is good at it.

facsimile (pl. facsimiles).

facsimile transmission *See* **fax**.

factious = relating to a faction (a group with a vested interest);

fractious = fretful, unruly, peevish. E.g.:

"The government refused the opposition party's factious demands."
"The parents ignored the child's fractious behaviour."

factitious = contrived, arranged, engineered (but nevertheless existing); **fictitious** = unreal, sham, counterfeit (non-existent). *See also* **fictional**.

factor, factorize, factorization.

factotum (pl. factotums).

faeces, faecal (but defecate, defecation).

Fahrenheit temperature (abbreviation °F) should normally be restated in Celsius (°C); for conversion factors, *see* **units**. If the text requires both, express them thus: 37°C (98.6°F).

faience

faint = weak, unclear, to lose consciousness; **feint** = false or distracting movement. In *feint rule*, meaning the narrowest line printed on a sheet of paper, the latter spelling is used with the former meaning.

fait accompli (italics) = something already done, an accomplished fact; plural *faits accompli*. The French terms should be avoided.

faker = someone who fakes; **fakir** = religious (usually Hindu or Muslim) mendicant or ascetic.

fall (verb) has the past tense **fell** and past participle **fallen**.

fallible

fallout (noun, one word).

falsehood = an untruth, a lie; **falseness** = deception, treachery, disloyalty; **falsity** = false assertion, quality of being false. E.g.:

"His excuse for being late proved to be a falsehood."
"He was found out through the falseness of his former friend."
"Inconsistencies revealed the falsity of his argument."

falsetto (pl. falsettos).

familiar, familiarize, familiarization. **Familiar** *to* = known to/by
(e.g. "The printing process is familiar to me"); **familiar**
with = having an understanding/working knowledge of (e.g. "I am
familiar with the process").

family relationships give rise to many terms, from great-
grandparents to great-grandchildren six generations later. Marriage
complicates the terminology by introducing "in-laws" (the
immediate relatives of one's husband or wife) into the relationships.
The diagram on the opposite page shows the names of one's
principal relatives. *See also* **cousin**; **half-brother**; **in-laws**; **step-**.

famous = well known for "good" deeds; **infamous** = well known for
"bad" deeds, notorious.

fantasy is the preferred spelling (not **phantasy**). **Fantastic** = unreal,
fanciful; its use to mean *excellent* is colloquial and should be
avoided.

farrago (pl. farragos).

Farsi *See* **Iran**.

far-sighted(ness) *See* **long sight**.

farther is the comparative of *far* and applies to distance in length or
time; **further** is also the comparative of *far*, but means *additional*.
E.g.:

"Birmingham is farther than Brighton from here."
"The article needs further editorial work."

fascia *See* **facia**.

fascinated *by* a person; **fascinated** *with* a thing or event.

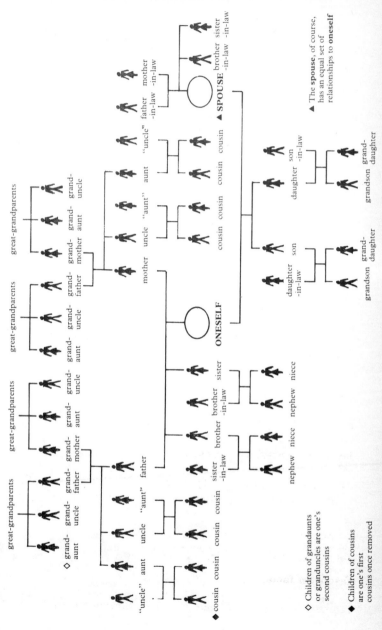

◇ Children of grandaunts or granduncles are one's second cousins

◆ Children of cousins are one's first cousins once removed

167

fat *See* **corpulent**.

fatal = leading to/causing death, disastrous; **fateful** = determined by fate. E.g.:

"He swallowed a fatal dose of poison."
"Turning back proved to be a fateful course of action."

fault, fallible (not faultable).

faun = Latin rural deity; **fawn** (noun) = young deer, a light yellow-brown colour; **fawn** *on* (verb) = to flatter in a servile way, to be obsequious.

fauna may have the plural *faunas* in biological texts (*see* **plurals**).

faux pas (italics) (pl. *faux pas*) = (an embarrassing) mistake (literally "false step"); the French form should be avoided. The English idiom is to *commit* a *faux pas*, or *make* a mistake.

fax = jargon for facsimile transmission, a method of electronically scanning text or graphic material and transmitting it (by telephone line or radio) to a receiving station where the image is reproduced on a television-type screen or as a photograph.

feasible = possible, practicable (it does not mean likely, probable). *See also* **viable**.

feed (verb) inflects *feed – fed – fed*.

feel inflects *feel – felt – felt*.

feint *See* **faint**.

feldspar is the preferred spelling of **felspar**.

fem. is the abbreviation of female or feminine.

female describes the sex of an organism; **feminine** describes the characteristics of a female (the corresponding terms are *male* and *masculine*). **Female** should not be used as a noun synonymous with *girl* or *woman*. *See also* **gender**.

femme fatale (italics) *See* **hussy**.

femur (pl. femurs, not femora).

fence, fencible.

feral = wild (after having been tame), uncultivated; **ferule** = flat stick used for corporal punishment; **ferrule** = strengthening metal ring or a rubber cap at the end of a stick.

ferment = to use yeast to convert sugar into carbon dioxide (which makes bread dough rise) and, if prolonged, alcohol (as in brewing and wine-making); **foment** = to apply a hot poultice to inflamed skin, such as a boil. Both words can be used figuratively to mean "to stir up (trouble)".

ferret, ferreter, ferreted, ferreting.

fertilize, fertilizer, fertilization (all uses).

fetch = to go some distance, find or retrieve something, and move it where required; **bring** = to move something from near at hand to where required. E.g.:

"Please go upstairs and fetch my book."
"Please bring me the book you are holding."

fetch off should not be used for **remove** (e.g. "That wine would fetch the varnish off the table" is incorrect usage). *See also* **bring**.

fête, fêted.

fetid is the preferred spelling (not **foetid**).

fetus The preferred spelling is **foetus**.

few = opposite of many; **a few** = "opposite" of none. E.g.:

"Few of the audience had heard the song before" (not many had heard it);
"A few of the audience had already heard the song" (which was new to many but not to all).

fewer *See* **less**.

fiancé(e)

fiasco (pl. fiascos).

fibreglass, fibre-optic (adj.), fibre optics (noun).

fictional = related to fiction; **fictitious** = not genuine, counterfeit, "made up". The meanings overlap *See also* **factitious**.

fiddle (noun) is both colloquial for violin and the preferred term for the instrument to people who earn their living by playing one; **fiddle** (verb) = to play the violin or, in slang, to cheat or swindle. Thus in formal writing it is safer to use *violin* or *play the violin*.

fidget, fidgeted, fidgeting, fidgety.

fight (verb) inflects *fight – fought – fought*.

figures of speech can add colour and interest to text. They must, however, be chosen with care to suit the probable readership. Most are idioms and illogical – and so cannot usually be translated literally into another language; and many modern writers of formal text avoid all but the common ones (such as analogy, metaphor and simile). Not all authorities agree on the types and naming of figures of speech; the following have separate articles in this Dictionary: **analogy; anticlimax; antithesis; antonomasia; apostrophe; bathos; climax; hypallage; hyperbole; irony; litotes; meiosis; metaphor; metonymy; oxymoron; paradox; personification; simile; syllepsis; synecdoche; zeugma.** *See also* **idiom**.

Fiji The derived adjective and noun is *Fijian*.

Filipino = people and language of the Philippines (pl. Filipinos).

filler (papermaking) *See* **loading**.

fillet, filleted, filleting.

fill in = to complete, insert into a gap; **fill out** = to enlarge or extend to a desired size/limit; **fill up** (often better merely as *fill*) = to add something to a "container" until it is full. E.g.:

"Fill in your name in the space provided"
"Fill out the row of plants until it is ten feet long"
"Fill (up) the glass with water".

filter = a device for separating a solid from a liquid; **philtre** = a love potion.

fimbria (pl. fimbriae).

final, finalize, finalization. **Final** (noun) = deciding event in sport or athletics; **finale** = conclusion of a play or piece of music.

find (verb) inflects *find – found – found*.

fine, finable.

Finland The derived adjective is *Finnish* and the noun (for the people) is *Finn*.

fiord is the preferred spelling of **fjord**.

fire-alarm, firearm, fireball, fire-bomb, firebrick, fire brigade, fireclay, fire-damp, fire-dog, fire-engine, fire-escape, fire extinguisher, fire-fighter, firefly, fire-guard, fire hydrant, firelight, fire-lighter, fireman, fireplace, fireproof, fireside, fire-water, firewood, firework.

first Both numbers 1 and 2 from a list should be referred to as the *first two* (not the *two first*). Similar style applies to *first three, first four*, and so on. **Last** follows the same rule. *See also* **latter**.

first aid (noun), first-aid (adj.), first-class (adj.), firstborn, first-floor (adj.), first-fruit, firsthand (adj.), first-rate, First World War (but use World War I).

firstly should be avoided; use instead **first** (*second*, *third*, and so on are preferred to *secondly*, *thirdly*, and so on).

First World War The preferred style is World War I.

fish usually has the plural *fish* ("They bought six fish"). When listing several types or species, use the plural *fishes* ("Cod and herring are the main fishes caught").

fistula (pl. fistulas).

fjord Use the spelling **fiord**.

fl. is the abbreviation of *floruit* (Latin, meaning "flourished") and of guilder(s) (from the Dutch *gulden florijn* = golden florin).

flaccid *See* **placid**.

flagrant *See* **blatant**.

flak = anti-aircraft fire, or (figuratively) repeated criticism. The spelling **flack** does not exist in standard English.

flambé (italics), *flambéed*.

flamingo (pl. flamingoes).

flammable *See* **inflammable**.

flan = open sponge-cake base, usually containing fruit; **pasty** = pastry envelope with a savoury filling; **pie** = pastry case with fruit or savoury filling and a pastry lid; **pizza** = bread base with a savoury topping usually based on cheese; **quiche** = open pastry case with a savoury filling usually containing eggs; **tart** = open pastry case usually with a fruit filling; **turnover** = pastry envelope with a fruit filling. These are the usual meanings, although a *pie* may also be cooked in a dish (not lined with pastry) with just a lid of pastry or, in a cottage pie or shepherd's pie, of potato. There are also various local variants and names, such as a *clanger* (a type of pasty, sometimes with a fruit-filled part as well as a savoury-filled part). *See also* **canapé**.

flannel, flannelled, flannelling, flannelly, flannelette.

flaunt = to display ostentatiously or proudly; **flout** = to disobey (a law or rule) openly and scornfully.

flèche

flee inflects *flee – fled – fled*.

flex, flexible, flexion (not -ection).

flier is the preferred spelling of **flyer**.

flimsy = editor's jargon for a carbon copy made on bank paper (*see* **bank**).

fling inflects *fling – flung – flung*.

floe = floating ice (pl. floes); it should not be confused with **flows**.

flong = a stereotype mould (not *flonge*).

flop = publishing jargon for an instruction to a reproduction house or printer to reverse an image left-to-right (that is, to produce a mirror-image version of what is supplied). Easily misinterpreted, this instruction is better put as "Please reverse left to right". **Lateral reversal** has the same meaning.

floppy disk = storage medium for computers consisting of a flexible plastic disc with a magnetizable coating on which data can be stored (by means of a write head) and from which it can be retrieved (using a read head) in a *disk drive*. The amount of data that can be stored on a floppy disk depends on its size (diameter) and whether it is *single-sided* or *double-sided*, or of *low density* or *high density*. "Floppies" and their associated equipment have the advantage of cheapness, light weight and portability over *hard disk* stores (but have much less capacity), and have much quicker average access times than small magnetic tape storage systems. Small floppy disks are sometimes known as *diskettes*. *See also* **hard disk**.

floor relates to a part of a building; each floor occupies a **storey** (the preferred spelling, not *story*), which generally relates to height. E.g.:

"Two floors of the ten-storey building are vacant."
In Britain and elsewhere in Europe, floors are usually numbered as *Ground, First, Second, Third*, and so on. The usual system in North America is *First Floor, Second Floor, Third Floor, Fourth Floor* and so on. The numbering of storeys is the same on both sides of the Atlantic, with the first storey at street level.

flora may have the plural *floras* or *florae* in biological texts (*see* **plurals**).

floruit (Latin, meaning "he/she flourished") has the abbreviation *fl.* (italics, with a full point).

flotation = keeping something afloat, floating a business (not *floatation*).

flounder (verb) = to struggle or make a mistake; **founder** = to sink, stumble. E.g.:

"The would-be rescuer floundered in the mud."
"The ship was holed and foundered on the rocks."

flout *See* **flaunt**.

flow *See* **floe**.

flu should be avoided as an abbreviation of **influenza** in formal writing.

fluid, fluidize, fluidity.

flux, fluxion.

fly (verb) has the past tense **flew** and past participle **flown**; **fly** (insect) has the plural *flies*; **fly** (an old type of carriage) has the plural *flys*. Other forms are flying, flier (not flyer).

flyover = road elevated to cross over another one; **overfly** = to fly over (in an aircraft); **underpass** = road that tunnels under another one; **pass under** = to cross beneath.

FM is the abbreviation of frequency modulation (in radio).

focus (pl. of noun is foci), focused, focusing (not focussed, focussing).

foetus (pl. foetuses), foetal.

foggy = with or hidden by fog; **fogy** (pl. fogies) = someone with old-fashioned ideas.

föhn (with an umlaut, preferred to foehn).

folio (pl. folios) = a page in a book or manuscript; abbreviations f. and ff. In a book, a right-hand folio (page) is called the *recto* side, and a left-hand one is the *verso*. *Folio* is also a printer's term for a page-number; rectos have odd numbers, versos have even ones. *See also* **leaf**.

folk is a plural word, and so the double plural **folks** should be avoided. *See also* **people**.

folk-dance, folklore, folk-song.

following should not be misused for **after** or **as a result of**; e.g. "I found an assistant following a newspaper advertisement" is ambiguous, and "Rationing did not immediately end following World War II" is incorrect. The former should have *as a result of*; the latter *after*.

foment *See* **ferment**.

fondue (italics)

font (of type in printing) The preferred spelling is **fount**.

fontanelle is the preferred spelling (not **fontanel**).

foolscap is a size of paper (named after the design of its original watermark). *See* **paper sizes**.

foot (pl. feet) In attributive constructions, the singular form should be used (e.g. "a six-foot wingspan" but "a wingspan of six feet", "its wings were six feet across").

foot-and-mouth disease, football, foot-brake, footbridge, foot candle, foot-fault, Foot Guards, foothill, foothold, footlight(s), footloose, footnote, footpath, footplate, foot-pound(al), footprint, foot-rot, footsore, footstep, footstool, footway, footwear.

footnotes The usual symbols to indicate footnotes are *, †, ‡ (asterisk, dagger or obelisk, and double-dagger), in that order, and are doubled for additional references (**, ††, ‡‡). If the number of references in one table or on one page exceeds six, use superscript numerals. If there are many references, number them sequentially and list them at the end of the section or chapter.

for- Words with the prefix *for-* include forbear (which *see*), forbid (forbade, forbidden), forever, forfend, forgather, forget, forgive, forgo (which *see*), forlorn, forsake, forswear, forward(s). *See also* **fore-**.

forasmuch (one word).

forbear (verb) = abstain, voluntarily avoid, exhibit forbearance; **forebear** (noun) = ancestor. The verb has the past tense **forbore** and past participle **forborne**.

forbid has the past tense **forbade** and past participle **forbidden**. **Forbidding** = discouraging (e.g. "a forbidding attitude"); **foreboding** = suggesting unpleasantness to come (e.g. "his attitude filled me with foreboding").

force, forceful (= vigorous, powerful, exerting/exhibiting force), forcible (= brought about by force, having force). E.g.:

"The spokesman made a forceful speech at the meeting."
"The protesters made a forcible entry to the meeting."

force majeure (italics).

forceps Unlike callipers, knickers, scissors, shears, trousers and so on (which are plural words), *forceps* can be either singular or plural.

fore- Words with the prefix *fore-* (meaning "before" or "in front of") include forearm, forebear, forebode, forecast, forecastle, foreclose, forecourt, fore-edge, fore-end, fore-father, forefinger, forefront, forego, foreground, forehand, forehead, foreland, foreleg, forelock, foreman, foremast, foremost, forenoon, forerunner, foresaid, foresail, foresee, foreshadow, foreshore, foreshorten, foresight, foreskin, forestall, foretaste, foretell, forethought, forewarn, foreword (of a book). *See also* **for-**.

forecast The preferred past tense and participle is **forecast** (not *forecasted*).

foreign words and phrases should be avoided wherever possible – if they are not well known, they require translation (hence Stephen Potter's recommendation, in a One-Upmanship context, 'to confuse, irritate and depress [an opponent] by the use of foreign words, fictitious or otherwise, either singly or in groups"). Many are listed and defined in this Dictionary, usually with the advice to avoid the foreign form. Foreign words that have become part of standard English should be typeset in roman face; others should be set in italics, with any necessary accents. Some, although totally assimilated and normally set in roman, retain their accents as an aid to pronunciation (e.g. café, fiancée, précis). The advice to avoid the use of foreign words is not intended to be xenophobic; and it can be argued that **jargon** (which *see*) confuses as much as overuse of non-English expressions. For plurals of foreign words, *see* **plurals**; for a list containing many exotic imports, *see* **dress**. *See also* **Americanisms**; **Arab words**; **Celtic words**; **Dutch words**; **French words**; **Hebrew words**; **Indian words**; **Italian words**; **Latin words**.

forensic = to do with the law or courts, hence *forensic medicine* = *medical jurisprudence*. The expression *forensic evidence* is tautologous, and usually means *scientific evidence*.

forfeit, forfeited.

forget has the past tense **forgot** and past participle **forgotten**.

forget, forgettable, forgetting, forget-me-not.

forgive, forgivable. **Forgive** has the past tense **forgave** and past participle **forgiven**.

forgo (= to relinquish, to do without), forgoing, forgone; **forego** (= to go before), foregoing, foregone.

form (noun) = shape, document with blanks to be filled in, school class, customary behaviour, etc.; **forme** = assembled type (in a *chase*) ready for printing or stereotyping.

formal, formalize, formalization.

formally = in a formal way; **formerly** = as before, in the past.

format = publisher's and printer's term for the size and shape of a book. For a book with a trimmed page size of 200mm by 280mm, for example, the format is stated as 200mm × 280mm. The first dimension (200mm) is the width of the page; the second (280mm) is the depth or height of the page, except in American practice which states the depth first and then the height (usually in inches). Such a shape is known as **portrait** or **upright** format; a page with a width greater than its depth is called **landscape** or **horizontal** format. *See also* **books; extent.**

former is preferred to the prefix **ex-** in such expressions as "former president John Jones", "his former wife", "her former boss" (not *ex-president, ex-wife, ex-boss*). *See also* **late; latter.**

formula (pl. formulas, except in some mathematical texts which use formulae).

forsake has the past tense **forsook** and past participle **forsaken**.

forte = a person's strong point; the Latin term should be avoided.

for the reason that = **because**, which should be used.

fortuitous = accidental, by chance; **fortunate** = favoured, lucky, prosperous.

forum (pl. forums).

fossil, fossilize, fossilization.

founder *See* **flounder**.

fovea (pl. foveae).

fracas has the same form in the singular and plural (although the pronunciation changes from "*frak-ah*" to "*frak-az*").

fractions can be a nuisance when preparing text for typesetting. Few typefaces have standard fractions other than those on a normal typewriter keyboard ($\frac{1}{4}$, $\frac{1}{3}$, $\frac{1}{2}$, $\frac{2}{3}$, $\frac{3}{4}$). Avoid "displayed" or "built-up" fractions except in scientific and mathematical works. Use the solidus (/) to form "shilling fractions", the aim being to form an expression that can be typeset on one line.

Thus: $\dfrac{1}{17}$ $\dfrac{3x}{y^2}$ $\dfrac{(a+b)^2}{x+y^2}$ $\dfrac{2c}{\sqrt{a+b}}$

should be expressed as:

$1/17$ $3x/y^2$ $(a+b)^2/(x+y^2)$ $2c/(a+b)^{\frac{1}{2}}$

In non-mathematical works, it is usually preferable to use decimal fractions, with the decimal point set on the line (like a full point or full stop), not above the line (i.e. 17.6, not 17·6). E.g.:

	2½ pints	1¾ inches	£6¼ million
become	2.5 pints	1.75 inches	£6.25 million.

Thus despite Winston Churchill's preference for "short words and vulgar fractions", most modern publishers advocate short words and decimal fractions.

framework, used to mean *circumstance* or *limitation* (e.g. "We will only negotiate within the framework of the existing guidelines"), is a vogue word and should be avoided. *See* **vogue words**.

franchise

fraternal, fraternize, fraternization.

fraught is archaic for **filled** (except in the cliché "fraught with danger/difficulties"); *filled* or *laden* should be used. **Fraught** survives in colloquial use as an adjective meaning *upset* or *anxious*.

free-and-easy, freeboard, free-born, free-for-all, freehand, freehold, free-lance, freeman, freemason, free-range, freestone, free-thinker, free trade, free-wheel, free will.

freeze has the past tense **froze** and past participle **frozen**.

French words One of the functions of the Académie Française is to examine "new" words and sanction official acceptance or rejection for the French language. English imports (termed Briticisms) are almost always banned in French (such as *le shopping, le weekend*). The English language, on the other hand, has never had an official review of foreign candidates for its vocabulary – these survive or not depending on the vagaries of usage. Thus words such as *café, leotard* and *pâté* are probably with us for ever, because they have no simple English equivalents – indeed they *are* English. At the time of writing, the British fashion trade (for example) employs *blouson* and *cagoule* for two types of lightweight jackets; only time and usage (or lack of it) will determine their fate. English dictionaries also contain many French words that have outgrown their usefulness, and often have better-understood English equivalents; their inclusion can give straightforward descriptive text an arty-crafty or pretentious flavour. Examples, just from those beginning with *m*, are manège, mélange, ménage, métier and milieu; this Dictionary includes many more of the latter type, usually with advice to avoid them. *See also* **foreign words and phrases; Latin words**.

fresco (pl. frescoes).

fresh should be used with care to mean **new** or **renewed**; e.g. "They agreed to fresh talks" is incorrect, whereas "fresh bread" and "fresh fall of snow" are correct.

freshwater (adj.), fresh water (noun), but seawater (adj. and noun).

friable = easily crumbled, or = can be fried (not the spelling *fryable*), so that only context distinguishes the two words.

frier The preferred spelling is **fryer**.

frightful/frightfully should be reserved for things or circumstances that invoke fright or fear, and not used as an intensifier (= *very*) or of something that is merely *unpleasant* or *disagreeable* (as in "I have a frightful cold", "I thought the talk was frightfully boring").

frolic, frolicked, frolicking, but frolicsome.

fry, fried, frying, fryer (not frier). *See also* **friable**.

ft is the abbreviation of foot (and feet).

fuchsia (plant named after Leonard Fuchs).

fuel, fuelled, fuelling.

-ful Quantities and measurements ending in *-ful* form the plural by adding *s*; e.g. *cupfuls, handfuls, spadefuls, spoonfuls* (not cupsful etc.).

fulcrum (pl. fulcrums).

fulfil, fulfilled, fulfilling, fulfilment.

fuller's earth, so-named because it was used for fulling (cleaning and finishing) cloth, does not have an initial capital letter.

full-length = not shortened; **full-scale** = not reduced in size/scope.

full point/full stop *See* **punctuation**.

fulsome = nauseous, excessive, insincere; it no longer means merely abundant or ample.

fumigate, fumigator, fumigation.

funeral, funereal (= like or appropriate to a funeral), funerary (= pertaining to a funeral).

fungus (pl. fungi), fungous (adj.), fungal (preferred to fungoid).

funnel, funnelled, funnelling.

fur, furred, furring, furry.

further *See* **farther**.

fuse, fusible (but fissionable in nuclear physics). **Fuse** should be used for all meanings (not *fuze*).

G

gabardine = durable (worsted) cloth; **gaberdine** = old name for a long loose cloak.

gabbro (pl. gabbros).

Gabon The derived adjective and noun is *Gabonese*.

gaff = fish-spear or hook for landing large fish; **gaffe** = blunder, especially a social one.

gage = token of defiance, challenge, pledge; **gauge** = specific measurement or measuring instrument.

gall bladder, gallstone.

gallery *See* **balcony**.

gallop, galloped, galloper, galloping (**galop** is the dance).

gallows is usually regarded as a singular word; "sets of gallows" achieves a plural construction.

gambit = an opening move that involves an apparent sacrifice but for long-term gain; **gamut** = musical scale, whole range, scope (as in Dorothy Parker's sarcastic comment about an actress: "She ran the whole gamut of her emotions from A to B").

gamble/gambling is applied to games of chance involving stakes, and by extension to any venture with an element of risk. **Gaming** has now an old-fashioned ring except when applied to a casino's *gaming tables*.

gambol, gambolled, gambolling (compare **gamble**, gambled, gambling).

game is now used generally to refer to any animals or birds killed for sport, large exotic ones being termed *big game* – it is no longer limited (in England) to deer, grouse, hares, partridges and pheasants (*see also* **quarry**); **gamy** = having the flavour of hung game; **gammy** = lame (preferred to the spelling *game*).

gamut *See* **gambit**.

gaol, gaoler. The preferred spellings are **jail**, jailer (although *gaol* is the official term).

garlic, garlicky.

garot = duck, tourniquet; **garotte** (preferred to *garrotte*) = ligature round the neck (to strangle criminals).

gaseous = of the nature of gas (e.g. "Earth's gaseous atmosphere"); **gassy** = full of gas (e.g. "Tonic water is a gassy drink").

gasoline *See* **petrol**.

gateau (pl. gateaux).

gaucho (pl. gauchos).

gaudy, gaudiness, gaudily.

gauge, gauging, gaugeable (compare **gage** (= pledge), gaging).

gay (= merry, bright, lively) should be avoided because of possible ambiguity with the modern usage meaning *homosexual* (adj. and noun). Derived words include gayness, gaiety, gaily.

gazebo (pl. gazebos).

gazette, gazetted, gazetteer. *See also* **anthology**.

gecko (pl. geckos).

gelatin is the preferred spelling (not **gelatine**).

gemma (pl. gemmae).

gender should be applied only to words, not to girls, women or female animals. *See also* **female**. Grammatical gender has largely passed from English. Sex-defining words do have two forms, of natural male and female gender. E.g.:

boy	girl	his	hers
he	she	man	woman
him	her	Mister (Mr)	Mistress (Mrs)

Other words, describing people, that retain gender usually denote occupation, position or (family) relationship. Examples include:

abbot	abbess
actor	actress
adulterer	adultress
author	authoress (but avoid)
baron	baroness
blond	blonde
boyfriend	girlfriend
bridegroom (or groom)	bride
brother	sister
conductor	conductress
deacon	deaconess
duke	duchess
emperor	empress
executor	executrix
father	mother
fiancé	fiancée
gentleman	lady
god	goddess
grandfather	grandmother
grandson	granddaughter
headmaster (etc.)	headmistress (etc.)
heir	heiress
hero	heroine
host	hostess
king	queen

lord	lady
manager	manageress
manservant	maidservant
marquis, marquess	marchioness
masseur	masseuse
mayor	mayoress (the mayor's wife)
patron	patroness
poet	poetess
prince	princess
sculptor	sculptress
shepherd	shepherdess
son	daughter
sorceror	sorceress
steward	stewardess
tailor	tailoress
testator	testatrix
uncle	aunt
usher	usherette
waiter	waitress
widower	widow

It is regarded as sexist by some people to emphasize the difference between men's and women's roles by using many of these words. Their habitual use by men is often branded as chauvinist. There are also many other compounds ending in -*man* or -*woman* (e.g. businessman, chairman, policeman, salesman). Some of these, particularly those lacking a -*woman* form (such as craftsman, draughtsman, fireman, foreman), have been objected to on sexist grounds, giving rise to compromise words such as *chairperson*. Where this might be a sensitive area, terms with a masculine preference should be avoided and "neutral" ones substituted, or the offending words recast to circumvent the problem (e.g. *fireman* becomes *fire fighter*, *policeman* becomes *police officer*, *workman* becomes *worker*). Masculine pronouns can often be avoided by making the sentence plural (e.g. "The applicant must sign his name before he begins to write" becomes "Applicants must sign their names before they begin to write").

Animal gender names, however, are not regarded as sexist. They are legion, and some are so unfamiliar as to be unhelpful unless the context makes their meaning clear. Some examples are:

billy-goat	nanny-goat
boar	sow (badgers, pigs)
buck	doe (antelopes, deer, rabbits)
bull	cow (cattle, elephants, seals)
bullock	heifer (calves)
cob	pen (swans)
cock	hen
dog	bitch
donkey	jenny
drake	duck
fox	vixen
goose	gander
hart/stag	hind (deer)
leopard	leopardess
lion	lioness
peacock	peahen
ram	ewe (sheep)
stallion	mare (horses)
tiger	tigress
tom	queen (domestic cats)

genealogy (not -ology).

general, generalize, generalization.

generate, generator.

genet = civet-cat; **jennet** = small Spanish horse.

genial *See* **congenial**.

genie has the plural genii; **genius** has the plural geniuses (not *genii*).

genitive *See* **gerund**; **punctuation** (apostrophe).

genteel = over- or affectedly polite (pejorative); **gentle** = mild, soothing (opposite of harsh, rough); **Gentile** = non-Jewish.

genteelism *See* **non-standard English**.

genuflect, genuflexion (not -ection).

genus (pl. genera). *See also* **Latin classification**.

geographical names *See* **compass directions; capitalization**.

gerbil is the preferred spelling of **jerbil**.

geriatric = concerning the health/welfare of elderly people (it does not mean *elderly* or *senile*); **gereatrics** = medical care of the elderly; **gerontology** = study of the processes of aging; **gerontocracy** = government by the aged.

Germany For the post-1945 nations, use **East Germany** (for the German Democratic Republic) and **West Germany** (for the Federal Republic of Germany).

gerrymander is the preferred spelling (not **jerrymander**).

gerund is a verb form ending in *-ing* used as a noun (e.g. "the coming of winter", "a strange happening occured"). Difficulties sometimes arise when the gerund is preceded by a pronoun or noun, which should have a genetive (possessive) form. E.g.:

"I looked forward to *his* coming" (not *him* coming, because I looked forward to the *coming*, not to him);
"He was annoyed at *its* breaking so soon" (not *it* breaking);
"She dreaded *John's* laughing at her" (not *John* laughing);
"She objected to *one's* smoking";
"I watched my *child's* gradual growing up";
"I watched my *children's* gradual growing up."

The last three, although strictly correct, seem stilted in comparison with:

"She objects to one smoking" (or "... to my smoking", or just
"... to smoking");
"I watched my child gradually growing up";
"I watched my children gradually growing up."

This form of construction is being increasingly used, although the
possessive is still preferred for a pronoun or proper name before a
gerund. Also a gerund, like the participle it resembles, is in danger
of being made unrelated to its "subject" (*see* **participles, related
and unrelated**).

get, gettable, get-at-able. **Get** (inflection *get – got – got*) = to obtain,
procure, acquire, attain to, receive, reach – which are preferred.
See also **got.**

Ghana The derived adjective and noun is *Ghanaian*.

ghastly = resembling death (of the same derivation as *ghost/ghostly*),
shocking, appalling; the word should not be used in a derogatory
way (to mean *unpleasant*). E.g.:

"After the accident he had a ghastly complexion" (correct);
"Have you seen that ghastly shirt he is wearing?" (incorrect).

ghetto (pl. ghettos).

gibbet, gibbeted, gibbeting.

giga- is the metric prefix for a thousand million times ($\times 10^9$), as in
gigahertz (*see* **units**).

gigo = acronym for *g*arbage *i*n, *g*arbage *o*ut, computer jargon which
acknowledges that the results obtained from poor data are often
equally poor.

gild = to cover with gold; **guild** = group of tradespeople, a society;
gilt = covered with gold; **guilt** = sinfulness, state of a lawbreaker or
wrongdoer. The preferred past tense and participle of **gild** is
gilded (not *gilt*).

gipsy The preferred spelling is **gypsy**.

give, givable. **Give** has the past tense **gave** and past participle **given**.

gladiolus (pl. gladioli).

glamour, glamorous, glamorize.

glasses (= spectacles) is a plural word. "A pair of glasses" achieves a singular construction.

glossary *See* **anthology.**

glue, glued, gluing, gluey.

glycerin is the preferred spelling (not **glycerine**); the substance is termed *glycerol* in chemistry.

gm is the abbreviation of gram (not g).

GMT is the abbreviation of Greenwich Mean Time.

gnaw has the preferred past tense and participle **gnawed** (not *gnawn*).

GNP is the abbreviation of gross national product.

gnu (pl. gnus); but the preferred term is **wildebeest** (pl. wildebeest).

go has the past tense **went** and past participle **gone**.

gobbledegook is a descriptive term for jargon, particularly that of officialdom and technology. *See* **jargon.**

godchild, god-daughter, goddess, godfather, God-fearing, god-forsaken, godhead, godless, godlike, godmother, godparent, godsend, godsent, godson, Godspeed.

goffer = heated iron for crimping hair; **gopher** = North American burrowing rodent, kind of wood.

going, as in the informal "the going rate for the job", is a poor substitute for **current,** which should be used.

golf-club (hyphen) is used for hitting a golf ball at a golf club (no hyphen) or golf course.

good (comparative *better*, superlative *best*), goodness, goodliness. Compounds include good afternoon, good-breeding, good-bye, good day, good evening, good-for-nothing, Good Friday, good-hearted, good-humoured, good-looking, good morning, good-natured, good night, good-sized, goods-train, goods van, goods yard, good-tempered, goodwill/good will (which *see*). *See also* **better**. **Good** is the opposite of *bad*; **well** is the opposite of *ill*; both can be the opposite of *unattractive*. E.g.:

"The workmanship is good" (good = unbad, i.e. high-quality);
"That food smells good" (good = attractive, i.e. appetizing);
"My son is now well again" (well = unill, i.e. healthy);
"The books look well on the shelf" (well = attractive).

good idea It is a good idea to avoid this expression.

goodwill = established custom/popularity of a business, often ascribed a monetary value (as an asset) when the business is sold; **good will** (adj. good-will) = kindly regard, well-wishing. E.g.:

"The price of the shop includes allowances for the stock and the goodwill."
"Much of his popularity stemmed from the fact that he was a man of good will."
Increasingly, the one-word spelling is being used for both meanings.

gossip, gossiper, gossiped, gossiping.

got is the past tense and participle of *get*. As a substitute for have, possessed, acquired, attained, arrived (at), achieved, and so on it should be avoided. *See also* **get**.

gourmand = lover of eating, a glutton; **gourmet** = connoisseur of wine or good food.

gracile is rare, and literary, for **slim** or **slender** (which are preferred); it should not be confused with **graceful** = elegant, becoming.

graffito (pl. graffiti).

grain (the seeds from a cereal crop) is ground to make meal which, after the husks are removed, becomes **flour. Corn** is an imprecise term for a cereal crop or its grain, but in American English is the term for **maize. Oatmeal** is the meal from oats; **flour** (unqualified) usually means wheat flour. **Cornflakes** and **cornflour** (= cornstarch) are made from maize (and **cornflower** is a blue-flowered plant that often grows in cornfields).

gram is the preferred spelling of gramme, and should be abbreviated to gm (not g); note also milligram (mg), kilogram (kg).

gramophone has come to refer to the earlier breed of machines (the first of which were called *phonographs*, now an Americanism); the modern version is *record player*.

granddad, grand-aunt, grandchild(ren), granddaughter, grandfather, grand master, grandmother, grand-nephew, grand-niece, grandparent, grandson, grand-uncle.

grand-parental = relating to grandparents; a new adjective coined by anology with *parental*, it fills a gap in the vocabulary. E.g.:

"Ageing parents take on a grand-parental role with their children's children."
Grandparenting (= acting as grandparents) is less acceptable, probably because *parenting* (on which it is presumably based) has yet to gain universal acceptance.

grant, granter (who grants), grantor (who makes a grant in law).

grapefruit has the same form in the singular and plural.

graphic display unit = another name for a visual display unit. *See* **VDU**.

grateful = feeling gratitude, thankful; **gratified** = pleased, satisfied, indulged.

gratis (italics) = without charge, free; the Latin term should be avoided.

grave (noun) = an accent (as in *crèche*), or a burial place; **grave** (verb) = to engrave, has preferred past tense and participle **graved**, although **graven** is retained as an archaic adjective (e.g. "a graven image"). *See also* **craven**.

graze, grazer (an animal), grazier (a keeper/breeder of grazers).

grease, greasy.

Great Britain consists of England, Scotland and Wales; the *United Kingdom* consists of Great Britain and Northern Ireland. *Eire* should be referred to as the Republic of Ireland. The terms *English* and *England* should not be used when *British* and *Britain* are intended. *See also* **British**.

great primer = obsolete name for 18-point type. For others, *see* **type sizes**.

Greek alphabet Greek letters, commonly used in mathematical and scientific texts, should be written by hand in copy for typesetting and the name of the letter(s) spelled out in the margin as a guide to the typesetter.

Name	Upper case	Lower case	Name	Upper case	Lower case
alpha	A	a	kappa	K	κ
beta	B	b	lambda	Λ	λ
gamma	Γ	γ	mu	M	μ
delta	Δ	δ	nu	N	n
epsilon	E	e	xi	Ξ	ξ
zeta	Z	z	omicron	O	o
eta	H	η	pi	Π	π
theta	Θ	θ	rho	P	r
iota	I	ι	sigma	Σ	σ

tau	T	τ	chi	X	χ
upsilon	Υ	υ	psi	Ψ	ψ
phi	Φ	ϕ	omega	Ω	ω

grief is the noun; **grieve** is the verb, giving *grievance* and *grievous* (not grievious).

griffin = fabulous beast (a winged bird-lion); **griffon** = kind of dog, bird of prey (vulture).

grill = to cook under direct heat, to cross-examine; **grille** = metal grating.

grind (verb) inflects *grind – ground – ground*.

grind to a halt is a cliché for to **end** or **stop**, either of which is preferred.

grisly = causing horror/terror, ghastly; **gristly** = having or like gristle; **grizzly** = grey, grey-haired.

grissini (Italian crispbread in the form of thin sticks) is a plural word, although like *lasagne, spaghetti* and other pasta names it is usually regarded as singular in English.

gristle = cartilage; **grizzle** = cry fretfully or self-pityingly.

groin = groove between lower abdomen and thigh, or an arch between ceiling vaults; **groyne** = breakwater.

grotto (pl. grottoes).

group terms *See* **collective words**.

grovel, grovelled, grovelling, groveller.

grow has the past tense **grew** and the past participle **grown**.

gsm is the abbreviation of grams per square metre, sometimes written g/m², the unit now generally used to specify the *substance* (weight) of a sheet of paper; also known as *grammage*. Paper of weight less than 60 gsm in known as *bank*; more than 60 gsm as *bond*; more than 220 or 225 gsm as *board*. *See also* **substance**.

guana = iguana, lizard; **guano** = sea-bird excrement.

guarantee is the only spelling of the verb and the preferred spelling of the noun (not **guaranty**). Other verb forms are *guaranteed* and *guaranteeing*, and a person who gives a guarantee is a **guarantor**.

guerrilla is the preferred spelling (not **guerilla**).

guild *See* **gild**.

guilder (abbreviation fl. = florin) is preferred to the Dutch form *gulden* for the money of the Netherlands.

guilt *See* **gild**.

gullible

gunboat, gun-cotton, gun dog, gunfire, gun-lock, gunman, gun-metal, gunpoint, gunpowder, gunroom, gun-runner, gunship, gunshot, gunsmith.

guttural (not gutteral).

Guyana The derived adjective and noun is *Guyanese*.

gybe/gibe *See* **jib**.

gymnasium (pl. gymnasiums, not gymnasia).

gypsy is the preferred spelling (not **gipsy**).

gyro (pl. gyros).

H

ha is the abbreviation of hectare.

habitable = "live-in-able"; **habitat** = usual place or region in which an animal or plant lives; **inhabit** = to live in; **inhabitable** = habitable; **uninhabitable** = "not live-in-able". *Habitable* is usually applied to dwellings, *inhabitable* to regions, *uninhabitable* to both.

habitué (italics) = frequenter, regular attendant; the French form should be avoided.

Habsburg is the preferred spelling (not **Hapsburg**).

hadj, haji (preferred to hajj, hajji).

haematite, haematology, haemoglobin, haemophilia, haemorrhage and other *haem-* words retain the first *a* in English (i.e. not *hem-*).

hairbreadth, hair's breadth, hairbrush, haircut, hair-do, hairdresser, hair-line, hair-net, hair-oil, hairpin, hair-rising, hair shirt, hair-space, hair-splitting, hairspring, hair-style, hairtrigger.

hale is archaic for **vigorous, healthy** – as in the cliché "hale and hearty" – and should be avoided; **hail** = frozen rain, a form of greeting (also archaic).

half may be singular or plural, depending on context. E.g.:

"Half (of) the text is unreadable."
"Half (of) the words are misspelled."

In each case, *of* is optional. The singular word *half* has the plural *halves* (e.g. "Buy two halves of cucumber"). Compounds ending in *-half* usually have *-halfs* as their plurals (e.g. right-half, right-halfs). *See also* the following entry.

half a dozen (noun), half-and-half, half an hour, half-back, half-baked, half-binding, half-blood (pejorative), half-bound, half-breed (pejorative), half-brother, half-caste (pejorative), half-cock, half-day, half dozen (adj.), half-empty (adj.), half-hearted, half holiday, half-hour, half-litre, half-mast, half measure, half moon, half nelson, half past, half pay, halfpenny, half-pint, half-pound, half-price, half-sister, half-term, half-timbered, half-time, half-title, halftone, half-truth, half-volley, half-way, half-wit(ted), half-yearly.

half-brother or **half-sister** is the child of one's parent who has remarried – i.e. half-brothers or half-sisters have one parent in common. *See also* **family relationships**; **step-**.

halftone = printed illustration containing an apparent range of tonal values, achieved by printing it in the form of many tiny dots of various sizes. Comparatively large dots produce dark tones, small dots create light tones. The density of dots is determined by the **screen size** (because originally halftone printing blocks or film were made by photographing a continuous tone original through a screen containing many small holes), specified as the number of dots in a given area; e.g. a 120-screen has 120 dots to the inch. In colour printing, each **separation** (i.e. the separate blocks or films for each colour and black) is made with the rows of dots running at a different angle (the *screen angle*), to avoid the creation of moiré patterns when printed.

halo (pl. haloes).

handful (pl. handfuls).

handicap, handicapped, handicapper, handicapping.

handkerchief (pl. handkerchiefs).

hang, hanger (who or which hangs), hangar (for aircraft), hangman (who executes criminals). A picture or pheasant is *hung*, a criminal is (or was) *hanged*.

Hapsburg The preferred spelling is **Habsburg**.

hara-kiri = a Japanese form of suicide (not **hari-kari**).

harass, harassed, harassing, harassment (not the common misspelling *harrass*).

hard (adj.) = unsoft, difficult. The logical related adverb is **hardly**, but this means **scarcely** and *hard* is also as an adverb meaning **strongly, with difficulty**. E.g.:

"The plastic table had a hard shiny surface" (adjective);
"She hardly knew him" (adverb);
"He hit the table hard enough to break it" (adverb).
There is a lot of difference between a loaf that is hard-baked and one that is hardly baked.

hard-and-fast, hardback, hard-baked, hard-bitten, hardboard, hard-boiled, hard cash, hardcore (noun), hard core (adj.), hard-headed, hard-hearted, hard hit, hard labour, hard-line (adj.), hard luck, hard-nosed, hard-of-hearing, hardship, hard shoulder, hardtack, hardtop, hard up (noun), hard-up (adj.), hardware, hard-wearing, hardwood, hard-working.

hardback = book with covers made from stiff card, usually covered by a binding material. *See also* **paperback**.

hard copy = computer term for text typewritten or printed on paper. To input hard copy (into a computer) it has to be manually keyed or electronically scanned (using an optical character reader); hard copy output is provided by a printer (as a printout). *See also* **OCR**; **printer**.

hard-disk = storage medium for computers consisting of a rigid circular plate with a magnetizable coating on which digitized data can be stored and retrieved by means of one or more read/write heads mounted over *tracks* or bands on the disk. A hard disk is generally larger, and therefore has a much higher storage capacity, than a *floppy disk*. A large computer may have several hard disks stacked in a hard disk store. *See also* **floppy disk**.

hardly none (= hardly not one) is incorrect for **hardly any**. Avoid using *hardly* in any negative construction.

hare-brained *See* **mad**.

harmonize, harmonization.

hassock *See* **cassock**.

hate, hatable.

haul, hauler (who or which hauls), haulier (whose job is to carry goods).

haute couture = high fashion, and *haute cuisine* = high-class cookery (both italics); the French terms should be avoided.

have inflects *have – had – had*.

he (and *him, his*) is the common gender pronoun in normal usage, even if the noun referred to could be a girl or woman (e.g. "A baby needs feeding when he is hungry", "A young child often counts on his fingers"). Sexist objections can be overcome by using *he or she* (or *him or her, his or her*), but this construction is clumsy and soon palls with repetition; it is best avoided. An alternative solution is to avoid gender by recasting in the plural (e.g. "Babies need feeding when they are hungry", "Many young children count on their fingers"). *See also* **gender**.

headache, headband, headboard, head-dress, headgear, head-first, head-hunting, headhunter, headlamp, headland, headlight, headline, headlong, headman, headmaster, headmastership, head mistress, head-note, head off (verb), head-on, headphones, headpiece, headquarters, head-rest, headroom, headscarf, headset, headship (preferred to headmastership), headsman, head start, headstock, headstone, headstrong, head teacher, headway, headwind.

headlines *See* **journalese**.

headquarters may be regarded as singular or plural.

hear inflects *hear – heard – heard*.

heartache, heart attack, heartbeat, heart block, heartbreak(ing), heartbroken, heartburn, heart disease, heart failure, heartfelt, heartless, heartrending, heart-searching, heart's ease, heartsick, heartsore, heartstrings, heart-throb, heart-to-heart, heartwarming, heartwood.

heave has the preferred past tense and participle **heaved**, although *hove* is retained as a (nautical) adjective and verb form (e.g. "hove to").

Heaven (initial capital) = the dwelling-place of God; heaven(s) = region in which the Sun, Moon, stars and so on (heavenly bodies) can be seen.

Hebrew *See* **Semitic**.

Hebrew words taken into English sometimes give trouble with plurals. As a rule, words of long standing take a normal "English" plural in -*s* (e.g. cherub/cherubs, seraph/seraphs, shibboleth/shibboleths), whereas rarer or more recent acquisitions retain the Hebrew plural in -*im* (e.g. goy/goyim, kibbutz/kibbutzim, teraph/teraphim). The combination of Hebrew and German which became **Yiddish** has also influenced English (with such words as bagel, golem, kibitzer, kosher, matzo, mazuma, nosh) and American (whose slang expressions schlep, schlock, schmaltz, schmo, schmuk, schnorer, shemozzle, and so on can also be encountered in Britain).

hectic, strictly, = affected by fever; many authorities regard its use to mean *rushed* or *extremely busy* as colloquial. *See also* **livid**.

hecto- is the metric prefix for a hundred times (× 10^2), as (shortened) in hectare (*see* **units**).

hedge, hedging.

heinous (not heinious).

heir = someone who inherits or succeeds to an estate/title; **heir apparent** = heir whose claim cannot be superseded; **heir**

presumptive = heir whose claim can be superseded after the birth of a child with a superior claim.

helix (pl. helices).

help (verb) someone *to* do something (the omission of *to* in this construction is usually regarded as an Americanism).

hemi- *See* **numerical prefixes**.

hence = from here, and so does not need another *from* (i.e. "from hence" is incorrect). **Hence** also = *from now* ("two years hence") and *for this reason* ("...hence my interest").

henceforth = **from this time/point on;** except in legal contexts, it should be avoided.

hendiadys = two words (often adjectives) joined by *and* used to convey a more complex idea. E.g.:

fast and furious	= furiously fast
hale and hearty	= heartily hale
nice and comfortable	= nicely comfortable
short and sweet	= sweetly short
well and truly	= truly well

Many of these are also examples of *dyads* (*see* **inseparable pairs**).

hepta- or **sept-** *See* **numerical prefixes**.

heredity (noun), hereditary (adj.), hereditable (= inheritable, which is preferred), heritable (= inheritable).

hereof, heretofore and **hereunto** are archaisms, still employed by the legal profession, for *of this, before* and *until this*, which should be used.

hernia (pl. hernias, not *herniae*).

hero (pl. heroes).

heroin = drug derived from opium; **heroine** = female hero.

hers (no apostrophe); *see* **one's**.

hesitate, hesitancy (= state of mind causing someone to hesitate), hesitation (= act of hesitating). E.g.:

"He could not decide whether to go ahead with the work, and the ever-increasing cost of the delays added to his hesitancy."
"Without hesitation, he authorised work to continue."

hew has the preferred past tense and participle **hewed**, although *hewn* is retained as an adjective (e.g. "hewn logs"). All are archaic for **chop/chopped** (down).

hexa- or **sex-** *See* **numerical prefixes**.

hickey = printer's jargon for a spot or other imperfection on a printed sheet, usually caused by dust or dirt (affecting separations, plate-making or printing). Various types include a *bull's eye* and a *doughnut* (a central spot with a pale or white ring surrounding it).

hidalgo (pl. hidalgos).

hide (verb) has the past tense **hid** and preferred past participle **hidden** (not **hid**).

hideous, hideousness (not hideosity).

hie, hied, hieing (*hie* is archaic for go quickly).

hieroglyph *See* **ideograph**.

high (adj. and adv.) is the opposite of low (e.g. high voice, flying high); **highly** = extremely (e.g. highly emotional state).

highbrow, highchair, high-class, high explosive, high fidelity (hi-fi), highflown, high-flying, high frequency, highjack(er), high jump, high-handed, highland(s), highlight, high-pitched, high pressure, high priest(ess), high-rise, high road, high school, high seas, high-spirited, high water, highway, highwayman.

hind leg, hindmost, hindquarters, hindsight.

hinder, hindrance.

Hindi *See* **Indian words**.

hinge, hinged, hinging.

hippopotamus (pl. hippopotamuses).

hire, hireable, hireling (= someone who is hired), hiring (= contract of hire). **Hire** = to pay for the short-term use of an item or service (e.g. hire a suit, a barman for the day, or a car for a week); **rent** = to pay for long-term use (e.g. rent a house, a stretch of river for its fishing rights); **lease** = a form of renting with certain legal implications, usually for a specified period (e.g. a three-year lease on a shop).

his *See* **he**.

historic = famous, important (in history); **historical** = of the nature of history—e.g. "A historical novel by a historic author." For the use of the indefinite article before *historic* and other words beginning with *h*, *see* **a or an**.

hitchhike, hitchhiker.

hither is archaic for **to here** (as in the cliché "come hither"), as **hitherto** is for **up to now**; both should be avoided.

HMS (roman capitals with no full points) is the abbreviation of Her Majesty's Ship. Ships' names should be typeset in italics (e.g. HMS *Beagle*, HMS *Victory*) and, after the first mention, can be referred to simply as *Beagle*, *Victory* (not the *Beagle*, the *Victory*).

Ho. is the abbreviation of House, but should be avoided.

hoard (noun) = store, collection of goods/provisions; **horde** = band of nomads, group of people.

hocus, hocused, hocusing.

hoe, hoeing.

hoi polloi (italics) (= ordinary people) literally means *the many* and purists claim that *the hoi polloi* (= the the many) should not be allowed – all the more reason for avoiding the Greek expression.

hold (verb) inflects *hold – held – held*.

hold up = lift up (with the hands), delay, stop and rob (carry out a hold-up); **uphold** = maintain, defend. E.g.:

"The captain held up the cup for the crowd to see it."
"The spokesman asserted he would uphold the law."

hole, holey (= with holes).

Holland is only part of the Netherlands, although often used for the whole country; strictly, *Netherlands* should be used.

holocaust = destruction by fire (*the Holocaust* refers to genocide of the Jews during World War II); the word should not be used for any other type of **disaster**.

hologram = three-dimensional photograph taken and viewed using lasers; **holograph** = handwritten document, in the writing of the signatory.

holy, holier, holiest, holiness, holily (= with holiness).

home-brew(ed), home-coming, home-grown, homeland, homeless, homely, home-like, homeliness, home-made, homesick, homespun, homestead, home town, homeward(s), homework.

homicide = the killing of one person by another; **murder** = deliberate killing of another; **manslaughter** = unintentional killing of another; **suicide** = killing oneself. Definite types of murder include *fratricide* (= killing one's brother), *genocide* (= killing a race of people), *infanticide* (= killing one's child), *matricide* (= killing one's mother), *patricide* or *parricide* (= killing one's father) and *regicide* (= killing a monarch). A recent introducton from psychology is the term **parasuicide** = an apparently attempted suicide in which the "victim" does not really mean to die.

homoeopathy (not homeopathy).

homogenize, homogeneous (not homogenous).

homonyms are two or more different words that are pronounced the same, often a source of confusion to learners of English. True homonyms are also spelled the same (words that merely sound the same are *homophones*; words merely spelled the same are *homographs*). Examples of the latter type are the future-forming verb *will* (= shall), the noun *will* (= testament) and the proper name *Will* (short for William); the nouns *seal* (= a tight closure) and *seal* (= an aquatic animal); and two remarkable verbs of opposite meaning, *cleave* (= to split apart) and *cleave* (= to stick together). To qualify as homonyms, the words must be of different origin and derivation; thus the various substantive meanings of *hand* (including the part of the arm below the wrist, a workman or seaman, and a unit for measuring the height of a horse) are not homonyms because they are derived from the same etymological source.

Homonyms with different spellings (properly called homophones) are much more common. A sample list follows with a very brief definition (of one meaning only) in parenthesis:

ail (be unwell)	ale (beer)
all (everything)	awl (hole-making tool)
altar (offertory table)	alter (change)
aught (anything)	ought (should)
beat (hit with a stick)	beet (vegetable)
beau (man friend)	bow (arch)
beer (drink)	bier (coffin carriage)
bight (wide bay)	bite (wound caused by teeth)
boar (male pig)	bore (drilled hole)
bole (base of tree)	bowl (basin)
bough (branch of a tree)	bow (bend forward)
by (near)	buy (purchase)

cede (give over to) — seed (from which plants grow)
cell (unit of living matter) — sell (retail)
cheap (inexpensive) — cheep (young bird's call)
choir (singers) — quire (paper)
cite (quote) — sight (sense of vision)
site (location)

cue (billiard stick) — queue (line of people)
dire (dread) — dyer (who dyes cloth)
doh (musical note) — dough (unbaked bread)
draft (sketch) — draught (volume of liquid)
earn (get pay for) — erne (eagle)
ewe (female sheep) — you (second person pronoun)
eye (organ of vision) — I (first person pronoun)
faint (fall unconscious) — feint (pretend)
fair (light-haired) — fare (tariff)
fate (destiny) — fete (gala)
feat (achievement) — feet (leg-ends)
fir (evergreen tree) — fur (animal hair)
flew (moved on wings) — flue (chimney)
fore (front) — four (2 + 2)
freeze (become very cold) — frieze (wall-band)
gait (way of walking) — gate ("door" in a fence)
gilt (golden) — guilt (sin)
gnu (wildebeest) — new (original)
groin (top of the thigh) — groyne (breakwater)
hail (frozen rain) — hale (healthy)
hair (tresses) — hare (rabbit-like animal)
hart (male deer) — heart (vital organ)
heal (get well) — heel (rear of foot)
hear (listen) — here (this place)
hie (hurry) — high (tall)
higher (farther up) — hire (pay to use)
hoar (frost) — whore (prostitute)
hole (gap) — whole (entire)
know (understand) — no (negative)
lade (to load) — laid (past tense of *lay*)
leaf (plant part) — lief (beloved)
liar (who tells lies) — lyre (harp)
loan (something borrowed) — lone (single)
made (fabricated) — maid (young woman)

mail (post)	male (man)
main (chief)	mane (horse's neck hair)
mean (tight with money)	mien (manner)
meat (flesh)	meet (gathering)
might (perhaps)	mite (trivial quantity)
naval (of a navy)	navel (umbilicus)
night (darkness)	knight ("Sir")
pail (bucket)	pale (light-coloured)
pain (hurt)	pane (window glass)
pall (gloom)	pawl (a catch)
peak (top of mountain)	peek (look)
peal (ring of bells)	peel (rind of fruit)
pear (fruit)	pare (slice)
place (location)	plaice (flat-fish)
plain (flat ground)	plane (smoothing tool)
pray (offer a prayer)	prey (hunter's victim)
raid (sudden attack)	rayed (having rays)
rain (water from the sky)	reign (ruling period)
real (genuine)	reel (spool)
roe (fish eggs)	row (tier or line)
role (part in play)	roll (cylinder)
sailer (sailing vessel)	sailor (seaman)
sale (market for goods)	sail (wind-catching cloth)
sane (not mad)	seine (fishing net)
scene (vista)	seen (viewed)
seam (join in cloth)	seem (appear)
sew (stitch)	sow (plant seeds)
slay (kill)	sleigh (sledge)
sloe (blackthorn bush)	slow (tardy)
soar (float on air)	sore (painful)
sole (base of foot)	soul (centre of emotions/morals)
staid (sober)	stayed (supported)
stair (step)	stare (peer at)
steal (rob)	steel (iron alloy)
straight (unbent)	strait (narrow)
tail (end part)	tale (story)
team (sports side)	teem (pour)
tear (water from eye)	tier (row)
their (belonging to them)	there (that place)
throe (spasm)	throw (hurl)

time (period)	thyme (herb)
tire (become weary)	tyre (rubber wheel rim)
toe (foot digit)	tow (pull along)
vane (wind-catching plate)	vain (conceited)
waist (narrowest part of the body)	waste (unused and discarded material)
wait (remain)	weight (mass)
war (armed conflict)	wore (dressed in)
way (path)	weigh (measure mass)
weather (atmospheric conditions)	whether (introducing choice)
wood (timber)	would (past tense of *will*)

Homonyms that might cause confusion are listed separately in this Dictionary, with fuller definitions. *See also* **antonym**; **pun**.

Homo sapiens (italics, initial capital letter).

Honduras The derived adjective and noun is *Honduran*.

Hong Kong (two words).

honour, honourable (= worthy of or motivated by honour); **honorary** (= conferred as an honour, or holding an office without reward or without performing the usual obligations).

honours A person is *awarded* a Nobel Prize, a VC or an OBE; *made* a CBE; *granted* a knighthood; *created* a life peer or a DBE. *See also* **capitalization** (Titles and ranks).

hoof (preferred plural *hoofs*).

hookah = Eastern tobacco pipe with a water trap, a hubble-bubble; **hooker** = small boat, rugby player, or prostitute (slang).

hope = desire (with expectation of achievement) for something good, optimistic anticipation ("the power of being cheerful in circumstances which we know to be desperate" – G. K. Chesterton). Strictly therefore the use of the word, and its corresponding verb, in a negative or pessimistic sense is at best colloquial (e.g. "I hope his application fails"). *See also* the next entry.

hopefully = in a hopeful manner. It does not mean *it is hoped that* or *let us hope*; e.g. "With the prospect of explaining his ideas to a group of intelligent people, he went to the meeting hopefully" is correct; "Hopefully it will not rain today" is incorrect. *See also* **optimistic**; **regretfully**; **thankfully**.

horrible/horribly should be reserved for things or circumstances that invoke *horror*, and not used of something that is merely **unpleasant** or **disagreeable** (as in "I made a horrible typing mistake"). *See* **horror**.

horrid originally meant bristly (as the poetic word *horrent* still does), but it has taken on the colloquial meaning of nasty, detestable (as in "Teacher was horrid to me at school today"). The word, which does not mean *horrible* (*see* **horror**), is probably best avoided.

horror = extreme repugnance and revulsion, a meaning it has largely retained even in *horror film*, although with additional associations of fear and dread. The same cannot be said of some of its derivatives, victims of journalism's "shock-horror". The basic meanings are: **horrible** = capable of evoking horror; **horrify** = cause horror (in someone); **horrific** = directly exciting horror. *Horrible* should not be used merely to mean disagreeable or detestable (as in "Did you eat any of that horrible salad?"). *Horrific* should not be employed merely to emphasize what follows it, with the sense *significant* (as in "Changing the goalkeeper at halftime could have horrific consequences"). *Horrify* should not be diluted to mean stir the emotions/conscience – except the emotion of horror (as in "Horrifying statistics highlight the increase in parking offences"). When horrific scenes follow a terrorist bomb explosion in a busy street, many headline writers find they have devalued the currency of *horror* and its derivatives (and promptly write about "unspeakable horror"). *See also* **horrid**.

hors-d'oeuvre(s) (italics).

horseback, horse-box, horse-chestnut, horseflesh, horsefly, horsehair, horse-leech, horse-mackerel, horseman(ship), horseplay, horsepower, horse-race, horse-raddish, horseshoe, horseshoe-shaped, horsetail, horsewhip, horsewoman, horsy.

hospice, an archaic word for a place of rest for travellers (often kept by monks or nuns), is a useful reintroduction for "a special hospital for the terminally ill."

hospitalize, a convenient if American-sounding short way of saying "put or take into hospital", can now be found in some English dictionaries; the action is **hospitalization**.

host = large number of people; it should not be applied to things (e.g. "He raised a host of objections" is incorrect).

hostelry is archaic for **inn** and precious for **pub** (or *public house*).

house-agent, house arrest, houseboat, housebreaker, house-dog, house-flag, housefly, household(er), housekeeper, housemaid, housemaster, house party, houseproud, house-surgeon, house style, house-to-house, housetop(s), housewarming, housewife, housework.

howbeit is archaic for **nevertheless**, which should be used. The similar **albeit** (= although it be, even if) does remain in currency.

however is, to purists, among the most misused (or, at least, misplaced) words. It should be placed in a sentence immediately after the significant thing/idea being emphasized. Examples are difficult to construct without a preceding sentence or clause. Suppose the initial sentence is "Most editors drink more beer than do designers", then, of the following sentences,

1. "However, most designers eat more food"
2. "Most designers, however, eat more food"
3. "Most designers eat more food, however",

(1) contrasts the whole of the two sentences, (2) contrasts "editors" and "designers" (as was probably intended) and (3) contrasts "beer" and "food". *See also* **ever**.

howsoever/whosoever/whomsoever (each one word). *See also* **ever**.

hr is the preferred abbreviation of hour, although h may be used in scientific texts.

human should be reserved as an adjective; **human being** is the preferred noun form. **Humankind** overcomes the objections to **mankind** (which *see*). **Humanize** is the verb (not -ise). **Humane** = kind. *See also* **race**.

hummus = (Greek) dish made from puréed chickpeas or lentils; **humus** (noun) = vegetable content of soil; **humous** (adj.) = to do with humus.

humour, humoured, humorous, humorist.

hussy (original meaning *housewife*) is an old-fashioned and derogatory term once applied to any woman from a *flirt* or *prostitute* to a *mistress* or *adultress* (*see* **gender**). The genteel *femme fatale* and coarser *trollop* are also archaic, and *hooker, scrubber, slag, tart* and *tramp* are vulgar colloquialisms. The Victorian euphemism "No better than she ought to be" often conveyed the intended meaning, for which there seems to be no acceptable modern equivalent.

hydrolysis, hydrolyse.

hydrometer = instrument for measuring the specific gravity (density) of a liquid; **hygrometer** = instrument for measuring the humidity of a gas (such as air).

hyena is the preferred spelling (not **hyaena**).

hygiene, hygienic.

hypallage Figure of speech in which a description properly fitting one part of a statement is applied to another part. E.g.:

"She gave him a reluctant smile";
(*she* was reluctant, not her *smile*).

hyper- = over, above, involving an excess; **hypo-** = under, below, involving a deficiency (e.g. hypertension = high blood pressure, hypotension = low blood pressure).

hyperbola is a curve (a conic section) described as *hyperbolic*; **hyperbole** is a figure of speech (exaggeration), described as *hyperbolical*.

hyperbole Figure of speech which uses (often gross) exaggeration for emphasis. E.g.:

"He made countless errors";
(no matter how many errors he made, given enough time they could be counted). The device, even used deliberately, could leave the reader with the impression that the writing is imprecise.

hypercritical = over-critical; **hypocritical** = pretending to be better than one is, insincere, false (from hypocrisy = deficient in judgement).

hyphen, hyphenation (not *hyphenization*). *See* **compound words**; **word breaks**.

hypnosis, hypnotism, hypnotize, hypnotic.

hypothesis (pl. hypotheses).

Hz is the abbreviation of hertz (the unit of frequency, equivalent to cycles per second). Multiples include kilohertz (kHz) and megahertz (MHz).

I

ibid. (italics) is the abbreviation of *ibidem* (= in the same place).

-ible *See* **-able and -ible**.

-ic/ics *See* **suffixes**.

Iceland The derived adjective is *Icelandic* and the noun (for the people) is *Icelander*.

ideal, idealism, idealize, ideology, ideological.

idée fixe (italics) = fixed idea, obsession; the French form should be avoided.

identical *with* (not identical *to*).

identify = establish the identity of; it should not be used to mean *find* or *discover* (e.g. "We must identify a new approach to the problem" is incorrect).

ideogram = another name for an **ideograph**.

ideograph = letter, character or symbol that stands for a thing, not for a spoken sound (e.g. an Egyptian hieroglyph); **logogram** = symbol for a complete word (e.g. an ampersand, & = *and*); **idiograph** = private symbol or trademark (such as a monogram). *See also* **monogram**.

idiom, in the sense of an established, usually colloquial expression characteristic of a language but incapable of literal interpretation, adds colour to English but should be avoided in "serious" or formal writing, particularly in text for translation into other languages. Some English readers may be unfamiliar with a particular idiom and, more importantly, idioms cannot be translated literally (they are metaphorical) and so place an unnecessary burden on co-edition translators – hence the well-known story that the expression "out of sight, out of mind" was once translated as "invisible idiot". The term idiom can be limited to a phrase and not be applied to a single word that takes on a new meaning. For example *battle-axe*, originally a formidable weapon, has come to mean also a formidable, haranguing woman. The expression *to lean over backwards for someone* is, however, true idiom because its meaning – not its literal one – is to go to extreme lengths to accommodate/please someone, and cannot be attributed to an existing or new meaning of any of the individual words in the phrase.

idiosyncrasy, idiosyncratic.

idle, idled, idling, idly.

idol, idolater, idolatry, idolize.

idyll, idyllic (preferred to idyllian).

-ie- *See* **-ei-**.

i.e. is the abbreviation of *id est* (= that is). It should not be confused with **e.g.** (which *see*).

if need be works with the present or future tense; the past requires *if need were*; e.g. "He corrects the work, if need be", "He will correct the work, if need be" but "He corrected the work, if need were". The last sounds so stilted, it might be better phrased as "He corrected the work as (or when) necessary".

if not Avoid ambiguous use of this term; e.g. "He made the fastest, if not the most accurate, changes to the text" might be damning with faint praise. The sentence should be written "He made the fastest, and the most accurate, changes ..." if that is what is meant. (The other meaning requires "... the fastest, but perhaps not the most accurate, changes ...").

igloo (pl. igloos).

ignite, ignitable, igniter.

ignoramus (pl. ignoramuses).

ignorant *See* **artless**.

il- *See* **negative prefixes**.

ileum = part of the small intestine (adj. *ileac*); **ileus** = intestinal obstruction (adj. *ileac*); **ilium** = the hip-bone (adj. *iliac*).

ill/illness is generally preferable to **sick/sickness** when referring to poor health; *sick* is used in references to vomiting. E.g.:

"He was ill for a long time."
"She died after a brief illness."
"The smell of petrol makes me feel sick."
"I was sick after eating some oysters."

A sufferer of a long-term illness can also be described as *sick*. E.g.:

"She nursed her sick child for three weeks."
"I was off sick for a fortnight."
Unwell is generally used of a mild illness ("I left early because I was feeling unwell"), and **poorly** (= unwell) now sounds old-fashioned ("He did look poorly").

ill-advised, ill at ease, ill-bred, ill-conditioned, ill-disposed, ill effects, ill-fated, ill-favoured, ill-gotten, ill health, ill humour, ill-humoured, ill-judged, ill luck, ill-mannered, ill nature, ill-natured, ill-omened, ill-tempered, ill-timed, ill-treat, ill-use (= ill-treat, not misuse), ill will.

illegal *See* **unlawful**.

illegible *See* **unreadable**.

illegitimate *See* **unlawful**.

illicit *See* **elicit**.

illude = to deceive, trick; **allude** = to refer to (casually); **elude** = to evade. The corresponding nouns are illusion (*see* **delusion**), *allusion*, and *elusiveness*. The adjective from *illude* is *illusory* (preferred to *illusive*); from *elude* it is *elusive* (preferred to *elusory*).

im- *See* **negative prefixes**.

image, imagine (= conjure up mental images), imagination (= repository of mental images), imaginary (= existing in the imagination), imaginitive (= capable of having or stimulating imagination). The last two should not be confused. E.g.:

"The illustration depicted imaginary creatures from Mars."
"The illustration made imaginative use of colour."

imago (pl. imagines).

imbibe is precious for **drink** and euphemistic for **drink alcohol**; it should be avoided.

imbrication *See* **embrocation**.

imbroglio (pl. imbroglios).

imbue (with) = permeate, fill; **instil** (in) = to infuse, introduce into. E.g.:

"His reassurance imbued the staff with confidence."
"Confidence was instilled in the staff by his reassurance."

imitate *See* **emulate**.

imitation art *See* **art paper**.

immanent = pervading, inherent; **imminent** = impending, threatening; **eminent** = famous.

immaterial = irrelevant, unimportant; **unmaterial** = not composed of matter (a meaning that is generally no longer applied to *immaterial*). E.g.:

"The slight differences in size were immaterial."
"A ghost is an unmaterial manifestation."

immeasurable = beyond measure (figuratively); **unmeasurable** = incapable of being measured (physically). Like *countless* and *innumerable, immeasurable* should not be used to describe things that can/could be measured. E.g.:

"She made an immeasurable contribution to the project" is acceptable;
"We had to walk an immeasurable distance to the village" is unacceptable.

immigrant/immigrate *See* **emigrant**.

immiscible (but note mix*a*ble).

immobile, immobilize, immobilization.

immoral *See* **amoral**.

immortal, immortalize, immortalization.

immovable (but immoveable in law) = cannot be moved (although once could be); **irremovable** = cannot be removed (having become established). E.g.:

"The rusty bolt was immovable."
"The wine stain was irremovable."
See also **mobile**.

immune *See* **exempt**.

immunity, immunize, immunization. **Immunity** = freedom from disease, harm or liability; **impunity** = freedom from penalty or punishment.

impact should be reserved for actual or figurative collisions, and not used as a stronger word for *effect* or *impression*.

impassable = cannot be passed; **impassible** = non-feeling.

impassioned/impassive *See* **dispassionate**.

impecunious is a euphemism for **short of money** or the colloquial **hard up**; it should be avoided.

impel, impelled, impelling, impellent.

imperial = concerning an empire or emperor; **imperious** = domineering, overbearing. E.g.:

"The imperial aspirations of British and Spanish explorers of the Americas."
"He alienated the staff by his imperious attitude."
Imperial is also the name of a standard size of paper. *See* **paper sizes**.

Imperial units *See* **units**.

imperil, imperilled, imperilling.

impetus (pl. impetuses).

impinge, impinging.

implicit *See* **explicit**.

imply *See* **infer**.

important is a grossly overworked word; chief, main, principal, significant could be used for a change. And if the intended meaning really is *of import*, an explanation of why or in what way should follow. For **importantly**, *see* **thankfully**.

imposition, in printing, is the arrangement of the pages of a signature (section of a book) on a printing plate in such a way that they are in the correct sequence after the printed sheet has been folded. Only two consecutive pages, which end up at the centre of a folded signature (e.g. pages 16 and 17 in a 32-page section), fall naturally adjacent to each other in the imposition scheme, which varies depending on the number of pages in the section and the way it is folded.

impossible/improbable *See* **possible** and **probable**.

impracticable = cannot be fulfilled or dealt with, unmanageable;
impractical = unpractical (which avoid), all right in theory but not
in practice.

impresario (pl. impresarios).

impression *See* **edition**.

imprimatur = licence to print or publish, a sanction (approval);
imprimature is obsolete for **impression** (of a book); *see* **edition**.

improve, improvable, improvement.

improvident = lacking provision for the future or foresight;
imprudent = ill-advisedly bold, incautious. E.g.:

"His unwillingness to save money proved to be improvident when
he lost his source of income."
"His investment in the new company proved to be imprudent when
it collapsed after a few months."

improvise, improviser (who improvises, in general), improvisator
(who improvises at speaking or playing a musical instrument),
improvisation.

impulse *See* **compulsion**.

in (no full point) is the abbreviation of inch (and inches).

in Avoid using this word for **within**, a use that can lead to ambiguity;
e.g. "I can have a bath in four minutes" and "Please edit this text
in four days" would both benefit from *within* for *in* to convey the
senses intended. Also avoid using **in** for **into**; "He jumped in the
lake" and "She walked in the room" both require *into* for *in*. In is
preferred to *at* in the construction "She was born in England/
London/Kensington/Cromwell Road."

in- *See* **negative prefixes**.

inadmissible

inadvisable = not recommended; **unadvisable** = not open to advice. E.g.:

"I thought that the proposed change to the schedule was inadvisable."
"I tried to pass on the information to the manager, but he proved to be unadvisable."

in any case should be avoided; use **anyway** (not *any way*).

inapt *See* **inept**.

inartistic = poor at appreciating art, lacking an artistic viewpoint; **unartistic** = lacking the talent/ability of an artist. E.g.:

"I found the exhibition of sculpture boring because I am inartistic."
"I find drawing a lifelike face impossible because I am unartistic."

in as much as, in so far as are preferred (as four separate words) to *inasmuch as* and *insofar as*.

in between (preposition) is usually a tautology (e.g. in "It was a colour in between blue and green", delete *in*); **in-between** (adj.) = intervening (e.g. "It was an in-between colour, neither blue nor green"); **in-between** (noun) = someone or something between two (specified) states/qualities (e.g. "He was neither man nor boy, merely an in-between") and should be avoided. *See also* **between**.

in-built, originally an Americanism, = **built-in**, which is usually to be preferred.

incapable relates to a permanent lack of ability; **unable** relates to a specific inability in terms of situation or time; e.g. "He was incapable of climbing the ladder because he had two artificial legs" (i.e. he never could) and "He was unable to climb the ladder because he had sprained his ankle" (but would be able to do so when his ankle healed).

incentive = that which incites to action (with the idea of reward for success); **inspiration** = that which inspires, stimulation (not necessarily for reward other than self-satisfaction); **instigation** = the act of inciting, impulse (with authoritarian overtones); **motivation** = that which motivates, makes move/happen (with no or merely neutral overtones). *See also* **induce**.

in charge of = in authority over; **in the charge of** = under the authority of. E.g.:

"The babysitter was in charge of the child."
"The child was in the charge of the babysitter."

incidentally (not incidently).

incise, incision.

inclose/inclosure The preferred spellings are **enclose/enclosure**.

include, inclusive, includible. *Include* should not be used to mean made up of, consist of, comprise – that is, to describe a complete group; *include* can refer only to an incomplete group.

incognito (pl. incognitos).

inconceivable, like *unimaginable* and *unthinkable*, are extreme words that have rapidly come into vogue. They should not be devalued merely to emphatic synonyms of such words as *impracticable, unacceptable, undesirable, unnecessary, unlikely* and *unwanted*.

incontinent = lacking self-control; **incontinently** = immediately.

incorrect (not uncorrect) is the opposite of *correct*; **uncorrected** is the opposite of *corrected*.

incorrigible

incredible = unbelievable; **incredulous** = unbelieving. The corresponding nouns are *incredibility* and *incredulity*. *See also* **credence; credible**.

incur, incurred, incurring.

indefensible is preferred to **undefendable**.

indefinable

indelible

index, meaning a list of topics at the end of a book, has the plural **indexes**; as a term for an exponent or power in mathematics, it has the plural **indices**. *See also* **anthology**.

Indian words Many words have entered the English vocabulary from the Indian subcontinent, often by way of the army or the British raj. Hindi, itself based on the Urdu word for India, has provided the most and there are others direct from Sanskrit and other modern languages of the subcontinent. As a check list of spellings (and for interest), here are some examples.

From Hindi:

bangle	dungarees	loot	shampoo
bungalow	gavial	mahout	Sikh
cheetah	guru	mina (bird)	sitar
chintz	gymkana	mugger	thug
chit	jodhpurs	(crocodile)	toddy
chutney	jungle	pundit	tom-tom
cot (bed)	juggernaut	pukka	topi
dekko	kedgeree	punkah	raj
dinghy	krait	puttee	verandah
dixie	kukri	sari	wallah

From Sanskrit: brahmin, mantra, raga, sandal (wood), stupa, yoga;
From Tamil: catamaran, cheroot, curry (food), mulligatawny, pariah, pappadam;
From Urdu: khaki, nabob, purdah, pyjamas, sepoy, shawl, tandoor, tandoori;
Others: kala-azar (Assamese), jute (Bengali), coir, copra, teak (Malayan), mongoose (Marathi), panda (Nepali).

India paper = extremely thin tough paper (made from rags and used for printing quality bibles, prayer books, and so on). *See also* **bible paper**.

indict = to accuse; **indite** = to write.

indigestible (not undigestible) = that cannot be digested;
  undigested = that has not been digested.

indiscipline (absence of discipline) but **undisciplined** (of someone
  lacking discipline).

indiscreet/indiscrete *See* **discreet**.

indiscriminate = heedless, lacking care; **undiscriminating** =
  lacking discrimination, lacking judgement. E.g.:

  "Her appearance suffers from the indiscriminate use of make-up."
  "She was undiscriminating in her choice of clothes for the formal
  occasion."

indispensable

indispose, indisposition (not indisposedness). **Indisposed** is
  precious for **slightly unwell**.

indite *See* **indict**.

individual (noun) should not be used to mean **person** (as in "a
  certain individual").

indoor is the adjective, **indoors** is the adverb. E.g.:

  "Squash is an indoor activity."
  "Squash is played indoors."
  Outdoor and **outdoors** are similar.

indorse The preferred spelling is **endorse**. *See also* **approve**.

induce = to bring on or into being, draw an inference (inductively);
  induct = to introduce; **inducement** = incentive, motive, that
  which induces; **induction** = bringing or drawing in, installation in
  office. *Induce/induction* also have technical meanings in electricity.

industry, industrial (pertaining to industry – of the e.g. engineering or manufacturing kind), industrious (diligent).

inedible *See* **edible**.

ineducable (not uneducatable).

inept = without skill, unfit, fatuous, futile; **inapt** = inappropriate, unsuitable, unaccustomed to; **unapt** = inapt. Close meanings that can, however, be distinguished. E.g.:

"The art student made a surprisingly inept attempt at drawing a face."
"The young art student was an inapt candidate for the senior designer's position."

inestimable *See* **estimable**.

in excess of seldom means more than **more than**.

inexplicable (= incapable of explanation) is preferred to **unexplainable**.

infallible

infamous *See* **famous**.

infant *See* **baby**.

infection/infectious refer to a disorder (disease) that can be passed from one person to another – by whatever means; **contagion/ contagious** refer to a disease that is passed on by contact (with an infected person, a carrier, or anything contaminated by pathogens); **infestation** is a disorder or circumstance that involves a "take-over" by insects, worms, parasites, and so on. An infestation that causes a disorder may or may not be infectious/contagious.

infer = to deduce, derive (as a consequence); **imply** = to hint, suggest, signify, express indirectly. One infers something *from* a statement, but implies something *with* (or *by*) a statement: what A implies, B infers. Note also the forms inferable, inferred, inferring, inference.

inferior *to* (not inferior *than*).

inferno (pl. infernos).

infiltrate = introduce (insidiously) a few items into a larger whole (such as a few men among a body of enemy troops or an idea into someone else's mind), to permeate; **insinuate** = introduce subtly or stealthily (such as oneself into favour or a thing into place), to suggest obliquely. Infiltrate does not need *into* (e.g. "The spy infiltrated the enemy camp"); insinuate needs *that* (e.g. "Are you insinuating that I am lying?").

infinitive, split *See* **split infinitive**.

inflammable (= capable of being set afire) is preferred to **flammable**. **Non-inflammable** (preferred to **non-flammable**) strictly means not capable of supporting flame although combustible – that is, treated in such a way that combustion cannot take place. Something that simply will not burn is **incombustible**. Thus petrol is inflammable, cotton fabrics can be made non-inflammable, and asbestos is incombustible.

inflate, inflater, inflatable.

inflect, inflective, inflexion. *See* **afflict**.

inflexible

inflexion (not -ection).

inflict *See* **afflict**.

inform = to give or pass information to; it should not be used to mean *advise, ask, instruct* or simply *tell*.

informant = someone who provides specific information or knowledge; **informer** = someone who provides information (usually about another) to the police or other authority.

infra-red (but ultraviolet).

infrequent is preferred to **unfrequent** (but use *un*frequented, not *in*frequented).

infusible (= unmeltable).

-ing *See* **gerund; suffixes**.

ingenious = clever (at contrivance); **ingenuous** = naive, innocent. **Ingenuity** is common to both, although **ingenuousness** is better of the latter. The French term *ingénu(e)* (unsophisticated or artless person) should be avoided.

inhabitable *See* **habitable**.

inherent = intrinsic, permanently existing in or as part of something; **innate** = inborn, native, natural; **congenital** = present at birth (although possibly of earlier origin); **inherited** = derived from a parent or predecessor.

inheritable is preferred to **hereditable**.

inhuman = cruel, unfeeling, lacking in humanity; **unhuman** = non-human (which is preferred). E.g.:

"The guards were censured for their inhuman treatment of the prisoners."
"The footprints were made by an unhuman creature."

initial, initialled, initialling.

initiate = admit someone to a select group (often with some sort of ceremony), make someone aware of the basic principles of a subject; the word should not be used merely as a synonym of **begin**. E.g.:

"He performed the rites that would initiate him into the secret society" (correct);

"The receipt of an order initiated the manufacturing process" (incorrect),
which is better put as "The manufacturing process began after receipt of the order."

ink-jet printer *See* **printer**.

in-laws is a convenient colloquialism for the relatives of one's husband or wife. **Brother-in-law** (pl. brothers-in-law) is the brother of your husband (or wife), often extended to mean also your sister's husband and even your sister-in-law's husband. **Sister-in-law** (pl. sisters-in-law) is your husband's (or wife's) sister, your brother's wife, or your brother-in-law's wife. **Father-in-law** is your spouse's father, and **mother-in-law** is your spouse's mother. *See also* **family relationships** (diagram).

in most instances = **usually**, which is preferred.

innate *See* **inherent**.

innings (at cricket) has the same form in the singular and plural. Baseball solves the problem by having *inning* as the singular (and *innings* as the plural).

innovation = something newly introduced; it is therefore tautologous to write "To the local people, the motor car was a new innovation" (delete *new*). **Innovative** should not be used as a modish alternative to **new** or **original**.

innuendo (pl. innuendos).

innumerable, like countless, should strictly be used only of things that cannot be counted (e.g. "The over-punctuated text contained innumerable commas" is incorrect). *See also* **enumerable**.

inoculation (with one *n* and one *c*, because it originally meant the insertion of a plant graft into a bud or eye: *in-oculus*); note also **vaccination** (with two *c*s, from *Vaccinia* = cowpox) and **immunization** (with a *z*).

in order that should be followed by *may* or *might*; e.g. "In order that no delay *will* occur" is incorrect.

in order to should not be used when plain *to* will do; e.g. in "I had to leave home an hour earlier than usual in order to meet the plane", the simpler ". . . than usual to meet the plane" works better.

-in or -ine As an ending of scientific or technical terms taken into more general use, *-ine* tends to be shortened to *-in* (e.g. adrenalin, gelatin, glycerin, lanolin, vitamin are the preferred forms); these spellings also reflect the preferred pronunciations.

inquire is the preferred spelling, not **enquire** (similarly **inquiry** is preferred to **enquiry**).

in rare cases is more briefly expressed as **rarely**.

in regard to, like *in relation to* and *in respect of*, seldom means more than **about**, which is preferred.

insanitary = unhealthy, unhygienic, likely to cause ill-health; **unsanitary** = lacking sanitation. E.g.:

"The army nurses fought a constant battle against sepsis in the insanitary wards of the field hospital."
"Their primitive homes were unsanitary, lacking any provision for the disposal of domestic or human waste."

insect is, strictly, an arthropod animal of the class Insecta. A typical mature insect has six legs, two antennae and three chief body parts (head, thorax and abdomen), although some of these features may be lacking at earlier (e.g. larval) stages. There are several other classes of arthropods, such as arachnids (spiders and their allies), crustaceans (including shrimps, crabs, and so on), diplopods (millipedes) and chilopods (centipedes), all of which have more than six legs. It is therefore incorrect to refer to members of these other classes as *insects*. The general American term **bug** (for insect) should be avoided except in reference to insects of the order Hemiptera, the true bugs (most of which feed by sucking sap or blood).

insensible = unconscious, lacking feeling/emotion; **insensitive** = incapable of reacting to sensation, unfeeling/unemotional. The latter is preferred to the former in their second meanings. **Nonsensical** = lacking in (common) sense, absurd. E.g.:

"The blow to the head knocked her insensible."
"She seemed insensitive to pain."
"Her proposal to omit the checking stage was a nonsensical suggestion."

inseparable pairs of words – often of similar meaning and many of which form clichés – should be avoided in formal writing. Known technically as *dryads*, many are archaic, and some are idiomatic and thus puzzling if taken literally. They are also irreversible – it is unnatural, and un-English, to say *change and chop* or *choose and pick*. A few common examples include:

chop and change	might and main
cut and thrust	odds and sods
fast and furious	part and parcel
fine and dandy	pick and choose
goods and chattels	pink and dimples
hale and hearty	short and sweet
home and dry	sweetness and light
hue and cry	time and tide
kith and kin	toss and turn
leaps and bounds	trials and tribulations
live and learn	well and truly

See also **hendiadys**.

inside of should be avoided; use plain **inside** (unless *inside* is a noun – e.g. "the inside of the box").

insidious (not insiduous) = spreading stealthily and secretly, possibly also treacherously; **invidious** = offensive, possibly also unjust; **perfidious** = treacherous (as in the French description of Britain as "perfidious Albion").

insignia is a plural word (Latin singular *insigne*).

insignificant = unimportant; it does not mean **small**.

insinuate = to imply in an underhand way, to hint at a flaw or fault in something; it is a pejorative term and should not be used as a synonym for the neutral **suggest**. **Insinuation** and **suggestion** are similarly related. *See also* **infiltrate**.

insipid, insipidness (not insipidity). *See also* **sapid**.

insist, insistent, insistence.

in situ (italics) = in (original) position; the Latin form should be avoided.

in so far as is preferred to *insofar as* (*see* **in as much as**).

insolate = to expose to sunlight; **insulate** = to isolate, block from a source of electricity, cold or sound.

insoluble describes something that cannot be dissolved or cannot be solved; it is preferred to **unsolvable** in the latter sense.

inspiration *See* **incentive**.

in spite of is better put as **despite** or **although** (but *see* **despite the fact that**).

instability (state of lacking stability) but **unstable** (not stable).

instal, installed, installing, installation, instalment.

instant = a very short time, now; **moment** = a slightly longer but nevertheless short time, very soon. E.g.:

"It will take me only an instant" (= very short time);
"Please do it this instant" (= now);
"It will only take me a moment" (= short time);
"I'll do it in a moment" (= soon).

Instantaneously = at the same time/instant, simultaneously; **instantly** = at once, at this instant, now. E.g.:

"The door banged and he dropped the saucer instantaneously."
"Please pick up that saucer instantly."

instigation *See* **incentive**.

instil, instilled, instilling, instillation, instilment (not to be confused with installation, instalment; *see* **instal**).

instinct, instinctive (= done/controlled by instinct, inborn, innate), instinctual (to do with instinct). The meanings of the two adjectives are much the same. E.g.:

"Suckling by a newborn baby is an instinctive reflex response."
"The suckling response in babies is instinctual."

Instinct is an innate ability, inherited by human beings and other animals – indeed one definition of non-human creatures hinges on the fact that much animal behaviour is totally instinctive.
Intuition, on the other hand, is purely a human attribute. It requires insight and is a product of the intellect which involves reasoning, unlike the automatic functioning of instinct. E.g.:

"He excelled at snooker with little or no coaching – he had a natural instinct for it."
"His intuition told him to play the blue ball, which turned out to be the correct choice."

instructional = giving instructions, educational; **instructive** = giving information, informative. E.g.:

"The students learned the technique by watching an instructional video film."
"The students found the video film instructive."

insure = to make an arrangement for the payment of money in the event of loss or injury; **ensure** = to make sure.

intaglio (pl. intaglios) *See* **cameo**; **printing processes**.

intangible

intelligence = innate mental (thinking) capacity; **intellect** = mental

development; **intelligent** = quick-witted, "bright";
intellectual = thinking, "brainy".

intelligible

intend, intendant, intendancy, intent, intention (= purpose) (not
intension, a term in logic).

intense = concentrated, extreme, dense, with strong emotion;
intensive = thorough, unremitting, exhaustive. E.g.:

"Even the glass melted in the intense heat."
"Meeting the deadline required an intensive effort by all the staff."

inter- = between, among; **intra-** = within; **infra-** = below, less than;
intro- = into. E.g. international, intravenous, infra-red,
introgression.

inter, interred, interring.

inter alia (italics) = among other things; the Latin form should be
avoided.

interesting is a word that, unqualified, raises the questions "to
whom and in what way?" Puzzling, dramatic, unusual, important
(used correctly), titivating, intriguing, full of character, strange,
exotic, curious, worthy of further investigation – all are better, if
somewhat wordier, alternatives.

interface = common boundary between two fluids or other states of
matter, an apparatus that links two electronic devices (such as an
IBM terminal and an ICL computer). The word should be
reserved for such technical meanings and not used to mean any
common ground or boundary between any two of anything. *See*
vogue words.

interject = interrupt (as an abrupt contribution to a conversation);
interpose = interject; **interpolate** = insert something (into a text
or conversation), estimate a value from other, surrounding values;
extrapolate = to extend (by estimation) a given set of values into

an unestablished area, to infer; **intersperse** = place things between or among others.

interment = burial (of a corpse); **internment** = confinement of an alien (in time of war). The corresponding verbs are *inter* and *intern*.

intermezzo (pl. intermezzi).

in terms of is a cliché generally to be avoided.

interpret, interpreter, interpretable, interpretation, interpretative (not interpretive).

interrelate, interrelated, interrelation, interrelationship.

interrupt, interrupter, interruption.

interstate = between two or more (political/territorial) states; **intestate** = having made no will (testament).

interval = length or period of time between two events; it should not be used merely to mean any period of time. E.g.:

"The schedule extended for two years, an interval regarded as too short" is incorrect;
"Between receipt of copy and dispatch of film is an interval of four months" is correct.

in the circumstances *See* **under the circumstances.**

in the event that = **if** (which is twelve letters shorter).

in the nature of should be avoided for *about, like* or *approximately*.

in the neighbourhood of = **near** or **round about,** either of which is preferred.

in the order of and **in the region of** should not be used to mean *about* or *approximately* (as in "Its length was in the order of 20 metres", "It cost in the region of £10,000").

intolerable = unbearable; **intolerant** = unwilling to endure something, likely to oppose those who differ or disagree.

in toto (italics) = entirely, completely (it does not mean in total or on the whole); the Latin form is often misused or misunderstood, and is therefore best avoided.

intramuscular, intra-uterine, intravenous.

inundate, inundation.

in vacuo (italics) = in a vacuum; the Latin term should be avoided in ordinary writing.

invalid (adj.) = not valid; **invalid** (noun) = someone who is ill. **Invalidated** = made not valid, made void; **invalided** = regarded as an invalid or unfit for duty; use **invalidation** of the former, **invalidity** of the latter.

invaluable *See* **valuable**.

inveigh = speak loudly against something; **inveigle** = tempt, entice or persuade someone into doing something.

invent *See* **discover**.

inverse = the direct opposite of something in order or direction, an inverted state or condition; **converse** = something (or an action) that is the exact opposite; **obverse** = counterpart/opposite of any fact; **reverse** = the opposite or contrary of something. All these words are close in meaning; *reverse* or *opposite* should be used when in doubt. Consider:

"His manner was the reverse of co-operative."
"The possession of flair without experience is the converse of the possession of experience without flair."
"The inverse of 1, 2, 3 is 3, 2, 1."
"He claims that men are more sensitive than women, whereas the obverse is often true."

(Technically, *reverse* = back, or non-head, side of a coin; *obverse* = front, or head side, of a coin.)

invert, inverter.

inverted commas English is one of the few languages in which inverted commas (or quotation marks) take the form of ' and ' or " and " (with the initial mark literally one or two inverted commas, resembling the figure 6 in shape, and the final mark identical with a normal comma or apostrophe). When checking printed proofs, editors and proof-readers should ensure that the initial mark is typeset correctly (especially if the typesetter is a non-English company) because in some other languages the initial mark may be identical with a comma and not inverted (i.e. ' and ' or " and "). Still other languages use totally different marks (such as « and » in Greek). *See also* **punctuation** (apostrophe); **punctuation** (quotation marks).

invest, investor.

in view of the fact that = **considering** or **because**, which are preferred.

invite is a verb; it should not be used as a noun to mean **invitation** (e.g. "I accepted her invite to the party" is incorrect).

in vitro, in vivo (italics).

involve is overused and should be deleted or replaced by a more precise verb. E.g.:

"The additional time involved will be two days" (delete *involved*).
"The cost involved in building the house..." (say "The cost of building the house").
"Much labour has been involved in cleaning" (say "Much labour has been expended on cleaning").
"The injury involved her leg" (say "She injured her leg" or "The impact broke/bruised/cut/fractured/ gashed/grazed/hurt/lacerated/ numbed/paralysed/severed her leg").

ion, ionize, ionization (and de-ionize).

ipso facto (italics) = **thereby**, which should be used.

IQ is the abbreviation of intelligence quotient.

ir- *See* **negative prefixes**.

Iran The derived adjective and noun is *Iranian*, which is preferred to *Persian* except in historical contexts (and expressions such as Persian carpet). The Iranian/Persian language is *Farsi*.

Iraq The derived adjective and noun is *Iraqi*.

irascible

iridesce, iridescent, iridescence, iridium (the metallic element).

iris (pl. irises).

Irish *See* **Celtic words; Scotland**.

Iron Age (initial capital letters).

ironic(al) = suggesting or expressing irony; it should not be overworked to mean *strange, paradoxical* or merely *unusual*.

irony = use of an expression that is capable of two interpretations; a literal one and the one intended. E.g.:

"Yes, children always know best"
(with the intended meaning that they do not). The use of irony can be disastrous for communication if the reader misses the point. Its aim is to make a point and perhaps to amuse, unlike **sarcasm**, which is intended to be hurtful. *See also* **satire**.

irradicate *See* **eradicate**.

irreconcilable, irreconcilement.

irregardless merely means **regardless**, which should be used.

irregular verbs *See* **verbs**.

irreligious = (deliberately) ignoring religious beliefs;
    unreligious = not holding/belonging to a religious faith. E.g.:

"I was offended by his repeated irreligious use of Christ's name."
"I admire church architecture although I am quite unreligious."

irrepairable = cannot be repaired, and **irreparable** = cannot be made
    good (from *repair* and *reparation* respectively) are now virtually
    synonymous.

irreplaceable

irresistible

irresponsible = rash, feckless; it does not mean *not responsible*. E.g.:

"Throwing the bottle out of the car window was an irresponsible
act."
but "Because of his mental state, he was not responsible for his
actions."
See also **unresponsible**.

irruption *See* **eruption**.

ISBN = abbreviation of International Standard Book Number.

-ise *See* **-ize or -ise**.

Islam is the preferred term for the religion of Muslims. **Muslim**
    (adj., preferred to *Moslem*) describes the people, **Islamic** (adj.)
    describes the religion, culture, and so on.

isn't (= is not) should be avoided in formal writing.

ISO = International Standard Organization, the authority which
    defines standard (ISO) paper sizes. *See* **paper sizes**.

isolate *See* **eliminate**.

Israel The derived adjective and noun is *Israeli*. *See also* **Semitic**.

issue (verb) takes *to* not *with* (e.g. write "Pens were issued to the staff" not "The staff were issued with pens", although ". . . were issued pens" is correct).

isthmus (pl. isthmuses).

Italian words in English relate mostly to the arts (particularly music) and to food. Long-standing nouns ending in -*o* tend to take the "English" plural in -*s* or -*es* (fresco, grotto, motto and volcano take -es; for a list containing -*s* plurals of Italian origin, *see* **plurals**). The following words form the plural with -*i*: graffito, incognito, libretto, literato, ovolo, scherzo, virtuoso. Words ending in -*a* generally form the plural with -*s*; e.g. breccia, gondola, pasta, piazza, pizza, plaza, trattoria, vista (although lira has the plural lire). They should be distinguished from words of Latin origin ending in -*a* that form the plural with -*ae* (although some assimilated Latin words also form plurals in -*s*) and Latin words that are already plural (e.g. candelabra, plectra, spectra, strata).

italic, italicize, italicization.

italics Italicize the names of ships (but keep HMS in roman type); names of newspapers, journals and magazines; titles of books, plays, films, television and radio programmes, operas, ballets, poems (e.g. *Paradise Lost*); and names of musical works (*see* **musical works**). Italicize also all foreign words and phrases that have not become part of everyday English usage (*see* **foreign words and phrases**). Avoid italics for emphasis; do not italicize the names of foreign streets or buildings, names of hotels or houses.

In the Latin nomenclature for plants and animals, only the names of genera, species and varieties/races should be italicized (*see* **Latin classification**). In genetics, genes should be typeset in italics (e.g. gene pairs *R*' and *r*'), but their products should be in roman (e.g. R'r' antibodies). Do not italicize geographical features of the Moon, planets, and so on. The following chemical prefixes are italicized: *cis-, trans-, dextro-, laevo-, n-, sec-, tert-, ortho-, o-, meta-, m-, para-, p-, meso-*. In a block of copy (such as a caption) typeset in italics, any words that would normally be italicized should be typeset in roman.

item, itemize, itemization. The verb **list** is preferred to *itemize*.

it goes without saying, like *needless to say*, is usually not worth saying.

its = genitive of it; **it's** = *it is* or *it has* and should be avoided in formal writing. *It's* should not be confused with its (as common an error as *her's* for *hers*). *See also* **one's**.

IU is the abbreviation of international unit (in which vitamins are quantified).

ivy (pl. ivies), ivied (= covered in ivy).

-ize or -ise The endings *-ize* and *-ization* are preferred to *-ise* and *-isation*. The following list of exceptions includes obvious as well as less obvious examples (with any related noun in parentheses). It also includes verbs ending in *-yse*. A simple rule of thumb is that if the verb can form a noun ending in *-ation*, then the verb should be spelled *-ize*; if an *-ation* noun is not possible, spell the verb *-ise*.

advertise (advertisement)
advise (advice)
analyse (analysis)
apprise
arise
baptise (baptism)
catalyse (catalysis)
chastise (chastisement)
circumcise (circumcision)
comprise (comprisal)
compromise
demise
despise (despisal)
devise (device)
dialyse (dialysis)
disfranchise (disfranchisement)
disguise
electrolyse (electrolysis)
emprise
enfranchise (enfranchisement)
enterprise

excise (excision)
exercise
franchise
hypnotise (hypnotism)
improvise (an exception to the -ation rule).
incise (incision)
merchandise
paralyse (paralysis)
patronise (patron)
premise
prise (verb)
promise
reprise
revise (revision)
summarise (summary)
supervise (supervision)
surmise
surprise
televise (television)
vasectomise (vasectomy)

J

jackanapes, jackass (= male ass; laughing jackass = Australian bird), jackboot(ed), jackdaw, jack-in-the-box, jack-knife, jack-of-all-trades, jack-o'-lantern, jack plug, jackpot.

jacket, jacketed, jacketing.

Jacobean = pertaining to James I or his reign; **Jacobian** = pertaining to the mathematics of Karl Jacobi; **Jacobin** = type of (Dominican) friar; **Jacobite** = follower of James (i.e. James II, Henry James or Jacobus Baradaeus).

jail/jailor are the preferred spellings (not **gaol/gaoler**, except in official use).

jam (noun) = blockage; **jamb** = upright part of a door.

japan (verb), japanned, japanning.

jargon has been defined by Eric Partridge as "the technicalities of science, the professions, the Services, trades, crafts, sports and games, art and Art." Many of the terms from publishing, printing and typesetting listed in this Dictionary are jargon. It is to be assiduously avoided in ordinary writing – it is bad style to talk shop to the uninformed reader. An editor might blench at being asked to cut two-thirds from a piece of highly technical text, yet this (contrived) 100-word sentence:

"Should the relative humidity of the ambient atmosphere in the machine's working environment decrease below the optimum level, the flexibility co-efficient of the base material of the punched paper tape and similarly that of the punched cards decreases, thus destabilizing their dimensions and inducing a degree of curvature; on the other hand, among the likely consequences of a higher than optimal ambient relative humidity is an inverse effect on the stretch co-efficient of the substrate of the punched cards with the result that their linear dimensions exceed the design parameters of the output device and cause its transport mechanism to malfunction."

can be edited to the following 34-word version (cited in slightly different form by Gowers as an example of anti-jargon):

"If the air in the computer room is too dry, paper tape may become brittle and cards may shrink and curl; if the air is too damp cards may expand and jam the card-reader."

without any loss of information but with a considerable increase in impact and understanding. *See also* **non-standard English; slang**.

jejune = barren, meagre, puerile; it is sometimes taken to mean unsophisticated or naive, a use that should be avoided.

jerbil The preferred spelling is **gerbil**.

jerrymander The preferred spelling is **gerrymander**.

jettison, jettisoned.

jewel, jewelled, jewellery (*jewelry* is an Americanism).

Jewish *See* **Semitic**.

jib (verb) = to balk, refuse, show objection; **jibe** is a spelling to be avoided either for **gybe** (= to swing a sail from one side to another) or for **gibe** (= to scoff (at), taunt, flaunt).

jigger (flea) The preferred spelling is **chigoe** (known as *chigger* in the United States).

jingo (pl. jingos), jingoism (= British chauvinism). **Jingo** is an archaic mild oath, as in E. E. Cummins'
"in every language even deafanddumb
                       ... by gorry
by jingo by gee by gosh by gum".

journalese = type of language favoured by popular (and sometimes less popular) newspapers. One reason for it is the desire to capture the reader's attention, often by the overuse of colourful words and superlatives (the "shock-horror" syndrome). Another reason is the need for brevity because of lack of space, particularly in headline writing, which often leads to the use of consecutive nouns ("Vicar in love-tug mercy dash"). Thus short words are pressed into service as synonyms for long ones; an investigation becomes a *probe*, a limitation a *ban* or *curb*, reductions are *cuts*, to resign is to *quit*, to criticize is to *slam*, and to discredit is to *gun for*. Puns may be used to catch attention or amuse (as in the classic misquotation of Keats: "Amid the Alien Porn").

journey = travels by land or air; **voyage** = travels by sea; **trip** = a short journey or voyage.

judgement (but strictly judgment in law).

judicial = relating to a court of law or a judge; **judicious** = of sound judgement, wise, prudent.

junction = a joining of roads or railway lines, a joint; **juncture** = a joining of events.

junta is the preferred spelling (not **junto**). This useful Spanish word has no short English equivalent, and should be pronounced in the English fashion (not *hun-ta*).

justification = typesetter's term for the technique of making all the lines of type in a page or column the same length (*measure*) by varying the spaces between words (*word spacing*) on different lines or, if necessary and permitted by the publisher, between individual letters of words (*letter spacing*). The resulting text is said to both *range left* (with all the lines of type aligning vertically at the left-hand margin) and *range right* (with all lines aligning vertically on the right). **Unjustified** setting may be ranged left (with *ragged*, non-aligning line-endings on the right, as in this book) or ranged right (aligning on the right but ragged on the left). Thus a typical typesetting instruction is:
"Please set main text in 10/12pt Univers medium justified across 18 picas."
This defines the type size and *leading* (space between the lines) [10-point type with 2 points of leading], the typeface [Univers] and its weight [medium], the line length [18 picas], with all the lines the

same length [justified]. Often the maximum and minimum word spacing is also specified. *See also* **point**.

justify = to excuse (give an excuse for), to exonerate; **rectify** = to correct. There is a world of difference between justifying a mistake and rectifying it.

juvenile = young, youthful; **puerile** = childish. An old man can have juvenile appetites and behave in a puerile way to satisfy them. *See also* **childish**.

K

k is an abbreviation of the metric prefix *kilo-* (which *see*); **K** is the abbreviation of kelvin (the unit of temperature of the "absolute" temperature scale) and is increasingly being used as an abbreviation of *thousand* when referring to sums of money (e.g. a salary of £15,000 a year may be referred to as £15K) or computer memory storage capacity (e.g. a 128K RAM machine), although originally in computers $1K = 2^{10} = 1,024$.

kale (a type of cabbage) is the preferred spelling of **kail**.

karri = Australian eucalyptus tree ("blue gum"); **kauri** = New Zealand "pine" tree; **cowrie** (preferred to cowry) = Asian and African mollusc and its shell.

katabolism The preferred spelling is **catabolism**.

keep (verb) inflects *keep – kept – kept*.

Kelt/Keltic The preferred spellings are **Celt/Celtic** (although the *k* pronunciation is the more usual).

ken is archaic for **knowledge** (as in the cliché "beyond/within his ken); *knowledge* should be used.

kerb (= kerbstone) is the preferred spelling of **curb** (as a noun).

kerning = typesetter's term for reducing (to less than normal) the spacing between letters in a typeset word, made relatively easy since the introduction of computer-controlled photosetting. It is often used to improve the appearance of words set in large (display) type sizes.

kerosene (not kerosine) is usually known as paraffin in Britain and is the name of similar petroleum hydrocarbons used as a fuel for gas turbine (e.g. "jet" aircraft) engines.

ketchup is the preferred spelling (not **catsup**).

keyboard, keyhole, key man, key-ring, keyword.

kg is the abbreviation of kilogram.

khaki

kibbutz (pl. kibbutzim).

kidnap, kidnapper, kidnapped, kidnapping.

kilo- is the metric prefix for a thousand times ($\times$ 10^3), as in *kilometre* (*see* **units**); **kilo** (pl. kilos) is an abbreviation of kilogram.

kilogram has the abbreviation kilo (pl. kilos) or kg.

kimono (pl. kimonos).

kin is old-fashioned for **relatives,** which is preferred.

kind should be regarded as singular (**kinds** being plural). E.g.:

"Some new kind of approach to the design is required."
"Some new kinds of designs are required."
See also **type of.**

kine- The preferred prefix is **cine-** (e.g. cinematograph).

king-sized

km is the abbreviation of kilometre.

kneel has the preferred past tense and participle **kneeled** (not *knelt*).

knit has the preferred past tense and participle **knitted,** although *knit* is used as frequently.

knot = nautical mile per hour (used for speeds of aircraft and ships); "a speed of 15 knots per hour" is therefore incorrect (write "speed of 15 knots").

know has the past tense **knew** and past participle **known**.

knowledge, knowledgeable.

Koran (initial capital letter).

kraft = type of strong, smooth brown paper produced from unbleached chemical wood pulp, used as wrapping paper. *See also* **paper**.

krona (pl. kronor) is Swedish money; **krona** (pl. kronur) is Icelandic money; **krone** (pl. kroner) is Danish or Norwegian money.

kudos is a singular word.

Kuwait The derived adjective and noun is *Kuwaiti*.

kW is the abbreviation of kilowatt.

L

l is the abbreviation of litre.

laager = camp or encampment; **lager** = light beer (*see also* **ale**).

label, labelled, labelling.

labium (pl. labia).

labour, laboured, laborious.

lace, lacy.

lachrymal, lachrymation, lachrymatory, lachrymose (not lacrimal, etc.).

lack *See* **absence**.

lackadaisical (= affected, listless) persists, whereas *lackaday* and *lackadaisy* have dropped out of circulation.

lacquer (printing) *See* **lamination**.

lacrimal etc. The preferred spelling is **lachrymal** etc.

lacuna (pl. lacunae).

lade (= to load with cargo) has the past tense and participle *laden*.

ladybird, lady-in-waiting, lady-killer, ladylike, lady-love, ladyship, lady's maid. Avoid using **lady** for **woman** in terms such as *woman doctor, woman traffic warden*.

laid *See* **lay**; **lie**.

laid = papermaking term for a pattern of parallel watermark lines impressed on one side of a sheet of paper by a *dandy roll* during manufacture. *See also* **paper**.

laisser-faire, laissez-faire (italics) survive as a short way of saying "government abstention from interference with individual action" (*Concise OED*).

lama = Buddhist priest; **llama** = South American camel-like mammal.

lamé

lamina (pl. laminae).

lamination, in printing = film of plastic (as a thin sheet) applied to paper or board after printing to improve appearance and wear-resistance (e.g. as on book jackets and record sleeves); **varnish** = shiny finish of a synthetic coating applied (initially as a liquid) to a printed sheet to improve gloss and finish (also called lacquer).

lamp-black, lampholder, lamplight(er), lamp-post, lampshade, lamp-shell.

land-agent, land-bridge, land-crab, landfall, land-grabber, landholder, landlady, land-line, land-locked, landlord, landlubber, landmark, land-mine, landowner, landscape, landslide, landslip, landsman, landward(s), land-yacht(ing).

landscape format *See* **format**.

languid = sluggish, lacking vigour, listless; **limpid** = clear, not turbid, untroubled.

languor = inertia, lassitude (adjectives languorous, languid; verb languish); **langur** = (sacred) Indian monkey.

lanolin is the preferred spelling (not **lanoline**).

Laos The derived adjective and noun is *Laotian*.

lapel, lapelled.

lapse *See* **elapse**.

large should not be used to qualify breadth, depth, distance, height or length (for which use **great**).

large number of = many; **large share of** = most. The shorter forms should be used.

large post = standard paper size of (in metric) 419 × 533 millimetres.

larger than *See* **as large as**.

largess is the preferred spelling (not **largesse**).

lariat = rope for tying up animals (it is not a **lasso**, which is a throwable rope with a noose at the end).

larva (pl. larvae).

larynx (pl. larynges).

laser printer *See* **printer**.

lasso (pl. of noun is lassos, 3rd. person singular present of verb is lassoes), lassoed, lassoing. *See also* **lariat**.

last can be ambiguous if used for **preceding**; e.g. "... referred to in the last four chapters" is strictly wrong if what is meant are the four before the one in which the statement is made ("the last four" are the four that end the whole book). **Last** describes the final item in a series, **latest** refers to the most recent (which may or may not turn out to be the last). For *last two* etc., *see* **first**. *See also* **latter**.

late = dead (as in "the late king"); it should not be used to mean *former* of someone who has relinquished an office or position (e.g. "the former president" is still alive but no longer in office, "the late president" is dead). *See also* **former**.

lateral reversal *See* **flop**.

lath = thin strip of wood; **lathe** = machine for turning wood or metal.

Latin classification (of plants and animals). Initial capital letters
(but not italics) are used for phyla, orders, classes and families, but
no initial capital for their anglicized equivalents; e.g. Arthropoda,
arthropods; Crustacea, crustaceans.
For both botanical and zoological classifications, genera, species
and subspecies/varieties/races are typeset in italics; all other
divisions are set in roman face. All but species and subspecies/
variety/race have an initial capital letter. Thus the Indian elephant
belongs to family Elephantidae of the order Proboscidea; it is genus
Elephas and species *maximus*. It is helpful to the reader to give the
common (popular, or vernacular) name, if one exists, as well as the
Latin name. The Latin name should appear in brackets
(parentheses) after the common name, if the equivalence is exact;
e.g. "rice (*Oryza sativa*)", but "the crop plant *Oryza sativa*".
Avoid capitalizing Latin names that have become part of common
English usage when they are used in a non-taxonomic way; e.g.
"the iris plant" but "the species *Iris versicolor*". A multiplication
sign (×) indicates a hybrid. Common names do not have capital
letters except for proper nouns or to avoid ambiguity; e.g. Red
deer, Toy poodle, Miniature Yorkshire terrier, Old English
sheepdog, Frisian, Arabian, Sussex blue.

Latin words In addition to words of Latin derivation – which form a
large part of the English language – English includes many
unaltered borrowings from Latin. Some are perfectly acceptable
(such as agenda, alga, alias, alibi, apex, aquarium, atrium, axis, to
list but a few from the *a* entries in this Dictionary). Apart from
presenting possible problems with plurals (*see* **plurals**), these are
useful words which have no simple "English" equivalents. The *a*
entries also contain *ab initio, ad hoc, ad infinitum, ad lib* and *ad
nauseam*, all of which parade their Latin origins by usually being
typeset in italics. These do have more familiar (and to many readers
easier to understand) English equivalents, and for this reason their
use is not recommended. It was overuse of such words that
prompted George Orwell to remark "A mass of Latin words falls
upon the facts like soft snow, blurring the outlines and covering up
the details." (*See also* **foreign words and phrases**.)

Some areas of science, particularly medicine and biology, legitimately have Latin or Latinized terms as part of their specialized vocabulary (*see*, for example, **Latin classification**).

latter = the second of two (but only two) things mentioned, near the end of a period of time ("the latter part of the week"). Latter should not be misused for **last**, which has to be used in reference to the final one of three or more things mentioned; e.g. "Of the two boys, John and Jim, he resembled the latter; among Ann, Betty and Catherine, he preferred the last." Similar rules apply to *former* and *first*.

laudable (not *laudible*) = worthy of praise; **laudatory** = containing or expressing praise. E.g.:

"The child's drawing was a laudable effort considering her age."
"The chairman made a laudatory speech about his retiring colleague."

launder, meaning to infiltrate stolen (or counterfeit) money into legitimate financial dealings, is a useful new metaphor.

lawful/legal *See* **unlawful**.

laws, scientific *See* **named effects and laws**.

lay (verb) is transitive ("lay something down"), inflexion: *lay – laid – laid* (compare *lie – lay – lain*). Note also *overlay – overlaid – overlaid*. *See also* **lie**.

lazaretto (pl. lazarettos).

lb is the abbreviation of *libra* (pound weight).

l.c. is the abbreviation of lower case.

le, as part of a proper name, generally has an initial capital letter; e.g. Louis Le Van, Charles Le Brun. Follow the style of the name's owner.

lead (verb) has the past tense and participle **led** (pronounced "led", as is the heavy metal spelled *lead*). Note that the verb **read** has the past tense and participle **read**, which is pronounced "red".

leading = typesetter's term for the space between lines of type, generally specified in *points* (*see* **point**). It can vary from zero (when the type is set *solid*) to several points, indicated by the type-size specification (e.g. "10/12pt" defines 10-point type with 2 points of leading between each line).

leading question *See* **question**.

leaf = sheet of paper, usually printed on both sides, constituting two pages; **page** = one side of the leaf of a publication (thus a 64-page book has only 32 leaves). *See also* **folio**.

lean The preferred past tense and participle is **leaned** (not **leant**).

leap The preferred past tense and participle is **leaped** (not **leapt**).

learn = to assimilate knowledge, to get to know something; **teach** = to impart/pass on knowledge; what A teaches B learns. E.g.:

"I want to learn to drive a car."
"He taught me to drive a car."

Like **lend** and **borrow** (which *see*), the two verbs are sometimes confused. The preferred past tense and participle of **learn** is **learned** (not *learnt*).

lease *See* **hire**.

leastways/leastwise are, according to the *OED*, dialect or vulgar for *or at least*, which is therefore preferred.

leave (verb) inflects *leave – left – left*.

Lebanon The derived adjective and noun is *Lebanese*.

lecture, lecturer, lecturership (but lectureship at Oxford University).

led *See* **lead**.

ledger = account book, method of fishing; **ledger-line** = type of fishing line; **leger line** = line to locate notes off the staff in music.

legal, legalize, legalization. *See also* **unlawful**.

legend *See* **fable**.

legible *See* **readable**.

legislation = laws or their enactment; **legislature** = law-making body of the State, the courts.

legitimate, legitimize (not legitimatize), legitimization. *See also* **unlawful**.

leisure, leisurely (characterized by leisure), leisured (having leisure).

lend inflects *lend – lent – lent*. *See also* **borrow; loan**.

lengthy should not be used when **long** is intended.

lenient, leniency (not lenience).

lens is a singular word (pl. lenses), originally meaning *lentil*. Its adjective *lenticular* is unfamiliar to many readers, with *lens-shaped* the awkward but more readily understandable alternative.

less and **fewer** *Less* denotes degree, quantity or extent (of something that is uncountable); *fewer* refers to number (of things that are countable). E.g.:

"Fewer trees, less timber."
"Less interest, fewer readers."
"Fewer sales, less profit."

lesser, like *less*, is a comparative of *little* (the superlative being *least*). *Less* usually denotes quantity or size (*see* **less**), whereas *lesser* generally qualifies significance or value. E.g.:

"Wendy takes less time than John to paint a wall."
"John is the lesser of the two painters."

lest is archaic for **unless** (or *for fear that, in case*), (as in the cliché "lest we forget"); the old term should be avoided.

letter space = typesetter's term for space introduced between the individual letters of a word to lengthen it, by effectively "stretching" it sideways, e.g. l e t t e r s p a c e. With text set as short lines (to a narrow *measure*), letter spacing may be employed in order to justify the lines (*see* **justification**). Conventionally in book setting, letter spacing is not used between letters set in *lower case* (small letters as opposed to capital letters, or *upper case*).

leuco- (white) is the preferred form of the prefix (except in *leukaemia*).

levee = a reception, or an elevated river bank (no accent).

level, levelled, levelling, leveller.

lexicon *See* **anthology**.

liable = answerable for, responsible; it should not be used to mean apt, capable or likely.

liaise, liaison.

libel, libelled, libelling, libeller, libellous. Libel is defamation by means of a statement made in writing (or, by extension, on radio or television – where programmes are assumed to be scripted), whereas **slander** is defamation by means of the spoken word. Slander is a civil offence, whereas certain kinds of libel can result in criminal charges.

liberal, liberalize, liberalization.

libido (pl. libidos).

libretto (pl. libretti).

licence (noun) = a permit; **license** (verb) = to authorize, grant a licence. The verb produces licensing, licensed, licensable, licensee;

the proper term for a shop that sells alcoholic drinks is an *off-licence* (with a hyphen and two *c*s).

lich- (= corpse) is the preferred spelling (not *lych-*) in compounds such as lich-gate, although the *y* form survives in some place-names (such as Lychpit, Hampshire).

lido (pl. lidos).

lie (verb) is intransitive ("lie under or on something"); inflexion: *lie – lay – lain* (compare *lay – laid – laid*). The confusion between *lay* and *lie* probably stems from the fact that the present tense of the former is the same as the past tense of the latter ("I lay the book down", present; "He lay on the floor", past). Note also *overlie – overlay – overlain*.

lifebelt, lifeblood, lifeboat, lifebuoy, life cycle, life-guard, life-jacket, lifelike, lifeline, lifelong, life-sized (preferred to life-size), lifespan, lifestyle, lifetime, life-work, life's work.

lifelong = for the span of life (e.g. "he had a lifelong interest in the theatre"); *livelong*, archaic/poetic for enduring, protracted, very long (as in the cliché "for the livelong day"), should be avoided.

ligature = a binding together, tying tightly round (a blood vessel, for instance); in typesetting, a ligature is a joining of two letters, such as æ and fl. **Digraph** = a two-letter combination that represents a single sound, such as *ch*, *ph* and *ae* (as in formulae) and the Old English æ (ash). **Diphthong** = the combination of two vowel sounds to form one sound, as in *gait* and *loud*. **Diaeresis** = the mark ¨ over a vowel, indicating that the vowel is pronounced separately, as in Noël. **Umlaut** = the mark ¨ over a vowel in German which modifies its sound, as in *Mann* and *Männer* (pronounced "man" and "menner"). Ligatures should be avoided and the letters separated (e.g. Caesar, naevus, phoenix, oesophagus), except in quotations of Old English, Icelandic, and so on.
Digraphs should also be avoided wherever possible (as in medieval), except in medical and other scientific terms

(archaeology, foetus, oestrogen). Diaeresis should also be avoided (e.g. naive, not naïve).

light (verb) has the preferred past tense and participle *lit* (not *lighted*), although *lighted* is retained as an adjective (e.g. "lighted candle").

light bulb (= electric lamp), light-fingered, light headed, lighthearted, lighthouse, light meter, lightship, lights out, lightweight, lightwood, light-year.

lightening = making less heavy; **lightning** is what precedes thunder.

light face (type) *See* **weight**.

light-year = the distance light travels in a year (9.46×10^{12} km or 5.88×10^{12} miles); it is thus not a measure of time but one of distance, which should be remembered when it is used figuratively (as in "The Christmas holiday seems light-years away", which is incorrect).

like, likeable, likely, likeness, likelihood, likeliness. *Like* should not be misused for *as*; e.g. "Do as I do" is the correct form of "Do like I do." Neither should *like* be misused for *such as*; e.g. "Mammals like cats and dogs" is correct only if the mammals referred to are attracted to cats and dogs; *such as* should be used in contexts such as this.

-like Longstanding words ending in *-like* have no hyphen (e.g. childlike, godlike, ladylike, workmanlike) unless the letter before the *l* in *-like* makes a hyphen necessary for readability (e.g. jelly-like protoplasm, mouse-like odour, shell-like ear, vice-like grip). More recent or temporary words ending in *-like* are usually hyphenated.

limbo (pl. limbos).

lime, limy (like lime); **Limey** = American slang for *Englishman*.

linchpin is the preferred spelling (not **lynchpin**); **lynch** = to execute someone without proper trial.

line, linable (= can be lined or aligned), linage (= number of lines), lineage = ancestry).

lineament = distinguishing mark, feature; **liniment** = embrocation, thin ointment.

line printer See **printer**.

lingerie is condemned by some as a genteel synonym of *underwear*, but the term also includes night-clothes and excludes men's clothes; it therefore seems to serve a useful purpose.

lingua franca *See* **accent**.

liqueur = strong sweet alcoholic drink; **liquor** = any alcoholic drink.

liquid, liquefy (= turn a gas into a liquid), liquefiable, liquefaction, (= the process of liquefying), liquidize (= turn a watery solid into a liquid or purée), liquidization, liquidate (= to kill, assassinate, wind up a company), liquidator. The word for turning a waterless solid into a liquid is *melt*; for incorporating a solid into a liquid (solvent) is *dissolve*. The potential pitfall among the words derived from *liquid* is failing to distinguish between *liqui-* and *lique-*.

liquorice (not licorice).

lira (pl. lire).

lissom, a little-used adjective meaning *lithe* (which should be used), is the preferred spelling (not *lissome*).

lit = typesetter's and proof-reader's abbreviation of *literal error*, a keyboarding mistake on a proof or printed page usually affecting only one or two characters.

literal = relating to the precise meaning (of words); **littoral** = neighbouring the shore; **literate** = able to read and write; **literary** = to do with literature. *See also* **lit**.

literally should not be used for emphasis and applied to something that cannot be taken literally. The word is particularly inapt when applied to a metaphor (which by definition cannot be taken literally), as in "He took me by surprise and I was literally frozen to the spot."

literato (pl. literati).

literature = the whole corpus of "quality" written works: drama, poetry and prose. The word has been devalued and taken over as part of salesmen's jargon to stand for any printed matter from a single-sheet press release to a thick trade directory (as in "I'll send you some literature about the new machine"), a use to be avoided.

lithe *See* **lissom**.

lithographic printing *See* **printing processes**.

litotes (a singular word) Figure of speech that relies on understatement, usually a way of meaning *yes* by saying *no* to the opposite. E.g.:

"She was not overdressed", "She is no fool"
(meaning she was scantily dressed, she is intelligent). *See also* **irony; meiosis**.

litre has the abbreviation l (no full point).

little-known etc. is hyphenated when adjectival (e.g. "little-known fact", "little-used technique") but unhyphenated when following a verb (e.g. "the artist is little known outside England").

live, liveable, liveable-in.

livelong *See* **lifelong**.

liven up The preferred term is **enliven**.

livid, strictly, = blue-grey, the colour of lead; many authorities regard its use to mean *extremely angry* as colloquial. *See also* **hectic**.

llama *See* **lama**.

llano (pl. llanos) = open plains (steppes) in northern South America; **pampas** = open grassland (savanna) in southern South America.

load has the past tense and participle **loaded**.

loading (or filler), in papermaking, = substance added to pulp to improve the opacity, stability and inking properties of the final paper. Loadings include china clay, calcium carbonate and titanium dioxide, and may make up to 30 per cent of the content of a high-quality paper. Optical brightners are also sometimes included in this category. *See also* **paper**.

loadstone is the preferred spelling (not **lodestone**, although *lodestar* is preferred to *loadstar*).

loaf (noun) (pl. loaves).

loan is a noun, not a verb (the verb is *lend*); one is granted a *loan* by somebody who *lends* one money.

loath/loathe *See* **loth**.

local, locality, localize, localization. **Local** = nearby; **locale** = scene of activity.

locate, location. **Location** = definite position, precisely where something can be found; **locality** = general situation or position of a thing or place, approximately where it can be found. **Locate** should not be used merely to mean *find*.

locomotive and train names should be italicized, with initial capital letters. E.g. locomotives: *King Henry V, Mallard, Rocket*; trains: *Cheltenham Flier, Golden Arrow, Orient Express*.

locum, the common shortening of **locum tenens** (= deputy, especially of a doctor), is a singular word (pl. locums); the full form would require the plural *locum tenentes*. **Locus** (= particular mathematical curve) is also singular (pl. loci).

lodestar is the preferred spelling (not **loadstar**, although *loadstone* is preferred to *lodestone*).

lodge, lodgeable, lodgement, lodging.

logogram = symbol that stands for a whole word or words, often called simply a **logo** in modern advertising and publishing. *See also* **colophon**; **ideograph**; **monogram**.

lone *See* **alone**; **lonely**.

lonely (= isolated, alone) is apparently formed from *alone* through the obsolete word *alonely*; its comparative and superlative are *lonelier* and *loneliest*. **Lonesome** (= solitary) is formed from *lone*, although most British people now regard its secondary meaning of *feeling lonely* as an Americanism. E.g.:

"He was marooned on a lonely island";
"The only tree in sight was a lonesome palm" (British/American);
"He soon became lonesome for his hometown in Kansas" (American).

See also **alone**.

long-ago (adj.), longboat, longbow, long-distance (adj.), long division, long-eared, longhorn, long johns, longhand, long jump, long-legged, long-lived, long-playing, long-range (adj.), longship, long-shore (adj.), longshoreman, long shot, long-sighted(ness), long-standing, long-suffering, long-term (adj.), longways, long-winded.

longitude (not longtitude).

long sight, long-sighted, long-sightedness (medical name *hypermetropia*). Far-sighted(ness) is best reserved to mean *good at anticipation*, and not used as a synonym for long-sighted(ness). *See also* **short sight**.

look over = to inspect, read through; **overlook** = to look over the top of, to look down on (from a higher position), to fail to see. (**Oversee** = supervise).

loose (verb) = to unbind, to undo, to set free; **loosen** = to slacken, to relax. (**Lose** = to mislay, to be unable to find.)

-l- or -ll- Verbs ending in -l preceded by a single vowel double the l before the suffixes -able, -ation, -ed, -er, -ery, -ible, -ing and -or (which begin with a vowel). E.g.:

annul	annulled, annulling
counsel	counselled, counselling, counsellor
distil	distillable, distillation, distilled, distiller, distillery, distilling

(exception *parallel*, paralleled, paralleling).

The l remains single before the suffix -ment. E.g.:

bedevil	bedevilment
enrol	enrolment
fulfil	fulfilment

Most words ending in -ll drop an l before the suffixes -ful, -ly, -ment, -some or other elements that begin with a consonant. E.g.:

all	albeit, almost, already, also, although, altogether, always
frill	frilly (not frill-ly = frillly)
full	fulfil, fully, fulsome
install	instalment
skill	skilful
will	wilful

The l remains double, however, before the suffix -ness. E.g.:

chill	chillness
dull	dullness
ill	illness
shrill	shrillness
still	stillness

See also **suffixes**.

lory = Asian parrot; **lorry** = goods road vehicle, a truck.

lose, losable. Lose inflects *lose – lost – lost*.

loth, an alternative spelling of **loath** (the adjective meaning reluctant, unwilling), prevents possible confusion with **loathe** (the verb meaning to detest, despise, hate).

lots of (= many, much, a great deal) should be avoided; **a lot of** is just acceptable.

lotus (pl. lotuses).

lour (a little-used word meaning to *frown*) is the preferred spelling (not **lower**), which also encourages the correct pronunciation (rhyming with *sour*, not "*low-er*").

love, lovable, love affair, love-bird, love-hate, lovely, love-in-a-mist, love-knot, love-letter, love-lies-bleeding, lovelock, lovelorn, lovers' knot, lovesick, love-song, love story, love token.

low (adj.) = not high, not loud; **lowly** (adj.) = humble, modest. The logical adverb from low is *lowly* (= in a low way), as in "He bowed lowly before her"; the logical adverb from *lowly* is *lowlily*, as in "He bowed lowlily before her." These difficulties can be avoided by using *low* instead of *lowly* (adv.) and *in a lowly manner* (or *humbly*) for *lowlily*. E.g.:

"He bowed low before her";
"He bowed before her in a lowly manner."
(A similar pronunciation problem occurs with godly/godlily, holy/holily, jolly/jollily and ugly/uglily).

low-down, low-lying.

lower *See* **lour.**

lower case = typesetter's and printer's term for small letters as opposed to capital letters or *upper case*. In proof-reading and type mark-up, it is usually abbreviated to l.c.

lowly, lowlier, lowliest, lowliness, lowlily (*see* **low**).

LPG is the abbreviation of liquefied (or liquid) petroleum gas.

lucerne is preferred to **alfalfa** for the fodder crop.

luggage *See* **baggage**.

lumbar = to do with the loins, the lower back (*lumbago* = pain in the loins); **lumber** = disused furniture, useless items, an Americanism for timber.

lunch = meal eaten about mid-day, a portable snack (e.g. "Take a packed lunch with you"); **luncheon** = formal lunch, usually with invited guests and possibly speakers (e.g. "a literary luncheon"); **brunch** = Americanism for a mid-morning meal that combines breakfast and lunch. *See also* **dinner**.

lunge, lunging.

lure *See* **allure**.

luxuriant = growing profusely or abundantly; **luxurious** = extravagant, rich. **Luxury** should be reserved as a noun, and not used as an adjective to mean *expensive* (as in "a luxury car").

lynch *See* **linchpin**.

lynx (pl. lynxes).

M

m is the abbreviation of metre.

macadam (even though it was named after John McAdam), or tarmacadam; *Tarmac* is a trade name.

machine finished (MF) = papermaking term for paper with a smooth surface produced by calendering (using polished rollers) on both sides. *See also* **paper**.

machine glazed (MG) = papermaking term for paper with a highly smooth surface, usually only on one side of the sheet. *See also* **paper**.

mackintosh (even though its inventor was Charles Macintosh, without a *k*).

macramé is the preferred spelling (not **macrami**).

mad = insane (and is an imprecise term now avoided by both the legal and medical professions). Colloquially *mad* can mean *angry* (e.g. "She makes me mad") or *impractical* (e.g. "A mad scheme"). The former colloquialism should be avoided in formal writing; the latter should be changed for another, more acceptable synonym (such as *illogical* or the more colourful *crackpot* or even *hare-brained*). **Mental** is a pejorative and slang term for describing somebody who is mentally ill (or somebody who is not!).

Madam = formal English form of address to a lady or other member of the nobility, abbreviated to **Ma'am** when addressing royalty; *Madame* (italics) = French form of address to a married woman; **madam** (no initial capital letter) = woman in charge of a brothel.

maestro has the preferred plural maestros (not maestri).

magic (adj.) = to do with magic; **magical** = entertaining, apparently caused by magic. E.g.:

"The pantomime fairy waved her magic wand."
"It was a magical moment: the fairy seemed to appear from nowhere."

magisterial = to do with a magistrate, authoritative, dictatorial; **magistral** = to do with a master.

magma (pl. magmata).

magnet, magnetic, magnetism, magnetize, magnetization.

magneto (pl. magnetos).

magniloquence is a lofty expression for *a lofty expression*, and often no more than a euphemism for **boasting**.

maharaja is the preferred spelling (not **maharajah**).

maize is the preferred term for the crop called **corn** in America; in English, *corn* is a general name for any cereal crop.

majority, like **major part**, should be avoided when it means merely most. *Majority* should be reserved for contexts in which there is a significant difference between a majority and a minority (and *major part* should be reserved for a contrast with *minor part*).

majuscule *See* **minuscule.**

make inflects *make – made – made.*

make-believe (noun), make believe (verb), makeready (noun), makeshift, make-up (noun), makeweight.

mako (pl. makos).

malapropism *See* **non-standard English.**

Malawi The derived adjective and noun is **Malawian.**

Malay words, derived from languages spoken today in Malaysia, Singapore and parts of Indonesia, were borrowed by and then assimilated into English during early colonial times. Today's survivors include:

amok	catechu	kapok
bamboo	cockatoo	orang-utan
batik	compound (enclosure)	paddy (rice)
cachou	gingham	sago
caddy (tea)	going	sarong
cassowary		

Some share origins with words in the Tamil language (*see* **Indian words**).

mal de mer is an old-fashioned euphemism for seasickness, which should be used.

male describes the sex of an organism; **masculine** describes the characteristics of a male (the "opposites" are *female* and *feminine*). *Male* is a poor synonym for *boy* or *man*.

malfunction *See* **dysfunction**.

Mali The derived adjective and noun is *Malian*.

malign (adj.) = injurious, evil (e.g. "malign influence"); **malignant** = actuated by great hatred, tending to go from bad to worse, cancerous (e.g. "malignant tumour"), Cavalier (i.e. pro-Charles I).

malnutrition has been condemned as officialese for "(virtual) **starvation**". The two words now have subtly different meanings. Someone with nothing to eat eventually dies of *starvation*; someone given the wrong type of food (such as a child fed only on polished rice) may suffer from *malnutrition* which, admittedly, can also end in death. Similarly **malnourished** = lacking in some essential dietary factor(s); **undernourished** = lacking enough food.

Malta The derived adjective and noun is *Maltese*.

mamba = poisonous African snake; **mambo** = lively Latin-American dance (or its music).

man has no initial capital letter in such expressions as Neanderthal man, Cro-Magnon man; *Man* should be capitalized when it is used as a generic term for the human race. *See also* **mankind**.

manage, manageable, management.

manakin = small Central American bird; **manikin** = little man, puppet, artist's jointed model; **mannequin** = person who models clothes.

mañana (with tilde).

mandrel = spindle, former on which to shape something; **mandrill** = large baboon.

manège = riding-school; **ménage** = household; both of these French forms should be avoided.

mango (pl. mangoes).

mangold is the usual spelling for the root vegetable, not **mangel**, although the full name is more often **mangel-wurzel** (not *mangold-wurzel*).

maniacal = like a maniac or madman; **manic** = exhibiting or provoking mania, a severe mental disorder characterized by euphoria and hyperactivity (often involving violence) out of proportion to the prevailing circumstances; the word should not be used just of any lively or happy mood, nor to describe someone who is merely unresponsible to reasoned argument. Similarly **mania** should not be applied to mere enthusiasm (e.g. "He has a mania for football") or unconventional behaviour. **Maniac** = a psychotic person exhibiting mania as a chief symptom, not just someone who behaves irresponsibly (as in "He drives like a maniac"). With all these words, the adoption of a scientific term for ordinary or figurative use has lost impact through overexposure. *See also* **paranoia**; **schizophrenic**.

manifesto (pl. manifestos).

mankind (= human race) has the pronoun *it*; **man** or **Man** (generically) has the pronoun *he*. The use of the term **humankind** overcomes sexist objections to *mankind*. *See also* **gender**; **human**.

mannish is properly applied to a woman who is unwomanly; it is not a synonym of **masculine** (*see* **male**). The corresponding term applied to men is *effeminate*.

manoeuvre, manoeuvred, manoeuvring, manoeuvrable, manoeuvrability.

manservant (pl. menservants).

manslaughter *See* **homicide**.

mantel = shelf over a fireplace; **mantle** = cloak.

manuscript, in publishing, = an author's original text or an edited version of it; it is now nearly always in the form of a *typescript* or computer *print-out*, contrary to the original meaning of manuscript (= something written by hand). The abbreviation of manuscript is MS (pl. MSS). *See also* **manuscript preparation**.

manuscript preparation All material for publication (i.e. typesetting) should be submitted in typescript form, using either a typewriter or a (legible) computer printer. Typewriting should have double-line spacing and be on white paper of "bond" quality, with generous margins left and right. A computer printer using continuous stationery should not be allowed to print close to or across the horizontal perforations. The whole manuscript should have its pages numbered consecutively. A page or pages added later should be numbered 25a, 25b, and so on (for example). If a page is deleted (say page 25), the previous remaining page should be numbered 24–25. Any hand-written amendments should be made legibly, with clear indications of their positions in the text.
A manuscript sent through the post should be clearly and correctly addressed, and securely packed. It is a sensible precaution – and a requirement in most editorial offices – to make and keep a copy of

anything sent by ordinary post; it is a tragedy when the only material result of several weeks or even years of work ends up as separate sheets of paper on the floor of the Dead-Letter Office. *See also* **corrections**.

manyfold is an adverb, and should not be used as an alternative to the adjective **manifold**. E.g.:

"Because of errors, the time taken was increased manyfold."
"Errors resulted in a manifold increase in the time taken."

Maori (pl. Maoris).

mare (pronounced "*mar-ay*"), a large flat area or "sea" on the Moon, has the plural **maria**.

marginal = to do with or written in the margin (of a page); it should not be used to mean **small**. E.g. "the cost of the extras was marginal" should be "...was small"); "marginal improvement" is better put as "slight improvement".

marijuana is the preferred spelling (not **marihuana**).

market, marketed, marketing.

marriage, marriageable.

marshal (not marshall), marshalled, marshaller, marshalling; the noun is also *marshal*.

mart is archaic for **market**, which should be used, although it survives in such expressions as "used car mart" (= second-hand car market).

marten = weasel-like animal; **martin** = swallow-like bird.

marvel, marvelled, marvelling, marvellous.

mask = covering for the face; **masque** = a masked ball (masquerade), old form of drama involving masked performers.

massif = group of neighbouring mountains; **massive** = bulky, solid, heavy, having a great mass. *Massive* should not be used to mean merely *large* or *huge*. E.g.:
"Stonehenge is built of massive blocks of stone" (correct);
"Stonehenge attracts a massive crowd of people each day" (incorrect).

master-class, master-mind, master of ceremonies, master-key, masterpiece, master-stroke, master switch, master-work.

masterful = imperious, high-handed; **masterly** = with the skill of a master.

mate, matey (preferred to maty), matily.

maté (tea).

mater *See* **pater**.

material, materially, materialize, materialization. **Material** (noun) = something from which things can be made, fabric; **material** (adj.) = to do with matter or a necessary factor in reasoning; *matériel* = paraphernalia of an army. **Materialize** = to become visible or real (from something insubstantial), as in "Gradually a human form materialized out of the mist"; the word should not be used to mean merely *happen* or *come about*.

mathematical text All mathematical symbols and formulae for publication should be typed or written in a clear and unambiguous way so that the typesetter is in no doubt what is required; for example, the numeral "one" should be distinguished from the letter "l", and zero from capital "O", if the typewriter fails to do so.
Greek letters (and other "foreign" characters and special symbols) should be written carefully and if necessary identified by name in the margin (*see* **Greek alphabet**). Horizontal fractions ($\frac{1}{2}$) should be used in preference to split fractions ($1/2$) in mathematical texts, but few type founts contain all fractions (*see* **fractions**).
In symbols, formulae and equations used in mathematical and

scientific works, variable quantities should be italicized and constant quantities set in a roman typeface. E.g.:

$$y = ax^2 + bx + c; \qquad E = mc^2; \qquad t = \pi\sqrt{\dfrac{l}{g}} \quad \text{or} \quad t = 2\pi(l/g)^{\frac{1}{2}}$$

Decimal points should be set on the line; e.g. 0.5, not 0·5. *See also* **figures**.

matinée (with accent), despite being French for a morning's worth, is English for an afternoon performance (of a concert, film, play etc.).

matrass = long-necked flask (obsolete); **mattress** = large, stuffed bag for sleeping on, large mat used in foundations of roads and buildings.

matrix (pl. matrices).

matt is preferred to *mat* or *matte* for the word meaning dull, unpolished; **matte** = (impure) product of the first smelting stage in metal extraction from an ore.

Mauritania The derived adjective and noun is *Mauritanian*.

Mauritius The derived adjective and noun is *Mauritian*.

maxilla (pl. maxillae).

maximum (pl. maxima), maximize, maximization.

may *See* **can**.

maybe (adv.) = perhaps (e.g. "Maybe she will come"); **may be** (two words) is a verb used in such constructions as "She may be late", "It may be that she will not come."

mayday (one word) = international distress signal (from French *m'aidez*).

mayonnaise

mb is the abbreviation of millibar.

Mc Proper names beginning with *Mc* should be alphabetized (and indexed) as though they begin with *Mac*.

mead = alcoholic drink made by fermenting honey, or a meadow (archaic); **meed** = reward (even more archaic).

mean (verb) inflects *mean – meant – meant*. For **mean** (noun), *see* **average**.

meaningful, as in "We have a meaningful relationship", is a vogue word to be avoided. *See* **vogue words**.

means (noun) = method of course of action; singular and plural are spelled the same.

meantime/meanwhile (each one word).

measles is a singular word; "cases of measles" achieves a plural construction.

measure, measurement, measurable. **Measure** = typesetter's and printer's term for the length of a line of text (and hence the width of a column). It is generally specified in *picas* (*see* **point**), although *ems* are also sometimes used (*see* **em**).

measurements *See* **figures; units**.

meat-eater (carnivore).

meatus (pl. meatuses).

mechanical = printer's jargon for camera-ready copy (CRC) – that is, an accurate paste-up of reproduction quality type matter and possibly (line) illustrations ready for film and plate-making.

mechanical paper = paper manufactured from mechanical pulp. *See* **mechanical pulp; paper**.

mechanical pulp = cellulose fibres for papermaking broken down from the raw material (such as wood) by grinding, rather than by a chemical process. As a result, it contains components of the wood other than cellulose (such as lignin) and is unsuitable for high-quality papers. *See also* **chemical pulp**; **paper**.

median *See* **average**.

mediate, mediator (= someone who, without authority, tries to bring together conflicting parties to resolve a dispute). *See also* **arbitrate**.

medieval (not mediaeval).

mediocre = neither good nor bad, of intermediate quality; the word should not be used to mean definitely *poor* or *bad*.

medium (spiritualist) has the plural *mediums*; a communications medium has the plural *media*. **Media** (pl. mediae) is also a technical term in phonetics and botany.

medium-sized is preferred to **medium-size** as the adjective; e.g. "A medium-sized dog", but "A dog of medium size".

meet is archaic for **fitting** or **seemly** (as in "it is meet so to do"); either of the modern alternatives should be used.

meet (verb) inflects *meet – met – met*. **Meet** a person or a date, but **meet** *with* disaster, approval and so on. The use of the latter to mean the former is an Americanism.

mega is the prefix for a million times ($\times 10^6$), as in *megawatt* (*see* **units**).

meiosis, in biology, = cell division that leads to the formation of gametes (sex cells); **mitosis** = cell division that forms two identical new (daughter) cells, the normal multiplication process.

meiosis, in writing, = figure of speech involving understatement, capable of misinterpretation unless used carefully. It is common in speech: E.g.:

"I can't say I like the design"

can mean "I think the design is inappropriate/poor/unacceptable." *See also* **litotes**.

mélange = mixture; the French form should be avoided.

mêlée, defined by Chambers as "a fight in which the combatants are mingled together", has no short English synonym and so the French form lives on.

melliferous = yielding honey; **mellifluous** = sweet-sounding (voice).

melt has the past tense and participle **melted**, although **molten** is retained for certain adjectival uses (e.g. *molten* lava, metal or rock but *melted* butter, ice or wax).

memento (pl. mementos).

memorandum (pl. memorandums).

memory, memorable, memorize.

mendacity = a lie (adj. *mendacious*); **mendicity** = begging (adj. and noun *mendicant*).

meniscus (pl. menisci).

-ment *See* **suffixes**.

mental *See* **mad**.

menu (pl. menus).

meretricious = gaudy, insincere, suitable for a whore; **meritorious** = deserving honour, praise or reward.

merino (pl. merinos).

merry-go-round (hyphens).

mesmerize

mestizo (pl. mestizos).

metal, metalled, metalling, metallurgy, metallurgist, metallize.
  Metal = usually shiny, dense, conducting elementary substance, or
  a mixture of such substances (an alloy); **mettle** = human spirit or
  courage (as in the cliché "put on one's mettle"). The latter is an
  aberrant, but accepted, spelling of the former.

metamorphosis, metamorphose.

metaphor = the most common figure of speech, involving the
  transfer of meaning of a word or words (which cannot then be taken
  literally). E.g.:

"The kettle is boiling" (the *water* boils, not the *kettle*);
"They were given a warm reception" (in which *warm* =
enthusiastic);
"They were given a lukewarm reception" (in which *lukewarm* =
unenthusiastic).

  Many metaphors are used unconsciously, and repeated
metaphorical use of a particular word soon becomes one of its
figurative uses (such as *warm* and *lukewarm* in the previous
examples). New or unfamiliar metaphors should generally be
avoided in text intended for translation into another language.
"Dead" metaphors, whose imagery belonged to former times and
should also be avoided (e.g. "at half-cock", "to bite the bullet",
"this sceptered isle"), should also be avoided. Another potential
pitfall is the mixed metaphor, in which two or more types of
inconsistent imagery are juxtaposed, often to ludicrous effect (e.g.
"We must grasp the nettle, put our shoulders to the wheel, and
leave no stone unturned"). *See also* **cliché; inseparable pairs.**

metastasis (pl. metastases).

meter = instrument/apparatus that measures; **metre** = basic unit of
  length in the SI (metric) system of units, the "rhythm" of poetry or
  music.

meticulous = overcareful, pernickety, fussy over trifles. It should not be used to mean merely *careful* or *scrupulous*.

métier = skilled ability or accomplishment (similar to *forte*), a calling; the French word should be avoided.

metonymy Figure of speech in which an object is made to stand for a different (associated but unnamed) object, concept or person. Examples used in courts of law include *bench* (= the judiciary), *brief* (= lawyer, defence counsel), *crown* (= the State), *silk* (= Queen's Counsel). The device differs from euphemism (*see* **non-standard English**), used merely to avoid the precise expression, or slang (such as *doing time, doing bird, doing porridge, inside, in jug, in stir* for "serving a prison sentence"). *See also* **slang; synecdoche**.

metric units *See* **units**.

mews (noun) has the same spelling in the singular and plural.

mg is the abbreviation of milligram(s).

MICR = acronym for *m*agnetic *i*nk *c*haracter *r*ecognition, a method by which printed letters and numbers can be "read" by a scanner and inputted to a computer. The characters have a form that can be read by a human being and are printed in an ink containing magnetic oxides that can be detected by the scanner's reading head. *See also* **E 13 B**.

micro- is the metric prefix for a millionth ($\times 10^{-6}$), as in *microfarad* (*see* **units**).

micron = unit of length equal to a millionth (10^{-6}) of a metre (abbreviation μ), also called a *micrometre*. *See also* **units**.

micro-organism is the general term for any organism that is too small to be seen with the naked eye. Chief of these are **bacteria**, which can be seen with the aid of an optical (light) microscope, and **viruses**, which can be made visible only by using an electron microscope. Also included are other microscopic organisms such as amoebas, rickettsia, various protozoa and minute fungi (moulds).

Disease-causing micro-organisms are known as *pathogens* or, in everyday language, *germs*; the term *microbe* is now seldom used.

mid should not be used for **amid**, which is itself archaic for **among** (the preferred term). **Mid-** is retained as a prefix meaning **middle**, taking a hyphen when attached to a word beginning with a capital letter; e.g. mid-Atlantic, mid-July, mid-Victorian. With most other roots, the hyphen is retained only as an aid to pronunciation; e.g. mid-air, midbrain, midday, mid-leg, midnight, mid-off, mid-on, mid-season, midships (and amidships), midshipman, midstream, midsummer, midway, mid-week, Midwest (of USA), mid-wicket, mid-winter. *See also* **midst**.

middle *See* **centre**.

Middle Ages (with initial capital letters).

midst and **in the midst of** are archaic for **among**, which is preferred.

migrant/migrate *See* **emigrant**.

mil = one-thousandth of an inch, or it stands for a millilitre. Since the former is a linear measure and the latter a liquid volume, there should be little probability of confusion; also **ml** is the preferred abbreviation of millilitre.

mile, mileage. Mile(s) should not be abbreviated; miles per hour can be abbreviated to mph. 1 mile = 1,760 yards (= 1.6093 km); 1 nautical mile (British) = 2,026.7 yards (= 1.8532 km); 1 nautical mile (international) = 2,025.4 yards (= 1.852 km). *See also* **knot**; **units**.

milieu = environment; the French term should be avoided.

militate (against) = to act as a powerful influence; **mitigate** = to lessen the intensity or severity of something. E.g.:

"His untidiness militated against his getting the job"
"His paralysis mitigated the untidiness of his appearance."

millennium (pl. millennia).

milli- is the metric prefix for a thousandth ($\times 10^{-3}$), as in *milligram* (*see* **units**).

milliard = 1,000 million, increasingly being called a **billion** (which *see*).

million should be spelled out in all numbers; e.g. "3 million cars", "12 million people", "37.5 million miles" and "£7 million". *See also* **billion**.

mimic, mimicked, mimicking.

min is the abbreviation of minute(s).

mina (= Asian bird) is the preferred spelling (not **myna** or **mynah**).

mineralogy (not -ology).

minimum (pl. minima), minimize. *See also* **diminish**.

minion = obsolete name for 7-point type. For others, *see* **type sizes**.

minority *See* **majority**.

minus should be confined to mathematical or scientific expressions, and not used as a synonym of *less* or *without* (e.g. "They all came, minus George" and "The car arrived minus its windscreen" are incorrect).

minuscule (not miniscule) = extremely small; its opposite **majuscule**, which should be used only of large handwriting, is rare.

misappropriate *See* **expropriate**.

mischief, mischievous (not mischievious).

miserable = very unhappy, wretched, feeling misery; the word should not be used as a general pejorative adjective. E.g.:

"The book had miserable sales" (*miserable* should be poor or disappointing);
"They gave us a miserable amount to eat" (*miserable* should be little or inadequate).

misogamy = hatred of marriage; **misogyny** = hatred of women; **misanthropy** = hatred of mankind.

misshape(n), misspell, misspend, misspent, misstate.

misremember *See* **disremember**.

misrepair *See* **disrepair**.

mistake, mistakable.

mistaken = in error, wrong; **misunderstood** = failed to understand. E.g.:

"I gave her directions but I was mistaken and sent her the wrong way";
"I gave her directions but she misunderstood and went the wrong way".

mitigate *See* **militate**.

mitre (verb), mitred, mitring.

mix, mixable; but note *immiscible* = (and is preferred to) unmixable. **Mix** is a well-known verb (meaning to combine thoroughly, intermingle), with **mix up** meaning to confuse. The usual noun forms are **mixture** (= the product of mixing) and **mix-up** (a confusion). A lesser-known word rapidly gaining currency is the noun **mix**, which often replaces its synonym *mixture* (e.g. "A strange mix of old and new").

ml is the abbreviation of millilitre(s).

mm is the abbreviation of millimetre(s).

mnemonic = memory aid. *See* **pneumatic**.

moat = defensive ditch full of water; **mote** = speck (of dust); **motte** = mound on which a castle (bailey) is built.

mobile, mobilize, mobilization. **Mobile** (adj.) = capable of moving (under its own power); **movable** = capable of being moved (by some external agency). Thus a mobile crane may be used to lift a movable container. **Immobile** = still, stationary, not moving (although capable of movement); **immovable** = incapable of being moved. E.g.:

"The young animal remained immobile, despite the close approach of the children."
"The heavy girder remained immovable, despite every attempt to lift it."

mode *See* **average**.

model, modelled, modeller, modelling.

modern, modernize, modernization.

modest should not be misused for **moderate**. *Modest* = bashful, retiring, unassuming, unobtrusive; *moderate* = unextreme, temperate, middling (of size), e.g. "He lived in a modest house of moderate size".

modicum is archaic for **small amount**; the Latin term should be avoided.

modish words *See* **vogue words**.

modus operandi (italics) = method of working; the Latin term should be avoided in ordinary writing.

modus vivendi (italics) = a truce before the parties settle their dispute; it does not mean *way of life* (even if the original Latin did), and should be avoided.

Mohamet etc. *See* **Muhammed**.

Mohammedanism The preferred term is **Islam** (which *see*).

moire = watered silk. The characteristic pattern of moire fabric (sometimes seen in printing when a halftone original is reproduced by the halftone process) is **moiré** (with an accent), which is also the spelling of the adjective. *See also* **halftone**.

molten *See* **melt**.

moment *See* **instant**.

momentary = occupying a moment; **momentous** = of great consequence. E.g.:

"The error revealed a momentary lapse in concentration."
"Pressing on proved to be a momentous decision."

momentum (pl. momenta).

money has the plural **moneys** (not *monies*, which would be the plural of *mony*). The preferred style for British currency is £10.75, £1,023.05 or 25p (no full point).

mongolism should be avoided; use instead Down's Syndrome or trisomy 21.

mongoose (pl. mongooses).

monogram = set of initials worked into a design; **monograph** = an article written about a single subject. *See also* **ideograph**; **logogram**.

mono- or **uni-** *See* **numerical prefixes**.

monster, monstrous.

Moon usually has a capital letter when referring to the Earth's natural satellite, especially in scientific contexts, but no capital in other uses. E.g.:

"The gravitational attraction of the Moon affects tides on Earth"; "Titan is one of the moons of Jupiter".

moose (pl. moose). *See also* **elk**.

moped (verb) = past tense and participle of verb *to mope*; **moped** (noun) = motorized bicycle.

moral, moralize. **Moral** = pertaining to correct behaviour; **morale** = state of mind regarding confidence or courage.

moratorium (pl. moratoriums).

mordant (adj.) = biting, caustic; **mordant** (noun) = substance for fixing dye into cloth; **mordent** = musical ornament.

more should not be misused for **other**; e.g. "he listed beer, cider, lager and many more examples" should be ". . . many other examples".

more/most *See* **comparative and superlative**.

more or less (no hyphens).

mores (= customs, conventions) is a plural word.

more than is preferred to **over** in references to number; "He wrote more than a hundred articles" not ". . . over a hundred articles". *See also* **above**.

morgue The preferred term is **mortuary**.

moribund = on the point of death; it does not mean merely *ailing, declining* or *dormant* (as in "The ship-building industry remained in a moribund state during the early 1980s").

Morocco The derived adjective and noun is *Moroccan*.

mortgage, mortgager (who grants a mortgage), mortgagee (who gets a mortgage), but mortgagor in law.

mortise, mortising. Note the noun is also *mortise* (not *mortice*).

mortuary is preferred to **morgue** for a building in which dead bodies are (temporarily) housed.

Moslem The preferred spelling is **Muslim** (*see also* **Islam**).

mosquito (pl. mosquitoes).

most is absolute; it should not be confused with **the most** (which is relative). E.g.:

"What I should most like to eat is kippers"
"Which do you like the most – kippers, bloaters or rollmops?"
Note that "Which do you like the more – kippers or bloaters?"
would be correct for a choice between two, but is stilted (better as
"Which do you prefer – kippers or bloaters?"

motif = recurring theme; **motive** = something that stimulates behaviour or action; **motivate** = provide with a motive, spur into action; **motivation** = providing with an incentive, the act of motivating.

motivation *See* **incentive; vogue words.**

motor, motorboat, motor bus, motor car, motor coach, motorize, motor-launch, motorcycle, motor scooter, motor torpedo boat (MTB), motor vehicle, motorway.

motorbike is colloquial for **motorcycle**, and should be avoided in formal writing.

motorway (= high-speed dual carriageway road restricted to certain vehicles/drivers) has various names outside Britain; e.g. autobahn (Germany), autopista (Spain), autoroute (France), autostrada (Italy), expressway/freeway (United States). When the foreign names are used in English, they should not be italicized and should be given normal English plurals in -*s* (e.g. autostradas, not *autostrade*).

motto (pl. mottoes).

mouse, mousy.

mouth is the form of the noun, and the verb (not *mouthe*).

move, movable (but moveable in law).

mow has the past tense and participle *mowed*, although *mown* is retained as an adjective (e.g. "the smell of mown grass").

Mozambique The derived adjective and noun is *Mozambican*.

mph is the abbreviation of miles per hour. But note **km/h**.

ms is the abbreviation of millisecond(s); **MS** is the abbreviation of manuscript (pl. MSS).

mucus (noun) = slimy fluid; **mucous** (adj.) = pertaining to mucus.

muffin *See* **crumpet**.

Muhammed is the preferred spelling for the name of the founder of **Islam** (which *see*).

mulatto (pl. mulattos).

multi- Compounds with *multi-* as a prefix have no hyphen unless the root word begins with *i* (e.g. multi-industrial). The *i* is sometimes omitted when the root word begins with *a* (e.g. multangular). *See also* **numerical prefixes**.

mumps is a singular word; "cases of mumps" achieves a plural construction.

murder *See* **homicide**.

musical works Subject titles should be typeset in italics; e.g. Gounod's *Faust*, Wagner's *Die Meistersinger*, Parry's *Judith*. But "New World" Symphony, "Eroica" Symphony, Beethoven's Choral Symphony, Ninth Symphony should be set in roman face. Opus 4, no. 2 or op. 4, no. 2 should be typeset thus.

Technical names of periods or styles should not have an initial capital letter; e.g. organum, descant, polyphony.

Names of instruments and organ stops should be in roman; e.g. cor anglais, cornet-à-piston, timpani, diapason, vox humana.

The terms leitmotif and motif should also be typeset in roman.

Muslim is the preferred spelling for the followers of **Islam** (which *see*).

must, as a noun meaning a necessity, essential or something that should not be missed (e.g. as in "Keeping to the schedule is a must" or "Do not miss the Turner exhibition at the Tate Gallery – it is a must") seems to be less in vogue than it once was, but nevertheless is probably best avoided in formal writing. **Must** is acceptable as a term for grape juice or new wine.

mutate, mutation, mutable (not mutatable).

mutual = shared both ways between two (or possibly more) – i.e. involving a two-way exchange; if something is possessed by both parties it is **common** to them. E.g.:

"The opponents' mutual hatred"
"The opponents' common belief in pacifism".

myna/mynah The preferred spelling for the Asian bird is **mina**.

mysterious = difficult to understand, secret, full of mystery;
mystical = beyond human understanding, symbolic in a spiritual or religious sense, to do with mysticism.

myth *See* **fable**.

N

naevus (pl. naevi).

naive, naivety (preferred to naïve, naïvety, *naïveté*).

name, nameable.

named effects and laws Scientific laws and principles, named effects, biological structures and disorders named after people, and so on should have an initial capital for the person but not the law. E.g.:

> Archimedes' principle
> Avogadro's hypothesis
> Boyle's law
> Charles' law (not Charles's law)
> Meckel's ganglion
> Ménière's syndrome
> Mossbauer effect
> Newton's law of motion
> von Graefe's sign
> von Recklinghausen's disease
> But the third law of thermodynamics
> Newton's second law of motion

See also **personal names**.

names *See* **aircraft names; astronomical terms; capitalization** (proper names, trade names); **car names; locomotive and train names; personal names; ships' names; space rockets and missiles; trade names** and the preceding entry.

nano- is the metric prefix for a thousand-millionth ($\times 10^{-9}$), as in *nanosecond*. (*See* **units**).

napkin is preferred to **serviette** for the square of cloth or absorbent paper used for wiping the fingers at meals, thus being consistent with the *napkin-ring* that sometimes holds it. *See also* **nappy**.

nappy is now preferred to **napkin** for the baby's garment.

narcissus (pl. narcissi).

nationalize, nationalization; note also *denationalize* (= "privatize" in the 1980s) and *renationalize*. **Nationalize** = put a company or undertaking under government ownership and management (such as, at the time of writing, the railways, coal and steel industries in Britain); **naturalize** = make an immigrant a citizen of the adopted country, giving him or her a new nationality.

native(s) Offence can be given by referring to aboriginal or indigenous peoples as natives (say *local people* or somesuch). *See also* **primitive**.

naturalism = action or system based on natural phenomena; **naturism** = nature-worship, nudism.

naturalize, naturalization. *See* **nationalize**.

naught is archaic for **nothing** (as in the cliché "come to naught"), and *nothing* should be used; **nought** = zero; **ought** = should (e.g. "You ought to know better than put *ought* for *nought*"). *See also* **aught**.

nausea = feeling of sickness; **nauseous** = causing one to feel sick; **nauseated** = made to feel sick. A disgusting smell may be nauseous, when the smeller is then nauseated. *See also* **ill/illness**.

nautical mile *See* **knot; mile**.

nautilus has the preferred plural nautiluses (not *nautili*).

N.B. is the abbreviation of *nota bene* (note well).

nearby is an adjective (e.g. "I hailed a nearby taxi"); **near by** is an adverb (e.g. "The taxi passed near by"), although the one-word form of the adverb is gaining ground.

nebula (pl. nebulae).

nectar, nectareous (= to do with nectar, preferred to the many alternatives), nectiferous (= producing nectar).

née

ne'er-do-well

negative prefixes Common prefixes meaning *not* include *a-*, *an-*, *il-*, *im-*, *in-*, *ir-*, *non-* and *un-*, to which may be added *dis-* in some of its uses. Originally *il-*, *im-*, *in-* and *ir-* were assigned to words of Latin origin, whereas *un-* was reserved for "English" words, a category that includes words that have been made English by a suffix such as *-able* (but not *-ible*), *-ed* and *-ing*. E.g.:

illegal	unlawful
illegible	unreadable
immodest	unashamed
impractical	unworkable
inaction	unactionable
indecisive	undecided
indigestion	undigested
irrational	unreasonable
irresolution	unresolved
irrespective	unrespected

Often two negative forms are equally acceptable (e.g. irreconcilable and unreconcilable), although sometimes they have different meanings. E.g.:

immaterial (= irrelevant)   unmaterial (= having no substance)
immoral (= lacking morals) unmoral (= not concerning morality)

In a similar way, *a-* or *an-* is (or was) regarded as a prefix for words of Greek origin, whereas *non-* is an English prefix. E.g.:

anaemia	nonconformist
anaesthetic	non-resident
analgesic	nonsense
asepsis	non-starter

Again different meanings can result; e.g. asexual (= biologically sexless) and nonsexual (= lacking sexual implications).
The prefix *dis-* can act as a negative prefix (e.g. disabled, disappear,

disorientated, dissatisfy), even if the original root no longer exists (e.g. the opposites of disappointed, disgruntled and dishevelled are not "appointed", "gruntled" and "hevelled"). *Dis-* can also form words with a different meaning from the corresponding *un-* version. E.g.:

disarmed (= having had weapons taken away)	unarmed (= not carrying weapons this time)
disinterested (= impartial)	uninterested (= not interested)
dismounted (= climbed down)	unmounted (= not in/on a mount)

A similar prefix in medical terms is *dys-*, as in dysfunction (compare with malfunction), dyslexia, dystrophy, and so on.

neglect, negligible.

negligee (= woman's flimsy dressing-gown) is preferred to **négligé**.

Negrillo (pl. Negrilloes).

Negrito (pl. Negritos).

Negro (pl. Negroes). *See* **black**.

neither is restricted to two things and is followed by *nor* (not *or*). *See* **either**.

neo-Gothic, neo-Platonism etc. (but neoclassical).

neologism = a new word. There are three main types: *borrowings*, that is words adopted from foreign languages (*see* **foreign words and phrases**); newly coined words, usually made up from existing word elements (e.g. *gasohol, quadraphonic*) or by analogy with an existing word (e.g. *grand-parental*); and *nonce-words*, made up (initially) for use on one occasion (such as Lewis Carroll's *chortle, galumph* and *jabberwocky*) and often then abandoned, such as some of the inventions of advertising agencies (e.g. "Have you Macleaned your teeth today?"). Some authorities also include among neologisms words that have fallen into disuse but are reintroduced with new meanings (e.g. *hospice*) and even current words ascribed new meanings (e.g. *aerobics*). Early in their careers, newly-coined words are sometimes distinguished by quotation marks (e.g. "unisex" haircut). Apart from the ephemeral nonce-words, neologisms serve a useful purpose if they fill a gap in the vocabulary and so enrich the language. Less justifiable are introductions that duplicate – and sometimes displace – perfectly good existing words. Whether they do so depends on usage; as in so many aspects of language development, time is the tester. *See also* **vogue words**.

Nepal The derived adjective and noun is *Nepalese* (preferred to *Nepali*).

net (free from deduction) is the preferred spelling of **nett**.

nether is archaic for **lower** (as in the cliché "nether regions"); *lower* should be used.

Netherlands should be used for the country (not **Holland**).

networking = technique in computers in which several terminals are linked to one central computer so that each can access or input data simultaneously.

neuron (nerve cell), not *neurone*.

neurotic used properly describes someone suffering from a type of mental disorder classified as a **neurosis** (pl. neuroses). As a synonym for *anxious, obsessive* or plain *nervous* it is grossly overworked (as in "There's no need to get neurotic about it"), and should be avoided in non-medical contexts. *See also* **manic**; **paranoia**.

neutral, neutralize, neutralization.

névé

never = not ever; e.g. "I never have a good seat at the theatre." It should not be used as an intensified negative when referring to a single occasion; e.g. "I never saw the beginning of last night's play" is incorrect (say "I did not see the beginning . . ."). E.g.:

"Did you ever steal apples as a child?" "I never did." (correct); "Did you spill that ink?" "I never did" (incorrect).

never-ending, never-failing, nevermore, nevertheless.

new *See* **innovative**; **newfangled**; **novel**.

new-blown, new-born, newcomer, newfangled, new-found, new-laid, New Moon, New World, New Year, New Year's Day.

newborn *See* **baby**.

newfangled (one word) = newly introduced but to no good purpose; it is thus pejorative and should not be used for the neutral **new**.

news is a singular word; "several items of news" achieves a plural construction.

news agency (such as AP, which supplies news), newsagent(s) (which sell newspapers), newsboy, news-cast(er), newsletter, newsmonger, newsprint, news-reader, newsreel, news-stand, News Theatre, newsvendor, newsworthy.

newsprint = insubstantial type of paper made entirely from mechanical wood pulp. *See* **mechanical pulp**; **paper**.

next of kin *See* **kin**.

nexus (pl. nexuses).

nice is so overused to mean *agreeable, pleasant* (not its original meaning) that the word is best avoided in this sense. "The skater's execution of the turn displayed a nice sense of timing" is correct usage (**nice** = exact, precise, accurate).

nicknames, unless well known or obvious, are usually identified by inverted commas (e.g. Hal "Scarface" Wilson, "Babyface" Nelson).

nigh = near, nearly or near to; **well-nigh** = nearly, almost. Both (particularly the former) have an archaic ring, and are best avoided.

night-blind(ness), night-cap, night-clothes, night-club, night-dress, nightfall, night-gown, nightjar, night-life, nightlight, night-long, nightmare, nightmarish, night nurse, night-school, nightshade, night-shift, night-shirt, night-spot, night-time, night-watch, nightwatchman.

nimbus (pl. nimbuses).

nitrogen, nitrogenous, nitrogenize.

nitroglycerine (not nitroglycerin), termed glyceryl trinitrate in chemistry and medicine.

nm is the abbreviation of nanometre.

no (pl. noes) ("The noes have it").

no. This abbreviation of *numero* (number) should be avoided. American texts commonly use the symbol #, but because this is also a proofreader's mark for *space* (e.g. "add 1-line #"), it should be carefully indicated in copy for typesetting that the symbol (and not a space) is required.

Nobel Prize (initial capital letters), Nobel Prize in chemistry etc. (no initial capital on chemistry); an exception is the Nobel Peace Prize.

noblesse oblige (italics) = imposes obligations (because of rank or position); the French form should be avoided.

nobody (preferred to *no-one*) is singular; e.g. "Nobody under the age of 16 is allowed."

noisome = disgusting, unhealthy (usually referring to a smell); it has nothing to do with *noise*.

no-man's land

nom de plume (italics) = pseudonym, pen-name; the French form was coined in England and should be avoided (the correct French equivalent is *nom de guerre*).

nomenclature, scientific, of plants and animals, *see* **Latin classification**.

nominal = to do with names or nouns, in name only ("a nominal price"); it should not be misused to mean approximate (e.g. "The experiment produced nominal results" is incorrect).

non- Nearly all compounds with the prefix non- have a hyphen (exceptions include nonconformist, nondescript, nonentity, nonplus, nonsense). *See also* **negative prefixes**.

nonce-word *See* **neologism**.

non compos mentis (italics) = of unsound mind; the Latin form should be avoided.

none is nearly always singular. E.g.:

"None of the workers *has* arrived yet" (none = not one).
"None *has* as much talent as this worker" (none = no-one, no person).
But compare:
   "None *is* so quiet as he who never talks"
and "None *are* so quiet as they who never talk".

none the less (three words) is the preferred spelling, although *nonetheless* (one word), standard in American, is rapidly gaining ground in Britain.

non-flammable/non-inflammable *See* **inflammable**.

non-linear

nonpareil = obsolete name for 6-point type. For others, *see* **type sizes**.

nonplus, nonplussed.

non sequitur is a statement, often presented as a consequence or conclusion, that does not logically follow from what precedes it. E.g. "It looked as if it would rain so I wore my red socks." Usually much less obvious than this example, non sequiturs should nevertheless be avoided.

non-standard English should be avoided in formal text, although opinions about what is standard inevitably differ. In terms of "non-acceptable" words for formal writing, there is a group consisting of cant, slang and colloquialisms. **Cant** is a type of jargon, usually the private language of crime and criminals, also called **argot** by some authorities. Many of its words have eventually become **slang** ("words and usages not accepted for dignified use" – Chambers Dictionary), which is the common linguistic coin of everyday speech. **Colloquialisms** also include words that are used mainly in informal speech. **Jargon** is the specialized language of science, technology, trade, commerce, and so on (*see* **jargon**).

Other informal expressions, which should be used only in conversation or personal letter-writing, include words such as *can't, don't* and *won't. Ain't*, described by some as colloquial, is condemned by others as an illiterate or dialect usage. **Dialect**, however, is best regarded as a regional vocabulary, sometimes involving new meanings of existing words and sometimes using words of its own. Thus in Cornwall a tourist is known in the local dialect as an *emmet* (a standard, if archaic, term for an ant), whereas in Devon the seasonal visitors are referred to as *grockles*. Words such as *emmet* (in its original sense) belong to the category known as **archaisms**, which are old-fashioned and should be avoided in modern formal writing (*see* **archaisms**).

There are various other isms in the lexicographer's vocabulary, including bowdlerism, euphemism, genteelism, malapropism and solecism. **Bowdlerism**, by definition an activity indulged in by editors rather than writers, is the (some would say unnecessary) removal from text of words and phrases that might offend a reader's sensibilities. It is close to **euphemism**, which is the use of a mild, and often twee, expression instead of one that might give offence. As a result the vocabulary is burdened with slang and colloquial synonyms such as House of Commons, WC, the smallest room, bathroom (American), cloakroom, convenience, the john, powder room, loo, karsi, lav, lavvy, toilet, thunder-box and even bog for the – to some people apparently unmentionable – *lavatory*. Indeed most euphemisms relate to bodily functions or sex. Again this sort of usage is similar to **genteelism** which, however, avoids what would be regarded as crude expressions such as *bog*.

A **solecism** is technically a breach of syntax, most often a complete misuse of a word, such as "She done it" or "The South American lama has four legs and a long neck". Examples of the latter type are also called **schoolboy howlers**. A solecism involving euphony and often humour is sometimes termed a **malapropism** (Mrs Malaprop, who habitually made this error, was a character in Sheridan's play *The Rivals*); a modern example is "Most people regard the threat of nuclear war as the ultimate detergent". Vocal gymnastics are also involved in **spoonerisms** (again named after their champion, Rev. William Spooner), in which initial letters or sounds of words are transposed, resulting in other real but incorrect words (e.g. "heaving the louse" for "leaving the house" and "well-boiled icicle" for "well-oiled bicycle"). *See also* **cliché**; **figures of speech**; **idiom**.

no-one (but *nobody* preferred)

nor *See* **neither**.

norm = pattern, standard, usual state/quantity (generally expressed as "the norm"); **normal** = agreeing with the standard, non-deviant (and various technical meanings in chemistry); **normality** = the state of being normal; **normalcy** = normality. As an alternative word for *normality, normalcy* (called an "ill-formed word" by Chambers Dictionary) would appear to be redundant and is probably best avoided. Other related words include normalize, normalization.

north, northern etc. *See* **compass directions**.

Northern Hemisphere (initial capital letters).

Northern Ireland *See* **Eire**.

North Pole (initial capital letters).

nosebag, noseband, nosebleed, nose-cone, nosedive, nosegay, nose over (verb), nose-piece, nose-ring, nose-wheel, nosy (not nosey).

nostrum (pl. nostrums).

nota bene (italics) (= note well) has the abbreviation N.B.

notable = worthy of notice or attention; **noted** = well-known, celebrated; **noticeable** = perceptible, claiming one's attention; **noteworthy** = worthy of note.

nothing is the opposite of *something*; **no thing** can contrast with *no person* (e.g. "Although many persons annoy him, no thing does").

notice, noticing, noticeable.

not only should always be followed, eventually, by **but** (...) **also**.

notorious = well known for misdeeds, infamous; **famous** = favourably well-known.

notwithstanding (one word).

nouns as verbs In the following examples:
   "He will chair the meeting"
   "She promised to gift her ring to her mother"
   "They will host the party"
   "Man the lifeboats"
   "She mothers that dog"
   "Paper over the cracks"
   "You can pocket the change"
   "I had to train it to London"
   man, mother, paper and *pocket* are recognized verbs, *chair* is accepted by most authorities, but *gift, host* and *train* (and many similar examples) should be avoided.

nova (pl. novae).

novel refers to kind, **new** refers to time, state or condition; e.g. "He uses a novel way of marking his comments" and "He used a new pen".

nowadays (one word).

ns is the abbreviation of nanosecond.

nuciferous describes a plant that bears nuts; **nucivorous** describes an animal that eats nuts.

nuclear is preferred to **atomic** in expressions such as nuclear energy, nuclear power, nuclear reactor, nuclear submarine, nuclear warhead.

nucleus (pl. nuclei).

number, like some other **collective words** (which *see*), may be singular or plural. It is usually singular when preceded by the definite article (e.g. "The number of errors was surprisingly small"), and plural when preceded by the indefinite article (e.g. "A number of errors were found"). In other constructions, *number* is singular or plural depending on whether it is regarded as a whole or distributively.

numbers *See* **figures, quantities and measurements**.

numbers and counting The following rules provide a guide to style in modern publications.

1. Cardinal numbers consist of the ordinary counting series one, two, three, four, and so on. The style for numbers over twenty is twenty-one, twenty-two, and so on (with a hyphen). At some stage in the series, it is usually necessary to change from numbers spelled in full to ones represented by numerals (e.g. 197 is briefer and more readable than one hundred and ninety-seven). Many editors/ publishers make this change after the number ten. Numbers larger than 100 should not be spelled in full except for the "round" numbers. E.g.:

432	987	1,234	23,456	345,678	4,567,890
but	a hundred	a thousand	a million		

Note that numbers larger than a thousand are comma'd off in groups of three, from the right; continental usage places full points, not decimal points (for which commas are used), instead of commas. Modern scientific typesetting uses narrow spaces instead of commas. Whole numbers of thousands or millions are best written as a combination of numerals and words. E.g.:

27 thousand   128 million   (not thousand*s*, million*s*).
Numerals should also be used to avoid a string of hyphenated words. E.g.:

"a 36-hour interval", not "A thirty-six-hour interval".

Beware of *billion*, which originally in Britain meant a million million but which in North America and increasingly in Britain means 1,000 million (formerly the British *milliard*). For this reason, the American "7 billion" should be written as 7,000 million". For a precise quantity – that is, a number followed by a unit – numerals should always be used. E.g.:

7 km   3 miles   120 bhp   1,200 mph   35°C.

Numerals should also be used for times of day, days of the month, years and dates E.g.:

3 p.m.   3 o'clock   15.00 hours   29 February 1988 (not 29th).

If style or position at the beginning of a sentence demands that a quantity be spelled out, the units should also be spelled in full. E.g.:

six metres   twenty horsepower   a thousand megawatts.

If there is a list of figures (in running text), use spelled-out numbers or numerals depending on the majority. E.g.:

> Two, four and seven . . .
> 26, 55, 72 and 273 . . .
> Three, eight and thirteen . . .
> 8, 9, 48, 49 and 438 . . .

In text prepared for translation or co-edition publication, quantities often have to be stated in two systems of units. The usual style is:

320 km (200 miles)   37°C (98.6°F)   1,000 ha (2,470 acres)

or, of course,

200 miles (320 km)   98.6F (37°C)   2,470 acres (1,000 ha)

Abbreviations of units may be typeset spaced (6 m), close-spaced (6 m) or close-up (6m), depending on the style required by the publisher. Roman numerals should be avoided, apart from World War I, World War II, rulers (Henry VIII, Elizabeth II), and books of the Bible (I Kings, II Kings).

2. Ordinal numbers, used for enumerating, are the series first, second, third, fourth, and so on (the *-th* ending is used from *fourth* upwards). In ordinary running text these should be spelled in full, although the abbreviations 1st, 2nd, 3rd, 4th, and so on may be used to save space in tabular matter. The style for numbers over 20 is twenty-first (21st), twenty-second (22nd), and so on (with hyphens). When used adjectivally, they all take a hyphen (e.g. "in the seventeenth century" but "a seventeenth-century building").

3. Dates See **time**.

4. Money See **money**.

5. Fractions See **fractions**.
See also **abbreviations**; **contractions**; **mathematical material**; **numerical prefixes**; **roman numerals**; **units**.

numerical prefixes generally have two possible forms, one derived from Greek and one from Latin.

prefix	Greek	Latin
half	hemi- (hemisphere)	semi- (semicircle)
one	mono- (monogram)	uni- (unique)
two	di- (dioxide)	bi- (biennial)
three	tri- (tripod)	ter- (tercentennial)
four	tetra-(tetrarch)	quadri- (quadrilateral)
five	penta- (pentangle)	quinque- (quinquereme)
six	hexa- (hexagonal)	sex- (sextant)
seven	hepta- (heptane)	sept- (September)
eight	oct(a)- (octagon)	oct(o)- (October)
nine		nona- (nonet)
ten	deca- (decathlon)	decem- (December)
many	poly- (polygon)	multi- (multiplex)
all	pan- (panacea)	omni- (omnipotent)

(For a tenth and below, and a hundred and above, *see* **metric**

prefixes.) Purists object to a mismatch of a Greek prefix and a Latin base (and vice versa), but the adoption of metric prefixes has made this inevitable. Examples of other hybrids from science include bichromate, bicycle, bimetallic, divalent, monorail, multipolar, quadriplegia, tetracyclic, tetravalent, trisect, trivalent and unicycle. *See also* **numbers and counting; units**.

nuncio (pl. nuncios).

O

-o For plurals of words ending in -*o, see* **plurals**.

oaf (pl. oafs).

oasis (pl. oases).

obese, obesity (not obeseness). *See also* **corpulent**.

objectionable (not objectional) = disagreeable, unacceptable, open to objection; **objective** = from a disinterested impersonal point of view (opposite of *subjective*). E.g.:

"The magistrate condemned the vandal for his objectionable behaviour."
"Because the incident involved my own family, I found it difficult to be objective in reporting the facts to the police."

objet d'art (italics) = small (usually practical) object of artistic merit.

obligatory hyphen *See* **discretionary hyphen**.

oblique (stroke) *See* **solidus**.

observe, observable, observance (= keeping customs, laws or regulations), observation (= noticing or seeing something), observant, observatory.

obsolete, obsolescent. *See* **ancient**.

obverse *See* **inverse**.

obviate = to get rid of, make unnecessary, neutralize; it should not be used to mean *lessen* or *reduce*. E.g.:

"Checking the printout should obviate the need for a second proof-reading stage" (correct);

"More careful keying should obviate the number of corrections at later stages" (incorrect).

occupy, occupier (who occupies e.g. a house permanently), occupant (who occupies e.g. a telephone box temporarily), occupation (= the act of occupying, employment); occupancy (= the state of an occupant).

occur, occurred, occurring, occurrence.

OCR is the abbreviation of *o*ptical *c*haracter *r*ecognition, a technique in typesetting which involves machine scanning of text (typewritten or printed) to convert the individual characters into electronic signals that can be displayed or manipulated by a computer, or drive a typesetting system. Scanning of existing printed text allows it to be re-formated (possibly in a different type size or typeface) before being reset.

octagon, octahedral (not *octo-*), but octogenarian, octopod, octopus (pl. octopuses).

octavo (pl. octavos, abbreviation 8vo) = printing term for an eighth of a sheet of paper, made by folding it in half three times. *See* paper sizes.

ocular, oculist, binocular(s). **Oculist** = a medically qualified specialist who treats disorders of the eye, an opthalmologist; **optician** = someone who sells spectacles, contact lenses and optical instruments; **opthalmic optician** or **optometrist** = someone who tests eyesight and prescribes spectacles etc.

-odd, as in 30-odd, needs a hyphen to avoid ambiguity with odd = strange (e.g. "The 30-odd members of staff" and "The 30 odd members of staff"); the construction should be avoided.

odour, odourless, odorous (and malodorous), odiferous, odorize, odorizer (and deodorize etc.).

-oe- This vowel sound, in words from Greek or Latin, should be written (and printed) as separate letters, not as the ligature *œ* (e.g.

302

amoeba, foetus, oedema, Oedipus, oestrogen). In a few words, the vowel has been reduced to a single *e* (e.g. ecology, ecumenic, fetid). *See also* **-ae-**.

OED, in this Dictionary and many others, is an abbreviation of the *Oxford English Dictionary*.

oesophagus (pl. oesophagi), oesophageal.

oestrus, oestrogen.

off-and-on, off-beat, off-centre, off-chance, offcut, offend, offhand, offhanded(ly), off-licence, offload, off-peak, offprint, offset, offshoot, off shore (noun), offshore (adj.), offside, offspring, off-stage, offstreet, off-white.

offer, offered, offering, offertory.

official (adj.) = with the force of recognized authority; **official** (noun) = someone holding office/position of authority; **officious** = too ready to offer unwanted advice, bossy (pejorative). E.g.:

"Only applications on official forms will be considered."
"He continued to meddle in our affairs and we soon tired of his officious manner."

officialese is another name for **beaurocratic English**.

offset printing *See* **printing processes**.

often Ambiguity should be avoided when using **often** to mean in many instances, usually or commonly; e.g. "Border Collies often have white tails" is better put as "Most Border Collies have white tails."

oftener/oftenest should be avoided; **more often/most often** are preferred.

oft-times is archaic and precious for **frequently**, which should be used.

oil-burner, oilcake, oilcan, oilcloth, oil-colour, oilfield, oil-fired, oil gauge, oil-meal, oil-painting, oil-palm, oil-seed, oil-shale, oilskin, oilstone, oil-tanker, oil well.

OK or **okay** is more than a century old and one of the most frequently used words in conversational English; but it is still colloquial and should be avoided in normal writing.

olden is archaic for **former** or simply **old** (as in the clichés "olden days", "olden times"), and should be avoided.

Oman The derived adjective and noun is *Omani*.

omelette is the preferred spelling (not **omelet**).

omnibus (pl. omnibuses); the term for the vehicle is almost invariably shortened to **bus** (pl. buses), except in the names of some long-established bus companies. *See also* **anthology**.

omni- or **pan-** *See* **numerical prefixes**.

omnipotent = all-powerful; **omniscient** = all-knowing.

on account of = because, which should be used.

one (pronoun) is impersonal, often used to express the speaker's or writer's views. Once introduced, it should be used consistently, but can sound over-formal and stilted, as in "One goes out of one's way to make the best of one's appearance." The construction is used here to circumvent the "personal" ring of "I go out of my way to make the best of my appearance." Another type of impersonal construction is exemplified by "One often hears it claimed that a high-fibre diet is good for one's health." This can be avoided by a general statement such as "Many people claim that a high-fibre diet is good for the health." On the whole, it is best to avoid the use of *one*. Less formal writing sometimes uses *you/your* or *they/their* as impersonal pronouns; e.g. "You cannot buy fresh fruit nowadays" and "They say it's going to be a bad winter." Purists object to the first device because the text appears to address the reader, and to the second because it raises the question "Who are the *they* referred to?"

one another *See* **each other.**

one of those should take a plural verb when it is the subject of a sentence (because *those* is the operative word). E.g.:

"He wrote one of those books that are seldom read"

(equivalent to "His book is among those that are seldom read", which presents no problem).

one or more is plural—fairly obvious when the phrase is the subject of a sentence, but less obvious when it is the object. E.g.:

"They will not all accept; one or more are bound to decline."
"Among the replies are one or more refusals."

one or two, or **a (something) or two**, is plural. E.g.:

"One or two are coming to dinner."
"A dog or two have barked."

one's is the only personal pronoun that takes an apostrophe (*hers, its, theirs, ours, yours* have none; neither does *whose*). But note **oneself** (not *one's self*).

ongoing, an overworked vogue word nearly always to be found in the company of *situation* (which *see*), should be avoided.

onionskin = translucent bank paper with a cockle finish, used when light weight is important (e.g. for sending by airmail). *See also* **bank.**

only Careful writers make sure that *only* qualifies only the word intended; "Make sure it qualifies only the word..." not "Make sure it only qualifies..."

on stream should be spelled, if it is used at all, as two words (not *onstream*). It is technical jargon (e.g. "The new machine will come on stream next week") and should be avoided in formal writing.

on the part of = **by**, which should be used.

onto and **on to** can be regarded as different. *Onto* means "to a place or position"; compare "He stepped onto the ladder" and "He walked on to the next house". When in doubt, *on to* should be used.

opacity, in papermaking and printing, describes the lack of transparency of a sheet of paper. Matter printed on a paper of high opacity does not show through on the other side of the sheet (*see* **show-through**).

operate, operator, operatable (= can be operated), operable (= can be operated on), operation, operative.

ophthalmia, ophthalmic, ophthalmology, ophthalmologist, ophthalmoscope. *See also* **oculist**.

opossum *See* **possum**.

opposite (noun) takes *of* (e.g. "*Yes* is the opposite of *no*"); **opposite** (adj.) takes *to* (e.g. "*Yes* is opposite to *no*"). *See also* **apposite**; **inverse**.

oppress, oppressor.

optimistic (believing that good will prevail) and **pessimistic** (always expecting the worst) reflect general attitudes and should not therefore be used as synonyms of *hopeful* and *unhopeful* when applied to a single occurrence. E.g. in "She was optimistic that the train would arrive on time", *hopeful* would be better; in "He was pessimistic that he would complete the task that day", *unhopeful* would be better.

optimum (adjectival) describes "the product of conflicting forces" (Gowers). The optimum rate at which a piece of text can be edited is not the fastest possible, but the rate that achieves the best compromise between the editor's conflicting desires for accuracy, quality, speed and sanity. So *optimum* should not be used as a grandiose synonym of *best*. **Optimal** may be preferred as an adjective (*optimum* is strictly a noun), but its correct use remains as described here. The pseudo-verb *optimize* should be avoided. The plural of *optimum* is *optima*. For *minimize, see* **diminish**.

option is an overworked alternative for **choice**. *See* **vogue words**.

-or, as a suffix with the approximate meaning "doer", forms the agent noun from a verb – that is, a noun that stands for the person or thing that performs an action. E.g.:

act	actor	invent	inventor
carburet	carburettor	operate	operator
contribute	contributor	protect	protector
create	creator	sail	sailor
exhibit	exhibitor	survey	surveyor

There are also many *-or* agent nouns with no associated English verb; e.g. censor, doctor, mentor, motor, tailor. All the *-or* nouns are, however, greatly outnumbered by those ending in *-er*, and some have both versions. Among these doublets, the *-or* form is generally used of inanimate objects, with the *-er* form reserved for human agents. E.g.:

conveyer (person)	conveyor (machine)
distributer	distributor (in a car)
resister	resistor (electrical)
senser	sensor (electronic)

or the *-or* form is the one usually favoured in legal usage. E.g.:

bailer (usual)	bailor (law)
deviser	devisor
relater	relator
releaser	releasor
voucher	vouchor

A different group of nouns in *-or* represent a state or condition. There is a much larger group ending in *-our*. E.g.:

ardour	flavour	odour	error
clamour	glamour	tumour	horror
colour	honour	valour	tremor
favour	humour	vapour	

The *-our* words can present spelling difficulties in their derived words, in which the *u* of *-our* is sometimes omitted; e.g. clamorous, coloration, glamorous, humorous, odorize, tumorous, valorous, vaporize.

oral = pertaining to the mouth; **verbal** = pertaining to words. (Gowers cites *oral contraceptive* and *verbal diarrhoea* as reminders of which is which). *See also* **aural**.

orang-utan (not any of the other spellings).

oratorio (pl. oratorios).

ordain = to order, decree, arrange, establish, admit (to holy orders); **ordination** = act of ordaining (to the ministry); **ordinance** = a rule, regulation, (temporary) law; **ordnance** = artillery, military stores. The original military surveyors gave their name to the Ordnance Survey (not Ordinance Survey).

ordinal numbers should be spelled in full in ordinary text (e.g. first, second, ninth, sixteenth, twenty-second, eighty-fourth). *See also* **numbers and counting**.

ore = metal-bearing mineral; **öre** = Swedish money; **øre** = Danish or Norwegian money. *See also* **krona**.

organdie = kind of dress fabric; **organza** = another kind of dress fabric.

organize, organization.

orient (verb, preferred to orientate), orientation, orienteering.

original = publisher's/printer's jargon for a photograph, transparency or piece of artwork as originally taken, drawn or supplied – not a copy, duplicate or (printed) reproduction; **dupe** = publisher's/printer's abbreviation of *duplicate*, a copy of an original illustration (usually a transparency).

ornamental describes something that decorates (something else); **ornate** describes something that is (highly) decorated.

orotund = having a full sound, pompous; **rotund** = plump, stout, rounded.

oscillate = to vibrate, fluctuate (regularly); **osculate** = to kiss.

ostensible = shown or professed outwardly; **ostensive** = indicating by direct demonstration, demonstrating. The words are interchangeable, particularly in adverbial form (*ostensibly, ostensively*). **Ostentatious** = showy, over-elaborate.

ostracize, ostracism.

other *See* **another**.

otherwise = *or else* should not be preceded by *or*; e.g. in "The boy will have to study hard, or otherwise he will fail the examination", delete *or*.

ought *See* **aught**; **naught**; **owe**.

ours (no apostrophe; *see* **one's**).

out- as a prefix does not usually take a hyphen except in such expressions as out-and-out, out-of-date, out-of-pocket, and out-of-touch, when they are used adjectivally.

outback, outbid, outboard, outbreak, outbuilding, outburst, outcast, outclass, outcome, outcrop, outcry, outdated, outdo, outdoor(s), outfield, outfit, outflank, outflow, outgo(ing), outgrow, outgrowth, outhouse, outlandish, outlast, outlaw, outlay, outlet, outline, outlive, outlook, outmanoeuvre, outmatch, outmoded, outmost, outnumber, out-of-date (adj.), out of doors, out-patient, outpost, outpour(ing), output, outrage, outrider, outrigger, outright, outrun, outrush, outset, outshine, outside(d), outsize(s), outskirts, outspoken, outstanding, outstay, outstrip, out-talk, outthrust, out-turn, outward(s), outweigh, outwit, outwork, outworn.

outdoor is an adjective (e.g. "outdoor sports"); **outdoors** is an adverb (e.g. "cricket is played outdoors"). *Indoor* and *indoors* are similar.

outline = a sketch, skeletal (preliminary) plan; **summary** = a short restatement, a summing up. One cannot, therefore, produce a summary of something that does not already exist in greater detail.

outré (italics) = extravagant, eccentric; the French form should be avoided.

outstanding = excellent, conspicuous, or not yet resolved or known. Care should be taken to avoid ambiguity from these different meanings; e.g. in "There was one outstanding reply to the questionnaire", *outstanding* could describe a reply conspicuous by its nature or one that has yet to be received.

over should be reserved to relate to position ("over the house") and should not be used to mean **more than**, relating to specific quantities ("more than four houses"). *See also* **above**; **all over**; **more than**.

over- Most words with the prefix over- are spelled as one word. Exceptions include over-active, over-anxious, over-careful, over-confident (-ence), over-determined, over-large, over-react, over-sensitive, over-shoe(s), over-trading, over-train, over-use, over-weighted (but overweight). Note the double *r* in such words as overreach, override, overrule, overrun.

overflow (verb) has the past tense and participle **overflowed**, not *overflown* – which is the past participle of *overfly* (past tense *overflew*). *See also* **flyover**.

overfly *See* **flyover**; **over-flow**.

overkill is a vogue word (e.g. "The employment of ten painters for one small room is an example of overkill"), and should be avoided. *See* **vogue words**.

overlay and **overlie** are analogous in declension to **lay** and **lie** (which *see*).

overly, an adverb from *over*, is described in the *Concise OED* – in the sixteenth meaning of *over* – as chiefly American and Scottish (as in

"I was not overly surprised when he lost his temper"). As a synonym for *too* it cannot even claim brevity, and lovers of polysyllables would probably substitute *excessively*.

overthrow *See* **throw**.

overview should be avoided in the sense *review* or *survey*.

ovolo (pl. ovoli).

ovum (pl. ova).

owe has the past tense and participle **owed**. The obsolete past tense **ought** (= should) has become an auxilliary verb in its own right; the obsolete past participle **own** (= belonging to oneself) has become an adjective.

owing to *See* **due to**.

owing to the fact that = **because**, which is preferred.

own *See* **owe**.

own-ends *See* **endpapers**.

oxygen, oxide, oxidation, oxidize

oxymoron Figure of speech which combines contradictory words for effect (e.g. optimistic pessimism, false truth, thundering silence). It is an effective literary device, but unless the context makes it absolutely clear that an oxymoron is deliberate, the figure of speech should be avoided. *See also* **paradox**.

oz is the abbreviation of ounce (and ounces).

Ozalid = proprietary copying process which gives a result resembling a blueprint, often used for proofing or printing film. A proof made from two or more films simultaneously is known as a *combined Ozalid*. In the United States, similar proofs are called **blues**.

P

p, the abbreviation of new penny or new pence, should be typeset close up to the numeral; e.g. 50p. The abbreviation is omitted for amounts of more than one pound; e.g. £1.75. *See also* **money.**

pace, pacey, pacier.

pace (italics) = with due respect to (someone who disagrees); this Latin term should be avoided.

package, packaged, packaging. **Package** = packet = small parcel; nowadays small items are *packaged,* not *packeted;* large items and suitcases are *packed.*

page, paging, paginate, pagination. *See also* **leaf.**

pagoda (pl. pagodas).

pail = bucket; **pale** (noun) = vertical piece of wood in a fence; **pale** (adj.) = lacking in colour.

pairs Some single objects consisting of two similar parts are known as pairs; e.g. binoculars, callipers, forceps, glasses (spectacles), jeans, knickers, pants, pyjamas, scissors, secateurs, shears, shorts, tights, tongs, trousers, tweezers. They are, however, plural words (e.g. "my glasses are broken", "these trousers are too tight") and to be represented unambiguously as a single item need to be prefixed by *pair of* (e.g. "she bought a new pair of jeans" because "she bought some new jeans" could mean one pair or more than one pair).

palaeo- (not *paleo-*).

palatal = pertaining to the palate (of the mouth);
palatial = pertaining to/resembling a palace.

palate = roof of the mouth; **palette** = artist's tablet for mixing colours on; **pallet** = straw bed, or wooden platform for carrying and moving goods (on a fork-lift truck); **pallatte** = a piece of head armour; **palet** = palea (botany), part of a flower; **pailette** = a spangle, metal foil used in enamel painting.

pale *See* **pail**.

pall = dark and gloomy (covering), a cloth spread over a coffin;
pawl = pivoted catch that engages the teeth of a ratchet.

palpate = to examine with the hands, by touch (noun *palpation*);

palpitate = to beat rapidly (noun *palpitation*).

pampas *See* **llano**.

pamphlet *See* **booklet**.

pan-, as a prefix meaning all or whole, added to an existing word usually has a hyphen; e.g. Pan-African Games, Pan-American Highway.

Panama The derived adjective and noun is *Panamanian*.

pancake *See* **crumpet**.

panda = bear-like animal; **pander** (to) = to gratify for base or evil purposes; **pamper** = to spoil, over-indulge (somebody).

pandit The preferred spelling is **pundit** (except as a formal Indian title).

panel, panelled, pannelling.

panic, panicked, panicking, panicky.

pantograph (not pantagraph).

Pantone = trade name of a colour-matching system consisting of a wide range of colours that can be closely matched by a conventional four-colour printing process.

papaya is preferred to **pawpaw** (or *papaw*) for the tropical tree and its fruit.

paper *See* **bulk; calliper; gsm; paper sizes; opacity; show-through; substance**.

paper = complex and versatile material used in the preparation and production of nearly all publications (as well as having a myriad other uses). Despite the introduction of electronic data capture, storage and retrieval, most readers still seem to prefer a user-friendly book to an impersonal machine – if only for portability. Even then, a request for "hard copy" from a computer often seems to result in yards of continuous stationery which has only a small part of its area occupied by letters or numbers. Like most other crafts originally carried out by hand, papermaking has been analysed by science and mechanized by technology. It has given rise to a bewildering number of terms, and it is the purpose of this short article to explain some of the common jargon associated with the production and use of paper in publishing. The major terms also have their own entries in this Dictionary.

Basically, paper is made by taking a fibrous raw material, pulping it in a large volume of water, and allowing the resulting slurry to filter through a fine wire mesh. This creates a thin mat of fibres which, when all the water has been removed, becomes paper. The fibres are microscopically small (consider the sheet of paper you are looking at now) but they interlock to give a material of surprising strength for its weight and thickness.

The final properties of a given sheet of paper depend on the type and mixture of fibres used and any chemical treatment of them, any substances added to the slurry before it passes onto the wire, the fineness and pattern of the wire mesh itself, any coatings applied to the surface of the paper, and the methods of treating the surface as the paper finally dries. Even with so many variables, the final product has to be manufactured to a predetermined thickness and quality, and ranges from boards and strong wrapping paper to gossamer-thin cigarette paper.

The chief sources of fibres for papermaking are wood (short-fibred hardwoods and long-fibred softwoods), rags (principally cotton), grass (such as esparto, manilla and straw) and waste paper. Various other vegetable fibres can be used (hemp, bagasse, kapok), as can mineral fibres and man-made materials (such as asbestos and regenerated cellulose). From all but the mineral sources, the basic material is cellulose fibre. This can be pulped *chemically* (using chemical treatment to remove the fibres from lignin or other natural binding agents), *mechanically* (using grinders to produce a pulp which contains natural materials in addition to the cellulose fibres), or by a combination of both. The fibres are then usually bleached, and blended with additives such as a *loading* (or filler), for example china clay or titanium dioxide (to improve opacity), and possibly a *sizing* (to modify inking properties). In addition to the moving wire mesh on the papermaking machine, there may be a hollow mesh cylinder called a *dandy roll*, which can apply a watermark or impress its texture on one surface of the paper, such as *wove* (a plain, fine woven texture) or *laid* (with parallel watermark lines). After being squeezed through rollers in the press section of the machine, the paper may be *calendered* on both surfaces by polished rollers, to give a smooth machine finish, or *glazed* on one side only. A second similar stage produces a highly polished, *supercalendered* paper.

The paper may also be *coated*, using a substance such as china clay mixed with a resinous binding agent, to improve opacity, smoothness and ink-holding ability. Sizing may also be applied as a coating. The chief methods are *roll coating* (using a roller), *blade coating* (using a thin steel blade to spread the coating evenly), *air-knife coating* (using a stream of high-pressure air) and *cast coating* (drying the coating over a hot polished roller).

Thus the description/definition of a given sheet of paper reflects the processes it has undergone during manufacture. *Mechanical* papers are made from the cheapest pulps and include *cardboard*, *newsprint* and *tissue*. Most are suitable for printing only by letterpress, although they can be improved by coating (e.g. for printing magazines). *Part-mechanical* papers contain some chemical (woodfree) pulp and are stronger, and (coated or uncoated) may be used for gravure and lithographic printing. *Woodfree* papers contain chemical pulp (with less than 10 per cent mechanical content). They may be *machine finished* (MF), *machine glazed* (MG), *supercalendered* (SC) on one surface (chromo paper) or both surfaces, *matt-coated*, *gloss-coated* (art paper) or *cast-coated*, the finish being suited to the required printing process and quality of the product (*see* **printing processes**).

General terms for common types of paper reflect their appearance or original use rather than their method of manufacture. Examples include *art paper*, *airmail*, *bible paper*, *cartridge*, *imitation art*, *India paper*, *onionskin*, and so on. Boards (that is, paper more than about 200 gsm in weight) include *artboard*, *chipboard* (a grey board made from waste paper), *lined chipboard* (with a usually white sheet added to one surface), *pulp board* (made from chemical woodpulp to its entire thickness on the papermaking machine and possibly coated) and *strawboard* (yellowish board made from straw pulp). Boards may also be made by combining plies of similar or different material, as in *drawing board* (with an outer surface of cartridge paper), *mounting board* and *pasteboard* or *ticket board*.

The description of a particular sheet of paper is completed by specifying its size (*see* **paper sizes**), thickness (*see* **calliper; bulk**) and weight (*see* **gsm; substance**). *See also* **opacity; show-through**.

paperback = book with covers made from thin (flexible) card. *See also* **hardback; perfect binding**.

paper punch/reader (computers) *See* **card punch; card reader**.

paper sizes Standard paper sizes (and the corresponding untrimmed book sizes) are now usually stated in millimetres, except in the United States (where inches are still usual). The names of the larger sizes are "metric" versions of the former "inch" sizes (*see* later). Standard sizes are based on the ISO (International Standards Organization) system (formerly DIN = Deutsche Industrie Norme) and designated A series, B series or C series (hence A4 etc.). A paper merchant or printer/binder can theoretically trim paper to any size, but at a cost, and even so-called standard sizes may vary among different sources. Smaller sizes are derived from the larger ones by cutting or folding; into four gives quarto (4to) and into eight gives octavo (8vo).

Common "metric" paper sizes (untrimmed) in mm

size	quad sheet	quarto (4to)	octavo (8vo)
metric royal	960 × 1,272	318 × 240	240 × 159
metric demy	888 × 1,128	282 × 222	222 × 141
metric large crown	816 × 1,056	264 × 204	204 × 132
metric crown	768 × 1,008	252 × 192	192 × 126

In the ISO system also, smaller sizes can be derived from larger ones by cutting or folding, thus halving the length of the larger side. The dimensions are in the proportion (longer side to shorter side) of $\sqrt{2}$ ($= 1.414$) to 1.

ISO system sizes

A series:	trimmed (in mm)	inches equivalent
A0	841 × 1,189	$33\frac{1}{8} \times 46\frac{3}{4}$
A1	594 × 841	$23\frac{3}{8} \times 33\frac{1}{8}$
A2	420 × 594	$16\frac{1}{2} \times 23\frac{3}{8}$
A3	297 × 420	$11\frac{3}{4} \times 16\frac{1}{2}$
A4	210 × 297	$8\frac{1}{4} \times 11\frac{3}{4}$
A5	148 × 210	$5\frac{7}{8} \times 8\frac{1}{4}$
A6	105 × 148	$4\frac{1}{8} \times 5\frac{7}{8}$
A7	74 × 105	$2\frac{7}{8} \times 4\frac{1}{8}$
A8	52 × 74	$2 \times 2\frac{7}{8}$
B series:		
B0	1,000 × 1,414	$39\frac{3}{8} \times 55\frac{5}{8}$
B1	707 × 1,000	$27\frac{7}{8} \times 39\frac{3}{8}$
B2	500 × 707	$19\frac{5}{8} \times 27\frac{7}{8}$
B3	353 × 500	$13\frac{7}{8} \times 19\frac{5}{8}$
B4	250 × 353	$9\frac{7}{8} \times 13\frac{7}{8}$
B5	176 × 250	$7 \times 9\frac{7}{8}$

The C series sizes are used for envelopes and folders designed to hold the A series sizes. For example:

C4 (229 × 324 mm) holds A4 flat
C5 (162 × 229 mm) holds A4 folded in half or A5 flat
C6 (114 × 162 mm) holds A5 folded in half or A6 flat

papier-mâché

Formerly in Britain (and currently in the United States) paper sizes were standardized in inches.

Former (and USA) paper sizes in inches

size	standard	quarto (4to)	octavo (8vo)
imperial	22 × 30	15 × 11	11 × $7\frac{1}{2}$
elephant	20 × 27	$13\frac{1}{2}$ × 10	10 × $6\frac{3}{4}$
royal	20 × 25	$12\frac{1}{2}$ × 10	10 × $6\frac{1}{4}$
small royal	25 × 19	$12\frac{1}{2}$ × $9\frac{1}{2}$	$9\frac{1}{2}$ × $6\frac{1}{4}$
medium	18 × 23	$11\frac{1}{2}$ × 9	9 × $5\frac{3}{4}$
demy	$17\frac{1}{2}$ × $22\frac{1}{2}$	$11\frac{1}{4}$ × $8\frac{3}{4}$	$8\frac{3}{4}$ × $5\frac{5}{8}$
crown	15 × 20	10 × $7\frac{1}{2}$	$7\frac{1}{2}$ × 5
foolscap	17 × $13\frac{1}{2}$	$8\frac{1}{2}$ × $6\frac{3}{4}$	$6\frac{3}{4}$ × $4\frac{1}{4}$
pot	$12\frac{1}{2}$ × $15\frac{1}{2}$	$7\frac{3}{4}$ × $6\frac{1}{4}$	$6\frac{1}{4}$ × $3\frac{7}{8}$

The sizes elephant, crown, foolscap and pot take their names from the design of the watermark originally incorporated in these sizes.

papier-mâché

paradox = apparently contradictory statement that appears at first sight to be illogical, but which can be resolved with further thought. E.g.:

"Flies are one of the largest and smallest groups of animals."

The use of paradox is a dangerous game if the reader does not know the rules.

paraffin *see* **kerosene.**

parallel, paralleled, paralleling, parallelogram, parallax.

paralysis, paralyse, paralytic.

parameter, a technical term in mathematics (usually meaning a variable quantity assigned a constant value in the case being considered), should be left to the mathematicians and not used as a vogue word for *aspect, consideration, factor* or just any *quantity*. Neither should it be confused with **perimeter**, also a mathematical term, meaning the distance round a closed two-dimensional figure but acceptably used of any other sort of *boundary* (which even then is a more familiar, and thus preferred, word).

paranoia = serious mental disorder involving delusions of persecution; the word (and its adjective **paranoiac**) should not be used of someone of a merely suspicious or mistrusting nature. *See also* **manic**.

parasite, parasitize, parasitism, parasitic.

parcel, parcelled, parcelling.

parenthesis (pl. parentheses). *See* **bracket; punctuation**.

par excellence (italics) = without equal, pre-eminent; the French form should be avoided.

parlous is an archaic form of **perilous** (as in the cliché "parlous state", which is often misused to mean *impecunious* or *hard-up*); *dangerous* or *perilous* should be used.

part = a fraction, constituent; **portion** = a share, specified component quantity. E.g.:

"She has taken over part of my job" (i.e. some of it);
"She has taken over my portion of the job" (i.e. all of it).
See also **proportion**.

part *from* = separate, leave; **part** *with* = give up. E.g.:

"She was reluctant to part from her friend so soon."
"He was reluctant to part with the money so quickly."

partial = relating to only a part (of something), or favouring one side in a contest/dispute (e.g. "a partial gastrectomy", "a partial point of view"); **partial** *to* = having a preference for (e.g. "She is partial to strawberries"); **partially** = in a biased manner, unfairly (opposite of *impartially*) (e.g. "We thought that the judge summed up partially"); **partly** = in part, incompletely (opposite of *completely*) (e.g. "The judge had only partly summed up before lunch") – there is great difference between a judge's *partially* summing up and *partly* summing up. As the Fowlers said: "... never write *partially* without considering first the claims of *partly*."

participles, related and unrelated Present or past participles should be located in a sentence in such a way that they relate to the correct subject (usually a noun). Failure to do this is a common error – the so-called dangling participle. E.g.:

"Looking over the fence, two horses were grazing" is incorrect unless it was extremely tall grass, so that the horses could bite it off and look over the fence at the same time. The participle phrase is misrelated to "two horses" and the sentence should be restructured:
"Looking over the fence, I saw two horses grazing" is correct.

A misrelated past (or perfect) participle is much more obvious. E.g.:

"Angered by the heckler, his voice shouted in reply" is incorrect. His voice was not angered, he was, so re-cast as:
"Angered by the heckler, he shouted in reply."

An unrelated participle "hangs" and does not relate to any real subject. E.g.:

"Ignoring errors involving participles, it is probably prepositions that cause the most trouble."
Here a spurious "it" dummies for the missing subject of the participle clause. The sentence can be salvaged only by re-writing:
"Except for participles, prepositions probably cause most errors."

particular should not be used with no particular reason (as in this sentence, from which it should be omitted).

part-mechanical = type of paper made from a mixture of chemical and mechanical pulps. *See* **chemical pulp; mechanical pulp; paper**.

passable = can be passed; **passible** = sensitive, exposed to suffering.

passed is the past tense and participle of the verb *to pass*; **past** is the adjective derived from it. E.g.:

"Did you see the car we passed?"
"I have had this car for the past four years."

passé = jaded, past his or its best; strictly, the French feminine form

passée should be used to refer to women, although both words are best avoided.

passim (italics) = everywhere, throughout, from this point onward; a concise term for readers who know what it means.

paste, pasty (resembling paste), pastry, pasty (a pastry), pasta (spaghetti etc.). *See also* **flan**.

pastel = chalky crayon; **pastille** = medicated sweet, incense pellet. *Pastil* should be avoided for either.

pasteurize, pasteurization.

pastiche = something (such as a painting or piece of music) made up from pieces of other works; **postiche** = superfluous addition(s) to an existing work, a forgery (originally a false hair-piece).

pastoral = relating to shepherds or pastors; **pastural** = (characteristic) of pasture; **pastorale** = pastoral piece of music.

pate = the top of the head; **pâté** = meat-paste.

pater, the Latin for father, is (like **mater** = mother) schoolboy slang, belonging to a former era.

pathetic should be reserved to describe objects, actions or situations that evoke *pathos* (pity, grief, sorrow), and not be used pejoratively or merely as a synonym for **mediocre** (which *see*).

patio (pl. patios).

patois

patrol, patrolled, patrolling.

patron = someone who commissions a work of art or who contributes (financially) to the arts, a protector (as in patron saint), a proprietor. The word should not be used to mean **customer**

(which *see*). Other forms are patronage, patronise (= to act as patron or customer, or to regard with condescension), patronising.

pave, pavement, pavior (who paves).

pay (verb) inflects *pay–paid–paid*.

pay-claim, pay-day, payload, paymaster, pay-off (noun), pay-out (noun), pay-packet, pay phone, payroll.

peace, peaceable, peaceful.

pease *See* **capers**.

peccadillo (pl. peccadillos).

pedal, pedalled, pedalling, pedaller (who pedals a bicycle).

peddle, peddled, peddling, pedlar (who peddles goods).

pejorative often, because of its usual pronunciation, attracts the misspelling *perjorative*.

pen-and-ink, pen-feather, pen-friend, penholder, penknife, penman(ship), pen-name, pen-pal.

penal, penalty, penalize, penology.

pencil, pencilled, pencilling.

pendant (noun) = something that hangs; **pendent** (adj.) = hanging.

pendulum (pl. pendulums).

penetrate, penetrable (not *penetratable*).

peninsula (noun) = narrow neck of land; **peninsular** (adj.) describes it.

penta- or **quinqui-** *See* **numerical prefixes**.

peony is the preferred spelling (not **paeony**).

people may be singular or plural. The singular *people* (= a nation or race) has the plural **peoples**; the plural *people* (= human beings) has the singular **person**. E.g.:

"As a group the British are insular, but so are many other island peoples."
"He is a strange person, but so are many people."

See also **folk; person**.

per *See* **a/an**.

per capita = "according to heads" (i.e. of each person) in a group or population (e.g. "a nation's per capita national debt ascribes an equal fraction of the debt to each member of the population"). It does not strictly mean *per head* (which would be *per caput*, singular), and is best avoided except in statistical data.

perceive, perceiver. **Perceptible** (preferred to *perceivable*) = able to be perceived, observable; **perceptive** = capable of perceiving, quick to notice, intelligent, E.g.:

"The replica was so like the original there was no perceptible difference."
"She was so perceptive that she noticed a difference between the replica and the original."

per cent (two words, no full point), not percent, per cent. or %, although the symbol may be used to save space in tables and captions; note that **percentage** is spelled as one word.

perchance is archaic for **perhaps** (= *maybe*), either of which should be used.

percolate, percolator (not perculator).

perfect, perfectible.

perfect binding, in book manufacture, is a technique in which the back (spine) of a *book block* is roughened and coated with hot-melt glue to hold the pages together and the cover (case) in position. The whole book is then usually trimmed to size (so that the covers are exactly the same size as the pages). A cheaper alternative to sewing, generally for limp or card covers (paperbacks), it is also known as **adhesive binding** or **cut-back binding**. *See also* **books**.

perfecter = a Catharist; **perfector** = a printing press (which prints on both sides of the sheet at the same time).

perfecting = method of printing on both sides of the sheet (or web) at once.

perfidious *See* **insidious**.

period (= full stop) *See* **punctuation**.

permanent *See* **temporal**.

permissible describes an allowed action or event, something that is unprohibited; **permissive** describes an attitude that allows things to be done or take place, even if they are not generally acceptable (as in "permissive society").

permit (verb) = actively give (formal) permission; **allow** = tolerate, sanction, let happen. Adjectives are *permissible*, *allowable*.

perpetrate = commit something outrageous; **perpetuate** = preserve, prolong (for ever). A man's actions may perpetrate a crime against society, and perpetuate a feeling of hostility towards himself.

perquisite *See* **pre-**.

per se (italics) = in itself (or him/herself or themselves); the Latin form should be avoided.

persecute = to hound, harass, punish (usually for moral, political or religious views); **prosecute** = to bring legal proceedings (against), follow up, pursue. Thus a tranvestite, Marxist or Jew may be *persecuted* (at certain times and in certain places), whereas a thief or a formal complaint against an official body may be *prosecuted*.

Persian *See* **Iran**.

persist, persistence, persistent. *See also* **consistent**.

person = any human being, child or adult (neutral connotation);
personage = somebody of importance (with slightly pompous
overtones); **personality** = somebody famous (with popular
overtones). The usual plural of *person* is *people*, although *persons*
may be used in formal and legal contexts; it is also the usual
American plural. *See also* **people**.

personable = of pleasing/pleasant appearance; **personal** = private;
personnel = staff (strictly a singular word, but often now used as a
plural). E.g.:

"The new office boy is a very personable young man."
"Managers should not make personal remarks about staff."
"The new office boy increased the number of personnel to 18."

personal names can enter the language and become words in their
own right (known as eponyms). When used as scientific units
(particularly common in science) they have no initial capital letter
and form plurals as if they were ordinary English words. The many
examples acknowledge the scientist's contributions:

ampere (amp)	André-Marie *Ampère*
angstrom	Anders *Ångström*
baud	Jean-Maurice *Baud*ot
becquerel	Antonie-Henri *Becquerel*
bel	Alexander Graham *Bell*
biot	Jean-Baptiste *Biot*
coulomb	Charles de *Coulomb*
curie	Marie *Curie*
debye unit	Peter *Debye*
farad	Michael *Farad*ay
gauss (pl. gauss)	Karl *Gauss*
gilbert	William *Gilbert*
henry (pl. henries)	Joseph *Henry*
hertz (pl. hertz)	Heinrich *Hertz*
joule	James *Joule*
kelvin	Lord *Kelvin*, William Thomson

lambert	Johann *Lambert*
maxwell	James Clerk *Maxwell*
mho	Georg *Ohm*, backwards
newton	Isaac *Newton*
oersted	Hans Christian *Oersted*
ohm	Georg *Ohm*
pascal	Blaise *Pascal*
poise	J. M *Poise*uille
röntgen	Konrad *Röntgen*
sabin	Wallace *Sabin*e
siemens (pl. siemens)	William *Siemens*
stokes (pl. stokes)	George *Stokes*
svedberg	Theodor *Svedberg*
tesla	Nikola *Tesla*
torr	Evangelista *Torr*icelli
volt	Alessandro *Volt*a
watt	James *Watt*
Weber	Wilhelm *Weber*

Personal names given to other things generally retain their initial capital letter until the word is totally assimilated into the language (e.g. cardigan, wellingtons). For a list of some of these, *see* **dress**. *See also* **Christian names; eponym; named effects and laws; trade names**.

persona non grata (italics) = an unacceptable person (originally in a diplomatic function). The Latin term should be avoided in ordinary writing, as should the rarer *persona grata* (= an acceptable person).

personification figure of speech in which an inanimate or abstract object is given human attributes. E.g.:

"The wind sings and sighs through the leafless trees."

The device belongs more to poetry than to formal writing, but can be an effective way of making a difficult point. *See also* **apostrophe**.

perspicuous describes an explanation that exhibits *perspicuity*, and so is clear, easy to understand, even obvious; **perspicacious**

describes someone who exhibits *perspicacity*, or clear-sightedness.
E.g.:

"I was able to follow the complex argument because of the
perspicuous nature of its presentation."
"I was able to follow the complex argument because of the
perspicacious nature of its presenter."
Perspicuous should not be confused with *conspicuous*.

persuade, persuadable, persuasible, persuasive, persuasion,
Persuadable/persuasible both = open to persuasion;
persuasive = able to persuade (someone else). E.g.:

"The customer proved to be persuasible and finally agreed to the
salesman's changes."
"The salesman was persuasive and obtained the customer's
agreement to the terms of sale."

Peru The derived adjective and noun is *Peruvian*.

peruse = to read thoroughly (not to read carelessly or incompletely).
See also **scan**.

petal, petalled.

petrol is preferred in English text to the American *gasoline* (preferred
to gasolene), known colloquially as *gas*. **Petroleum** is the mineral,
and includes crude oil and natural gas. *See also* **kerosene**.

pH (lower case p, Capital H) is used in chemistry to express the
acidity (or alkalinity) of a solution. (It is the negative logarithm of
the hydrogen ion concentration.) A pH of 7 is neutral; a pH of less
than 7 is acidic; a pH of more than 7 is alkaline.

phalanx = wedge-shaped formation of troops (pl. phalanxes), or a
bone in the finger or toe (pl. phalanges).

phantasy The preferred spelling is **fantasy** (which *see*).

pharmacopoeia

phenomenon (pl. phenomena, often misused as a singular) gives the adjective *phenomenal*, which means to do with a phenomenon or apprehension by the senses. The use of the word to mean *remarkable* is therefore strictly incorrect and certainly overdone (as in "Her contribution made a phenomenal difference to the week's output").

Philippines The derived adjective and noun is *Filipino*.

phobia (pl. phobias) = mental disorder (classified as a neurosis) involving morbid fear (of something); the adjective is **phobic**. The many examples range from *acrophobia* (= fear of heights) to *xenophobia* (= fear of strangers). None of the words should be used for mere *dislike* (as in "He has a phobia about going out in the rain").

phone should be avoided as an abbreviation of telephone in formal writing.

phoney (if it must be used) is the preferred spelling of **phony**.

-phth- This element is often misspelled in such words as diphtheria, diphthong, ophthalmia, naphthalene, phthisis, etc. (especially if mispronounced "diptheria", etc.).

phylum (pl. phyla).

piano (pl. pianos).

pica = a printer's measure. In Britain and the United States, 1 pica = $\frac{1}{6}$ inches (= 0.166044 inches or 4.212 mm), and is equal to 12 *points*. In Continental Europe, the nearest equivalent is the cicero (= 4.511 mm). Picas are used to specify the measure (width) of a column or page of type (i.e. the length of the typeset lines of text) or the length of a rule (*see* **rule**). The widths of illustrations may also be given in picas, to achieve an exact range on the width of adjacent text, although it is more usual to convert these dimensions to millimetres. A pica is sometimes incorrectly referred to as an *em*, which strictly is the width of a lower case m in a designated typeface and type size (thus an em equals a pica only for a 12-point face). *Pica* is also an obsolete name for 12-point type in general (*see* **type sizes**). *See also* **cicero; didot; em; point**.

picaresque = to do with a **picaroon** (= vagabond, someone who lives by his wits). The latter word is obsolete, and the former should (very strictly) be reserved to describe seventeenth-century fiction (novels) that featured Spanish rogues (pícaros). The words are included because of possible confusion with **picturesque** (= quaint, picture-like); their only common feature is their foreign origin.

piccolo (pl. piccolos).

picket, picketed, picketing. *See also* **pique**.

picnic, picnicked, picnicking, picnicker.

pico- is the metric prefix for a million-millionth ($\times 10^{-12}$), as in *picofarad* (*see* **units**).

pie (food) *See* **flan**.

pie, or **printer's pie** = confused mixture of type, usually obtained by tipping typeset characters (after printing) into a jumbled heap rather than distributing them (*see* **diss**). *See also* **sort**.

pièce de résistance (italics) = the best item; the French form should be avoided.

pigmy The preferred spelling is **pygmy**.

pikelet *See* **crumpet**.

pilau (rice) is the preferred spelling, not *pillau, pilaw* or *pilaff*.

pilot, piloted, piloting.

pimento (pl. pimentos).

pincushion, pin-head, pin-hole, pin-money, pin-point, pinprick, pinstripe, pin-table, pintail (duck), pin-up (noun), pin-wheel.

pincers = tool for gripping nail-heads, etc.; **pinchers** = people who pinch; **pinschers** = kinds of dog.

pique = resentment (noun), to annoy (verb) – piqued, piquing; **piqué** = thick cotton fabric; **piquet** = card-game; **picket** = pointed stave, guard.

pirouette

pistachio (pl. pistachios).

pity, pitied, pitying, piteous, pitiable, pitiful. **Piteous** = stimulating pity; **pitiable** = deserving pity, contemptible; **pitiful** = feeling pity, despicable. The words, of similar meaning, tend to be used in a pejorative way, as in the second and third examples that follow. E.g.:

"He commented on the piteous state of the old beggar."
"She laughed at my pitiable attempts to draw a face."
"Pressure of work is a pitiful excuse for lateness of delivery."

pivot, pivotal, pivoted, pivoting. *See also* **vogue words**.

pixie (= fairy) is the preferred spelling (not **pixy**).

pizza *See* **flan**.

pl. is the abbreviation of plural.

placable = easy to appease or pacify, mild; **placeable** = can be placed or positioned; **placatory** = conciliatory (of actions or things, not people).

placebo (pl. placebos).

place-names in text for publication should be checked against any maps in the same work and the spelling on the maps followed for style. As a general rule, foreign place-names should be anglicized in ordinary text. *See also* **compass directions**.

placid (= calm) may explain why **flaccid** (= limp) attracts the misspelling *flacid* and mispronunciation "flassid" (instead of "*flak-sid*").

plagiarism, plagiarist, plagiarize. Plagiarism is lazy, unethical and illegal. Under English law, permission to publish copyrighted material is required if it exceeds 10 consecutive lines or 300–400 words, is more than 800 words in total (non-continuous text), exceeds 40 lines or a quarter of a poem, or is an illustration or tabular matter. Most publishers seek permission to quote any published material, of whatever extent. Copyright is usually effective for 50 years after the death of the copyright holder.

plague, plaguing, plaguy, plaguily, plaguesome.

plaid = woollen (often tartan) cloth; **plait** = braided strands (of hair, rope or straw).

plaintiff = person who brings a legal action (against the *defendant*); **plaintive** = mournful, sad-sounding. Both derive from the archaic word **plaint** = a lamentation, complaint.

planchet = blank metal disc from which a coin is struck; **planchette** = pencil on wheels used at seances.

plane = a flat surface (and a carpenter's tool, a tree); **plain** = a flat area of land (and unattractive, uncomplicated).

planetarium (pl. planetariums).

planographic printing *See* **printing processes**.

plantain = low-growing weed, or tropical "tree" that bears banana-like fruit (two different plants with the same name).

plastic = synthetic polymer that can be cast or moulded; the former use of *plastics* as an adjectival form (e.g. "a plastics container"), to distinguish it from the older adjective *plastic* = mouldable, should be avoided (e.g. "plastic bag", "plastic doll", "plastic flowers", "plastic tubing" are current usage – a fact possibly unwelcome by a plastic surgeon).

plate, platy (= plate-like, formally *laminar*).

plateau (pl. plateaux).

plateful (pl. platefuls).

platypus (pl. platypuses).

plausible

play-acting, play-actor, playback (noun), playbill, playgoer, playground, playhouse, playmate, play-off (noun), play-pen, plaything, playtime, playwright.

plectrum (pl. plectra).

plexus (pl. plexuses).

plimsoll is the preferred spelling of **plimsole** (= a light, canvas shoe); **Plimsoll line** = marking on a ship's hull near the waterline, which indicates the freeboard (maximum permitted loading) allowed.

plum, plummy (= like or having plums).

plumb, plumbic (= like lead).

plunge, plunging.

plurals Words taken from foreign languages, particularly French, Greek and Latin, generally take the "foreign" plural.

Examples:	amenuensis	amenuenses
	bureau	bureaux
	carcinoma	carcinomata

codex	codices
corpus	corpora
genus	genera
graffito	graffiti
meninx	meninges
omentum	omenta
phenomenon	phenomena
plateau	plateaux
polypus	polypi
protozoon	protozoa
radius	radii
sarcoma	sarcomata
septum	septa
spermatozoon	spermatozoa
stoma	stomata
stratum	strata

Increasingly, however, some such words are taking an "English" plural:

alibi	alibis
aquarium	aquariums (not aquaria)
cornea	corneas (not corneae)
medium	mediums (but media used in "the news media")
pharynx	pharynxes (not pharynges)
referendum	referendums (not referenda)
ultimatum	ultimatums (not ultimata)
Note also: mongoose	mongooses (mongeese is incorrect)
octopus	octopuses (octopi is incorrect)
platypus	platypuses

Two forms of plurals are sometimes retained for different usages (the more "scientific" usage usually retains the classic plural):

antenna	antennas (radio)
	antennae (zoology)
appendix	appendixes (of books)
	appendices (of intestines)
genius	geniuses (clever people)
	genii (spirits)

333

index	indexes (of books)
	indices (powers or exponents in maths)
lemma	lemmas (themes)
	lemmata (seed husks)

Occasionally the adopted word is already (strictly) plural although used in a singular sense, and an *s* is added to re-pluralize it:

fauna	faunas
flora	floras

The word *data* is also generally regarded as a singular word, particularly in computer terminology (e.g. "data is obtained"); it then has no plural.

One should be careful to pluralize the correct element in compound words.

Examples:	aide-de-camp	aides-de-camp
	court martial	courts martial
	man-o'-war	men-o'-war
	mother-in-law	mothers-in-law
NOTE:	manservant	menservants (pluralize both elements)
	spoonful (etc.)	spoonfuls (not spoonsful)

Proper names are pluralized in the normal way by adding *s* or *es*.

Examples:	Toms, Dicks, and Harrys
	a collection of Herculeses
	the Joneses
	four Hail Marys
	there were two Beatrixes

NOTE: henrys (plural of henry, the unit of inductance)

Some words have the same form in both singular and plural (e.g. deer, sheep). Letters, numerals and abbreviations without full points form the plural by adding *s*.

Examples:	There are eight *E*s in this sentence.
	There are two twos in 22.
	The early 1980s resembled the mid-1930s.

Seven MPs included four VCs, but only two had A-levels.

NOTE: the plural of MS (manuscript) is MSS; that of St (saint) is SS.

Abbreviations with full points should be pluralized by adding 's.

Examples: He engaged two Q.C.'s.

All applicants' c.v.'s were considered.

NOTE the following exceptions:

p.	pp. (pages)
f.	ff. (folios)
v.	vv. (verses)
w.	ww. (words)
sp.	spp. (species)

Abbreviations and contractions of units and measurements should *not* be pluralized.

Examples:

1 in	3 in	1 ft	4 ft
1 ml	18 ml	1 cwt	7 cwt
1 sec	30 sec	1 hr	24 hr

See also **abbreviations; contractions**.

Of the 128 words ending in *o* in the following list, 93 form the plural by adding *s*, 27 take *es* to form the plural, and others form a plural ending in *i*—so there is no obvious general rule.

albino	albinos	lido	lidos
alto	altos	limbo	limbos
archipelago	archipelagos	literato	literati
armadillo	armadillos	llano	llanos
arpeggio	arpeggios	maestro	maestros
bamboo	bamboos	magneto	magnetos
banjo	banjos	mango	mangoes
bolero	boleros	manifesto	manifestos
bravado	bravados	memento	mementos
bravo	bravos	merino	merinos
bronco	broncos	mestizo	mestizos
buffalo	buffaloes	mosquito	mosquitoes
calico	calicos	motto	mottoes
cameo	cameos	mulatto	mulattos

canto	cantos	negrillo	negrilloes
cargo	cargoes	negrito	negritoes
casino	casinos	negro	negroes
cello	cellos	nuncio	nuncios
cockatoo	cockatoos	oratorio	oratorios
comedo	comedoes	ovolo	ovoli
commando	commandos	patio	patios
concerto	concertos	peccadillo	peccadillos
contralto	contraltos	photo	photos
credo	credos	piano	pianos
crescendo	crescendos	piccolo	piccolos
curio	curios	pimento	pimentos
dado	dados	pistachio	pistachios
dago	dagoes	placebo	placebos
desperado	desperadoes	poncho	ponchos
dingo	dingoes	portfolio	portfolios
dodo	dodos	portico	porticos
domino	dominoes	potato	potatoes
dynamo	dynamos	potto	pottos
echo	echoes	proviso	provisos
embargo	embargoes	quarto	quartos
embryo	embryos	radio	radios
Eskimo	Eskimos	ratio	ratios
falsetto	falsettos	salvo	salvos
fiasco	fiascos	scenario	scenarios
flamingo	flamingoes	scherzo	scherzi
folio	folios	seraglio	seraglios
fresco	frescoes	shako	shakos
gabbro	gabbros	shampoo	shampoos
gaucho	gauchos	silo	silos
gecko	geckos	solo	solos
ghetto	ghettos	soprano	sopranos
graffito	graffiti	stiletto	stilettos
grotto	grottoes	studio	studios
halo	haloes	taboo	taboos
hero	heroes	tango	tangos
hidalgo	hidalgos	tattoo	tattoos
igloo	igloos	tiro	tiros
imago	imagines	tobacco	tobaccos
imbroglio	imbroglios	tomato	tomatoes

impresario	impresarios	tornado	tornadoes
incognito	incognitos	torpedo	torpedoes
innuendo	innuendos	torso	torsos
intaglio	intaglios	trio	trios
Jingo	Jingoes	two	twos
kilo	kilos	veto	vetoes
lasso	lassos	virago	viragoes
lazaretto	lazarettos	virtuoso	virtuosi
libido	libidos	volcano	volcanoes
libretto	libretto	zero	zeros

Plurals of words ending in *f* also defy logic, although sometimes the form of the plural distinguishes a noun from a verb. The following are the preferred forms:

belief	beliefs (*believes* being a verb form)
brief	briefs
calf	calves
chief	chiefs
delf	delfs (*delves* being a verb form)
dwarf	dwarfs
elf	elves
gulf	gulfs
half	halves
handkerchief	handkerchiefs
hoof	hoofs
leaf	leaves
loaf	loaves (verb form is *loafs* = idles)
oaf	oafs
proof	proofs (*proves* being a verb form)
relief	reliefs (*relieves* being a verb form)
roof	roofs
scarf	scarves (verb form is *scarfs* = joins)
self	selves
serf	serfs
sheaf	sheaves
shelf	shelves
spoof	spoofs
thief	thieves
turf	turfs

wharf	wharfs
wolf	wolves
woof	woofs

plus should be reserved for actual or implied mathematical expressions, and not used merely as a synonym for *and*. E.g.:

"The cost is £7,200 plus interest at 32 per cent" is correct (if expensive);
"The cost includes the car plus all accessories" is incorrect.

p.m. is the abbreviation of *post meridiem* (= afternoon).

pneumatic refers to air or air pressure (e.g. pneumatic drill);
pneumonic refers to the lungs (e.g. pneumonia); **mnemonic** is a memory aid (e.g. "Run off you girls, boys in view" is a mnemonic for the letters ROYGBIV, the inital letters of the colours of the rainbow – *see also* **acronym**).

pochette, in publishing, = a pocket-sized book (pocketbook).

pocket, pocketed, pocketing.

podium (pl. podia).

poetess Most women who write poetry prefer to be called a *poet*. *See also* **gender**.

point = printer's measure. In Britain and the United States, 1 point = $\frac{1}{72}$ inches (0.013837 inches or 0.351 mm). In Continental Europe, 1 didot point = 0.376 mm. Type sizes and rule widths are usually specified in points, although large (display) sizes may be given in mm. The equivalent (for "English" points) are as follows:

5 points	= 1.755 mm
6	= 2.106
7	= 2.457
8	= 2.808
9	= 3.159
10	= 3.510
11	= 3.861

12	$= 4.212$ ($= 1$ pica)
14	$= 4.914$
16	$= 5.616$
18	$= 6.318$
24	$= 8.424$ ($= 2$ picas)

12 points $= 1$ pica ($= \frac{1}{6}$ inches or 4.212 mm), sometimes incorrectly called an *em*. *See also* **cicero; didot; em; pica; point**.

points of the compass *See* **compass directions**.

poison = substance that injures the health of a living organism (or, by extension, injures anything else, such as the mind or an industrial catalyst); **toxin** = poison released (in the body) by a micro-organism such as bacterium; **venom** = poison secreted by an animal. The corresponding adjectives are *poisonous*, *toxic* and *venomous*; the first two are synonyms in general use, the last is often employed figuratively. **Antitoxin** and **antivenin** are medical terms for antidotes to specific kinds of poisoning.

poky = confined, cramped (not pokey).

pole, polarize, polarization.

police car, police constable, police-court, police-dog, police inspector, policeman, police officer, police sergeant, police state, police station, policewoman.

policy = general course of action or conduct, or an insurance contract; **polity** = form of government, the State.

politic = prudent, judicious, cunning, crafty, expedient; **political** = pertaining to politics. E.g.:

"His comment about company security was a politic criticism of the management."
"The councillor's comment about national security was a political, rather than personal, response."

polypus has the preferred plural polypuses (not *polypi*), although the simpler word **polyp** (pl. polyps) is now more common.

339

Polythene is a trade-name for the plastic polyethylene.

pomander *See* **pot-pourri**.

pommel = a knob on a sword-hilt or saddle; **pummel** = to hit repeatedly.

pom-pom = rapid-firing, self-loading (anti-aircraft) gun; **pom-pon** = spherical tuft or flower so shaped (as are some types of dahlias).

poncho (pl. ponchos).

popular, popularity, popularize.

popular names (of plants and animals) *See* **Latin classification**.

pore (verb) = study closely, gaze attentively at (usually with *over*); **pour** = make or allow liquid to flow in a stream (usually with *out* or *away*), rain heavily.

-p- or -pp- Monosyllabic words ending in *-p* preceded by a single vowel usually double the *p* before the suffixes *-able, -ant, -ed, -er, -ing, -ish*, and *-y* (which begin with, or effectively are, a vowel). E.g.:

flip	flippant
fop, up	foppish, uppish
whip	whippable, whipped, whipper, whipping, whippy

The *p* remains single if preceded by a long or double vowel, E.g.:

reap	reapable, reaped, reaper, reaping
sheep	sheepish
sleep	sleeper, sleeping, sleepy

With polysyllabic words taking these suffixes, the choice of *-p-* or *-pp-* depends on where the accent falls. If it is on the last syllable, the rule is as for monosyllabic words; e.g. entrapping, equipping, unshipping. If the last syllable is unaccented, the *p* is not normally doubled; e.g. chirruping, enveloping, galloping, hiccuping, walloping. (Exceptions include handicapping, kidnapping, sideslipping, worshipping). Neither is the *p* doubled, in monosyllabic or polysyllabic words, before the suffixes -ful or -ment; e.g. development, entrapment, equipment, worshipful. *See also* **suffixes**.

portentous = ominous, foreboding an unusually calamitous event; **pretentious** = florid, showy, pompous.

portfolio (pl. porfolios).

portico (pl. porticos).

portion *See* **part; quota**.

portmanteau (pl. portmanteaus, not portmanteaux).

portrait format *See* **format**.

position (noun) = location, precise place; **position** (verb) = to place, to locate precisely (but this use should be avoided). As a vogue word (which *see*), *position* passes for *circumstance* or the equivalent vogue word *situation* (e.g. "If I were in your position" = "If I were you").

positive should not be used as an emphatic synonym of *sure* or *certain*; it should be reserved for contexts in which it contrasts with *negative* (which need only be implied). E.g. in "Are you positive she said she would come?" substitute *certain* for *positive*. "His positive approach to the project encouraged the others" is correct usage (although *positive approach to* is probably better put as *enthusiasm for*).

positively = in a positive (as opposed to negative) manner; it should not be used as an intensifier. E.g. in "The talk was positively boring" delete *positively* (or substitute *extremely* or *very*). "He reacted positively and granted my request" is correct, if slightly tautological, usage.

possessives *See* **gerund; punctuation** (apostrophe).

possible and **probable** (like *possibly* and *probably*) should not be confused, but sometimes are. **Possible** = capable of existence or occurrence; **probable** = likely to occur. Thus, theoretically, nearly all things are possible, but perhaps only a few are probable. Similarly, it is often argued that nothing is impossible, but even the most optimistic have to agree that some things are highly improbable.

possibility that ... may/might is a tautological construction, as in "There is a possiblity that the train may be late." Correct versions include "... a possibility that the train will be late" and the simpler "The train may be late." *Might* would be wrong in all the examples.

possum is colloquial (in Britain and the United States) for **opossum**, which should be used.

post-bag, post-box, postcard, post-classical, post code, post-date(d), post-free, postgraduate, post-haste, posthorn, posthouse, Post-Impressionist, postman, postmark, postmaster, postmistress, post mortem (pl. post mortems), postnatal, post office, post-paid, postscript, post-war, postwoman. When the prefix, *post-* means after or behind, there is generally a hyphen (except in post mortem, postscript).

poste restante = accommodation address, a place where letters are left until called for; *accommodation address* should be used.

posterior is a euphemism for **backside, behind** or **buttocks**, any of which is preferred; **derrière** is twee and colloquial, **bum** is vulgar and slang.

postiche *See* **pastiche**.

postlims *See* **prelims**.

postscript, an afterthought added below the signature of a letter, is preceded by the abbreviation PS (*post scriptum*). Further postcripts are denoted by PPS, PPPS and so on.

pot (preferred to pott), in papermaking, is a size of paper (named after the design of its original watermark). *See* **paper sizes**.

potato (pl. potatoes).

poteen is the preferred spelling for the illicit Irish whiskey (not *potheen*).

potent = powerful, strongly influential; **potential** = latent, possible but not necessarily real.

pot-pourri = mixture, medley; the French term should be avoided. A pot-pourri of herbs or petals is known as a **pomander**.

potto (pl. pottos).

pouf (= a soft, stuffed ottoman or footstool) is the preferred spelling (not *pouff*, *pouffe* or *pouffé*).

p.p. is the abbreviation of per pro. or per proc., which is itself the abbreviation of *pro procurationem* (by the agency of, for and on behalf of).

ppi = abbreviation of pages per inch, the term used in the United States for the thickness (bulk) of a sheet of paper. *See* **bulk**.

practicable = able to be done/achieved (in practice); **practical** = concerned with or adapted to actual practice, efficient (in action), practised. E.g.:

"The use of half-sized photocopies was not practicable (= was impracticable) because our machine's maximum reduction is only 60 per cent."
"The use of photocopies instead of bromides was a practical way of reducing costs."
Practical should not be misused for *virtual*. E.g.:

"Obtaining consistently good photocopies from our machine is a practical impossibility" (*practical* should be *virtual*) Similarly, **practically** should not be misued for *virtually* or *nearly* or *almost*; as A. P. Herbert says *practically* often means *not practically* (e.g.

you cannot get somewhere "practically on time" or be "practically awake" or "practically first in a queue').

practical/practically *See* previous entry.

practice is the noun; **practise** is the verb (although Americans economize and have only *practice* for both).

pray = to address (a prayer) to a deity; **prey** = an animal that is hunted (by a predator). The "target" of a human hunter is usually called the **quarry**. *See also* **predate**.

pre-, as a prefix meaning *before*, usually takes a hyphen only before elements beginning with *e* or another vowel (e.g. pre-arrange, pre-election), pre-engage(ment), pre-establish, pre-exist(ence), pre-ignition, pre-ordain). Exceptions include pre-Cambrian, pre-cancerous, pre-Christian, pre-cook, pre-date, pre-glacial, pre-heat, pre-med(ication), pre-menstrual, pre-Raphaelite, pre-select(or), pre-shrink, pre-stress(ed), pre-tax, pre-war. **Pre-** is usually superfluous in such compounds as precondition, preplanned, prerequisite, in which the idea of "beforeness" is carried in the main part of the word (most conditions, plans and requisites have to be considered before the event). Thus a "necessary precondition" is merely a *condition*, "detailed preplanning" is merely *planning* and an "essential prerequisite" is usually only a *requisite*. **Prerequisite**, if it must be used, should not be confused with **perquisite** (often shortened to *perk*) = extra payment, more often in kind than in cash, for a task.

precede = go before (in time or place); **proceed** = go forward, go on (with). The related nouns are *precedence* (which *see*), *procedure* (= method of going forward) and *progress* (going forward).

precedence = superiority (in order); **precedent** = previous example that establishes a ruling; e.g. "Giving precedence to the Managing Editor (on his birthday) should not establish a precedent."

precentor = cathedral musician-in-chief; **preceptor** = teacher.

pre-Christian, pre-Classical, pre-Colombian, etc.

precipitously = very steeply; **precipitately** = very hurriedly. As Partridge says, the only way of leaving a room precipitously is to jump out of the window.

précis (= a textual abstract) can be used as a verb; if it must be so used, the past tense and participle is **précised** ("pray-seed") and the present participle is **precising** ("pray-seeing").

predate = to date before the actual writing, to antedate. As a verb meaning to prey upon (as a back-formation from predator) the word has not found favour, and should be avoided. Acceptable derived words include predatory (preferred to predaceous, predacious or predative) and *predation* (preferred to predacity).

predilection (not predilection) seldom means more than **preference** (not prefrence, preferrence), and should be avoided.

pre-dominant *See* **dominating.**

preface = an introduction to a book, about the book, written by the author(s) or general editor; **foreword** = an introductory piece written by someone other than the author (indeed it may be about the author and not about the book itself). In a book containing both a preface and a foreword, the former usually precedes the latter; both should follow the **contents** (if any).

prefer, preferred, preferring, preferable, preference. The first four forms take *to*; *preference* takes *for*.

prefix *See* **numerical prefixes; units.**

prehensible = can be grasped; **prehensile** = can grasp.

prejudgement

prejudice, correctly prounounced, does not attract the misspelling *predudice*. **Prejudice** *against* or *in favour of* = bias; **prejudice** *to* = disadvantage, detriment.

prelims = publisher's abbreviation of **preliminary matter** (also called **front matter**), the pages at the beginning of a book that may include a half-title, title-page, copyright/acknowledgements, contents, foreword and introduction. They may have no folios (page numbers) or have folios typeset in lower case roman numerals (i, ii, iii, iv, and so on). Unfolioed prelim pages may or may not be included in the page numbering of the whole book; thus the first main page of a book with eight pages of prelims may have 1 or 9 as its folio. By analogy, the jargon term for the **back matter** or *end matter* of a book (such as a bibliography, glossary or index) is **postlims**. These pages are usually numbered consecutively as a continuation of the main book folios. *See also* **books**.

premier = first (in importance, order or time); **première** = first performance (of a film, play, etc.).

premise (verb) = to state first, to prefix; **premise** (noun) = a proposition (something stated first for later discussion); **premises** = buildings (it has no singular); **premiss** = premise (noun).

premium (pl. premiums).

preoccupy and **preoccupation** take *with* (not *by*).

prepositions Pedants abhor a preposition at the end of a sentence; to paraphrase Winston Churchill, it is something up with which they will not put. The absurdity of this last clause is proof that avoidance of prepositional sentence-endings usually requires a complete recasting of the sentence; alternatively, let them stand – what is wrong with "it is something they will not put up with"? Most of the enlightened authoritories now allow this construction. Prepositions and adverbs connected phrasally with verbs are called phrasal verbs; in this way *go* can be modified into *go away*, *go down*, *go in*, *go into*, *go off* and *go up*, all of which convey meanings different from plain *go*.

pre-school child *See* **baby**.

prescribe = appoint, order, advise; **proscribe** = ban, prohibit, condemn.

present-day is overworked for *present* or *contemporary* (or *today's*).

presently = soon (e.g. "She will be here presently"). The word is also often used to mean *at present* (e.g. "She is presently in the other room"), which purists continue to resist.

press agent, press-button (but push-button preferred), press conference, press-cutting, press-fastener, press gang (noun), press-gang (verb), pressman, press-stud, presswork.

pressure, pressurize (= raise to high pressure), pressurized (= under additional/high pressure). Thus the contents of an aerosol can are pressurized, although the word should not be extended figuratively to people (who may, however, be pressed, pressured or under pressure).

prestigious (not prestigous) = having prestige, esteemed, or high standing; **prodigious** (not prodigous) = unusually large, monstrous. An author's task in compiling a reference book can be prodigious; after publication, he or she may hope that the book becomes prestigious.

presume, presumable, presuming. For **presumably,** *see* **supposedly.** *See also* **assume.**

presumptuous is usually spelled correctly by people who do not mispronounce it *presumtious.*

pretend, pretence, pretension, pretentious, pretentiousness. **Pretence** = the act of pretending; **pretension(s)** = claim, aspiration, pretext; **pretentiousness** = claiming (too) much. Note that the spelling *pretention* does not exist.

pretension *See* **pretend.**

prevaricate = evade, mislead; **procrastinate** = postpone, put off. E.g.:

"When asked a direct question he prevaricated and turned the conversation to the weather."

"When asked to mow the lawn he procrastinated and said he would do it at the weekend."

prevent, preventive (not preventative). **Prevent** someone *from* doing something, or prevent someone*'s* doing something are the correct forms. E.g.:

"She prevented him from going" is correct;
"She prevented him going" is incorrect;
"She prevented his going" is correct.

previous to should not be used as a preposition; e.g. "Previous to the new typist's coming..." should be "Before the new typist came...". *See also* **prior to**.

pre-war

price, pricey.

priceless *See* **valuable**.

prima facie (italics) = at first sight; except in legal contexts, the Latin form should be avoided.

primeval

primitive People should not be described as primitive, which is regarded as derogatory in this context.

principal = main, chief; **principle** = an origin, source, theoretical basis. Reminder: *Principal = Head* or *chief* (of a college).

printer, in computers, is an *output device* which produces *hard copy* (characters printed on paper, often in the form of continuous stationery). Commonly used printers include a *dot-matrix printer* (in which the individual characters consist of a pattern of small dots), a *line printer* (which prints a line of type at a time at high speed), a *daisy-wheel printer* (which prints very legible typewriter-type characters, but is relatively slow), an *ink-jet printer* (which "paints" characters using an electrostatically controlled jet of minute ink droplets) and a *laser printer* (which uses a laser beam to "burn" characters onto paper, and is capable of giving a good representation of various type styles). Early proofs, such as galleys or first pages, from computerized typesetting systems may be provided as printouts. The choice of printer depends on cost and on the speed and clarity of characters required; a laser printer is often best on both of the last two counts.

printing processes can be broadly classified into three kinds: relief, planographic and intaglio. In **relief** processes, the characters to be printed are raised above the surface of the printing plate; typical examples are letterpress and its derivatives Monotype and Linotype, now used mainly for newspapers. **Planographic** processes include lithography (jargon *litho*), in which a photographic method is used to make part of the (usually aluminium) printing plate accept ink – the part carrying the characters to be printed – while the remainder of the plate remains ink-free. In **intaglio** processes, the printing ink is held in indentations below the level of the plate and transfers to paper pressed hard against it. Engravings, etchings and gravure are printed in this way. A **flat-bed** press uses flat printing plates; a **rotary** press uses curved or cylindrical plates. In a **direct** process, the inked printing plate presses directly onto the paper; in an **offset** process, the ink is transferred to a second plate or cylinder before being printed onto the paper. Printing presses may be **sheet-fed** (i.e. they print on individual sheets of paper) or **web-fed** (using a continuous ribbon of paper fed from a reel). A complete description of a particular printing process generally combines several of the terms described here; e.g. a four-colour web offset litho process.

printout (computers) *See* **hard copy; printer**.

prior as an adjective is correct (as in "a prior arrangement"), but **prior to** as a preposition is not ("prior to receiving your letter" should be "before receiving...").

prise = to force apart/open; **prize** = a reward (in a competition).

pristine = old and unspoiled, persisting and untouched. It should not be used to mean merely *fresh* or *new*.

probable *See* **possible**; **probe**.

probe, probeable (with an *e*, to prevent confusion with *probable*).

proceed, procedure, procedural, proceeding(s) (noun), proceeds (noun). **Proceed** = go forward, continue; **progress** (verb) = go forward, make something carry on; **process** (verb) = prosecute, put something through a prescribed procedure or process. E.g.:

"The guard signalled the driver to proceed."
"The manager must progress the job at each stage."
"The clerk processes the forms as they come in."

proceed should not be used as a pompous synonym for *go*, *walk*, *drive* etc. or to add weight to a simple statement, devices sometimes (at least in popular fiction) part of a policeman's vocabulary. E.g.:

"As I was proceeding down the High Street, I apprehended the accused."
"When I apprehended the accused, he proceeded to run away."
See also **precede**.

procrastinate *See* **prevaricate**.

procure = to win, gain, obtain by effort or contrivance (obtain for immoral purposes); **secure** = to make safe, obtain for certain. Both are stronger forms of the neutral *obtain* and the slovenly *get*.

prodigious *See* **prestigious**.

produce, producer, producible; **product**, productive, productivity (preferred to productiveness).

Prof. is the abbreviation of Professor, when used as a title, but should be avoided in narrative text.

profess, professor (abbreviation of the title is Prof.).

proffer, proffered, proffering (not preferred, preferring).

proficient *See* **efficient**.

profit, profited, profiting.

prognosis (pl. prognoses). *See* **diagnosis**.

programme (but computer program), programmer, programmed, programming.

progress *See* **proceed**.

project (noun and verb), projector.

proliferate = to increase rapidly (and greatly), not merely to increase.

prolific should describe the creator, not the creation. E.g.:

"She was prolific in her output of articles" (correct);
"Her output of articles was prolific" (incorrect).

promise, promissory.

promote, promotor.

prone = lying face downwards; **prostrate** = lying face downwards (in a faint); **recumbent** = lying down; **supine** = lying face upwards. **Prone** (to), in the sense having a proclivity or tendency (to), is becoming overworked and is often misused for *susceptible* (to) e.g. "People of the district are prone to sleeping sickness" is incorrect (even though they probably do finish up face downwards!), although "... are prone to contracting sleeping sickness" is just about acceptable.

pronounce, pronouncing, pronounceable, pronouncement, pronunciation.

proof (verb) has the past participle **proofed**. *See also* **prove**.

proof reading Standard proof-reading marks were originally defined in British Standard 1219. According to this system, all instructions to the typesetter and printer should be circled; additions or corrections should be inserted in the margin, or given on an attached sheet (keyed by a letter of the alphabet). A new standard, BS 5261, was introduced in 1976. It uses only symbols as marginal instructions (for international recognition), although many of the marks are the same as those in BS 1219. The accompanying table compares the most frequently used marks in each standard. Many people in publishing still use the old system; obviously, a mixture of the two should be avoided. Proofs should be marked in ink or ball pen, not pencil; for colour coding, *see* **corrections.**

propaganda is singular (and has no plural).

propel, propelled, propeller, propelling. **Propellant** is the noun (= something that propels); **propellent** is the adjective (= relating to that which propels); e.g. "Nitrogen is used as a propellent gas in some aerosols; others have fluons as propellants."

proper names *See* **capitalization**.

prophecy is the noun; **prophesy** is the verb.

proportion = a stated relation (in terms of magnitude) between one thing and another, ratio, due relation; e.g. "He mixed tonic with gin in the proportion of three to one." It should not be misused for *portion*, *part* or *number*; e.g. "The greater proportion of children have bad handwriting" is incorrect, at least in the use of *proportion* – it should be written "Most (= a large number of) children have...". A *proportion* of usually means merely **some**.

proposal = an offer (of marriage), a plan; **proposition** = terms of an enterprise (business proposition), something propounded, a promise.

proprietary (not proprietory) = of a proprietor or property, patented, trade-marked; **proprietry** does not exist; **propriety** = decency, rightness, conformity with convention (opposite *impropriety*).

Proof-reader's marks

action	mark in text	mark in margin	mark in text	mark in margin
	From BS 1219	*From BS 1219*	*From BS 5261*	*From BS 5261*
Editorial changes				
insert letter(s) or words(s)	⋏	new letter(s) or word(s)	⋏	new letter(s) or word(s)
insert new (omitted) copy	⋏	**insert copy attached Ⓐ**	⋏	⋏ Ⓐ
insert comma	⋏	⸲	⋏	⸲
insert semi-colon	⋏	⸵	⋏	⸵
insert full point	⋏	⊙	⋏	⊙
insert colon	⋏	⊙	⋏	⊙
insert apostrophe	⋏	ˊ	⋏	ˊ
insert single quotes	⋏⋏	ˊˊ	⋏⋏	ˊˊ
insert double quotes	⋏⋏	ʺʺ	⋏⋏	ʺʺ

353

action	mark in text	mark in margin	mark in text	mark in margin
	From BS 1219		*From BS 5261*	
insert question mark	⅄	?/	⅄	?
insert exclamation mark	⅄	!/	⅄	!
insert parentheses	⅄ ⅄	(/)/	⅄ ⅄	( )
insert (square) brackets	⅄ ⅄	[/]/	⅄ ⅄	[ ]
insert hyphen	⅄	|-|	⅄	|-|
obligatory hyphen at end of line	⅄	|=|	⅄	
insert en rule	⅄	1/N or ⊡en	⅄	⊡en
insert em rule	⅄	1/M or ⊡em	⅄	⊡em
insert elipsis	⅄	...	⅄	...
insert oblique stroke	⅄	/ (solidus)	⅄	⊘
spell out abbreviation or numeral in full	encircle character(s) to be spelled out	(spell out)		

354

Instruction	Textual mark	Marginal mark
delete	cross through characters to be deleted	᷂
delete and close up	cross through characters to be deleted and mark ⌒	(ᷟ)
ignore this correction (leave as printed)	– – – under word(s) or letter(s) to remain	stet
correction is ended	none	/(to separate more than one correction on one line)

Typeface changes

Instruction	Textual mark	Marginal mark
change to italics	—— under word(s) or letter(s) concerned	ital
change to small capitals	═══ under word(s) or letter(s) concerned	s.c.
change to capitals	≡≡≡ under word(s) or letter(s) concerned	caps
change to lower case	encircle word(s) or letters concerned	l.c.

action	mark in text	mark in margin	mark in text	mark in margin
	From BS 1219		*From BS 5261*	
change to bold face	~~~ under word(s) or letters concerned	(b.f.)	~~~ under word(s) or letters concerned	∼
change to roman face	encircle word(s) or letters concerned	(rom)	encircle word(s) or letters concerned	Ⴔ
wrong type fount	encircle character(s) to be changed	(w.f.)	encircle character(s) to be changed	⊗
damaged character(s)	encircle character(s) to be changed	×	encircle character(s) to be changed	×
Type position changes				
start new paragraph	[before first word of new paragraph	(n.p.)	[before first word of new paragraph	⌐
do not start new paragraph here	between the paragraphs	run on	between the paragraphs	⌇
make or insert superior character	⌄	Ɣ under letter required	⌄	Ɣ under letter required
make or insert inferior character	⌃	Λ over letter required	⌃	Λ over letter required

356

Proofreaders' Marks

Instruction	Marginal mark	In-text mark	Description
use ligature	(ae)	()	joining letters to be changed
do not use ligature	write out separately	/	through ligature
delete space between words or letters	()	⊃	bridging the space
insert space between words or letters	#	⌄	
delete space between lines	less #	(	connecting the lines
insert space between lines	#	>	between the lines
make word spacing equal	eq #	|	between words of line
reduce word spacing	less #	|	between words of line
insert space between letters	letter #	|||	between the letters
make letter spacing equal	eq #	vvv	between the letters

action	mark in text	mark in margin	mark in text	mark in margin
	From BS 1219		*From BS 5261*	
make line spacing equal	> between the lines \ ^ ^	eq #		
transpose	between elements to be transposed	trs	between elements to be transposed	
centre across measure	astride element(s) to be centred	centre	astride element(s) to be centred	
indent one em				1 *em*
indent two ems				2 *ems*
move right	to left of text to be moved		to left and right of text to be moved	
move left	to right of text to be moved		to right and left of text to be moved	
take over character(s) to next line		t.o.		

358

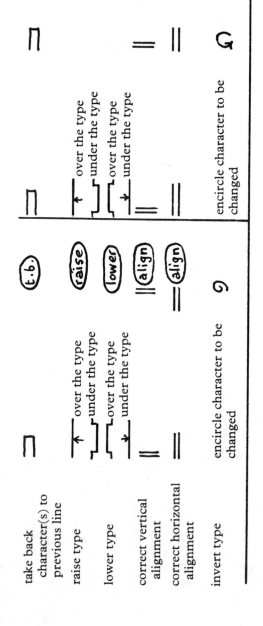

take back character(s) to previous line		
raise type	over the type / under the type	
lower type	over the type / under the type	
correct vertical alignment		
correct horizontal alignment		
invert type	encircle character to be changed	

t.b. · raise · lower · align · align

encircle character to be changed

pro rata = in proportion; the Latin form should be avoided.

proscribe *See* **prescribe**.

prosecute *See* **persecute**.

prospectus (pl. prospectuses).

prostrate *See* **prone**.

protagonist = a principal character (actor) in a story or incident. It does not mean *champion*, *advocate* or *supporter* of something; i.e. it is not the opposite of **antagonist** – it is from *protos* = first (fore-), not *pro* = in favour of (for).

protect, protector.

protégé (pl. protégés).

protest (verb) needs a preposition – which is *against*, not *at*.

protozoon (pl. protozoa).

protract, protractor.

prove (verb) has the past participle **proved**, although **proven** is often used in law. The adjectival form is also *proven*. E.g.:

"He proved his assertion."
"He was a proven friend."
See also **proof**.

provided that should introduce a stipulation (and in this use is preferred to **providing**); e.g. "I said I would write the article provided that he edited it." *Provided that* should not be used for *if*; e.g. "I will go away on Monday provided that it does not rain" should be "...if it does not rain."

provident = thrifty, frugal (providing for the future); **providential** = unexpectedly lucky (the result of divine providence). E.g.:

"Through the provident use of fuel, we were able to cook every day for a week."
"Through the providential discovery of the key, we were able to unlock the door."

proviso (pl. provisos) = stipulation; the Latin form should be avoided.

provocative *See* **evocative**.

prowess = daring, bravery (not merely *mastery* or *skill*).

prudent = displaying prudence, cautious, discreet; **prudential** = taking prudence into account. E.g.:

"Faced with the problem he took the prudent course, but later regretted not taking the riskier alternative."
"Prudential decisions are not always the best decisions."

pry = enquire, peer (into), be nosey; it does not mean **prise** (open).

PS is the abbreviation of *post scriptum* (written after).

psyche, psychic, psychiatry, psychoanalysis, psychoanalyse, psychology, psychedelic (illogical, but preferred to *psychodelic*).

publicize = to make an effort to get something widely known (often using a medium such as advertising); the result is **publicity**.
Publish = to issue in printed form; the result is **publication**. Most publications benefit from publicity.

pudendum (pl. pudenda).

puerile *See* **juvenile**.

pun is a (humorous) play on words, a device that depends for its effect on a double meaning (often involving homonyms, which *see*), such as the classic:

> Q: "When is a door not a door?"
> A: "When it's ajar."

Used very occasionally, puns can be effective in informal (and journalistic) writing; used to excess, they soon elicit groans. They should be avoided in formal text, and not even allowed to happen accidentally (e.g. "the swallow is a swift bird", "large noses ran in his family", "a lone idea about borrowing money"). *See also* **journalese**.

pulp board = papermaking term for board made entirely from wood pulp (*see* **chemical pulp**). Uncoated it is used for cartons and packaging; coated pulp board may be printed on and is used for greetings cards, paperback book covers, and so on. *See also* **cardboard**; **paper**.

punctilious (with one *l*) = scrupulously observant of details; **punctual** = scrupulously observant of an appointment time; people who are the former are always the latter.

punctuation Authorities continue to argue about punctuation. Today common sense and readability (not, as in former times, read-out-ability) should be the guide. As a general rule, punctuation should be kept to a minimum.

1. *Full point* A full point (also called a full stop or period) marks the end of a sentence, which has been defined as the complete expression of a thought. So this is a sentence. And so is this. And this.
   A full point is also used to terminate an abbreviation, such as "etc.", "a.m.", "fig." (*see* **abbreviations**).
   Do not put a full point after an exclamation mark or a question mark (which *see*, later).
   A full point hand-written on a typescript or proof is indicated thus: ⊙ For decimal point, *see* **fractions**.

2. *Comma* Commas are for sense, not decoration.
   Unless the clauses in a compound sentence are short and of similar form, a comma should be used before the conjunction, especially if there is a change of subject. E.g. "Most of the editors who work in reference book publishing are more than 80 years old, whereas most of the designers are under 20." The sentence "Editors work and designers play" needs no comma. Two or more adjectives which independently modify the same noun should be separated by commas: "a long, muddy river", "a small, round table", "a huge, hairy, green monster". If

"and" could be substituted for the comma (and the sentence still make sense), then a comma should probably be used. But if the combination of the second adjective and the noun are modified (jointly) by the first adjective, no comma is necessary: "a long white dress", "a small red ball".

Parenthetic nouns and phrases should be enclosed between commas: "The chief editor, John Jones, refused to accept the article", or "*My Life in Publishing*, a best-seller for ten years, was John Jones' first book". Pairs of dashes or parentheses (brackets) can be used as an alternative to commas in this type of sentence. But no commas are required in such constructions as "The editor John Jones refused to accept...", or "The best-seller *My Life in Publishing* was John Jones's first book", in which the identifying noun is used in a restrictive sense.

Clauses or phrases relating to a previously stated subject should be enclosed between commas: "The editor is admired, and even respected, by his colleagues".

Comma off items in a list, but not preceding "and" or "or": "Her favourite names were John, James and George", "She could not stand John, James or George". But if one or more items in a list contain "and", use a comma before the final "and": "The books included *The Animal World*, *Men and Machines*, and *Physics Today*". If one or more items in a list include a comma, use semicolons to separate the items: "The books included *Animals, Vertebrate and Invertebrate*; *Unicellular Organisms*; and *Man, Matter and Energy*".

Normal style for large numerals is to comma off in threes to the left of the (implied) decimal point: "2,300 people", "£1,473,000", "the conversion factor is 1,560.764", "12, 125.8432" (note no commas after the decimal point). Modern scientific setting often employs a thin space instead of a comma in large numerals. Do not use a comma in dates, for which the style is "13 November 1937" (not 13th).

Use a comma after "that is" and "for example":
"All three women were present – that is, Jane, June and Joan."
"Many names begin with J: for example, Jane, June and Joan."

3. *Semi-colon* A semicolon is a stronger stop than a comma, but not as strong as a full point. Preserve the relation between two related sentences by using a semi-colon (but no conjunction): "Modern punctuation is complicated; modern grammar is non-

existent.'' The inclusion of a conjunction would reduce the semicolon to a comma: ''Modern punctuation is complicated, but modern grammar is non-existent.'' If the sentences are not related, a full point should be used: ''Modern punctuation is complicated. Modern motor cars are expensive.''
Use semicolons to separate items in a list when individual items contain commas or are lengthy (see previous examples under *Comma*).

4. *Colon* A colon is no longer used as a stop or pause in a sentence (for which the comma and semicolon serve). A colon should be used to introduce a list or an example: ''He had three main interests: wine, women and song.'' To test if such a colon is correctly used, try replacing it with the word, ''namely''; do not follow such a colon with a dash. A colon may also be used to emphasise the contrast yet relationship between two related sentences (as in the first use of a semicolon described previously).

5. *Parentheses* (brackets). Use parentheses to enclose a definition or equivalent, as in the heading to this paragraph. Use them also to enclose an abbreviation following the term(s) abbreviated: ''The World Health Organization (WHO)'', ''The British Broadcasting Corporation (BBC)''. Use parentheses to give equivalents in a second system of units ''The road was 80 km (50 miles) long''. Use them also to enclose dates: ''Jones, John (1912–1985), was a well-known editor.''
''During World War II (1939–1945), John Jones served in the army.''
''At the end of World War II (1945), John Jones returned to publishing.''
Use parentheses round letters or numerals in lists and captions: ''There are three types of material: (1) animal, (2) vegetable and (3) mineral.''
''They can be specified in terms of (a) mineral content or (b) water content.''
''The exterior view (A) shows the skin texture, whereas the cross-section (B) reveals the internal anatomy.''
Apart from these technical uses, parentheses enclose an afterthought or an aside which is not crucial to a sentence (and can be omitted without altering the meaning), as in this

sentence. Pairs of commas set off similar phrases or clauses, but set them off less completely. Pairs of dashes set them off more completely, if less formally. Compare:

"He rode the bicycle, a green one, as fast as he could."

"He rode the bicycle (it was a green one) as fast as he could."

"He rode the bicycle – which was bright green – as fast as he could."

(see also later examples under *Dashes*.)

Only parentheses can be used to set off a whole sentence:

"He rode the bicycle as fast as he could. (It was a green bicycle with red handles.)

See also **brackets**.

6. *Dashes* Use a dash before "that is":

"Many great apes are bipedal – that is, they can walk upright on their hind limbs."

Use a dash before a summarizing final clause:

"Wine, women and song – these were his main interests."

Use dashes to enclose an afterthought or aside which bears little relation to the rest of the sentence:

"He rode the bicycle – which was bright green – as fast as he could."

Use dashes also around parenthetic expressions which would normally be set off with commas but which themselves contain commas:

"He rode the bicycle – an ancient, rusty, green one – as fast as he could."

(See also previous examples under *Parentheses*.)

7. *Quotation marks* Double or single quotation marks may be used; editors should find out and follow the publisher's style. If no guidance is given, use double quotation marks (") and single quotes (') for quotations within quotations:

He declared: "I have to agree with Henry Ford, 'History is bunk' ". Any punctuation marks belonging to the quoted text should be enclosed within the quotation marks; punctuation marks belonging to the sentence as a whole are kept outside. Interpolations in quotations should be set in brackets (i.e. square brackets, not parentheses):

He said: "The man [John Jones] is a scoundrel."

Omissions in quotations should be indicated by ellipses (. . .):

He said: "The man is a rascal . . . and a scoundrel."
Use quotation marks round words or phrases that are being ascribed new or unfamiliar meanings:

Notes in the mid-range are regarded as "safe".

Known to chemists as a "condensation" reaction, it . . .
(If overused, this device becomes tedious. Italicization is often a better alternative in constructions such as the second one:
Known to chemists as a *condensation* reaction, it . . .).
See also **inverted commas**.

8. *Apostrophe* An apostrophe is used to show possession (form the genitive case), normally by adding *'s*; e.g. John Brown's body, the dog's claws, NATO's ability, sheep's clothing, mens' stupidity, actress's dress. Exceptions are the pronouns hers, its, theirs, ours and yours, although one's does have an apostrophe. Possessives of plurals ending in *s* are formed by adding merely the apostrophe; e.g. victims' bodies, the two dogs' dinners, the Joneses' children, the actresses' dresses. Some modern usage omits the apostrophe from phrases containing possessive plurals; e.g. in two weeks time, four days holiday.
Most singular, monosyllabic proper names ending in *s* take an additional *'s* to form the possessive; e.g. Jones's car, St James's gospel, Strauss's waltzes. The additional *s* is usually omitted with di- and polysyllabic names; e.g. Williams' book, Adams' design. It is also omitted with Greek and French names (in which such an *s* would not be pronounced); e.g. Archimedes' principle, Charles' law. Possessives of proper names applied to products tend to drop the apostrophe; e.g. *Chambers Dictionary*, Clarks shoes, Smiths crisps.
Usage favours also the omission of an unpronounced *s* in other possessive forms; e.g. conscience' sake, appearance' sake, convenience' sake, goodness' sake, old times' sake (plurals consciences' sake, appearances' sake).
An apostrophe should be used in forming plurals where it is necessary to avoid confusion; e.g. *p's* and *q's*, *do's* and *don'ts*, *set-to's*.
Plurals of "ordinary" abbreviations do not need an apostrophe; e.g. BAs, MBEs, MPs, UFOs.
An apostrophe is used to indicate that a letter or letters have been omitted; e.g. *it's* (= it is), *don't* (= do not), although these abbreviated forms should be avoided in formal writing. No

apostrophe is needed in the following:
bus, cello, flu, fridge, phone, plane, teens.
See also **'s**.

9. *Question mark* Do not normally use any other punctuation
(except quotation marks) immediately after a question mark.
For example, compare the punctuation in this sentence:
He wondered briefly whether to go, but decided not to.
And this one containing a question:
He asked himself "Should I go?" but quickly answered "No".
where the expected comma after the question mark is omitted.

10. *Exclamation mark* Do not use exclamation marks except in
quotations or in names or titles that have an exclamation mark
as part of the names; e.g. *Hello, Dolly!*, Westward Ho! Do not
use a full point immediately after an exclamation mark.

11. *Hyphen see* **compound words**; **word breaks**.

pundit is the preferred spelling (not **pandit**).

pupa (pl. pupae).

pupil = someone who attends school; **student** = someone who attends
university or other institution/course of higher education. Because
the ages (and standards) at which young people – even old people –
make such attendance, *student* is the preferred blanket term for all
but the youngest of them.

purchase, purchasable, purchaser.

purée

purloin is usually a euphemism for **pilfer** or **steal** (and of these two,
the former is often a euphemism for the latter); *purloin* should be
avoided.

purposely = intentionally, on purpose; **purposefully** =
determinedly, with specific purpose. E.g.:

"He wrote small purposely, to save paper."
"She canvassed purposefully on behalf of the candidate."

put an end to = **kill** or **stop**, either of which is usually preferred.

putrefy, putrefaction, putrescent.

pygmy is the preferred spelling of **pigmy**.

pyjamas is the preferred spelling (not **pajamas,** which is an Americanism).

pyrolysis, pyrolyse.

Q

quad = printer's abbreviation for **quadrat**, a spacing-piece used in typesetting (employed to indent lines, such as beginnings of paragraphs, or to fill out the blank part of short lines). Widths of quad spaces are usually specified as *en*, *em*, *two-em* or *three-em*, often written as, for example, 2-em indent or space (#). Traditionally, an en quad is called a *nut*, and an em quad a *mutton*. In papermaking, a quad sheet size is four times a standard size of paper (e.g. a quad crown sheet has each dimension twice as large as a crown sheet). *See also* **paper sizes**.

quadraphony (not quadriphony, quadrophony).

quadri- or **tetra-** *See* **numerical prefixes**.

qualifying adverbs, such as *almost*, *possibly*, *probably*, *rather* and *somewhat*, should be used sparingly or they lose their effectiveness. Many editors employ them – indeed some are encouraged to do so – to introduce a slight doubt into what would otherwise be a definite statement with no exceptions. E.g.:

"The common cold is the most prevalent disease" may be edited to "The common cold is probably the most prevalent disease" (just in case it is not), which is better than alternative ways of hedging such as "Many experts believe that the common cold is the most prevalent disease" or "It may well be that the common cold is . . ." *Almost*, *rather* and *somewhat* should not be used to qualify an incomparable adjective, such as *perfect* or *unique*. For example it is nonsense to talk of a "rather unique machine"; either the machine is the only one of its kind (= unique) or it is not. *Possibly unique* (implying considerable doubt) and *probably unique* (implying only little doubt) are acceptable constructions.

quandary is the correct spelling (not quandry, despite the usual pronunciation).

quantitative = relating to quantity or number; **qualitative** = relating to quality or composition.

quantity (correctly applied to something that is uncountable) should not be misused for **number** (applied to something that can be counted). E.g.: "a quantity of sand" but "a number of bricks".

quantum (pl. quanta).

quarrel, quarrelled, quarrelling, quarreller, quarrelsome.

quarry = a (wide) hole in the ground from which sand, gravel, stone or minerals are excavated; or the "prey" of a hunter (two distinct words with the same spelling).

quarter-binding (a type of bookbinding with the spine only in a different material), quarter-day, quarterdeck, quarter-final, quarter-light, quartermaster (title abbreviates to QM), quarter-plate, quarter sessions, quarter-staff.

quarto (pl. quartos, abbreviation 4to) is a printing term for a fourth of a sheet of paper, made by folding a standard size in half twice. *See* **paper sizes**.

quatercentenary (not quartercentenary), quaternary.

queer = strange, odd, quaint; the modern slang usage meaning *homosexual* (adj. and noun) makes *queer* a word to use with care, at least for the time being.

query (verb) should not be used to mean *ask* (e.g. "I queried her about her childhood" is incorrect); the verb can, however, be used to mean *raise doubts about* (as in "The surveyor queried the dimensions of the house"). **Query** (noun), in typography, is an alternative name for **question mark**.

question is part of two idioms that are commonly misused. To *beg the question* = to prove an assertion by means of another (different) assertion. (Fowler's example is that "democracy must be the best form of government because the majority are always right"); it does not mean to avoid giving a straight answer. A *leading question* is one phrased in such a way as to help elicit the required answer, and for this reason is not allowed in a court of law (e.g. "Would you say that the confusion of the accused was consistent with drunkenness?"); it does not mean a searching question or one that strikes at the nub of a problem.

queue, queued, queuing. *See also* **cue**.

quiche *See* **flan**.

quick is an adjective meaning speedy; **quickly** is an adverb meaning speedily. E.g.:

"He wanted to make a quick escape."
"He wanted to escape quickly."
The coloquial use of *quick* as an adverb should be avoided (as in "She had to run quick to catch the bus"). The archaic use of *quick* to mean "alive" persists only in the cliché "the quick and the dead".

quiescent = inactive, motionless; **quiet** = free from or not emitting sound or noise.

quieten, quieting (= quietening).

quire = (nominally) 25 sheets of paper, $\frac{1}{20}$ of a *ream*; **choir** = group of singers; **coir** = coconut fibre.

quit has the past tense **quitted** and past participle **quit**.

quite = completely, entirely; it should not be used to mean **moderately** or *somewhat*. E.g.:

"The job is quite finished" (correct);
"The job is quite interesting" (avoid).

qui vive (italics) = **alert**; the French term should be avoided.

quiz (pl. quizzes), quizzed, quizzing, quizzer, quizmaster.

quoin is the preferred spelling of **coign** for a corner-stone and the only one for the wedge that locks type in a forme (both words are old versions of *coin*, whose pronunciation they still share).

quorum (pl. quorums, not quora).

quota = an allocation, predetermined share or portion (*see* **portion**); e.g. "She did not drink her quota of wine" is incorrect unless it was a two-glasses-of-wine-per-person-and-no-more-and-no-less kind of a party. *Quota* is a singular word (pl. quotas); it is not the plural of **quotum** – a little-used synonym of quota.

quotation marks *See* **punctuation**.

quotations should be transcribed accurately, keeping the original spelling and punctuation. In quoting poetry, reproduce also the type layout/line breaks if possible. *See also* **ellipsis; punctuation** (quotation marks); *sic*.

quoth is archaic for **said**, and should be avoided.

qwerty is an acronym for the first six letters on a normal computer or typewriter keyboard, used to describe such a keyboard.

R

rabbet (verb = to make a woodwork joint), rabbeted, rabbeting.

rabbi (pl. rabbis).

rabbit (verb = to catch rabbits), rabbited, rabbiting, rabbiter.

race should be used with care. The inhabitants/citizens of a country are rarely of one race (e.g. the Germans are a *nation* or *people*, most of them belonging to the Caucasian *race*). In ordinary contexts, to refer to blacks or Asians as a race is pejorative and regarded as **racism** (preferred form to *racialism*). It is also incorrect to refer to members of a particular religious faith as a race (e.g. there is no Jewish race or Moslem race). The *human race* is a correct term to distinguish people from other animals. *See* **racism**.

racism should be assiduously avoided in all writing (and editing). Among the most controversial terms in this context are the names used by one group of people to describe members of another group. Some are neutral (unintended) and acceptable, some dubious, some derogatory (intended) and unacceptable, and some downright offensive. Terms in the last two categories are generally regarded as racist. Sensitive writers do not use them, and editors should be aware of the pitfalls in dealing with texts from writers who do. Three broad groups can be compiled; terms in the "dubious" category should be used only with care.
Neutral/acceptable Black/black, Coloured (South Africa only), gaucho, gentile, mestizo, mulatto.
Dubious Aussie, Brit, Eurasian, infidel, Jock, Kiwi, Murphy, Negro, Negress, Negrillo, Negrito, paddy, pommy, Springbok, Taffy, Tyke.
Racist Abo, Anglo-Indian, Argie, Bosch, Chinaman, Chink, colonial, coloured, coon, Croakie, dago, darky, diddy, Frog, gippy, gook, goy, greaser, gringo, Guinea, gypo, Hun, half-breed, half-caste, honky, Iti, Ivan, Jap, Jerry, Jim Crow, Kaffir, Kanook, Kike, Kraut, Limey, munt, Newfie, nigger, nig-nog, Nip, Octaroon, Paki,

polak, quadroon, sambo, Sassenach, Scand, spade, spik, Swartz, tink, wetback, wog, wop, Yank, Yid.

rack *See* **wrack**.

racket is the correct spelling of all meanings (not **racquet**).

radical = basic, fundamental, root or stem of a word, an active unit if a chemical compound; **radicle** = embryonic root of a seed.

radio (pl. radios), radioed, radioing, radioactive, radioactivity, radio-carbon (etc.), radiography, radio-isotope, radiology, radiotherapy.

radius (pl. radii).

rag content = papermaking term for the proportion of the pulp, and hence of the fibres in the finished paper, that is derived from (usually cotton) rags. An *all-rag paper* is made entirely from rags. *See also* **paper**.

rainbow, rain-cloud, raincoat, raindrop, rainfall, rain-gauge, rainforest, rainhat, rainproof, rainstorm, rain-water.

raise is transitive (e.g. "Raise your arms"); **rise** is intransitive (e.g. "I saw the balloon rise in the sky"); **raze** = to lay level with the ground (e.g. "The building was razed by the fire"); **arise** = to occur, come into existence ("The meeting should finish early, as long as nothing unexpected arises"). **Raise** can also = bring up (young), rear; some authorities insist that animals are *raised*, whereas human children are *reared*. **Raisable** = can be raised; **risible** = laughable, silly. Of all the words discussed, only *rise* can be used as a noun (an employee applies for a *rise*; *raise* is an Americanism in this context).

raison d'être (italics) = reason/purpose of existence; the French form should be avoided.

râle (= abnormal chest sound).

RAM = abbreviation of random access memory, the data storage of a computer from which any item can be recalled in a virtually constant (and quick) access time. In lay terms, it takes the same time to look up anything in a RAM store. *See also* **CP**.

rancour, rancorous.

random access memory (computers) *See* **RAM**.

rapped is the past tense and participle of the verb to *rap*; **rapt** is an adjective from *rapture*; **wrapped** is the past tense and participle of the verb to *wrap*. E.g. knuckes may be *rapped*, an audience may be *rapt*, and a parcel may be *wrapped*.

rarefy, rarefaction.

rarely ever = rarely (which is preferred). **Rarely or ever** is nonsense and incorrect for **rarely or never** (or *rarely if ever*). One of these last two is intended in "Layout artists can rarely or ever draw straight lines." *See also* **seldom ever**.

rarity *See* **scarcity**.

rat-catcher, rat-flea, rat-poison, ratrace, ratsbane, rat's-tail, rat-tail, rat-trap.

ratchet, ratcheted, ratcheting.

rate, ratable, rating.

ratio (pl. ratios).

rational = sane, judicious, logical, showing/accepting reason (opposite to *irrational*); **rationale** = basic principle, theoretical explanation; **rationalize** = to make rational. E.g.:

"His bigotry closed his mind to rational argument."
"He gave tiredness as the rationale for his poor performance."
"He rationalized his poor performance by claiming to be tired."

raze *See* **erase**; **raise**.

razzmatazz is an Americanism which some American dictionaries no longer include. The consensus of those that do indicates the spelling given, although British dictionaries offer also the alternatives *razmataz* and *razzamatazz*. The word is used less frequently than it once was, and if it must be used the preferred spelling is the American one.

Rd is the abbreviation of (a named) Road.

re should not be used in formal writing to mean **about** or **concerning**.

re-, as a prefix meaning again, takes a hyphen when the root word begins with an *e* or when the resulting compound word could be mispronounced or confused with another word. E.g.:

re-cede (= give back)   recede (= shrink)
re-collect (collect again)   recollect (= remember)
re-cover (cover again)   recover (= get better)
re-count (= count again)   recount (= narrate)
re-dress (= dress again)   redress (= compensate)
re-do, re-done
re-echo
re-edit
re-elect
re-enter
re-establish
re-examine
re-export
re-fuse (= fuse again)   refuse (= decline offer)
re-heat
re-lay (= lay again)   relay (= pass on)
re-route
re-serve (= serve again)   reserve (= keep for later)
re-sign (= sign again)   resign (= relinquish)
re-soluble (= dissolvable again) resoluble (= capable of resolution)
re-sort (= sort again)   resort (= turn for help)
re-strain (= strain again)   restrain (= hold back)
re-turn (= turn again)   return (= to give/go back)

The use of *again* with any of the *re-* words in the first column is a tautology that should be avoided (*see* **tautology**).

read has the past tense and participle **read** (pronounced "red"). Thus it is not possible, out of context, to determine the tense and punctuation of the simple sentence "I read books". *See also* **lead**.

readable = interesting to read; **legible** = written or printed clearly, can be read without difficulty.

reafforest(ation) is preferred to **reforest(ation)**.

realize, realizable, realizer, realization.

really, like *actually* and *definitely*, is overworked as an intensifier. Good writers make sure *really* is really needed – this sentence does not need the second one.

ream (verb) = to enlarge a hole or bore; **ream** (noun) = (nominally) 500 sheets of paper (= 20 quires), although in printing reams of 480 and 516 sheets are also used.

reason (why) should be followed by *is that*; e.g. "The reason editors make mistakes is that they . . ." *Why*, however, is superfluous and should be omitted. *See also* **cause**.

rebel, rebelled, rebelling.

rebuff = reject (an offer of help), repulse; **rebuke** = censure, reprove; **rebut** = disprove an allegation by answering in kind; **refute** = prove beyond all doubt that an allegation is wrong. E.g.:

"She felt hurt because he rebuffed her offer to assist him."
"He rebuked her for making the error, even though she offered to correct it."
"She rebutted his accusation by pointing out that he had made similar errors."
"She refuted his allegation of carelessness by showing him that the previous version was free from errors when she passed it on."

rebuke *See* **rebuff**.

rebus (pl. rebuses).

rebut, rebutted, rebutting, rebuttal. *See also* **rebuff**.

recall = deliberately to remember; **recollect** = suddenly to remember, or succeed in remembering. E.g.:

"You must try to recall her name."
"Now that I see her photograph, I recollect her name is Maria."

receipt = paper acknowledging that money has been paid; **recipe** = list of ingredients and method for cooking/preparing a dish. The former word is no longer used for the latter.

receive, receiver (all meanings), receivable (describes someone or something that can be received), receptive (describes someone who is willing or readily able to receive new ideas), recipient (someone who receives).

received English, or received pronunciation (RP), was originally a term coined by Alexander Ellis and embodied in Daniel Jones's description of the socially acceptable non-regional English accent associated with public schools, Cambridge and Oxford Universities, the educated speech of the Home Counties.

recherché

reckless = without heed of the consequences, rash; **ruthless** = without compassion/mercy, unscrupulous. E.g.:

"The driver was reckless in his disregard of the speed limit."
"The employer was ruthless in her disregard for people's feelings."

recognize, recognizable, recognizance.

reconcile, reconcilable, reconciler, reconciliation.

reconnaissance

reconnoitre, reconnoitred, reconnoitring.

record player *See* **gramophone**.

recourse = turning to someone or something for help; **resource** = a reserve (which can be drawn on, especially when in difficulty); **resort** = expedient, something that can provide help. *Resource* and *resort* overlap in meaning; they should not be misused for *recourse*. E.g.:

"They were reassured that they always had recourse to the military in times of trouble."
"They were offered the resources of the military in times of trouble."
"They could turn to the military as a last resort in times of trouble."

rectify *See* **justify**.

recto = right-hand page of a book; **verso** = left-hand page.

rectum (pl. rectums).

red admiral, red-belly, red biddy, red-blooded, redbreast, red-breasted, redbrick (adj.), red cabbage, redcap, red carpet, redcurrant, redeye, red face, red-faced, red hair, red-haired, red-handed, redhead, red-headed, red-heat, red herring, red-hot (adj.), red lead, red-letter day, red-light (adj), redpoll, red-shank(s), redskin, red tape, red-water fever, red wine, redwing.

redolent (= odorous, smelling) requires *of*.

reduce, reducer, reducible (not reductible), reductant. *See also* **deplete**.

redundancy in language *See* **tautology**.

refer, referred, referring, referable, referrer, reference, referral, referee. **Refer** does not need the preposition *back* (write "refer to" not "refer back to").

reference marks *See* **footnotes**.

referendum (pl. referendums).

reflect, reflectible (= able to be reflected, as light is), reflective (= able to reflect, as a mirror is, hence *reflection*), reflector; **reflexive** = of a reflex or reflex action, a grammatical term.

reforest(ation) The preferred form is **reafforest(ation)**.

refract, refractor, refractable (preferred to refrangible).

refraction *See* **diffraction**.

refute *See* **deny**; **rebuff**.

regalia is a plural word (and has no singular).

regenerate, regenerator.

regime (no accent) = administration, government; **regimen** = a course of treatment (such as a diet).

register, registrable (not registerable), registrar, registry (but Register Office).

register = printing term for the accurate superimposition of two or more coloured images to form a composite one. Accurate alignment is facilitated by *register marks* outside the image area. Misaligned images are termed *out of register*.

regret, regretted, regretting, regrettable (describing something that causes regret), regretful (describing the state of having regret). *See also* **regretfully**.

regretfully (= with regret) should not be used for **regrettably** (= to be regretted). *Regretfully* has become a vogue word, used (incorrectly) to given an apologetic tone to a statement (e.g. "Regretfully the item you require is out of stock", in which *regrettably* is intended and "I am sorry but . . ." would be better). *See also* **hopefully**; **thankfully**.

regulate, regulator (all meanings).

relapse, relapsable.

relate, relater (who relates), but relator in law (who informs authority).

relations *with* someone, not relations *to*. *See also* **family relationships**.

relative (noun) is preferred to **relation** when referring to a member of a family (e.g. "We are going to stay with my wife's relatives").

release, releaser (who releases), but releasor in law (who grants a release).

relevant, relevance (and irrelevant, irrelevance). *See also* **material**.

relic = object of historical interest, souvenir; **relict** = widow.

relief printing *See* **printing processes**.

reluctant = unwilling to act; **reticent** = unwilling to talk, reserved. E.g.:

"When asked to attend the conference, he was reluctant to go." "During the heated debate, she was too reticent to state her view."

remainder *See* **balance**.

remit, remitted, remitting, remittal (= referring a legal case to another court), remittance (= payment of money), remission (= shortening of a prison sentence), remissible, remitter (who gives), remittee (who receives).

remove, removable.

remunerate = to pay recompense; **renumerate** = to count again; **enumerate** = to count (the number of). E.g.:

"I shall remunerate you for doing the job."

"To avoid further mistakes, I shall renumerate the things to be done."

"Before you start, I shall enumerate the things to be done."

rend, an archaic verb for to **tear**, inflects *rend – rent – rent*.

render, rendible (but *translatable* preferred, unless of fat).

rendezvous (pl. rendezvous); the verb form is he (or she) rendezvouses.

renounce, renounceable, renunciation (preferred to renouncement).

rent *See* **hire**; **rend**.

reorganize, reorganization.

repair, repairable (= can be repaired), reparable (of a loss that can be made good), reparation.

repast is precious for **meal**, which is preferred.

repel, repelled, repelling, repeller, repellent (adj. and noun, preferred to repellant), repulsive. **Repel** = drive back (opposing forces), refuse (an offer), or offend the senses, cause repugnance; something that drives back is *repellent*, something that causes repugnance is *repulsive*. **Repulse** also = drive back or rebuff, but does not form the adjective *repulsive* (which is reserved for the meaning defined previously). E.g.:

"She repelled his amorous advances."
"He accepted her repellent response."
"She found his behaviour repulsive."
"The garrison repulsed the enemy attack."

replace, replaceable. Replace something *by* something else (not *with* or *for*); A is replaced by B, not B with or for A. **Substitute** something *for* something else, not *with* or *by*; A is substituted for B, not with or by B. Thus *replace* = take the place of; *substitute* = put in the place of. E.g.:

"Please replace Wendy by Maria on the team"
and "Please substitute Maria for Wendy on the team"
convey the same meaning.

reply = an answer; **retort** = a sharp reply, retaliation; **riposte**
= sharp witty reply, repartee.

reprehend, reprehensible.

represent, representable (also re-present, re-presentable),
representation, representative (adj. and noun); *representive* does not
exist.

repress, represser, repressible, repression.

reprint *See* **edition.**

reproduce, reproducible, reproducer, reproduction.

reproof (verb) = to proof again; **reprove** = to rebuke; **reproof**
(noun) is common to both.

repulse *See* **repel.**

repute, reputable, reputation.

require, requirement, requisition, requisite. *Requirement(s)* = a need
or condition; *requistion* = a written order for something that is
needed; *requisite* (noun) = something that is needed; *requisite*
(adj.) = required. E.g.:

"A science degree is a requirement for the post."
"He made a requisition for a new desk."
"Driving experience is a requisite for the job of milkman."
"He lacked the requisite experience."
See also **pre-.**

reredos (pl. reredoses).

research *in* or *into* a subject (not *on*).

reserve, reserver (but reservor in law), reservist, reservable (= can be reserved); also re-serve (= serve again), re-servable (= can be served again).

resin = natural gum from plants or an artificial substitute used in paints and plastics. The natural resin used on violinists' bows, boxers and ballet dancers' shoes, and gymnasts' hands is known as **rosin**.

resist, resister (= someone who resists), resistor (= that resists electric current), resistance (no longer used for *resitor* in electronics), resistant, resistible.

resolve, resolvable (and re-solve, re-solvable).

resort *See* **recourse**.

resource *See* **recourse**.

respect, respector, respectable (= worthy of respect), respectful (= showing respect), respective (= pertaining to, appropriate), respectively (= in the order previously listed/stated).

respirate, respirator, respiration.

respond, responsive, responsible. **Responsible** = accountable (for) (e.g. "She was responsible for approving designers' layouts"), or cause of (e.g. "A broken suspension was responsible for the crash"). Care is needed to avoid the first meaning being mistaken for the second (e.g. "The office manager is responsible for holes in the carpet."). *See also* **irresponsible**.

restaurateur (not restauranteur).

restive = intractable, unco-operative; **restless** = unsettled, uneasy, never still.

restore, restorer, restorable, restoration.

restrain *See* **constrain**.

resume, resumable.

résumé (with two accents).

reticent *See* **reluctant**.

reticulum (pl. reticula).

retina (pl. retinas).

retort *See* **reply**.

retrace, retraceable.

retract, retractor, retractable (= retractile).

retrieve, retrievable, retriever, retrieval.

retrospective = looking back, in retrospect; **retroactive** = acting backwards (in time).

retroussé

revel, revelled, revelling, reveller.

revenge *See* **avenge**.

reverend = deserving reverence; **reverent** = showing reverence.

reverse, reversible, reversal. **Reversal** = a turning back or the other way round, should not be confused with **reversion** = a return to a previous state or condition. The former is from *reverse*, the latter from *revert*. E.g.:

"In the second game our team won 2–1, a reversal of the score in the first game."
"The patient's behaviour seemed like a reversion to childhood."
See also **revert**.

revert, revertible, reversion. *See also* **reverse**.

review = survey, formal inspection, critical opinion on a book, film or play; **revue** = entertainment (usually on stage), generally with humorous sketches and songs. *See also* **overview**.

revise, revisable, revision.

revive, revival, reviver (who revives = brings back to life), but revivor in law.

revoke, revocable, revocation.

revolt, revolution(ary), revolutionize.

reward *See* **award**.

rhesus factor abbreviates to Rh-factor; also Rh-positive, Rh-negative (abbreviated further to Rh +, Rh − if necessary).

rhinoceros (pl. rhinoceroses).

rhombus (pl. rhombuses).

rhyme is the preferred spelling (not **rime**, except when *rime* = frost).

rhyming slang *See* **slang**.

riches is usually regarded as a plural word (e.g. "Riches are a common goal of ambitious people").

rick (verb) is the preferred spelling (not **wrick**), for the verb meaning to twist or sprain.

rickettsia (pl. rickettsiae) is a type of disease-causing micro-organism.

ricochet, ricocheted ("*riko-shayed*"), ricocheting ("*riko-shaying*").

rid, ridding, riddance. The preferred inflexion of the verb is *rid – rid – rid*. *See also* **ride**.

ride, riding, ridable. The inflexion of the verb is *ride – rode – ridden*. *See also* **rid**.

rider *See* **corollary**.

right-angle, right-angled, right-handed(ness), right-minded, right-of-way, right-whale, right-wing(er).

rigor (= unresponsiveness, stiffness, chill), rigor mortis; **rigour** (= strictness, over-exactness), rigorous, rigorousness.

rill = a stream; **rille** = a valley on the Moon.

rime The preferred spelling is **rhyme** (for the poetical device), although *rime* is correct for a type of frost.

ring (verb = to sound a bell) has the past tense **rang** (not *rung*) and past participle **rung**. **Ring** (verb = to encircle, put a ring round something) has the past tense and participle **ringed**.

riposte *See* **reply**.

rise has the past tense **rose** and past participle **risen**. *See also* **raise**.

risible *See* **raise**.

risky = hazardous, potentially dangerous; **risqué** (with an accent) = bordering on impropriety.

risotto (pl. risottos).

ritual, ritualize, ritualization.

rival, rivalled, rivalling.

rivet, riveted, riveting (not rivetted, rivetting).

road-bed, roadblock, road-hog, road-map, roadside, road-works, roadworthy, roadworthiness.

rodeo (pl. rodeos).

role (no circumflex) = part in a play, function in an event/process;
   roll (noun) = register, list of names, anything of cylindrical shape.

roll coating = papermaking term for a method of applying a coating
   to paper during manufacture using a roller. *See also* **paper**.

roman describes upright type (as in these words), as opposed to **bold**
   or *italic*.

Roman Catholic *See* **Catholic**.

roman numerals should be avoided except as part of a monarch's
   name (e.g. Charles II, Henry VIII), book of the Bible (e.g. I Kings,
   II Kings), in the terms World War I and World War II, and in
   certain technical conventions (such as the numbering of the cranial
   nerves and valence in chemistry). Lower-case roman numerals are
   sometimes used for folios (page numbers) on the preliminary
   matter in books (i.e. i, ii, iii, iv, etc.). The "modern" roman
   numerals are:

   I = 1, V = 5, X = 10, L = 50, C = 100, D = 500, M = 1,000.

rondo (pl. rondos).

röntgen (preferred to roentgen).

roof (pl. roofs).

-r- or -rr- Monosyllabic words ending in -*r* preceded by a single
   vowel double the *r* before *y* or a prefix beginning with a vowel.
   E.g.:

   blur   blurred, blurring, blurry
   stir   stirrable, stirred, stirrer, stirring

   The *r* remains single if preceded by a long or double vowel. E.g.:

   bear   bearable, bearing
   moor   moored, mooring
   wear   wearable, wearing

With polysyllabic words, the choice of -r- or -rr- depends on where the accent falls. If it is on the last syllable, the rule is as for monosyllabic words; e.g. debarring, disinterring, occurring, preferring (exceptions include inferable, preferable, referable, severable, in which the accent changes, and registrable, in which the spelling changes). If the last syllable is unaccented the r is not doubled; e.g. capering, entering, motoring, offering, suffering. Neither is the r doubled, in monosyllabic or polysyllabic words, before suffixes that begin with a consonant; e.g. bothersome, dapperly, deferment, fearful, interment, tearfully.

rosary = string of (55 or 165) beads for "telling" devotions; **rosery** = rose garden.

rosé (wine)

rosin *See* **resin.**

rostrum (pl. rostrums).

rota (pl. rotas).

rotate, rotor (= rotating part of machinery), rotary (= having a circular motion), rotatable (= capable of rotary movement), rotator (= a muscle that rotates a joint), rotatory (= causing, or in, rotation), rotational (= acting in rotation), rotative (= turning like a wheel, produced or caused by rotation). *Rotatory* has largely replaced *rotary*, and can be used for *rotative*.

rotisserie (not rôtisserie).

rotund *See* **orotund.**

roué

rough-and-ready, rough-and-tumble, roughcast, rough house, roughneck, rough-rider, roughshod, rough-spoken.

round about should be avoided to mean approximately, near (e.g. "She is round about two metres tall", "He lives round about here''). In the first example, *round about* means merely *about*; in the second, it means *near*. **Roundabout** (one word) is a large traffic island at a junction or intersection of roads, or a merry-go-round.

rouse *See* **arouse**.

rout (verb) = to put to flight; **route** (verb) = to direct along a particular path.

roux = mixture of flour and fat; **rue** = to be sorry, regret.

rpm is the abbreviation of revolutions per minute.

rps is the abbreviation of revolutions per second.

rue, rueful, rueing.

rule = typesetter's term for a line to be printed (originally a thin strip of metal of type height, resembling a metal rule). The thickness of a rule is generally specified in *points* (*see* **point**), and may be horizontal, vertical or a box rule (forming a closed square or rectangular box around text or an illustration). For display setting, a *swell rule* (which is fatter at the middle) may be specified.

rumen (= cow's stomach), ruminate, ruminant (= animal that chews the cud), ruminator (= person who chews things over).

run (verb) has the past tense **ran** and past participle **run**.

runabout, runaway, run-down, runoff (noun), run-of-the-mill, run-on (noun).

running head = publisher's term for a book, chapter, section or article title (or a combination of two of these) repeated at the tops of pages of a book. In alphabetically arranged works (e.g. a dictionary), the first three letters of an article or entry only may be used as running heads, but most readers find it more helpful to have the whole word. In such works, it is conventional for the left-hand running head to be the title of the first article beginning on that page, and the right-hand running head to be the last article on that page. An article that extends for more than a whole page has its title repeated in the running heads.

rural = pertaining to the country(side) (opposite of *urban*);
rustic = pertaining to countryfolk, unsophisticated, roughly made. E.g.:

"Some foxes abandon a rural environment and live on the outskirts of cities."
"His origins were obvious from his rustic manner of speech."

Russia should be used for the nation before November 1917; references after that date should be to the **Soviet Union** (abbreviate to USSR if necessary in tables etc.). The corresponding adjectives are *Russian* and *Soviet*.

ruthless *See* **reckless**.

S

s, in scientific works, is the abbreviation of second(s). In other texts **sec** should be used, if an abbreviation has to be employed.

**$**, the dollar sign, should be avoided when there are only occasional references to currency (when dollar(s) should be spelled out). In either case, unless the context makes it clear, write US dollar ($) or Australian dollars etc., at least at first mention. For large amounts, note the style of 300 million dollars, $300 million.

's forms the possessive (genitive case) of nouns – e.g. cat's, (singular) Jones's, (plural Joneses'), women's – *see* **punctuation** (apostrophe); the possessive of only one pronoun (*one's*, which *see*); a short form of *is* – e.g. it's (= it is), there's (there is); a short form of *us* – e.g. let's (= let us); an abbreviation of *God's* – e.g. the exclamations 'sdeath (= God's death), 'strewth (= God's truth). The exclamations and abbreviated forms such as *it's*, *there's* and *let's* should be avoided in formal writing.

Sabbath (initial capital letter); it is not necessarily synonymous with *Sunday*.

saccharin = artificial substitute for sugar; **saccharine** = sugary.

sacred = holy; **sacrosanct** = inviolate, secure from infringement or abuse.

saddle-stitching = method of binding (slim) books or magazines using a wire staple or staples through the centre fold of the pages; **side-stitching** = method of binding by stapling through the side of a book, magazine or book section (signature) close to the spine, also called *stabbing*. Binding method using thread is called *sewing*.

safety-belt, safety-catch, safety curtain, safety film, safety glass, safety lamp, safety-match, safety net, safety-pin, safety razor, safety-valve.

saga (pl. sagas).

sailer = a sailing vessel (e.g. "that yacht is a good sailer"); **sailor** = member of a ship's crew (not necessarily on a sailing ship), a seaman, someone in the Navy.

Saint has the abbreviation **St** in personal and place-names (St John, St Albans, St Helens). The French female **Sainte** has the abbreviation **Ste**; **San** abbreviates to **S**; **Santa** abbreviates to **Sta**; none has a full point. The abbreviation of *Saints* is *SS*. Names beginning with *St* are alphabetized as if *Saint* were spelled in full (*see* **alphabetization**).

sake (noun) usually has no plural (e.g. "for our sake", "for the animal's sake") and constructions such as *for all their sakes* should be avoided (say "for the sake of them all") – note also the idioms *for goodness' sake, for conscience' sake*; **sake** (preferred to *saki*) = Japanese rice wine; **saki** = South American monkey.

salami = Italian (etc.) sausage; **salmi** = game stew.

salary *See* **wage**.

sale, saleable.

salt-cake, salt-cellar, salt-glaze, salt lake, salt-marsh, salt-mine, salt-pan, saltpetre, saltspoon, salt water (noun), salt-water (adj.) (but seawater, noun and adj.).

salubrious = beneficial to one's health, healthful; **salutary** = beneficial to one's morals; **salutatory** = welcoming.

salvage (noun) = property rescued from hazard; **selvage** (not *selvedge*) = reinforced edge of a length of cloth.

salve (verb), = to save property from hazard, gives the words *salvage* and *salvor* (= one who savages); **salver** = a tray. The word for to save a person (people) from hazard is **rescue**.

salvo (pl. salvos).

same denotes (exact) identity; **similar** implies (mere) likeness. The reply "No, similar" to the question "Same again?" is, however, that of a thirstless pedant.

sanatorium (pl. sanatoriums).

sanatory = healing, of healing; **sanitary** = concerned with the promotion of health, concerned with drainage and sewerage.

sanction (verb) = to give approval to, authorize; **sanction** (noun) = something that makes an oath binding, penalty for non-obedience of a law. The verb does not mean "to impose sanctions" and the noun does not mean "ban" or "embargo", although the politicians' "impose economic sanctions" threatens to change the distinctions.

sanctum (pl. sanctums).

sandal, sandalled.

sandbag, sandbank, sandbar, sand-blast(ing), sand-castle, sand-dune, sandfly, sand-glass, sandman, sandpaper, sandpiper, sand-pit, sandstone, sandstorm, sand-trap, sand-yacht.

sanserif describes a typeface with no serifs. *See* **seraph**.

Sanskrit *See* **Indian words**.

sapid = palatable, with an agreeable flavour; its opposite is **insipid** (which *see*).

sarcasm *See* **irony**.

sarcoma (pl. sarcomata).

sari (pl. saris).

Satan (initial capital letter).

satire (= exposure of vice or folly, through ridicule), satirize, satirist;

satyr = a woodland god; **satyriasis** = the male equivalent of nymphomania.

Saudi Arabia The derived adjective and noun (for the people) is *Saudi*.

sauté, sautéd, sautéing.

savanna (not **savannah**).

save is archaic (and affected) for **except** or **bar** (as in "all save one"); *except* should be used.

saw (verb = to cut with a saw) has the past tense **sawed** and past participle **sawn**. *See also* **see**. **Saw** (noun) = a saying.

say inflects *say – said – said*.

s.c. is the abbreviation of small capital (letters). The letters or words should be marked in text for typesetting by double underlining, thus: <u>small capitals.</u>

scale, scaler (who or which scales), scalable; **scalar** = a real number in mathematics.

scallop, scalloped, scalloping (not scollop, even though it reflects the pronunciation).

scan = to examine closely, scrutinize (it does not mean to glance at casually or hurriedly). *See also* **peruse**.

scandal, scandalize.

scanner = machine that electronically scans coloured originals (transparencies or prints/artwork wrapped round a drum) and produces separations for printing four-colour halftones. *See also* **separations**. An optical character reader is also sometimes called a scanner (*see* **OCR**).

scarcity = a temporary lack of a necessity; **scarify** = to scratch, lacerate, cause to become scarred; **rarity** = a long-term or permanent lack of something. E.g.:

"There is a scarcity of fresh vegetables in winter."
"Foxes are a rarity in London."

"Fresh fruit is scarce in winter."
"Foxes are rare in London."

scare (verb) is transitive. *Scared of* should not be misused for *afraid of* or *frightened by*; e.g. correct usage is "Some children are afraid of the dark and frightened by spiders; the dark and spiders scare some children."

scarf (pl. scarves).

scenario (pl. scenarios) is a vogue word to be avoided. *See* **vogue words**).

sceptic (= someone who disbelieves or holds profound doubts) is the preferred spelling of **skeptic**; **septic** = pertaining to sepsis or putrefaction.

scherzo (pl. scherzi).

schizophrenic describes someone with a severe psychotic disorder who has lost contact with reality (schizophrenia). The word should not be used of mere **ambivalence** or to describe frustration caused by a **dilemma**. *See also* **maniacal**; **paranoia**.

school-book, schoolboy, schoolchild, schoolfellow, school-friend, schoolgirl, school bus, school-days, school-leaver, schoolmaster, schoolmistress, schoolroom, schoolteacher.

schoolboy howlers *See* **non-standard English**.

scientific laws *See* **named effects and laws**.

scissors is a plural word; "a pair of scissors" achieves a singular construction.

scone *See* **crumpet**.

Scotland is inhabited mainly by Scots, many of whom speak with a Scottish accent; it is not unknown for them to drink Scotch (whisky, without an *e*). Neither the people nor their language should be referred to as Scotch. The term *Scotch* is also retained for Scotch pancakes and Scotch eggs. Note: in a general biographical work, especially if it is for international consumption, the nationality of someone born in Scotland (or Wales or Ireland) after the respective Act of Union should be given as *British* – Wales after 1543, Scotland 1707 and Ireland 1800.

screen angle/size *See* **halftone**.

scrim = open-weave cloth used in bookbinding; it is glued to the spine of the book block before the covers are added, giving strength to the "hinge" in the binding where the book opens.

scrimmage = a (spontaneous) tussle; **scrummage** = a set formation at rugby football.

script (typeface) *See* **cursive**.

scrutinize

scull = a short, light oar or the boat employing it; **skull** = the bones of the head.

sea-bed, seaboard, sea-borne, sea breeze, seafarer, seafaring, seafood, sea-going, seagull, sea-horse, sea-level, seaplane, seaport, seascape, sea serpent, sea shell, sea-shore, seasick(ness), seaside, sea-urchin, seawater (noun and adj.), seaway, seaweed, seaworthy, seaworthiness.

séance (with accent).

sear = to scorch; **seer** = a prophet; **sere** = a catch in a gun-lock.

search and spell = facility on some word processors and typesetting computers that allows a given word or combination of letters to be accessed from its memory store (and displayed if necessary) so that a spelling can be checked or changed throughout the file for consistency.

seasonable = appropriate to a given season (as log fires in winter); **seasonal** = characteristic of a given season (as is hay fever in summer).

seasons (spring, summer, autumn, winter) do not normally have an initial capital letter.

sec is the preferred abbreviation of second, although **s** may be used in scientific works.

secateurs (not sécateurs) is a plural word; "a pair of secateurs" achieves a singular construction.

Second World War The preferred form is **World War II**.

second-best, second childhood, second-class (adj.), second-cousin, second-floor (adj.), second-hand (adj.), second-in-command, second nature, second-rate (adj.), seconds-hand (on a watch), second-sight, second wind.

secret = hidden, unrevealed, confidential; **secrete** = to hide, to produce a substance. The former gives the adjective *secretive*; the latter the adjective *secretory*. E.g.:

"Biologists have tried to discover the secret of hormone production in the human body."
"He secreted the results of his researches into hormones."
"The pancreas secretes the hormone insulin."

section (of a book) *See* **signature; working**.

seduce, seducible (not seductable), seducer (not seductor), seduction (preferred to seducement).

see/see also *See* **cross-references**.

see has the past tense **saw** and past participle **seen**. *See also* **saw**.

seek inflects *seek – sought – sought*. Unlike **look**, seek does not need
for (e.g. "Seek a way out", "look for treasure").

seesaw (no hyphen).

seize = grasp, take hold of (possibly using force); **siege** = using forces
to surround a building or town. E.g.:

"He seized his assailant by the throat."
"They lifted the siege when the enemy troops surrendered."

seldom ever = seldom (which is preferred). **Seldom or ever** is
nonsense and incorrect for **seldom or never** (or *seldom if ever*);
one of these last two is intended in "Editors seldom or ever have
legible handwriting". *See also* **rarely ever**.

self-ends *See* **endpapers**.

sell inflects *sell – sold – sold*.

selvage *See* **salvage**.

semi- Most compound words with this prefix have a hyphen;
exceptions include semibreve, semicircle, semicolon, semifinal,
semiquaver. *See also* **numerical prefixes**.

semi-colon *See* **punctuation**.

semi-monthly/semi-weekly *See* **biannual**.

Semitic = concerning the Semites or the Arabic, Aramaic, or Hebrew
languages; **Hebrew** = an (early) Israelite or their language or its
modern version as spoken in Israel; **Hebraic** = concerning the
Hebrews or their language; **Jewish** = concerning Jews;
Israeli = concerning modern Israel. **Anti-Semitic** is commonly
used to mean **anti-Jewish**.

send inflects *send – sent – sent*.

Senegal The derived adjective and noun is *Senegalese*.

senhor (italics) = Portuguese for Mr; *senhora* = Portuguese for Mrs; *senhorita* = Portuguese for Miss. *See also* **señor**; **signor**.

señor (italics) = Spanish for Mr (pl. *señores*); *señora* = Spanish for Mrs; *señorita* = Spanish for Miss. *See also* **senhor**; **signor**.

sensible = showing or using common sense; **sensitive** = easily affected or stimulated.

sensual = lewd, voluptuous, concerning sexual gratification; **sensuous** = emotionally concerned with or received by the senses, alive to the pleasures of sensation; **sensory** = biologically concerned with the senses or sensation; **sensitive** = easily stimulated, responsive.

sentence, in grammar, is difficult to define. One definition makes a sentence "a complete expression of a thought". In writing or printing, a sentence begins with a capital letter and ends with a full stop (point, or period). Thus this is a sentence. And so is this. And this. In normal writing, however, it is usual for a sentence to include a verb, the most common simple sentence structure being subject + verb + object (as in "The boy kicked the ball"). Sentences without verbs attract criticism, and should therefore be avoided in formal writing.

sentiment = emotion, feeling, opinion; **sentimentality** = exaggerated feeling, false emotion.

sentential = to do with a (grammatical) sentence; **sententious** = in an affectedly pithy, brief or formal way (usually of writing), or moralistic in tone (usually of speech). The latter word is sometimes misused to mean *unconvincing*, *specious* or simply *wordy*.

separate, separator, separable (not separatable), separation.

separations = printer's term for a set of four films corresponding to the cyan (blue), magenta ("red"), yellow and black components of a full-colour original illustration. They are made using a camera and coloured filters, or by an electronic scanner. They may initially be continuous-tone or directly screened (and so consist of many tiny black dots of various sizes). The screened separations are used to make plates for printing four-colour halftones. *See also* **scanner**.

septic *See* **sceptic**.

septum (pl. septa).

sérac (with accent).

seraglio (pl. seraglios).

seraph (pl. seraphs, preferred to seraphim) = highest-ranking angel;
serif (preferred to seriph or ceriph) = short cross-line at the end of a stroke of a letter, as in this capital **I**. A typeface lacking this feature is called a *sanserif* face.

serf (pl. serfs).

sergeant is the preferred spelling of **serjeant**, except in historical titles such as *serjeant-at-arms*.

serial *See* **cereal**.

series (pl. series).

serif *See* **seraph**.

serious = earnest, of importance, life-threatening, not light-hearted;
serous = to do with or resembling serum (the watery component of blood). E.g.:

"The child had only a slight temperature, but the doctor regarded the illness as serious enough for hospital treatment."
"The wound remained wet because of leakage of serous fluid."

serum (pl. serums).

service, serviceable.

serviette The preferred term is **napkin**.

sesqui- Little-used prefix meaning one-and-a-half (as in sesquioxide, sesquiplane). *See* **numerical prefixes**.

session *See* **cession**.

set (noun), = block of stone or wood used for paving and (formerly) surfacing roads, is the preferred spelling (not **sett**); **sett** = badger's burrow.

seta (pl. setae).

set-back, set-off, set piece, set-screw, set square, set-to, set-up.

settee/sofa *See* **couch**.

settle, settler (who settles), but settlor (who makes a settlement in law).

sew has the past tense **sewed** and past participle **sewn**. *See also* **sow**.

sewage is the stuff in the pipes; **sewerage** is the system of pipes that carry sewage.

sewing = method of bookbinding in which the signatures (sections) are fastened together with thread. *See also* **saddle-stitching**.

sexism *See* **gender; mankind**.

Seychelles The derived adjective and noun is *Seychellois*.

s.g. is the abbreviation of specific gravity.

shake has the past tense **shook** and past participle **shaken**.

shako (pl. shakos).

shall and **will** *Shall* is the normal, "neutral" way of forming the first person future tense (I shall go, we shall go), and *will* forms the normal second and third persons (you, he, she, it or they will go);

used in this way they express what Partridge calls "mere futurity". For emphasis, the roles are reversed: E.g.:

"I will get there" = "I am determined to get there";
"He shall not suffer" = "He must not suffer";
"Thou shalt not kill" is a command (well, Commandment);
"We will finish on time" – or else.

shammy is an accepted spelling which reflects the pronunciation of the alternative spelling **chamois** when it is applied to a type of soft leather.

shampoo (pl. shampoos), shampooed, shampooing.

shape, shapable.

shard (a piece of broken pottery) is preferred to **sherd**.

shave has the preferred past tense and participle **shaved**, although *shaven* is retained as an adjective (e.g. "a shaven chin").

she/her should not be used in reference to ships or countries (use *it* or *its*).

sheaf (pl. sheaves).

shear has the preferred past tense and participle **sheared**, although *shorn* is retained as an adjective (e.g. "a shorn sheep").

shears (noun) is a plural word. "A pair of shears" achieves a singular construction.

sheath (noun) = a holder (e.g. of a dagger), scabbard, part that encloses; **sheathe** (verb) = to place in a sheath, to enclose.

sheep-dip, sheepdog, sheep-farmer, sheep-pen, sheepshank, sheep tick, sheep's-head, sheep-shearer, sheepskin.

sheikh is the preferred spelling (not **sheik, shaik** or **shaikh**).

shelf (pl. shelves).

shellac, shellacked, shellacking.

sherif (preferred to shereef) = Muslim leader; **sheriff** = British Crown's representative in a county, American law officer (of a county).

shew/shewn Do not use these archaic spellings; use **show/shown**. The old form persists in *shewbread*.

Shiah = Muslim sect whose members are known as **Shiites** (sometimes represented as *Shi'ites*).

shine, shiny. *Shine* inflects *shine – shone – shone*.

shingles (the virus disease) is a singular word; "cases of shingles" achieves a plural construction.

shipbuilder, shipbuilding, shipmate, ship-owner, shipshape, shipwreck, shipwright, shipyard.

ships' names should be typeset in italic with an initial capital letter; e.g. *Queen Mary*, HMS *Beagle*, SS *Mauritania*. A ship should be referred to as *it*, not *her*. *See also* **HMS**.

"shock-horror" *See* **horror**.

shoe, shod (not shoed), shoeing.

shoot inflects *shoot – shot – shot*.

shop assistant, shop-boy, shop-fitter, shop-front, shop-girl, shopkeeper, shop-lifter, shop steward, shop-walker.

short *See* **brief**.

short sight, short-sighted, short-sightedness (medical name *myopia*). *See also* **long sight**.

should is the normal past tense of *shall*, as **would** is of *will*. Thus as auxiliaries indicating tense they follow the same rules as do *shall* and *will* (which *see*). E.g.:

"I thought that if I kept going, I should get there soon."
"I hoped that you would come too."
"He said that he would let me know."
Transposing *should* and *would* conveys emphasis (but tangles with the subjunctive). E.g.:

"I knew that if I kept going I would get there on time."
"I thought that you should come, too."
"He admitted that he should let me know."

shoulder-head *See* **subheadings**.

shovel, shovelled, shovelling, shoveller, shovelful (pl. shovelfuls).

show (verb) has the past tense **showed** and preferred past participle **shown**. Do not use *shew/shewed/shewn*.

show business, show-case, show-down, showgirl, showground, show house, showjump(ing), show-off (noun), showman, show-piece, show-place, showroom.

show-through = term in printing and papermaking that describes the faint appearance on a printed page of letters or images printed on the other side of the sheet (which show in mirror image). It occurs because the paper is too transparent (i.e. its *opacity* is too low). *See* **opacity**.

shrewd now almost always means of good judgement, often demonstrating foresight (noun *shrewdness*). For this reason its former meanings relating to the mouse-like *shrew* (i.e. bad-tempered, biting) are best avoided.

shrink has the past tense **shrank** and past participle **shrunk**, although *shrunken* is retained as an adjective (e.g. "a shrunken head").

shut describes the physical action of doing something; **close** (verb) is the general opposite of to *open*. E.g.:

"The dog will escape, so please shut the gate at once."
"Please close the cupboard door when you have finished."

shy (= to throw), shied, shying; **shy** (= bashful), shyer, shyest, shyness.

SI is the abbreviation of Système International (d'Unités), the formal "metric" (metre-kilogram-second) system of units. *See* **units**.

sic (italics) (= thus, Latin) usually indicates that an odd-looking word is being quoted exactly. E.g.:

"The editor wrote to the author criticizing his grammer (*sic*)." It is also used to indicate ironic comments.

side-arm(s), side-bet, sideboard, sideburns, side-car, side-dish, side-door, side-drum, side-effect, sidelight, sideline, sidelong, side-road, side-saddle, side-show, side-slip, side-step, side-street, side-table, side-track, side valve, sideways,

side-head *See* **subheadings**.

siege *See* **seize**.

sign, signatory.

signal, signalled, signalling, signaller.

signature = printed and folded sheet that forms part of a book, often consisting of 16, 24 or 32 pages; also called a *section*. *See also* **imposition**; **working**.

signor (italics) = Italian for Mr (pl. *signori*); *signora* = Italian for Mrs; *signorina* = Italian for Miss. *See also* **senhor**; **señor**.

silhouette

silica, silicate, siliceous.

silicon is a metalloid chemical element (Si), used to make semiconductors (silicon chips), and is the main component of silica (sand) and quartz; **silicone** is a type of silicon-containing plastic, valued for its lubricating, heat-resisting or water-proofing properties.

silk-screen printing = method of printing which uses a stencil supported on a fine screen; the ink is squeezed through the small holes in the screen. Formerly called *serigraphy*.

silo (pl. silos).

similar *See* **analagous**; **same**.

simile (pl. similes) = figure of speech involving an obvious and direct comparison between two things, often using the word *like* or *as*. E.g.:

"Electrons orbit an atomic nucleus like planets orbiting the Sun." Like **analogy** (which *see*), simile can be a useful way of explaining unfamiliar concepts. Overworked similes, reduced to the level of clichés, should be avoided (e.g. "as deaf as a post", "as drunk as a lord", "dying like flies"). *See also* **cliché**.

simplistic, used to mean *oversimplified*, is a vogue word to be avoided. *See* **vogue words**.

simply, used to mean **merely**, can lead to ambiguity, as in "He was simply careless." The different uses are compared in:
    "he worked simply" (= in an uncomplicated way)
and "He simply worked" (= only worked, and did not recite poetry at the same time).

simulate = pretend, copy, imitate, appear to be; **assimilate** = absorb, take in, become like. E.g.:

"Some textured plastics simulate the appearance of leather."
"Many children assimilate the mannerisms of their parents."

since, in the sense *because*, needs care with tenses; e.g. "What an improvement since we have used the new machine" should be ". . . since we used the new machine."

sine qua non (italics) = an essential condition; except in legal contexts, the Latin phrase should be avoided.

sing has the past tense **sang** and past participle **sung**.

Singapore The derived adjective and noun is *Singaporean*.

singe, singed, singeing.

sink has the past tense **sank** and past participle **sunk**, although *sunken* is retained as an adjective (e.g. "sunken eyes").

sinus (pl. sinuses).

siren is the preferred spelling of **syren**.

sirocco is the preferred spelling (not **scirocco**).

-sis Nouns ending in *-sis* (e.g. genesis, hypothesis, synthesis, thesis) form the plural *-ses* (e.g. geneses, hypotheses, syntheses, theses).

sister-in-law *See* **in-laws**.

sit inflects *sit – sat – sat*.

situate should be avoided an as adjective meaning **situated**.

situation is a versatile if imprecise word which can mean location, place, condition or even circumstances surrounding a fact or event. Perhaps because of this imprecision it is often associated with another, precise, word but contributes nothing and serves only to fog what is already there. If the other word is also a vogue word, whole vogue phrases can be created. The many examples include "crisis situation", "ongoing situation" (or "ongoing crisis situation"), "feedback situation" (or "ongoing crisis feedback situation"), and so on. *See* **vogue words**.

size, sizable (= able to be sized; it does not mean *fairly large*).

-sized is preferred to **-size** in such expressions as life-sized model, medium-sized house.

sizing in papermaking = substance added to reduce the absorbency of the final paper and improve its inking properties in printing. *Internal sizing*, such as a resin or alum, is added to the pulp before it is made into paper; *surface sizing*, such as starch, is coated on the surface of the paper during the finishing processes. Depending on the amount of size used, a paper is termed *unsized* (e.g. blotting paper and paper towelling), *slack-sized* (e.g. newsprint), *medium-sized* (e.g. most uncoated papers) or *hard-sized* (e.g. paper for high-quality lithographic printing). *See also* **paper**.

ski (pl. skis), ski'd (past tense of verb, not *skied* = past tense of to sky), skiing, skier (who skis; someone who skys a ball is a *skyer*).

skilful and **skilled** both = having/showing skill, but the latter should be reserved to describe labour, crafts and technical skills (a skilful editor but a skilled plumber). Note that *skilful* has only two *l*s.

skull *See* **scull**.

slang includes words and expressions that are still a long way from becoming formally accepted into standard English. Slang terms are usually invented to reinforce group identity to the exclusion of outsiders and may become **colloquialisms** (which *see*) before, perhaps, emerging as members of the formal vocabulary. Specialized slang includes argot, cant and jargon, each of which comprises expressions that are (sometimes deliberately) understandable only to the initiated (*see* **jargon; non-standard English**). In Britain, rhyming slang – particurly that of Liverpool and London – provides an insight into the adoption of new meanings for existing words. A few examples (collected in London during one week) from so-called Cockney rhyming slang illustrate this; the final slang expression is often only part of a rhyme on the word it replaces, and thus utterly confusing strangers (e.g. *apples* = apples and pears = *stairs*).

Final form	Intermediate form	Meaning
apples	apples and pears	stairs
arris	Aristotle	"bottle"
	armoured rocks	socks
barnet	Barnet Fair	hair

bird	bird-lime	time (in prison)
	boat race	face
boracic	boracic lint	skint
bottle	bottle and glass	class
	brass tacks	facts
	bull and cow	row
bushel	bushel and peck	neck
butchers	butcher's hook	look
china	china plate	mate
conan	Conan Doyle	boil
	daisy roots	boots
Derby Kelly	Derby Kelly	belly
dicky	dicky bird	word
	dicky dirt	shirt
dog	dog and bone	telephone
elephants	elephant's trunk	drunk
farmers	Farmer Giles	piles
	frog and toad	road
George	George Raft	draught
Germans	German bands	hands
ginger	ginger beer	queer
gooses	goose's neck	cheque
	Gregory Peck	cheque
Jacks	Jack's alive	five (pounds)
	jam-jar	car
Jimmy	Jimmy Riddle	piddle
	half-inch	pinch (steal)
loaf	loaf of bread	head
minces	mince pies	eyes
mutton	Mutt and Jeff	deaf
Nelsons	Nelson Eddys	readies (banknotes)
	north and south	mouth
	pen and ink	stink
	pig's ear	beer
plates	plates of meat	feet
porkies	porky pies	lies
rabbit	rabbit and pork	talk
Richard	Richard III	bird
	Rosy Lee	tea
	round the houses	trousers

	rub-a-dub	pub
Ruby	Ruby Murray	curry
sausage	sausage and mash	cash
Sweeney	Sweeney Todd	Flying Squad
	skin and blister	sister
	tea-leaf	thief
titfer	tit for tat	hat
tod	Tod Sloan	own
	Tom and Dick	sick
tom	tom-foolery	jewellery
	trouble and strife	wife
	two and eight	state
whistle	whistle and flute	suit

Thus expressions such as "I need a new whistle but I'm boracic, and won't have a sausage until I cash a gooses" can be translated! Slang expressions are among the most volatile in the language, living a short but gay life or gradually gaining acceptance, as within recent times have *bedrock*, *exploit*, *frontal attack*, *globetrotter*, to *hedge*, to be *stumped* and to *tackle*, whose slang origins are now largely forgotten.

slatternly *See* **slovenly**.

slay has the past tense **slew** and past participle **slain**. Like the verb *slaughter* (except when used to describe killing animals for meat), it has an archaic ring to it and should not be used merely as an alternative for *kill*.

sledge = platform on runners for moving goods or people, usually over ice or snow (a *toboggan*); **sleigh** = passenger-carrying sledge pulled by animals; **sled** is a technical word or an Americanism for *sledge*.

sleep (verb) inflects *sleep – slept – slept*.

sleight = cunning, dexterity (as in *sleight of hand*); **slight** (noun) = disrespectful affront or disregard, insulting indifference; **slight** (adj.) = flimsy, lacking significance, small (e.g. "a slight increase in weight").

slide (verb) inflects *slide – slid – slid (not slidden)*.

slight *See* **sleight**.

sling (verb = to throw) has the past tense and participle **slung**. When **sling** = to put on or into a sling, the past tense and participle is **slinged**.

slink inflects *slink – slunk – slunk*.

slip-case = protective slip-in board box for a book or books which leaves the spine(s) showing. The slip-case may be plain, printed or covered (in book-binding material).

slivovitz is the preferred spelling (not **slivovic, slivovica, slivowitz**).

slovenly = untidy, dirty; **slatternly** = unclean, untidy, loose (morals). The former can be applied to anyone; the latter should be reserved for women and girls.

sly, slyer, slyest, slyly.

small capitals = capital letters the size of the x-height of normal lower case letters in the same typeface, marked in text for typesetting by double underlining and usually abbreviated to small caps or s.c. *See also* **x-height**.

small pica = obsolete name for 11-point type. For others, *see* **type sizes**.

smell (verb) The preferred past tense and participle is **smelled** (not *smelt*).

smite (archaic for to *strike*) has the past tense **smote** and past participle **smitten**. **Smitten** is the most commonly used of the three, as in "smitten with plague" or colloquially just "smitten" (with love).

smoke, smokable, smoky.

smooth Verb form is **smooths** (not *smoothes*).

snoek is preferred to **snook** for the edible fish (usually barracouta).

snowball, snow-berry, snow-blind(ness), snow-drift, snowdrop, snowfall, snowflake, snow-goggles, snow leopard, snowman, snow-plough, snowscape, snowshoe.

so, much overworked for *therefore*, needs care to avoid ambiguity; e.g. "It was her first article, and she was so painstaking" could mean either "she was therefore painstaking" or "she was extremely painstaking".

sobriquet = **nickname**, which is preferred.

so-called (adj.)

sociable = naturally inclined to be with others, company-seeking, affable; **social** = consisting of or relating to groups of (friendly) people, to communities, to society.

socialize

-soever is used as an affix to add vagueness to *how, what, where, who* (howsoever, whatsoever, wheresoever, whosoever).

soirée

solemn, solemnize.

solid-state (adj.).

solidus or **virgule** = an oblique stroke (or shilling stroke), as in *13/4d*, *and/or* and *15/16*; plural *solidi*. *See also* **fractions**.

solo (pl. solos).

solve, solvable (= can be solved); **soluble** = can be dissolved.

Somalia The derived adjective and noun is *Somali*.

sombrero (pl. sombreros).

some should not be misused for part; e.g. "He wasted some of the time day-dreaming" should be "... part of the time day-dreaming."

somebody, something and **sometime** should be distinguished from **some body, some thing** and **some time** (although the first pair are seldom confused). E.g.:

"Somebody must be responsible for the error."
"The wine would benefit from some body."
"Something is wrong with the table."
"It was not an animal; some thing did that damage."
"It must have happened sometime in the night."
"Take some time and make sure you get it right."

Some day should always be spelled as two words (*someday* is an Americanism).

sonar (no initial capital letter).

songbird, songbook, song-cycle, song-hit, songthrush, songwriter.

soprano (pl. sopranos).

sort = typesetter's term for a character that is not part of the normal fount of a typeface (which consists mainly of letters, numerals and punctuation marks). Typical sorts include fractions and mathematical and scientific symbols. The availability (or non-availability) of the necessary sorts often influences the choice of typeface for a particular text. Mathematical characters are sometimes called *pi sorts*.

sort of *See* **type of**.

sortie, sortied, sortieing.

so that should = *with the result that*; it should not be used to mean *in order that*. E.g.:

"She worked late so that the work was completed" is correct usage;

"She worked late so that she could complete the work" is poor usage;
"She worked late so that her boss was impressed" is ambiguous – with the result that, or in order that, the boss was impressed?

sotto voce (italics) = as an aside, under one's breath; the Italian expression should be avoided.

souflée

soupçon = a pinch, suspicion (of), minute quantity; the French word should be avoided.

South Africa has English and Afrikaans as its official languages. Afrikaans, based originally on Dutch, has contributed several words to the standard English vocabulary. *See* **Dutch words**.

south, southern etc. *See* **compass directions**.

Southern Hemisphere (initial capital letters).

South Pole (initial capital letters).

Soviet = to do with the Soviet Union – i.e., the USSR post-1917; **Russian** = to do with Russia or the Russian Empire pre-1917.

Soviet Union See **Soviet; Russia**.

sow (verb) has the past tense **sowed** and past participle **sown**. *See also* **sew**.

space rockets and **missiles** Capitalize the name and use Arabic numerals; e.g. Atlas, Exocet, Saturn 5, Titan 3. Space programmes are similar; e.g. Gemini 3, Apollo 13. Note also terms such as ABM (anti-ballistic missile), ICBM (intercontinental ballistic missile) and SAM (surface-to-air missile).

spacious = roomy, having plenty of space; **specious** = plausible yet deceptive, insubstantial. E.g.:

"He had a spacious office, large enough for three people."

"His argument was specious and based on a false assumption."

spaghetti, and most of the names of the other types of pasta, is a plural word in its original Italian but is normally regarded as singular (and has no plural) in English.

spate = flood, torrent; it should not be used to mean merely more than usual, slight excess (as in "The spate of thefts increased the crime rate by two percent").

spatula (pl. spatulas).

speak has the past tense **spoke** and past participle **spoken**.

special, specialize, speciality (general and cooking), specialty (legal and medical).

specially = specifically, for a certain purpose; **especially** = particularly, outstanding. E.g.:

"The article was specially written for this book."
"It is a good book, especially the article written by him. It is especially good."

special typefaces Foreign languages, Old English, scientific and mathematical symbols, and so on that require special typefaces should be typed or written with such clarity that their forms and positions cannot possibly be misunderstood by the printer. *See also* **mathematical material**.

specie = coined money; it has no plural. **Species** = member of an interbreedable group of plants or animals (one category down from genus, one up from variety or race; *see* **Latin classification**). *Species* is the singular and plural form; the corresponding abbreviations are *sp.* and *spp.*

spectacles (= glasses) is a plural word. "A pair of spectacles" achieves a singular construction.

spectral = like a ghost (from *spectre*), or pertaining to a spectrum.

spectrum (pl. spectra).

speculate, speculator.

speed (verb) inflects *speed – sped – sped*.

spell (verb) has the preferred past tense and participle **spelled** (not *spelt*).

spelling Much of this Dictionary is to do with spelling, and for specific queries see the word concerned. For some general spelling rules (and their exceptions), *see* **-l- or -ll-**; **negative prefixes**; **-p- or -pp-**; **-r- or -rr-**; **suffixes**; **-t- or -tt-**; **verbs**.

spend inflects *spend – spent – spent*.

sperm has the preferred plural **sperm** (not **sperms**). It is derived from *spermatozoon* (pl. spermatozoa).

spice, spicy.

spike, spiky.

spill (verb) has the preferred past tense and participle **spilled**, although *spilt* is retained as an adjective (e.g. "spilt milk").

spin (verb) inflects *spin – spun – spun*.

spin-dry, spin-drier (not spin-dryer).

spiral binding = method of binding (usually single sheets) using a helical plastic or wire spring through holes in the top or the side edge of the pages; **wire binding** = similar to spiral binding but using a loop of wire through slots parallel to the bound edge.

spiritual = pertaining to the spirit, mind or soul; **spiritous** = alcoholic. *See also* **temporal**.

spirt/spurt/squirt all mean to spout, shoot out in a sudden jet or stream. The first two are merely spelling variations, with *spurt* being more common.

spit (verb) has the past tense **spat** and preferred past participle **spit** (not *spat*).

split infinitive This construction is to be avoided, but that may not always be possible without creating an awkward or stilted sentence. E.g.:

"He used to continually interrupt" is better than "He used continually to interrupt" and more direct than "He used to interrupt continually." In a sentence such as "He expects to more than double his output" the infinitive cannot be unsplit without changing the sense ("He expects to double more than his output?"). From this it can be concluded that to unnecessarily split an infinitive is not good style. As Douglas Adams said (*The Hitch Hiker's Guide to the Galaxy*): "... all dared ... to boldly split infinitives that no man had split before".

spoilt (verb) has the preferred past tense and participle **spoiled**, although *spoilt* is retained as an adjective meaning *marred* or *damaged*.

sponge, spongeable, spongy.

spoonful (pl. spoonfuls).

spouse is archaic for **husband** or **wife**, although convenient when the sex cannot be indicated and common in legal texts.

spring (verb) has the past tense **sprang** and past participle **sprung**.

spring (as a season, no initial capital letter), springbok, springtide (= springtime), spring tide (= tide of greatest height).

spry, spryer, spryest, spryness, spryly.

spurt *See* **spirt**.

square brackets *See* **brackets**.

square roots etc. The square root sign (vinculum) should be
avoided except in special mathematical setting; use parentheses and
fractional powers instead. E.g.:

$$\sqrt{xy}, \qquad \sqrt[3]{x}, \qquad \sqrt[3]{y^2}$$

should be given as $(xy)^{\frac{1}{2}}, \qquad x^{\frac{1}{3}}, \qquad y^{\frac{2}{3}}.$

squirt *See* **spirt**.

SS (capitals, no full points) is the abbreviation of Saints (plural) and
of Steam Ship (e.g. SS *Mauritania*). *See also* **ships' names**.

St is the abbreviation of Saint and Street.

stabilize, stabilizer.

stable = firm, steady, established, constant; **static** = unmoving,
stationary, unchanging. The meanings overlap, but the words are
not interchangeable in usages such as:

"A tall building must have a stable foundation."
"The weather was too poor for flying, so the crowd could see only a
static display of aircraft."

stadium (pl. stadiums).

staff has the usual plural **staffs,** but *staves* in music.

stage-coach, stagecraft, stage door, stage fright, stage-manage(r).

staid = solemn, humourless; **stayed** = supported/propped up,
remained.

stalactite = calcium carbonate (limestone) formation that hangs from
the ceiling of a cave; **stalagmite** = similar formation that grows up
from the floor of a cave. Both are formed extremely slowly by the
evaporation of dripping water containing dissolved minerals.

stanch = to stem (stop the flow); **staunch** = true.

stand (verb) inflects *stand – stood – stood*.

standard, standardize, standardization.

stanza (pl. stanzas).

star, starred, starring, starry (compare stare, stared, staring, stary).

start (verb) should not be used for **begin** when referring to inanimate objects; e.g. "He starts work on Monday" but "The article begins on p. 24."

state, stater (= one who states, old Greek coin), stator (= stationary part of a machine).

states of the USA *See* **US states**.

static *See* **stable**.

stationary = static, unmoving; **stationery** = writing materials.

status quo = the previous position, and has come to mean also *the present position* (e.g. "return to the status quo", "maintain the status quo"); it is therefore tautological and incorrect to write "return to the former status quo" or "maintain the present status quo". The Latin form should, however, be avoided.

staunch *See* **stanch**.

stave (verb) has the preferred past tense and participle **staved**, although *stove* is still used for broken in barrels or ships' hulls (e.g. "The rocks stove in the ship's hull").

Ste is the abbreviation of the French (female) Sainte.

steal has the past tense **stole** and past participle **stolen**.

steamboat, steam-driven, steam engine, steam-hammer, steam iron, steamroller, steamship (but Steam Ship, abbreviated to SS, in a ship's name), steamtight, steam train, steam turbine.

stencil, stencilled, stenciller, stencilling.

step- = prefix added to a family relationship which acknowledges the remarriage of a parent. **Stepchild** (stepdaughter or stepson) = spouse's child by a former marriage; **step-parent** (stepfather or stepmother) = one's parent's second or subsequent spouse after remarriage; **stepbrother/stepsister** = child of one's step-parent. *See also* **family relationships**; **half-brother**.

sterile = incapable of reproduction, germ-free; **sterilized** = made incapable of reproduction (although formerly able), made germ-free (although formerly contaminated). Other forms are sterilize, sterilizer, sterilization.

stet = instruction (on a typescript or proof) to a typesetter to ignore a previous instruction for amendment (*stet* = Latin "let it stand"). The word is written at the end of the line in the margin, and the letters or words concerned underlined with a broken line.

stick (verb) inflects *stick – stuck – stuck*.

stigma = brand, part of a flower (pl. stigmas), one of Christ's wounds (pl. stigmata) or their miraculous reappearance in someone else.

stile = vertical member forming the edge of a door, a step over a fence; **style** = a pen, custom, manner. The latter gives rise to *stylize*. *See also* **stylish**.

stiletto (pl. stilettos), stilettoed, stilettoing.

still life (pl. still lifes).

stimulant = a substance (such as a drug) that produces or increases activity; **stimulus** (pl. stimuli) = something that arouses a nerve or sense organ; **stimulation** = excitement, arousal.

sting (verb) inflects *sting – stung – stung*.

stink (verb) has the past tense *stank* and past participle *stunk*.

stoep = South African veranda; **stoop** = container for holy water (and an Americanism for a front porch).

Stone Age (initial capital letters).

stopcock, stop-gap, stop-go, stop-off (noun), stop-over (noun), stop-press, stop valve, stop-watch.

store, storable.

storey and **story** *See* **floor**.

straight = unbent, direct; **strait** = narrow, close (hence strait-jacket).

straightaway/straightforward (each one word).

strata is plural (singular *stratum*).

strawboard = papermaking term for yellowish board produced using unbleached pulp made from straw. Its uses include backing for stiffened envelopes (for mailing photographs etc.) and boards for the cases (covers) of hardback books. *See also* **paper**.

streamline(d)

strew has the preferred past tense and participle **strewed**, although *strewn* is retained as an adjective (e.g. "a floor strewn with petals").

stria (pl. striae), striated, striation.

stride has the past tense **strode** and past participle **stridden**.

strike (verb) has the preferred past tense and participle **struck**, although *stricken* is retained as an adjective (e.g. "a stricken ship").

string (verb) has the preferred past tense and participle **strung**, although *stringed* is retained as an adjective (e.g. "stringed instruments").

stripe, stripy.

strip line *See* **cut line**.

strive has the past tense **strove** and past particle **striven**.

student *See* **pupil**.

stupefy, stupefaction.

sty = pig house (pl. sties); **stye** = pimple at the base of an eyelash (pl. styes).

style *See* **stile**.

stylish = smart, fashionable; **stylized** = unnatural, conformist. *See also* **stile**.

stylus (pl. styluses, of record players).

sub- Most words with this prefix are now spelled as one word (without a hyphen); e.g. subatomic, subclass, subheading, and so on. Exceptions include sub-basement, sub-branch (and others with two *b*s), sub-edit(or), sub-lieutenant, sub-plot.

subconscious = only partly aware, not firmly part of the consciousness (of the mind); **unconscious** = in a faint, completely unaware, carried out without conscious thought. The psychological meanings (stated last in each case) can also be used as nouns. **Subliminal** = below the threshold of consciousness; it has recently come into prominence in the term *subliminal advertising*, a proscribed technique of introducing advertisements as single frames interlaced in a film or video programme (which pass too rapidly to register on the consciousness).

subject to = liable to, exposed or open to, particularly something disadvantageous; **addicted to** = given to a harmful practice or habit, often leading to physical or psychological dependence.

subheadings within printed text can be of various kinds. The most prominent is a cross-head, which is centred over the measure (width) of a column or page, usually with a line space above it. A *boxed head* is ranged left (aligning with the left-hand margin of the text) and may be a *side-head*, with the text continuing on the same line, or a *shoulder-head*, on a line of its own. There may or may not be a line space above and below a boxed head, which should be distinguished typographically by being set in a different type style to that of the text (in capitals, small capitals, italics or bold face), possibly also in a different typeface or a larger size, or both. Text below a shoulder-head is usually set full out (with no paragraph indent). Widows and widowed lines should be avoided above a box head (*see* **widow**). In quality publications, there should normally be at least two or three lines of text below a subheading near the bottom of a column or page, and a similar number above a subheading near the top of a column or page, although some publishers allow a subheading to fall at the top as long as it is not immediately below an illustration.

subnormal *See* **abnormal**.

subpoena (pl. subpoenas), subpoenaed, subpoenaing.

subsequent to = **after**, which is preferred.

substance, in papermaking, is a term that refers to the weight of a given type of paper, formerly arrived at by weighing a designated number of sheets of a particular size. Thus a substance of (s/o) "double crown 30lb/516" corresponds to the weight (30lb) of 516 sheets of paper measuring 20 by 30 inches. This method of expressing substance has been largely superseded by the *gsm* (grams per square metre) system. *See also* **bulk**; **gsm**; **paper sizes**.

substantial = having substance/solidity, of real value, existing; it should not be used to mean merely **large**.

substitute *See* **replace**.

substratum (pl. substrata).

suchlike

sudden, suddenly, suddenness. The expression *all of a sudden* (= suddenly) should be avoided.

sue, sued, suing.

suede (no accent).

suffer *from* a disorder, not **suffer** *with*.

sufficient, like **adequate**, seldom means other than plain **enough**.

suffixes The major difficulty with suffixes concerns the spelling of the resulting word, particularly the change (if any) to the termination of the root word when the suffix is added. Here are some rules.

1. *-able or -ible* A special case with no simple rules. *See* **-able and -ible**.

2. *-ed and -ing* Monosyllabic words ending in a consonant preceded by a single vowel double the consonant on adding *-ed* or *-ing*. E.g.:

bag	bagged	bagging
bar	barred	barring
con	conned	conning
fob	fobbed	fobbing
ham	hammed	hamming
knit	knitted	knitting
pad	padded	padding
slap	slapped	slapping
stab	stabbed	stabbing
thud	thudded	thudding

Exceptions include *bus – bused – busing* and words ending in *w*, *x* or *y*:

fix	fixed	fixing
sew	sewed	sewing

Other monosyllabic forms do not normally double the consonant:

foil	foiled	foiling
heal	healed	healing
sort	sorted	sorting
spurt	spurted	spurting
vamp	vamped	vamping

425

Polysyllabic words with a stress on the last syllable follow the double consonant rule:

allot	allotted	allotting
occur	occurred	occurring
prefer	preferred	preferring
preplan	preplanned	preplanning
refer	referred	referring
remit	remitted	remitting

Exceptions are words ending in *w*, *x* or *y*:

allow	allowed	allowing
annoy	annoyed	annoying
relax	relaxed	relaxing

The last consonant is generally not doubled, however, if the final syllable is unaccented (unless the consonant is an *l*):

ballot	balloted	balloting
bias	biased	biasing
focus	focused	focusing
market	marketed	marketing
proffer	proffered	proffering
profit	profited	profiting
rivet	riveted	riveting

but

channel	channelled	channelling
enrol	enrolled	enrolling
level	levelled	levelling
travel	travelled	travelling

(exceptions include *appeal*, *parallel* and *repeal*).

3. *-er and -est* With monosyllabic words, these two suffixes follow the same rules as for *-ed* and *-ing*. E.g.:

hot	hotter	hottest – double consonant
low	lower	lowest
lax	laxer	laxest
coy	coyer	coyest
damp	damper	dampest

no doubling

Polysyllabic adjectives generally form the comparative and superlative using *more* and *most* (not *-er* and *-est*). *See* **comparatives and superlatives**.

4. *-ic and -ics* Certain adjectives ending in *-ic* become nouns on the addition of an *s*. E.g.:

acoustic	acoustics
athletic	athletics
ceramic	ceramics
economic	economics
geriatric	geriatrics
mathematic	mathematics
narcotic	narcotics
politic	politics
semantic	semantics

Many of the nouns are regarded as singular (e.g. "acoustics is a branch of physics", "semantics is the study of the meanings of words") but "cosmetics are becoming increasingly expensive".

5. *-ize, -ise and -yse See* **-ize or -ise**.

6. *-ment* Words ending in *-dge* retain the *e* when the suffix *-ment* is added. E.g.:

abridge	abridgement
acknowledge	acknowledgement
estrange	estrangement
judge	judgement (but judgment in law)
lodge	lodgement
prejudge	prejudgement

7. *-s, -es, -ies, and -ves* Most English words, including those ending in *-e*, *-ee* or *-y* preceded by a vowel, form plurals by adding *s*. E.g.:

comb	combs
dome	domes
employee	employees
key	keys
monkey	monkeys
ploy	ploys

Words ending in -*s* or -*x* form the plural by adding -*es*:

loss	losses
box	boxes

(exception *ox*, plural *oxen*).

Words ending in -*y* preceded by a consonant change the -*y* to -*ies* to form the plural:

try	tries
lorry	lorries
pony	ponies

8. *Words ending in -f* form the plural by adding -*s* or by changing the -*f* to -*ves*. For a list of examples, *see* **plurals**.

For plurals of foreign words and words ending -*o*, *see* **plurals**. *See also* **-l- or -ll-**; **-or**.

sugar beet, sugar-bowl, sugar-cane.

suggest, suggestible, suggestive.

suit = a set of armour, clothes or cards, or a court action; **suite** = a set of furniture, related pieces of music, or adjacent rooms.

summary *See* **outline**.

summons (law), summonsed (= issued with a summons).

sumptuous is usually spelled correctly if it is not mispronounced "sumptious".

Sun (the star of our Solar System) has an intial capital letter, as have the words Solar System, when referred to as an astronomical object. In other meanings and in compounds – of which there are many – sun has no capital; e.g. sunbathe, sun-baked, sunbeam, sun-bonnet, sunburn(ed), sundew, sundial, sundown(er), sun-dress, sunflower, sun-glasses, sun-god, sun-hat, sunlight, sunrise, sunroof, sunset, sunshade, sunshine, sunspot, sunstroke, sun-tan, sun-trap, sun-up, sun-worship.

super- Most words with this prefix are spelled as one word (without a hyphen). An exception is *super-ego*.

supercalendered (SC) = papermaking term for paper with a highly smooth surface on one or both sides of the sheet produced by two stages of calendering (using polishing rollers). *See also* **paper**.

superficial = concerning only the surface, shallow; **superfluous** = extra to requirement, more than enough, redundant, E.g.:

"Despite his experience, his knowledge of the basic principles is only superficial."
"We are moving to smaller premises, so please throw away any superfluous stock."

superintend, superintendent, superintendency.

superior to (not superior *than*).

superlatives *See* **comparatives and superlatives**.

supersede (not *supercede*) = to take the place of; **surpass** = to do better, do better than; the two words are not synonyms.

supervise, supervisor.

supine *See* **prone**.

supper *See* **dinner**.

supplement (noun) = an addition to something previously thought to be complete; **complement** (noun) = an integral part, that which completes the whole; both words also have special meanings in mathematics. **To supplement** = to augment or add something to; **to complement** = to complete by adding an essential part, to supply what is (obviously) wanting. *Supplementary* and *complementary* are the corresponding adjectives. **Compliment** = an expression of praise, regard or flattery.

supposedly should not be misused for **presumably**; e.g. in "Fred was supposedly to blame", *presumably* is presumably intended.

suppress, suppressor.

supra-, a prefix meaning above, does not take a hyphen except in *supra-axillary, supra-orbital*.

surmise

surplus (pl. surpluses).

surprise = to take off guard or unawares; **astonish** is stronger; **astound** is even stronger; **amaze** is strongest. The corresponding nouns are *surprise, astonishment, astoundment* and *amazement*. One of the stronger words should not be used when mere *surprise* is intended.

surrender, surrenderer (*-er*, even in law).

survive, survivor.

susceptible

suspend, suspender(s), suspension.

swat = to hit (a fly); **swot** = to study hard.

Swaziland The derived adjective and noun is *Swazi*.

swear has the past tense **swore** and past participle **sworn**. *See also* **curse**.

sweep (verb) inflects *sweep – swept – swept*.

swell (verb) has the past tense and participle **swelled**, which can mean *increased*; **swollen** is used adjectivally to mean *increased to a harmful extent* (e.g. "a swollen ankle").

swim (verb) has the past tense **swam** and past participle **swum**.

swing (verb) inflects *swing – swung – swung*.

swinging = oscillating; **swingeing** = chastising.

swivel, swivelled, swivelling.

swop is preferred to **swap** for the colloquial verb meaning *exchange*.

sycamore = large ornamental maple tree (*Acer pseudoplatinus*);
    sycomore = Mediterranean fig tree (*Ficus sycomoros*).

syllable, syllabication (not syllabification).

syllabus (pl. syllabuses).

syllepsis Figure of speech that links the literal use of one word and a
    metaphorical use of another. E.g.:

"They held hands and their breath when they met."
Like a **pun** (which *see*), syllepsis is best reserved for deliberate
humorous effect. *See also* **zeugma**.

symbol, symbolize.

sympathy Have sympathy *for*; be in sympathy *with*; sympathize
    with; be sympathetic (or unsympathetic) *to*.

symposium (pl. symposia).

synchronize

syncope = omission in pronunciation of the sound(s) of letters in the
    middle of a word. Thus the nautical terms *boatswain* and *coxswain*
    (originally *cockswain*) are pronounced *bosun* and *coxun*. This
    phenomenon has allowed *bosun* to become an accepted alternative
    spelling (but not, so far, *coxun*). Note also *forecastle* (pronounced
    foke-sel).

syndrome is a medical term for a group of characteristic symptoms.
    Its figurative use has inflated its status to that of a vogue word
    (which *see*).

synecdoche = figure of speech in which a key part of something is made to stand for the whole of it. E.g.:

"The face that launched a thousand ships"
(in which *face* stands for "Helen of Troy").

synonyms = two or more words of the same meaning. They are uncommon in a rich vocabulary such as that of English (Fowler refers to *gorse* and *furze* as "that very great rarity, a pair of exact synonyms", a fact that resulted in at least one dictionary defining each only in terms of the other). Usually the terms *synonym* and *synonymous* refer to words that are almost the same in meaning, often more dependent on context than consideration of words in isolation. Thus the words *usually* and *often* are sufficiently synonymous to be transposed in the previous sentence without significantly changing its meaning.

synopsis (pl. synopses).

synthesis, synthesize, synthetic.

syren The preferred spelling is **siren**.

syringe, syringeing.

system, systematic (= pertaining to or according with a system, logical, planned), systemic (= pertaining to or affecting the nervous system, or applying to the body as a whole), systematize.

T

table-cloth, table-knife, tableland, table-linen, table-maid, table-mat, tablespoon, tablespoonful(s), table tennis, table-top, table-ware, table wine.

tableau (pl. tableaux).

taboo (pl. taboos), tabooed, tabooing (preferred to **tabu**). *Taboo words* are those that are considered inappropriate for use in polite company.

tabulate, tabulator.

tachograph = instrument in the cab of a lorry or coach for recording on a card the speed of a vehicle and the time for which it is driven; **tachometer** = rev(olutions) counter, instrument for indicating speed of rotation; **tachygraph** = Medieval shorthand; **tachymeter** = instrument for locating points in surveying.

tactics is plural; it has no singular.

taenia = tapeworm or ribbonworm; **tinea** = ringworm (caused by a fungus).

tail-back, tail-board, tail-end(er), tail-gate, tail-lamp, tail-light, tail-off (noun), tailpiece, tailpipe, tailplane, tailstock.

take has the past tense **took** and past participle **taken**.

take umbrage is an archaism and cliché for **take offence**, which should be used.

talisman (pl. talismans, not talismen).

tamarin = small South American monkey; **tamarind** = tropical tree with edible pods.

tame, tameable.

Tamil *See* **Indian words.**

tampon = cotton-wool plug (for a wound or body orifice);
  tampion = plug for the muzzle of a gun; **tompon** = tampion;
  tompion = kind of early watch.

tam-tam = orchestral gong; **tom-tom** = American Indian or African
  drum.

tangible

tango (pl. tangos).

tantalize, tantalization.

tarantella = lively dance (originating in Italy), thought to mimic the
  effect of being bitten by a **tarantula** spider.

tarsus (pl. tarsi).

tart *See* **flan.**

tattoo (pl. tattoos), tattooed, tattooing, tattooer, tattooist.

taut = tight; **taught** = past tense and participle of the verb **to teach.**

tautology is unnecessary repetition. Common phrases that are
  usually tautologous (and therefore should be avoided) include:

added bonus	lose out
adequate enough	meet/merge/mingle/mix together
all alone	minute detail
assemble together	more especially
burn down/up	more preferable
check out/up	nearly dead (although *near death*
circle round	is acceptable)
climb up	joint partnership
close proximity	new innovation
close down/up	newly created

close/thorough scrutiny
collect/combine/connect together
completely/totally destroyed
completely/totally surrounded
continue on
cut back
divide off/up
drink down/up
each and every
earlier on
end result
end up
equally as
file away
final completion
finally/ultimately end in
finish up
first/initially conceived/founded
first prototype
follow after
free gift
from hence(forth)
future prospects
gather together
general consensus
head up
hurry up
if and when
in between
indirect allusion
join/link together
later on
lend out

opening gambit
original source
over again
past history
pay off
plan ahead
polish up
reason why
refer back
renew/repeat again
rest up
return/revert back
rise up
root cause
round ball
self-confessed
send on
settle up
sit down
solitary isolation
still remain
trigger off
true facts
try out
twice (etc.) over
ultimate conclusion
unite together
unless and until
usual habit
watch out for
whether or not
raze to the ground

In many pairs, the second word (often a preposition) can be omitted.

taxi (verb), taxied, taxiing. **Taxi** (noun) has the plural *taxis*.

tea-bag, tea-break, tea-caddy, teacake, tea-chest, tea-cloth, tea-cosy, teacup, teacupful(s), tea-garden, tea-house, tea-leaf (tea-leaves), tea-party, teapot, tea-room, tea-rose, tea service, tea-shop, teaspoon, teaspoonful(s), tea-table, tea-time, tea-towel, tea-tray, tea-trolley, tea-urn.

teacake *See* **crumpet**.

teach inflects *teach – taught – taught*.

tear (verb) has the past tense **tore** and past participle **torn**.

technical expressions Many "ordinary" words have been taken over by science, technology and crafts and given a special meaning; e.g. *transparency*, the state of being transparent, is used for a positive photographic image on (colour) film, also called a *slide* or *diapositive*. But the traffic has been two-way, and some technical expressions have been adopted into the general vocabulary with non-technical meanings; e.g. *catalyst*, in chemistry a substance that (in small quantities) accelerates a reaction without taking part in it, is used figuratively for something or someone who initiates an act, particularly one that was previously bogged down. Such exchanges can enrich the vocabulary without the need to invent new words (*see* **neologisms**). Care should be exercised, however, in using borrowed technical expressions, particularly if they are employed merely for novelty, emphasis or exaggeration (such as the misuse of the psychological terms manic, paranoiac and schizophrenic and various others included in this Dictionary).

technics is obsolete for **technology** (= the study and practice of applied science), as **technic** is for **technical** (= to do with applied science or engineering). Someone with technical skills is a **technician**, who applies various **techniques** in his work; *technique* also describes the skills/methods of an artist or musician. A *technician* often works in a narrower field than an **engineer**; a **mechanic** generally deals only with mechanisms (e.g. computer engineer, dental technician, car mechanic), although the terms are interchangeable.

teenage, teenaged, teenager (*see also* **baby**).

teeth is the noun; **teethe** is the verb.

teetotal, teetotaller, teetotalism.

televise, television ("No good will come of this device. The word is half Greek and half Latin" – C. P. Scott).

tell inflects *tell – told – told*.

temperature conversions *See* **units**.

temperance *See* **abstain**.

templet is the preferred spelling (not **template**).

tempo (pl. tempos).

temporal, = to do with the time or relating to a lifespan (opposite of *spiritual*, *eternal*), gives the adverb **temporally**; **temporary**, = of short duration, fleeting, transient (opposite of *permanent*), gives the adverb **temporarily**. The spellings of the adverbs are sometimes confused. A derived verb is **temporize** = to play for time, hedge, negotiate (compare with *extemporize* = to play/speak without preparation). **Temporal** also means to do with the temple(s) (at the side of the head). *See also* **transient**.

tendency to (not tendency *for*).

tensimeter = instrument for measuring vapour pressure; **tensometer** = instrument for measuring elasticity (by stretching).

tepid = luke-warm, half-hearted; **torpid** = sluggish, lethargic, inactive.

tera- is the metric prefix for a million million times ($\times 10^{12}$). (*See* **units**).

terminus (pl. termini), terminate, terminator, termination. Also note terminal (noun) used of an airline terminus (airport).

ter- or tri- *See* **numerical prefixes**.

terrible should be reserved for things or circumstances that invoke *terror* and not used of something that is merely **unpleasant** or **disagreeable**. Similarly **terribly** should not be used as a meaningless intensifier (as in "She was terribly pleased").

terrorize, terrorist.

test-bed, test case, test drive, test flight, test match, test pilot, test-tube (baby).

tetchy

tête-à-tête = private (conversation); the French term should be avoided.

textual = pertaining to text; **textural** = pertaining to texture.

Thailand The derived adjective and noun is *Thai*.

than Apart from *other, otherwise, else* and *elsewhere*, the only words that can be followed by *than* are comparatives (e.g. older, younger, better than). So beware of using *than* as a preposition in such construction as "He is richer than her" which, strictly, should be "... richer than she (is)".
Do not misuse *than* for **as**; e.g. "Twice as many errors had been made than in the other article" is incorrect – it should read "... had been made as in the other article."

thankfully = in a thankful way. It should not be used to mean *let us be thankful* (that). E.g.:

"He took the drink thankfully" is correct;
"Thankfully, there is more time" is incorrect.
This misuse is currently in vogue (*see also* **hopefully, regretfully**) but is not (yet) acceptable in good writing – it may, however, go the way of that other common "sentence adverb" *importantly*, which has more or less gained acceptance: "More importantly, the mayor will be there."

that and which *See* **which**.

theca (pl. thecae).

theirs (no apostrophe). *See* **one's**.

their, there and they're have only pronunciation in common (*see* homonyms). **Their** is a possessive pronoun meaning *of them* (e.g. "They paid for their tickets"). **There** usually indicates position, and is thus an adverb (e.g. "I used to go there"), although it can also be a pronoun (e.g. "There is a bad smell in this room"). **They're** is a contraction of *they are* (e.g. "They're over there!"), and should be avoided in formal writing.

thence is archaic for **from there**, which should be used.

thenceforth is archaic for **from that time on(ward)** which, although longer, is preferred. *See also* **thereafter**.

theory, theorize.

thereafter = after a particular (designated) time (e.g. "He made his views known and thereafter said no more"). It has an archaic ring and can usually be replaced by *from that time* or *from then*. Similarly **thereof** = *of that* and **theretofore** = *up to that time* (or **before**). *See also* **thenceforth**.

there are many is correct (not *there is many*).

thesis (pl. theses).

thief (pl. thieves).

think inflects *think – thought – thought*.

this/these Usually these demonstrative pronouns should not be used as the subject of a sentence; they should be made into adjectives modifying a noun. E.g.:

"This is a sign of vague writing" should read "This error is a sign of ..."

thither is archaic for **to there** (as in the cliché "hither and thither"), and should be avoided.

tholus (pl. tholi).

thorax (pl. thoraxes), thoracic.

though *See* **although**.

thrash = to flog, beat soundly (transitive), move about violently (intransitive); it also means to **thresh** (corn), but *thresh* should be used for this meaning (and threshing machine etc.). **Thrash out** = to discuss/debate exhaustively.

threshold (not threshhold).

thrive has the past tense and participle **thrived** (not *throve, thriven*) although *thriven* (= developed, succeeded) is sometimes used as an adjective.

throe = spasm, violent pang (usually used in the plural – e.g. "throes of starvation"); not to be confused with **throws**.

thrombus (pl. thrombuses, not thrombi).

throughout *See* **all over**.

throw (verb) has the past tense **threw** and past participle **thrown** (paralleled by its compounds *overthrow* and *underthrow*). *See also* **throe**.

thymus (pl. thymuses).

tibia (pl. tibias).

tie, tying, tied.

tilde = mark over Spanish *n*, as in cañon, mañana, Señor, vicuña.

till should not be used for **until**.

time, timeable. Some of the compounds are time-and-motion, time
bomb, time-consuming, time exposure, time-fuse, time-honoured,
time-lag, time-lapse (adj.), time-limit, timepiece, time-saving, time-
scale, time sharing, time-sheet, time-signal, time-signature, time-
switch, timetable, time-worn (adj.), time zone.

time (dates, months, days) The preferred style is: 13 November
1986; November 1986; 13 November ; 56 BC; AD 56; the eighteenth
century (not 18th century, unless unavoidable in captions); an
eighteenth-century house; 1980s or the eighties (not 1980's, 80's or
'eighties).
The form 5/11/86 (or 5.11.86) should be avoided, which in Britain
means 5 November but which in the United States means 11 May.
The international system is 1986–11–05 (for 5 November).
In ranges of years, both years should be given in full: 1400–1419
(not 1400–19), 1986–1987 (not 1986–7).

Names of months should be given in full in text, but may be
abbreviated to save space in tables thus:
Jan Feb Apr Aug Sept Oct Nov Dec
(March, May, June and July in full).
Names of days should be given in full in text, but may also be
abbreviated thus in tables:
Sun Mon Tues Weds Thur Fri Sat.
Time should be given thus:
8 a.m. (not 8.00am); 8.30 p.m.; half past three; nine o'clock; 10hr
14 min; 14.00 or 14.00hr ("14 hundred hours"); 18.20 or 18.20hr.

Biographical dates: birth and death dates should be given, unless
identified as otherwise; e.g. Queen Victoria (1819–1901) but Queen
Victoria (reigned 1837–1901). Use the terms flourished, died and
born in text but *fl.*, *d.* and *b.* with life dates and in captions,
annotations and time charts. If a date is not known with precision,
use c. (*circa*), not "?"
If both birth and death dates are obscure then the style is
(*c.*1250–*c.*1300) not (*c.*1250–1300).
If the subject is still alive the preferred style is (1949–), not (born
1949). Two character spaces should be left after the dash, unless
the subject was born in the nineteenth century, when four spaces
should be left after the dash. (In this way, both spaces will accept
the death date in a subsequent revision without the need to re-set
more than one line.)

times *See* **x** (multiplication sign).

timid/timorous *See* **apprehensive**.

timpano = orchestral kettledrum (pl. timpani); **tympanum** = the ear-drum, semicircular panel over a door (pl. tympana).

ting (= to ring), tinged, tinging; **tinge** (= to tint/colour), tinged, tinging. The spellings of the past tenses and present participles of each verb are the same.

tiny, tinier, tiniest.

tip-toe, tiptoed, tiptoeing.

tire is the verb; **tyre** is the preferred spelling of the noun (as in bicycle tyre). *See* **tyre**.

tiro (pl. tiros) (not *tyro*).

tissue = type of absorbent paper made from mechanical pulp. *See* **mechanical pulp; paper**.

titillate = to arouse pleasure in; **titivate** = to smarten up, tidy oneself.

title(d)(= name(d)). The preferred verb is **entitle(d)**.

titles and ranks *See* **capitalization; honours**.

to and fro is the adverb (e.g. "the piston moved to and fro"); **to-and-fro** is the adjective (e.g. "to-and-fro motion"); **toing and froing**.

tobacco (pl. tobaccos).

toboggan *See* **sledge**.

to boot is archaic for **moreover** or **in addition**, either of which is preferred.

tocsin = an alarm; **toxin** = a poison (of biological origin).

today, tomorrow and **tonight** are the preferred spellings (not **to-day, to-morrow** and **to-night**.).

... to death Expressions such as **burned to death**, *choked to death, drowned to death, hanged to death, shot to death, starved to death, strangled to death* and *suffocated to death* should be selected carefully. The addition "... to death" is redundant after *drowned, hanged, strangled* and *suffocated* because drowning, hanging, strangling and suffocation ultimately cause death. The addition can be justified in the other expressions because burning, choking, shooting and starvation, while possibly causing severe injury or ill-health, do not necessarily lead to death.

toga (pl. togas).

Togo The derived adjective and noun is *Togolese*.

tolerant *of* is correct (not tolerant *to*).

tolerate, tolerable (not toleratable).

tomato (pl. tomatoes).

tom-tom *See* **tam-tam**.

ton, in Britain, is 2,240 pounds weight; **ton** in the United States, is 2,000 pounds (= a short ton); **tonne** is 1,000 kilograms (= 2,204.62 pounds). The term *metric ton* should not be used for **tonne**.

Tonga The derived adjective and noun is *Tongan*.

tongs, like scissors and trousers, is a plural noun; "a pair of tongs" achieves a singular construction.

top brass, topcoat, top dog, top drawer (noun), top-drawer (adj.), topdress (verb), top-dressing, topgallant, top-hat, top-heavy, top-knot, topless, top-level (adj.), top-line, topmast, topmost, topsail, top-secret, topside, topsoil, top table.

tophus (pl. tophi).

torment, tormentor.

tornado, (pl. tornadoes).

torpedo (pl. torpedoes).

torso (pl. torsos).

-t- or -tt- Monosyllabic words ending in -*t* preceded by a single vowel double the *t* before *y* or a prefix beginning with a vowel. E.g.:

pot	pottable, potted, potter, potting, potty
skit	skitter, skitting, skittish

The *t* remains single if preceded by a long or double vowel. E.g.

heat	heatable, heated, heating
sprout	sprouted, sprouting

With polysyllabic words, the choice of -*t*- or -*tt*- depends on where the accent falls. If it is on the last syllable, the rule is as for monosyllabic words; e.g. allotting, besotting, remitting, submitting. If the last syllable is unaccented, the -*t*- is not doubled; e.g. balloting, combating, defeating, exhibiting, interpreting, marketing, mistreating, rabbiting, riveting. Neither is the *t* doubled, in monosyllabic or polysyllabic words, before suffixes that begin with a consonant; e.g. fitful, commitment.

tortuous = twisting and turning, not straightforward; **torturous** = cruel, causing pain.

torus (pl. tori).

touché (italics, with an accent).

toupee (not italic and with no accent).

tour de force (italics) = feat of skill or strength; the French form should be avoided.

tournedos (pl. tournedos).

tourniquet

towards is preferred to **toward**.

to whit is an archaism for **namely**, which should be used.

toxin *See* **poison; tocsin**.

trace, traceable.

trachea (pl. tracheae).

trade, tradeable.

trade-in (noun), trade mark, trade name, tradesman, trades-people, tradeswoman, trade union (pl. trade unions, but TUC = Trades Union Congress), trade unionism, trade wind.

trade names or proprietary names (and trade marks) still in current use should be spelled with an initial capital letter. Long-standing ones that have entered the language (i.e. have become generic names) are usually spelled as ordinary words with no initial capital. For example, each of the following was once a trade name:

aspirin	caterpillar (track)	linoleum
autogiro	celluloid	melamine
bakelite	duralumin	mimeograph
barathea	escalator	polythene
brilliantine	gramophone	nylon
carborundum	gunk (slang)	rayon

Some trade names that are, in everyday language, acquiring generic status are listed here, but they are still registered trade names and should be capitalized when they appear in print.

*Araldite	* + Biro	CinemaScope
+ Ascot	+ Boeing	Coalite
Aspro	*Calor gas	*Coke (drink)
Bendix	Celanese	+ Cow gum
*Benzedrine	*Cellophane	Dacron

445

Durex
Ektachrome
Elastoplast
*Formica
Freon
*+Hoover
*Jeep
*Klaxon
*Kodak
Land-Rover
Leica
Letraset
*Levis
Librium
Linotron
*Linotype
*Lysol
*+Martini
*Monotype

*Muzak
*Nembutal
*Neoprene
*Novocaine
*Ouija
Ozalid
Pentothal
*+Perrier
*Perspex
*Photostat
*Plasticine
Polaroid
Pomagne
*Primus
*+Pullman
Pyrex
*Rexine
*Roneo
*Scotch tape

*Sellotape
*Spam
Sweetex
Tampax
*Tannoy
Tarmac
*Technicolor
Teflon
*Terylene
*Thermos
*Triplex
*Valium
*Vaseline
*Velcro
*Wimpy
*Xerox
*+Yale lock
Y-Front(s)
*Yo-Yo

Names marked * are listed in the *Concise OED* (although not all with an initial capital). Most trade names are based on a set of initials or are invented words (*see* **acronym**; **neologism**); the ones marked + are unaltered personal names or place-names. *See also* **drug names**.

traffic, trafficked, trafficking, trafficker.

train names *See* **locomotive and train names**.

traipse is the preferred spelling (not **trapes**).

trammel, trammelled, trammelling.

tranquil, tranquillity, tranquillize, tranquillizer (the single *l* spelling is an Americanism).

transatlantic (not trans-Atlantic or Transatlantic).

transcend, transcendent, transendence.

transcendent = surpassing, supremely excellent; **transcendental** = idealistic, visionary, beyond human experience.

transfer, transferred, transferring, transferrer (transferror in law), transferee, transference, transferable.

tranship, transhipment are preferred to the more logical **transship**, transshipment.

transient = of short existence, passing, fleeting (*see also* **temporary**); **transitional** = in a state of change or passage, intermediate (with the implication of short-lived); **transitory** = lasting for a very short time, rapidly vanishing.

translate, translator, translatable.

translucent describes the optical property of a material that, while allowing the passage of light, diffuses it; **transparent** describes a material that allows the unimpeded passage of light. The associated nouns are *translucence* (preferred to translucency) and *transparency* (preferred to transparence), also used for a colour positive photograph (a "slide").

transmit, transmitter, transmissable (preferred to transmittable).

transonic (not transsonic).

transpire = to become known, to come to light, to leak (of information). It should not be used to mean simply to **happen**. E.g.:

"After the evidence had been accepted it transpired that there had been collusion between the witness and the accused" is correct; "Let us wait for next week's delivery and see what transpires" is incorrect.
Transpiration = respiration – like exchange of gases in plants.

transport = method of moving people or goods; **transportation** = punishment that involved moving people to another continent. The latter has not yet superseded the former in English (as it has in American).

447

transsexual (not transexual).

trapes The preferred spelling is **traipse**.

trapezium (pl. trapeziums).

trauma (pl. traumas, not traumata).

travel, travelled, travelling.

tread (verb) has the past tense **trod** and preferred past participle
   trodden (not *trod*).

trek, trekked, trekking.

tremendous/tremendously should be reserved for things that are
   overpowering or *fearful*, and not used to mean *excellent* or *very large*
   (as in "I heard a tremendous record yesterday", "We collected a
   tremendous amount of money").

tremor (not tremour).

triceps *See* **biceps**.

trio (pl. trios).

trip *See* **journey**.

triple, triplet, treble. *See* **double**.

triumph, triumphal (pertaining to triumph); **triumphant**
   (= conquering, pertaining to a winner).

trivia is a plural word; it has no singular.

troop = group of soldiers; **troupe** = group of performers;
   trooper = soldier; **trouper** = professional performer.

trousers is a plural word. "A pair of trousers" achieves a singular
   construction.

trust, trustee, trusting (= having trust in), trustful (= lacking suspicion), trustworthy (= reliable, worthy of trust), **Trusty** is archaic for **trustworthy,** particularly when applied to a person; it survives in various clichés (such as "my trusty steed/companion" for a horse/dog).

try to do something is formally correct (not *try and do*). Increasingly, *to* is being omitted (e.g. "Please try and complete the work").

tsar is the preferred spelling of **tzar** and **czar**.

tsetse (one word).

tsunami

tuba (pl. tubas) = deepest pitched orchestral brass instrument; **tuber** = swollen, underground part of a plant (such as a dahlia or potato).

tumour, tumorous.

tumulus (pl. tumuli).

tune, tuneable. *See also* **attune**.

tunnel, tunnelled, tunnelling.

turbid = cloudy, muddy, unclear; **turgid** = swollen. Good writing is neither turbid nor turgid.

turf (pl. **turfs**) = grass sods for making a lawn; **turves** = blocks of peat.

Turkish *See* **Arabic words**.

turnabout, turnbuckle, turncoat, turn-down (adj.), turnkey, turn-out (adj.), turnover, turnpike, turn-round (noun), turnstile, turnstone, turntable, turn-up (noun).

twain is archaic for **two** (as in the expression "never the twain shall meet"); *two* should be used.

tweezers is a plural word; although *tweezer* is given as the singular in the *OED*, few people would say "Please pass me the tweezer". The preferred singular construction is "a pair of tweezers".

twilight, twilit.

'twixt should not be used for **between**.

two first *See* **first**.

tympanum (pl. tympana). *See* **timpano**.

type of (like *kind of*, *sort of*) usually takes a singular noun. E.g.:

"It was the type of dog that . . ."
"He is the kind of person who . . ."
"This is the sort of example . . ."
The expressions *types/kinds/sorts of* should have a plural noun. E.g.:

"There were many types of dog on show"
"They remind me of the kinds of people who . . ."
"This guide contains all sorts of examples"

typesetting terms and instructions *See* **justification; leading; letter space; measure; point; proof-reading; rule; underlining; word space**.

type sizes are nearly always specified in *points*, although large (display) faces may be given in millimeters (*see* **point**). Formerly, common type sizes were given names; here are examples of some of the obsolete terms:

4 point	brilliant	9 point	bourgeois
4½ point	diamond	10 point	long primer
5½ point	agate or ruby	11 point	small pica
6 point	nonpareil	12 point	pica
6½ point	emerald	14 point	English
7 point	minion	18 point	great primer
8 point	brevier	48 point	canon

See also **cicero**; **didot**.

typo = editor's and typesetter's jargon for **typographical error**, a misspelling caused by an error in typesetting.

tyrant, tyranny, tyrannize, tyrannical.

tyre is the usual English spelling for the air-filled rubber case round the wheel of a bicycle, car etc. (*tire* being an Americanism in this sense), although the *OED* and others give *tire* as the preferred spelling for a metal band shrunk onto the rim of a wooden wheel. The *y* spelling avoids possible ambiguity between the verbs *retyre* (to put on a new tyre) and *retire* (to withdraw or go to bed).

tyro The preferred spelling is **tiro**.

tzar The preferred spelling is **tsar**.

U

U-boat, U-turn (capital U and a hyphen).

u.c. is the abbreviation of upper case (= "capital letters"), marked in text for typesetting by triple underlining, thus: <u>upper case</u>. *See also* **underlining**.

Uganda The derived adjective and noun is *Ugandan*.

ugli = grapefruit-like fruit (pl. uglis).

ugly, uglier, ugliest, ugliness, uglily.

UHF is the abbreviation of ultra-high frequency.

Ulster *See* **Eire**.

ultimatum (pl. ultimatums).

umlaut = German accent mark, as in röntgen, Müller. It can be avoided (if, for instance, a typeface does not include the characters) by adding an *e* to the *o* or *u* (e.g. roentgen, Mueller).

un- *See* **negative prefixes**.

unable, inability. *See also* **incapable**.

unadvisable *See* **inadvisable**.

unanimous (unanimity) = of one mind; **single-minded** (single-mindedness) = of one view to the exclusion of all others. It takes two or more people to be unanimous; one person may be single-minded.

unarmed *See* **disarmed**.

unauthorized

unaware is the adjective; **unawares** is the adverb. E.g.:

"She was unaware of his presence in the room."
"He jumped out and took her unawares."

unbalance(d) *See* **balance**.

unbeknown is archaic for **unknown** (as in the cliché "unbeknown to him"); *unknown* should be used.

unbiased

unchangeable

uncircumcised

uncle = brother of one's parent and, by extension, husband of one's aunt. *See also* **family relationships** (diagram).

unconscious *See* **subconscious**.

uncooperative (no hyphen).

uncoordinated (no hyphen).

uncorrected *See* **incorrect**.

unction, unctuous = greasy, oil (not unctious); **unguent** = ointment.

under *See* **beneath**; **above**.

under- Most compounds with this prefix are spelled as one word. Exceptions include under-secretary, under-sexed, under-sized, under way (as a vessel on the move, not *under weigh*).

underhand = sly, secret, "sneaky"; **underhanded** = undermanned.

underline is a poor synonym of **emphasize**.

underlining in a manuscript or typescript for publication should be avoided to convey emphasis because it will be interpreted as an instruction to the typesetter. Single underlining indicates letters or words that are to be set in italic face (e.g. <u>see also</u> would be set as *see also*); double underlining, such as <u>AD</u> or <u>DICTIONARY</u>, indicates small capital letters (AD; DICTIONARY); triple underlining (<u>NATO, HEADING</u>) indicates large (= normal text face) capital letters (NATO, HEADING). A wavy line (underlining) indicates bold face (black) type (**underlining**). *See also* **proof reading**.

underpass *See* **flyover**.

understand inflects *understand – understood – understood*.

understatement *See* **litotes; meiosis**.

undertake has the past tense **undertook** and past participle **undertaken**.

under the circumstances, although not incorrect when properly used, is often misused for **in the circumstances**. The latter is correct in reference to mere situation, the former in reference to the performance of an action affected by the circumstances; e.g. "In the circumstances the meeting could not take place" and "He had a broken wrist and, under the circumstances, could not type." When in doubt, use *in the circumstances*.

underthrow *See* **throw**.

underwrite has the past tense **underwrote** and past participle **underwritten**.

undeveloped countries, or underdeveloped countries, are better referred to as developing countries.

undiscriminate *See* **indiscriminate**.

undo has the past tense **undid** and past participle **undone**.

uneatable *See* **edible**.

unequal takes *to*, not *for*. E.g.:

  "The editor was unequal to the task."

unequivocal (not unequivocable), unequivocally (not unequivocably).

unexceptionable *See* **exceptionable**.

unexplainable The preferred term is **inexplicable**.

unfertilized = not fertilized; **infertile** = incapable of being fertilized or of fertilizing; e.g. "the fertile female moth remained unfertilized because all the males were infertile" (although *sterile* would be better here than infertile; *see* **sterile**).

unforgettable

unfrequented is preferred to **infrequented**, but **infrequent** is preferred to **unfrequent**.

unilateral, **bilateral** and **multilateral** are better put as one-sided, two-sided and many-sided, unless being used as technical terms in diplomacy or physiology.

unionized = having a trade union; **un-ionized** = not ionized.

unjustified setting *See* **justification**.

unique = only one of its kind, and so should not be qualified by words such as *rather*. *See* **qualifying adverbs**.

United Kingdom *See* **Great Britain**.

units The two chief systems of units in common use are the Imperial System (used in Britain and, with a few modifications, in the United States, where they are generally referred to as Customary Units) and the Metric (or SI, Système International) System. The following tables list the chief units in each of the systems, and give factors for converting various measurements from one system to the other.

Imperial System

Basic units are the foot (ft), pound (lb) and second (sec).

Linear:
    12 inches (in) = 1 foot (ft)
    3 feet (ft) = 1 yard (yd)
    $5\frac{1}{2}$ yards (yd) = 1 pole
    22 yards (yd) = 1 chain (= 4 poles)
    220 yards (yd) = 1 furlong (= 10 chains)
    1,760 yards (yd) = 1 mile (= 8 furlongs; = 5,280 feet)

Nautical:
    6 feet = 1 fathom
    120 fathoms = 1 cable (= 720 feet)
    5,080 feet = 1 nautical mile (6,076.1 ft International and US)
    3 nautical miles = 1 league (= 3.456 statute miles)
    60 nautical miles = 1 degree
    (a speed of 1 nautical mile per hour = 1 knot)

Square:
    144 square inches (sq in) = 1 square foot (sq ft)
    9 square feet (sq ft) = 1 square yard (sq yd)
    $30\frac{1}{4}$ square yards (sq yd) = 1 perch
    40 perches = 1 rood
    4 roods = 1 acre (= 4,840 sq yd)
    640 acres = 1 square mile (sq mile)

Volume:
    1,728 cubic inches (cu in) = 1 cubic foot (cu ft)
    27 cubic feet (cu ft) = 1 cubic yard (cu yd)

Capacity:
    4 gills = 1 pint (= 20 fluid ounces)
    2 pints = 1 quart (= 40 fl oz)
    4 quarts = 1 gallon (= 160 fl oz)
    2 gallons = 1 peck
    8 gallons = 1 bushel (= 4 pecks)
    8 bushels = 1 quarter (= 64 gallons)
    1 barrel (oil) = 50.4 gallons (= 42 US gallons)

Capacity (Apothecaries'):
    60 minims = 1 fluid drachm
    8 drachms = 1 fluid ounce
    16 fluid ounces = 1 pint
    8 pints = 1 gallon

Weight (Avoirdupois):

        27.344 grains = 1 dram (7,000 grains = 1 pound)
        16 drams = 1 ounce (oz)
        16 ounces (oz) = 1 pound (lb)
        14 pounds (lb) = 1 stone
        2 stones = 1 quarter (= 28 pounds)
        4 quarters = 1 hundredweight (cwt) (= 112 pounds)
        20 hundredweight (cwt) = 1 ton (= 2,240 pounds)

Weight (Apothecaries'):

        20 grains = 1 scruple
        3 scruples = 1 drachm
        8 drachms = 1 ounce

US units (Customary Units)
As Imperial except for:

        1 pint = 16 fluid ounces (= 0.8 Imperial pints)
        2 pints = 1 quart (= 32 fluid ounces; 0.8 Imperial
          quarts)
        4 quarts = 1 gallon (= 128 fluid ounces; 0.8 Imperial
          gallons)
        1 ton = 2,000 pounds (= 0.8939 long, or Imperial,
          tons)

Metric (more properly Système International d'Unités, or SI units)
Basic units are the metre (m), kilogram (kg) and second (sec). Other
units are formed by adding prefixes, which are also used for
forming multiples and submultiples of derived units.

Prefix	*Symbol*	*Example*
pico- = $\times 10^{-12}$ (million-millonth)	p	pF (picofarad)
nano- = $\times 10^{-9}$ (thousand-millionth)	n	ns (nanosecond)
micro- = $\times 10^{-6}$ (millionth)	μ	μF(microfarad)
milli- = $\times 10^{-3}$ (thousandth)	m	mg (milligram)
centi- = $\times 10^{-2}$ (hundredth)	c	cm (centimetre
deci- = $\times 10^{-1}$ (tenth)	d	dl (decilitre)
deca- or deka- = $\times 10$ (ten times)	da	decametre
hecto- = $\times 10^{2}$ (hundred times)	h	ha (hectare)
kilo- = $\times 10^{3}$ (thousand times)	k	kg (kilogram)
mega- = $\times 10^{6}$ (million times)	M	MW (megawatt)
giga- = $\times 10^{9}$ (thousand million times)	G	GHz (gigahertz)
tera- = $\times 10^{12}$ (million million times)	T	

Examples:

picofarad, microfarad (farad)

nanometre, micron (= micrometre), centimetre, (metre), kilometre

microgram, milligram, (gram) kilogram

(hertz) kilohertz, megahertz, gigahertz

Note: 1 hectare = 100 acres

1 square kilometre = 100 hectares

Conversion factors

Imperial to metric:

	To convert		*Multiply by*
Length:	inches	to millimetres	25.4
	inches	to centimetres	2.54
	inches	to metres	0.245
	feet	to centimetres	30.48
	feet	to metres	0.3048
	yards	to metres	0.9144
	miles	to kilometres	1.6093
Area:	square inches	to square centimetres	6.4516
	square feet	to square metres	0.0929
	square yards	to square metres	0.8316
	square miles	to square kilometres	2.5898
	acres	to hectares	0.4047
	acres	to square kilometres	0.00405
Volume:	cubic inches	to cubic centimetres	16.3871
	cubic feet	to cubic metres	0.0283
	cubic yards	to cubic metres	0.7646
	cubic miles	to cubic kilometres	4.1678
Liquid:	fluid ounces	to millilitres	28.5
	pints	to millilitres	568.0 (473.32 for US pints)
	pints	to litres	0.568 (0.4733 for US pints)
	gallons	to litres	4.55 (3.785 for US gallons)
	To convert		*Multiply by*
Weight:	ounces	to grams	28.3495

	pounds	to grams	453.592
	pounds	to kilograms	4.536
	pounds	to tonnes	0.0004536
	tons	to tonnes	1.0161

Metric to Imperial:

Length:

	millimetres	to inches	0.03937
	centimetres	to inches	0.3937
	centimetres	to feet	0.032808
	metres	to inches	39.37
	metres	to feet	3.2808
	metres	to yards	1.0936
	kilometres	to miles	0.6214

Area:

	square centimetres	to square inches	0.1552
	square metres	to square feet	10.7636
	square metres	to square yards	1.196
	square kilometres	to square miles	0.3861
	square kilometres	to acres	247.1
	hectares	to acres	2.471

Volume:

	cubic centimetres	to cubic inches	0.061
	cubic metres	to cubic feet	35.315
	cubic metres	to cubic yards	1.308
	cubic kilometres	to cubic miles	0.2399

	To convert		*Multiply by*
Capacity:	millilitres	to fluid ounces	0.0351
	millilitres	to pints	0.00176 (0.002114 for US pints)
	litres	to pints	1.760 (2.114 for US pints)
	litres	to gallons	0.2193 (0.2643 for US gallons)

459

Weight:	grams	to ounces	0.0352
	grams	to pounds	0.0022
	kilograms	to pounds	2.2046
	tonnes	to pounds	2204.59
	tonnes	to tons	0.9842 (1.1023 for US, or short, tons)

Temperature

The two most common temperature scales are Fahrenheit (on which water freezes at 32° and boils at 212°) and Celsius (also called Centigrade, on which water freezes at 0° and boils at 100°). Interconversion between the two scales is straightforward if it is remembered that the zeros on the two scales are 32°F apart and that the Fahrenheit scale packs 180° between the two fixed points, whereas the Celsius scale has only 100° – Fahrenheit degrees are 180/100 = 9/5 times "smaller" than Celsius degrees.

So, to convert a Fahrenheit temperature to a Celsius one,

SUBTRACT 32 AND MULTIPLY BY $\frac{5}{9}$

(i.e after subtracting 32 from the Fahrenheit temperature, multiply by 5 and divide this product by 9 – or multiply by 0.556 using a calculator).

To convert a Celsius temperature to Fahrenheit,

MULTIPLY BY $\frac{9}{5}$ AND ADD 32

(i.e. multiply by 9 and divide by 5 – or multiply by 1.8 if using a calculator – and add 32 to the result).

Examples:

To convert 59°F to Celsius:

$59°F = (59 - 32) \times \frac{5}{9}$
$= 27 \times \frac{5}{9}$
$= 15°C.$

To convert 15°C to Fahrenheit:

$15°C = (15 \times \frac{9}{5}) + 32$
$= 27 + 32$
$= 59°F$

To convert 23°F to Celsius:

$23°F = (23 - 32) \times \frac{5}{9}$
$= -9 \times \frac{5}{9}$
$= -5°C.$

To convert $-40°C$ to Fahrenheit:

$-40°C = (-40 \times \frac{9}{5}) + 32$

$\qquad = -72 + 32$

$\qquad = -40°F$ (the point at which the two
temperature scales coincide).

To convert $37°C$ to Fahrenheit:

$37°C = (37 \times \frac{9}{5}) + 32$

$\qquad = (\frac{333}{5}) + 32$

$\qquad = 66.6 + 32$

$\qquad = 98.6°F$ (which is why "normal" human body temperature
was changed from 98.4°F to 98.6°F, to make
it exactly 37°C).

United States is the preferred name, although USA (not U.S.A.) may be used in tables, etc. *See also* **America**.

unlawful = against the law of the land, or against religious or moral law; **illegal** = against the law of the land; **illegitimate** = not recognized by the law, born outside marriage (bastard).

unless should not be misused for **except**; e.g. in "Ball pen may be used unless you are marking up bromide proofs", *unless* should be *except* (when).

unmanageable

unmeasurable *See* **immeasurable**.

unmistakable

unnameable

unobservant *See* **oblivious**.

unparalleled

unpractical *See* **impractical**.

unreadable = too obscure or dull to read (with comparative ease); **illegible** = indecipherable. E.g.:

"The article was so badly written that it was unreadable by anyone but an expert in the subject."

"The letter was so badly written that it was illegible to everyone but the writer."

unrelated participles *See* **participles**.

unresponsible = not in the position of responsibility; **irresponsible** = undependable, feckless, lacking a responsible attitude; **unresponsive** = failing to respond (not irresponsive).

unridable (= cannot be ridden).

unrivalled

unsaleable

unscalable

unserviceable

unshakeable

unskilful

until such time as = **until,** which should be used.

untraceable

unused *See* **disused**

unwieldy (not unwieldly).

up-and-coming, up-and-down, upbeat, upbraid, upbring(ing), up-country, update, up-draught, up-end, upflow, upflung, upgrade, upheaval, upheave, upheld, uphold, upkeep, upland, uplifted, up-line, up-market, upraise, upright, uprising, uproar, uproot, upset, upshot, upside-down, upstage, upstairs, upstart, upstream, upstroke, upsurge, uptake, upthrust, up to date (noun), up-to-date (adj.), uptown, up-train, uptrend, upturn, upwards, upwind.

uphold inflects *uphold – upheld – upheld. See also* **hold up**.

upper case = typesetter's and printer's term for capital letters, as opposed to small letters or *lower case*. In proof-reading and type mark-up, it is usually abbreviated to u.c.

urban = pertaining to a city; **urbanize**, urbanization; **urbane** = courteous, civil, blandly polite.

Urdu (not Hindustani) is the preferred term for the official language of Pakistan. *See also* **Indian words**.

use, usable.

used is the past tense and participle of the verb **use** (= employ); e.g. "The editor used the wrong word." As an adjective, its principal modern meaning is *second-hand* (e.g. "a used car"). In both senses, the *s* in *used* is generally pronounced like a *z* ("*you-z'd*"). **Used to** = did habitually at one time, or accustomed to; e.g. "The editor used to make mistakes", "I became used to his mistakes". In these senses, *used* is generally pronounced with a sibilant *s* (to rhyme with *juiced*). It is bad style to employ both meanings in the same sentence; e.g. "The editor used to use a pencil," "I got used to him using a pencil" (say "The editor used to write in pencil", "I have become accustomed to his using a pencil"). Note also **ill-used** = mistreated.

usage = mode of use, habitual practice or custom. It should not be used merely to mean *use* (noun). E.g.:

"Increasing usage of the photocopier contributed to extra costs" is incorrect;
"Rough usage of the photocopier contributed to its breakdown" is correct.

USSR (not U.S.S.R.) is the abbreviation of the Union of Soviet Socialist Republics, for which the preferred name is Soviet Union; USSR may, however, be used in tables etc. *See also* **Russia**.

US states The names of American states should be spelled in full in formal writing, although the context may allow abbreviations after place-names (e.g. Chicago, Ill.) and in tables and captions. The following table lists official abbreviations (US style prefers full points after abbreviations and contractions) and the U.S. Postal Service's ZIP (= Zoning Improvement Plan) Codes for correspondence.

State	Abbreviation	ZIP Code
Alabama	Ala.	AL
Alaska	–	AK
Arizona	Ariz.	AZ
Arkansas	Ark.	AR
California	Calif.	CA
Colorado	Colo.	CO
Connecticut	Conn.	CT
Delaware	Del.	DE
Florida	Fla.	FL
Georgia	Ga.	GA
Hawaii	–	HI
Idaho	Ida.	ID
Illinois	Ill.	IL
Indiana	Ind.	IN
Iowa	Ia.	IA
Kansas	Kans.	KA
Kentucky	Ky. or Ken.	KY
Louisiana	La.	LA
Maine	Me.	ME
Maryland	Md.	MD
Massachusetts	Mass.	MA
Michigan	Mich.	MI
Minnesota	Minn.	MN
Mississippi	Miss.	MS
Missouri	Mo.	MO
Montana	Mont.	MT
Nebraska	Nebr. or Neb.	NE
Nevada	Nev.	NV
New Hampshire	N.H.	NH
New Jersey	N.J.	NJ
New Mexico	N. Mex or N.M.	NM
New York	N.Y.	NY
North Carolina	N.C.	NC

North Dakota	N. Dak. or N.D.	ND
Ohio	O.	OH
Oklahoma	Okla.	OK
Oregon	Ore. or Oreg.	OR
Pennsylvania	Pa. or Penn.	PA
Rhode Island	R.I.	RI
South Carolina	S.C.	SC
South Dakota	S. Dak. or S.D.	SD
Tennessee	Tenn.	TN
Texas	Tex.	TX
Utah	Ut.	UT
Vermont	Vt.	VT
Virginia	Va.	VA
Washington	Wash.	WA
West Virginia	W.Va.	WV
Wisconsin	Wis.	WI
Wyoming	Wyo.	WY

uterus (pl. uteri).

utilize, utilization. **Utilize** = make good/profitable use of: it should not be used merely to mean *use* or *employ*.

uttermost the defunct Old English *ut* (= out) had the comparative *utter* and the superlative *utmost*. *Uttermost* is therefore an absurdity and should be avoided. In current usage, **utter** = extreme, complete (e.g. utter darkness, utter stranger); **utmost** = greatest or highest degree, number or amount; most extreme (e.g. with the utmost care).

V

v is the abbreviation of versus.

vacant *See* **empty**.

vaccine, vaccinate, vaccinator, vaccination (from *Vaccinia*, cowpox).

vacuum (pl. vacuums), although *in vacua* sometimes in science.

vagary (not vagiary), = a diversion or caprice, is a noun (pl. vagaries).

vagina (pl. vaginas, not vaginae).

vagueness *See* **ambiguity**.

vain, vanity (preferred to vainness).

valance = pelmet or curtain; **valence** = chemical bond(ing).

valet, valeted, valeting.

valour, valorous.

valuable = having intrinsic value; **valued** describes something regarded as having value; **invaluable** = priceless, valuable to a high degree (the opposite of *invaluable* is *valueless*; of *priceless* is *worthless*).

van and **von,** as part of a proper name, do not usually have a capital *v* (except at the beginning of a sentence). Follow the style of the name's owner.

vapour, vaporize, vaporization, vaporizer, vaporous.

variegated

various *See* **different**.

varix (pl. varices), varicose.

varnish (printing) *See* **lamination**.

vas deferens (pl. vasa deferentia). The alternative term *sperm duct* avoids the Latin plural.

vasectomy, vasectomise.

VDU = abbreviation of visual display unit, the television-type screen on a computer input or output terminal which displays alphanumeric characters (letters and numbers) or graphic images (diagrams etc.).

vegan (= a strict vegetarian who eats no animal products) appears to have passed into the language and no longer needs an initial capital letter.

vein, venous (= pertaining to veins), venose (= having prominent veins).

veld is the preferred spelling (not veldt).

vena cava (pl. venae cavae).

venal = able to be bought over, corruptly mercenary; **venial** = pardonable, trivially wrong.

vend, vendible, vendor (who sells), vendee (who buys), vending machine.

vengeance *See* **avenge**.

venom/venomous *See* **poison**.

venture *See* **adventure**.

venue = meeting place, not merely any place.

veracious = truthful; **voracious** = greedy, with an insatiable appetite. E.g.:

"He was veracious to the point of hurting people's feelings."
"Even three portions did not satisfy his voracious appetite."

veracity should be avoided as a pretentious synonym of **truth** or **truthfulness**.

veranda (pl. verandas) is the preferred spelling of **verandah**.

verbal *See* **oral**.

verbalize, verbalization.

verbal noun *See* **gerund**.

verbatim = literally, word for word; the Latin term should be avoided.

verbiage = use of too many words in writing; **verbosity** = use of too many words in speaking.

verbs Most English verbs inflect – i.e. form the past tense and participle – by adding *-d* or *-ed* to the infinitive (or by changing *-y* to *-ied*); they are known as weak verbs. E.g.:

tame (present)	tamed (past)	tamed (participle)
bang	banged	banged
worry	worried	worried

Verbs that do not follow this pattern are termed *irregular* (the most notorious being *to be*). One group of irregular verbs, which could be considered to be all too regular, have the same form for the present (infinitive), past and past participle. They include beset, bet, burst, cast, cost, cut, lit, hit, hurt, let, put, read, rid, set, shed, shred, shut, slit, split, thrust, upset. With *read*, the pronunciation changes for the past tense and participle, although the spelling remains the same.
Another group have irregular past tenses and participles although, as with regular verbs, they take the same form (e.g. *bleed – bled –*

bled, fight – fought – fought and *stand – stood – stood*). A third
category includes verbs – the thoroughly irregular ones – whose
past tense and participle differ (e.g. *break – broke – broken, ring –
rang – rung* and *wear – wore – worn*).

Some older forms of past participles are no longer used as such but
have been retained as adjectives; e.g. the verb *to melt* is now regular
(*melt – melted – melted*) but its old participle *molten* is retained as an
adjective (e.g. molten iron). The declensions of common irregular
verbs of the second and third types described here – known as
strong verbs – are given in this Dictionary under each verb, with an
additional note about any adjectival use of defunct or alternative
participles.

vermilion (not vermillion).

vermin is a singular word; it has no plural.

vernacular name (in biology) = common name. *See* **Latin
classification**.

verso = left-hand page of a book; **recto** = right-hand page of a book.
See **books**.

vertebra (pl. vertebrae).

vertex = uppermost point, apex; **vortex** = whirl, as in a tornado or a
whirlpool. When the words are used scientifically, their plurals are
vertices and *vortices*; when used figuratively, they can be pluralized
to *vertexes* and *vortexes*.

very Overuse of *very* (and other intensifers) should be avoided, and it
should not be misued for **much** to modify a past participle; e.g. "It
is very improved" should be " . . . much improved".

veto (pl. vetoes).

VHF is the abbreviation of very high frequency.

via = by the way of, and refers to the direction of a journey or voyage, not the means of travel; e.g. "He went via the train" is incorrect; "He travelled to Paris via London" is correct.

viable describes the ability of a plant or animal to continue its existence; it should be reserved for that meaning. Thus "viable alternative" = "workable alternative" (or, even better, "choice"); "more economically viable" = "cheaper"; "viable solution" = "practicable solution". Often **viability** means little more than **feasibility** (*see* **vogue words**).

vibrate, vibrator.

vice versa (not italic, no hyphen).

vicious = wicked, spiteful (full of vice); **viscous** = thick, sticky (of a liquid), syrupy.

victimize, victimization.

victuals, victualler, victualling. **Victuals** is archaic (and imprecise) for **food**, which is preferred.

vicuña (with a tilde).

vide (italics) = see, consult (instruction in text); the Latin term should be avoided – use *see* or *see also* instead.

vie, vied, vying.

vigour, vigorous.

villain = a person who is evil; **villein** = a serf.

villus (pl. villi).

vintage, originally applied only to wine, is now acceptable to describe anything old (e.g. a vintage car).

violate, violable (not violatable), violator.

virago (pl. viragoes).

virgule *See* **solidus**.

virtual/virtually *See* **almost; practicable**.

virtuoso (pl. virtuosi).

virus (pl. viruses).

visage is precious and archaic for **face**, which is preferred.

vis-à-vis (italics) = face-to-face, with reference to, regarding; the
   French form should be avoided (*about* is often a good substitute).

viscera is plural (singular viscus).

visible

vista (pl. vistas).

visual display unit *See* **VDU**.

visualize, visualizer, visualization.

vitamin Style is vitamin A, vitamin D, etc. with a lower case *v* and
   capital A, D etc. In vitamin B_6 the 6 is set as a small inferior
   numeral – the type mark-up is B_6.

viz is an abbreviation of *videlicet*, Latin for **namely**, which is
   preferred.

vocalize, vocalization.

vogue words suddenly come into fashion, enjoy a short but gay life
   of overuse and misuse, and then usually fade away. Some writers
   and speakers adopt them to demonstrate that they are "with it",
   but such words can be habit-forming and seriously damage the
   health of the language. Many are imprecise, many usurp perfectly
   good and precise alternatives, and a few persist and become

established. Several are listed (and condemned) in this Dictionary; for an example, *see* **situation**. The following words seem to be particularly popular (at this moment in time): aspect, aspirations, ball game, basically, bottom line, charisma, confrontation, cut-off (noun), dialogue, dimension, environment, escalation, framework, grass roots, grey area, hopefully, in-depth, interface, meaningful, motivation, option, overkill, parameter, pivotal, position, pragmatic, problem, scenario, shortfall, simplistic, syndrome, thankfully, viability.

One of the most entertaining features of Bruce Fraser's many contributions to Gowers' *Complete Plain Words* is the "buzz-phrase generator". Most lists of vogue words can fulfil a similar function: from the preceding list, choose any three words and generate an impressive (if gobbledygook) phrase, such as:

"Grass-roots aspect of the dialogue",

"A ball-game figure for the key parameters of the present option",

"A simplistic scenario which nevertheless represents grass-roots motivation".

Now it is your turn to find a viable framework which will hopefully motivate my readers into adopting a pragmatic approach to prevent the escalation of the buzz-word syndrome, and so develop a meaningful environment for an ongoing solution to the dialogue problem.

Or perhaps you can find a way to stop people from using vogue words.

volcano (pl. volcanoes).

volte-face = an about turn; the French form should be avoided.

volume (paper thickness) *See* **bulk**.

voluptuous (not voluptious).

von *See* **van**.

vortex *See* **vertex**.

vote, votable.

vouch, voucher (a ticket), vouchor (who vouches in law).

voyage *See* **journey**.

vulcanize, vulcanization.

vulgarize

W

W is the abbreviation of watt; kW = kilowatt, MW = megawatt.

wadi (a dry river bed) has the plural wadis.

wage (noun) usually used as the plural **wages** = payment to a non-professional employee; professional employees earn a **salary**.

wage-earner

wagon (not waggon), wagoner, wagonette, wagon-lit (pl. wagon-lits).

wait is intransitive; **await** is transitive. E.g.:

"Editors sometimes have to wait for galley proofs."
"Editors sometimes have to await the arrival of galley proofs."

waive = forgo, relinquish, disperse with; **wave** = move (the hand) backwards and forwards, flutter. The corresponding nouns are *waiver* and *waver*.

wake/waken *See* **awake**.

wallaba = South American timber tree; **wallaby** = Australian marsupial, a small type of kangaroo; **wallaroo** = large type of kangaroo.

wane *See* **wax**.

want of = lack of (e.g. "for want of a nail the structure collapsed") is archaic and should be avoided; the noun **want** is best reserved to mean **poverty**.

wapiti (pl. wapitis). *See also* **elk**.

war-cloud, war crime, war-cry, war damage, war-dance, war-drum, warfare, war-game, war-gaming, war-god, warhead, war-horse, warlord, warmonger, war-paint, war-path, warship, wartime, war-worn.

-wards is the preferred ending (not *-ward*) on such adverbs as *afterwards, backwards, forwards, towards, upwards,* etc. The preferred adjectival forms are *backward, forward,* etc. (e.g. "move backwards" but "a backward movement").

warn = to give notice of impending danger or unpleasantness; it should not be used for giving notice of merely neutral or pleasant happenings. E.g.:

"I have to warn you that no bonus will be paid."
"I have to advise you that a large bonus will be paid."
Correct usage is to warn *against* danger, not *of* it.

warrant, warranter (but warrantor in law), warrantee (who warrants), warranty (which warrants).

waste, wastable, wasteful, waste paper (noun), waste-paper (adj.), waste-pipe, waste product. **Waste** = useless expenditure or consumption, squandering, and the (non-) products thereof; **wastage** = loss by use, decay, evaporation, leakage, etc. The latter should not be used merely in an attempt to dignify the former.

watchcase, watch committee, watch-dog, watchful, watchglass, watchmaker, watchman, watch-spring, watch-tower, watchword.

water-bath, water-bed, water-beetle, water-bottle, water-borne, water-butt, water closet, water-colour, watercourse, watercress, water diviner, waterfall, waterfowl, waterfront, water gas, water-glass, water-hen, water-hole, water-jacket, water-level, water-lily, water-line, waterlog(ged), water-main, waterman, watermark, water-melon, water-mill, water-pipe, water-polo, waterproof, water-pump, watershed, waterside, water softener, waterspout, water supply, water-table, watertight, water-tower, waterway, water-wheel, water-wings, waterworks.

wave *See* **waive**.

waveband, waveguide, wavelength, wave number.

wax, meaning to **grow** or **increase**, is an archaism that should be reserved for describing the Moon in the first half of the lunar month (after which it attracts the partner archaism **wane**).

way-out (= unusual, unconventional, excellent) is at best colloquial and at worst slang; it should be avoided.

-ways is usually not hyphenated as a suffix (e.g. broadways, edgeways, endways, lengthways). *See also* **leastways/leastwise; -wise**.

weal (= a raised area on the skin left by a whip or a skin disorder) is the preferred spelling (not **wheal** or **wale**). **Wale** = a ridge on fabric, a horizontal timber; **wheal** = a Cornish (tin) mine.

wear (verb) has the past tense **wore** and past participle **worn**.

weather = local climate; **wether** = castrated sheep; **whether** = conjunction that introduces the first of two alternatives (the second of which is preceded by *or*).

weave has the past tense **wove** and past participle **woven**.

wed, although the origin of the word *wedding* and its compounds, should not be used as a verb meaning *to marry* (which is preferred).

weep inflects *weep – wept – wept*.

weigh = to measure the weight (mass) of something. The nautical expression "to weigh anchor" means "to raise the anchor"; this probably accounts for the misuse of *weigh* for *way* in the expression "get under way" (= "start moving").

weight of a typeface is an indication of its "blackness". A *light* face is not as prominent as its *medium* version, which in turn is not as prominent as its *semi-bold* or *bold* versions. *See also* **condensed face; expanded face**.

weir (= dam).

welch *See* **welsh**

well- as a prefix takes a hyphen in adjectival forms; e.g. well-meaning, well-intended, well-known (as in "a well-known author" but "the author is well known"). Note the hyphen in the nouns well-being, well-doer, well-wisher, and the absence of a hyphen in wellnigh.

wellnigh = **near** or **nearly**, which are preferred.

welsh (= to fail to pay a debt) is the preferred spelling (not **welch**).

Welsh *See* **Celtic words; Scotland**.

wench is archaic for **girl**, and should be avoided.

wend is archaic for to turn, direct one's steps (as in the cliché "wend one's way"), and should be avoided. Its past tense, *went*, has been taken over by the verb to *go*.

werewolf is the preferred spelling (not **werwolf**).

west, western etc. *See* **compass directions**. Note the West, Western countries, Western world (with a capital *W*).

Western Hemisphere (initial capital letters).

West Indian words that have been assimilated into English include some from local Carib languages and others that early immigrants took there from Africa. For examples, *see* **Americanisms**.

w.f. is the abbreviation of wrong fount (in typesetting).

wharf (preferred plural *wharfs*).

what, as a subject, can be regarded as singular or plural, depending on the number of the "object". E.g. "What he wants is help" and "What he needs are helpers" are both correct; in the first sentence *what* stands for *that which*, and in the second sentence it stands for *those which*.

whatever and **whatsoever** are each one word.

whatnot = piece of furniture with shelves; **what not** = other things. E.g.:

"The aspidistra was in a pot on the whatnot."
"The room was full of aspidistras, antimacassars and what not."

when, misused for whereas, leads to ambiguity; e.g. "When editors shuffle words, designers manipulate colours" – meaning?

whence is archaic for **from where**, which should be used.

whereas implies contrast; **while** means "contemporaneous(ly) with". The latter is often misused for the former (or for merely *and*). E.g.:

"He prefers Mozart while I prefer Bach" should be
". . . whereas I prefer Bach".
"Jim played the violin while Pat played the cello" is correct only if they both played at once; compare:
"Nero fiddled while Rome burned".

which and **that** The word *that* should be used to introduce a definitive or restrictive clause, which cannot be omitted from the sentence without greatly altering its meaning; e.g. "I always buy the books that he recommends." (Not books generally but only those defined by the *that* clause.) The word *which* should be used to introduce a non-restrictive clause, which gives extra information (and the rest of the sentence can stand without the *which* clause). *Which* can be preceded by a comma, *that* cannot: "I always buy his books, which are well written." (The clause does not limit "his books" but gives a reason – because they are well written – or adds new information – and they are well written.) The distinction between *which* and *that* is increasingly being blurred – and ignored. *See also*, **who, whom, whose** and **who's**.

of which *See* **who, whom, whose** and **who's**.

while should be used consistently in preference to **whilst**.

while = at the same time as; it should not be misused for *whereas* or *although* or even plain *and*. E.g.:

"Fred bought the first drink while Jack bought the second" *and* is intended;

"Fred bought the crisps while Jack had to pay for all the drinks" *whereas* is intended;

"Fred finished his beer while the others played cards" *while* is intended.

whir (the sound of a whirling object, to make such a sound) is the preferred spelling (not **whirr**).

whisky is the drink from Scotland; that from Ireland, Canada or the United States is spelled **whiskey**.

white, whiten, whitening (= making white; a pigment), whiting (= a fish; powdered chalk).

white admiral, white arsenic, whitebait, whitebeam, white-beard, whitecap, white-collar (adj.), white elephant, white-faced (adj.), whitefish, white flag, white gold, whitehead, white-headed (adj.), white heat, white-horse, white-hot (adj.), White House, white lead, white lie, white light, white man, white metal, white noise, white-out, white paper, white pudding, white slave(r), white spirit, whitethorn, whitethroat, white vitriol, whitewash, white-water, white whale, white wine.

whither is archaic for (to) **where,** which should be used.

whizz (to make the sound characteristic of a missile flying through the air) is the preferred spelling (not **whiz**).

who, whom, whose and **who's** *Who* is the nominative (subjective) case, *whom* is accusative (objective) and *whose* is genitive (possessive). *Who* and *whom* are reserved for persons (i.e., *that* should not be used for people: e.g. "men who", not "men that"). But *whose* can be used for *of which* and avoids stilted constructions; e.g. compare "The machine, the complex components of which are made of plastic, manufactures biscuits" and "The machine, whose

complex components are made of plastic, manufactures biscuits."
(And compare both with "The machine, which has plastic complex
components, makes biscuits.") The case of the pronoun is
determined by its role in a clause or sentence. Consider the
following examples:

"The editor who erred is my friend" (*who* is nominative, the
subject of "erred").
"The man whom you criticized is my friend" (*whom*, accusative, is
the object of "criticized").
"He criticized whoever made errors" (*whoever*, nominative, is the
subject of "made").
"He criticized whomever he chose" (*whomever*, accusative, is the
object of "chose").
"He criticized the editor whose work contained errors" (*whose*,
possessive, refers to "editor": "... the editor, the work of
whom...").
"Whom do men say that I am?" is incorrect (a rare example of an
error in the Bible).
Who's is a contraction of *who is*, and should be avoided.
See also **one's**.

whole, wholly.

widgeon is the preferred spelling for a type of duck (not **wigeon**).

widow = jargon term for a single word on a line of text.

wildebeest (preferred to **gnu**) is spelled the same in the singular and
plural.

wile (verb), archaic for to trick, coax or beguile, should be avoided,
although the plural noun *wiles* (= cunning) persists; **wily** = full of
cunning, crafty; **while** (verb), usually with *away*, means to pass
without boredom (e.g. "I read a magazine to while away the time").

wilful (with only two *l*s).

will and **shall** *See* **shall** and **will**.

will-o'-the-wisp

win inflects *win – won – won*.

wind (verb) inflects *wind – wound – wound*.

winter, wintry.

wire binding *See* **spiral binding**.

-wise should usually be hyphenated as a suffix (e.g. end-wise, cross-wise), except in clockwise, likewise and stepwise. Constructions such as work-wise, time-wise should be avoided. *See also* **leastways/leastwise**; **-ways**.

wisent *See* **bison**.

with and by The former should be used of the instrument and the latter of the agent. E.g.:

"He was flattered with a kiss."
"She was flattered by an admirer."

withal (not withall) is archaic for **beside** or **nevertheless**, either of which is preferred.

withhold, withheld (two *h*s).

within *See* **in**.

with regard to, like *with relation to* or *with respect to*, seldom means more than **about**, which is preferred.

wivern is the preferred spelling (not **wyvern**).

wolf (pl. wolves).

wolverene is the preferred spelling of the American weasel (not **wolverine**).

womanize

wonderful = evoking wonder; it should not be used as a vague superlative (as in "We had a wonderful time on holiday").

wondrous (preferred to wonderous) is archaic for **wonderful** (which *see*), and should be avoided.

wont is an archaism for custom or habit (as in the cliché "as was his wont") and can be carelessly read as *won't* (= will not); *custom* or *habit* should be used.

won't should not be used for **will not** in formal writing.

woo, woos, wooed, wooing, wooer.

wood-alcohol, wood-anemone, wood-ant, wood-ash, woodbine, woodblock, wood-borer, -boring, wood-carver, -carving, woodcock, woodcraft, woodcut, wood-cutter, -cutting, wood-engraving, wood-flour, wood-grouse, wood-hyacinth, woodland, wood-lark, wood-louse (wood-lice), woodman, wood-naphtha, wood-nymph, woodpecker, wood-pigeon, wood-pulp, woodruff, wood-screw, woodshed, woodsman, wood-warbler, woodwind, woodwork, wood-worm.

wooded = covered in trees (e.g. "The wooded slopes of the mountain"); **wooden** = made of wood, lacking life or animation (e.g. "The carpenter used a wooden mallet", "The addict's face retained a wooden expression"); **woody** = to do with a wood (of trees), having the appearance/properties of wood (e.g. "We rested in a cool woody glade", "Each large carrot had woody fibres along its centre").

woodfree = type of paper made (almost entirely) from mechanical pulp. *See* **mechanical pulp**; **paper**.

wool, woolly (= resembling wool, fluffy, unclear), woollen (made of or pertaining to wool), woolliness.

word breaks There are two main rules that govern where, in a single word, a hyphen may be inserted so that the word may be split over

482

two lines of text. The rules are cited below, but note also that there are some words that simply cannot be broken, and different rules may apply to foreign words.

The rules are:

1. Insert the hyphen where the word breaks naturally into two or more elements:

hum-bug   mari-time   thim-ble

This is a simple matter in compound nouns:

cup-board   fat-head   pot-hole

And is just as simple after prefixes and before suffixes:

anti-macassar	care-less	con-tempt
establish-ment	fellow-ship	hand-some
inter-vention	loveli-ness	per-vade
peri-helion	pot-hole	pre-clude
retro-grade	skil-ful	sub-vert
trans-gression	vibra-tion	widow-hood

If possible, avoid two-letter elements, although this may be difficult in tightly set jusified copy:

de-fer   ex-cept   re-tain

Beware also of elements that may vary in combination:

palaeo-artic	but	palae-ontology
ortho-paedic	but	orth-optic

But there are some exceptions in which breaking the word into component elements is not correct; the guiding principle is readability.

2. Insert the hyphen so that each element of the broken word can be pronounced correctly at sight (often between a double consonant);

travel-ling   exceed-ingly
horri-ble, terri-ble (not: hor-, ter-)
batt-ling (not: bat-tling or battl-ing)
miss-ile (not: mis-sile, as in mis-guided)
fu-ture (not: fut-ure, but avoid two-letter elements)

483

tet-rarch, oli-garch (but mon-arch, matri-arch)
oper-ation (not: ope-ration or opera-tion)

For reasons of pronunciation, particularly of stress, there are
occasions when the hyphen cannot be inserted following the rule
(1) above, although it may still be possible to break:

persever-ance (not: per-severance or perse-verance)
perti-nent (not: per-tinent)
predi-cate (not: pre-dicate, although pre-dicatively)
consul-tation (not: con-sultation, although con-sultant)
tran-sition or transi-tion (not: trans-ition)

For reasons of stress, there are some words that should not be
broken:

period   detail   prefect
perfect (adjective; although the verb can be split, per-fect)
epitome

Other words cannot be split because the fragments would consist of
unpronounceable elements:

angry   guidance   hungry
mission   panache   session

or create misleading elements:

leg-end   mans-laughter   read-just   reap-pear   the-rapist

3. In typewritten copy mark *obligatory* hyphens that happen to come
at the end of a line thus: =

(e.g. ... and they co =
operated in marking the copy.)

word processor = small computer with a keyboard (for input), a
VDU screen (for displaying text) and possibly a printer (for
producing hard copy) which is programmed to store text and enable
it to be retrieved and manipulated (edited) as required. In many
word processors, files of text can be *dumped* (stored) on floppy
disks, and reintroduced into the machine's central processor (CP)
for later amendment if necessary.

word space = typesetter's term for the space between the words in a line of text. The sizes of word spaces may be varied from line to line to make them all set to the same length (*measure*)—that is, to justify the lines (*see* **justification**). In unjustified setting, in which the lines are allowed to have different lengths, equal word spaces are generally employed (as in this book).

work (verb) has the past tense and participle **worked**, although the form *wrought* is used adjectivally (to describe metals).

workaday, work-bag, workbench, workbox, workday, work-force, workhouse, workman, workmanlike, workmanship, workmaster, work-mate, work-out, work-people, workpiece, workroom, worksheet, workshop, work-table, work-to-rule (noun).

work at = make an intensive or prolonged effort, is a modern cliché (e.g. "The only way he will pass his final examination is to work at it"); it is best avoided.

working Printer's term for a printed sheet of paper that can be folded to form a group of pages, usually for a book. If the whole sheet is used (with no waste), it is termed as *even working*, which usually results in groups of pages in multiples of four (such as 16 or 32 pages, made by folding a sheet two or three times). The folded sheet may form a *section* or *signature* of a book, and several sections may be bound together to form a *book block* ready for *casing in* (attaching the cover, *see* **hardback**; **paperback**; **perfect binding**).

world-weary, worldwide.

World War I and **World War II** are the preferred forms (not The Great War, First World War, Second World War).

worship, worshipped, worshipping, worshipper.

worthwhile is the adjectival form, but **worth while** following a verb. E.g.:

"A worthwhile task creates job satisfaction."
"Fair wages make working worth while."

would-be (hyphen) = aspiring.

wrack = type of seaweed; all other meanings should use the spelling **rack** (= ruin; stress; support, grating or shelf; toothed bar; torture machine).

wreath (noun) = a bunch or circlet of flowers; **wreathe** (verb) = to encircle, to garland (as with flowers); **wrath** = violent anger.

wrick The preferred spelling is **rick** (for the verb meaning to twist or sprain).

wring inflects *wring – wrung – wrung*.

write has the past tense **wrote** and past participle **written**.

wrought *See* **work**.

wych-elm, witch-hazel (two names for the same plant.)

wyvern *See* **wivern**.

X

x (multiplication sign) should not be used for **times** in expressions
such as "shown magnified 500 times" (i.e. not " × 500"), nor for **by**
in "a room 8 metres by 6 metres" (i.e. not "8 × 6 metres").

-x- or -ct- *See* **-ection**.

X-chromosome (capital X, hyphen).

Xerox is the trade name of a type of photocopying machine and
should have an initial capital letter. Increasingly it is being used as
a generic verb (e.g. "I have xeroxed the typescript"); *photocopy* is a
better alternative (e.g. "I have photocopied the typescript").

x-height, in typography, is the height of the body of lower-case
(non-capital) letters, ignoring the ascenders and descenders. An
ascender projects above the x-height (as in the vertical stroke of a
letter b); a descender projects below it (as in the vertical stroke of a
letter p). The x-height, typically, is the height of a letter x.

Xmas should be avoided as an abbreviation of Christmas.

X-rays (capital X, hyphen), X-ray (adj.).

Y

-y Nouns ending in *-e* generally drop the *-e* when forming adjectives ending in **-y** (e.g. bony, cagy, crazy, icy, racy, spongy). Exceptions include bluey, dicey, gluey and holey.

Yank = (an American) has acquired derogatory overtones, as has **Yankee** (= New Englander), except in historical references.

yapp = type of limp bookbinding in which the covers overlap the edges of the pages. *See also* **books**.

Y-chromosome (capital Y, hyphen).

yd is the abbreviation of yard (and yards).

Yiddish *See* **Hebrew words**.

yodel, yodelled, yodelling, yodeller.

yoga = Hindu philosophical meditation; **yogi** (pl. yogis) = someone who practises yoga.

yoghurt is the preferred spelling of the fermented milk food.

yonder is archaic and poetic for (**that**) **over there**, which is preferred.

you can be used as an impersonal pronoun, much less formal than *one* (e.g. "You have to be mad to work here", "The sights you see these days"). It should be avoided in formal writing, if only because it can appear to address the reader directly. *See also* **one**.

yours has no apostrophe (*see* **one's**).

yucca is preferred to **yuca** as the spelling of the Central American agave plant.

-yse/-yze *See* **-ize or -ise**.

Yugoslavia (not Jugoslavia). The derived adjective and noun is *Yugoslav* (not Yugoslavian).

Z

Zaire The derived adjective and noun is *Zairian*.

Zambia The derived adjective and noun is *Zambian*.

zero (pl. zeros).

zeugma = figure of speech in which an adjective (or verb) is made to refer to two nouns, only one of which is strictly appropriate. E.g.:

"With heavy hearts and memories"
(in which an adjective meaning *sad* is omitted before *memories*). *See also* **syllepsis**.

zig-zag, zig-zagged, zig-zagging.

zinco = printer's jargon for a zinc printing plate (zincograph), usually reserved for line illustrations rather than the more expensive copper plates (used for halftones).

zoo (pl. zoos).